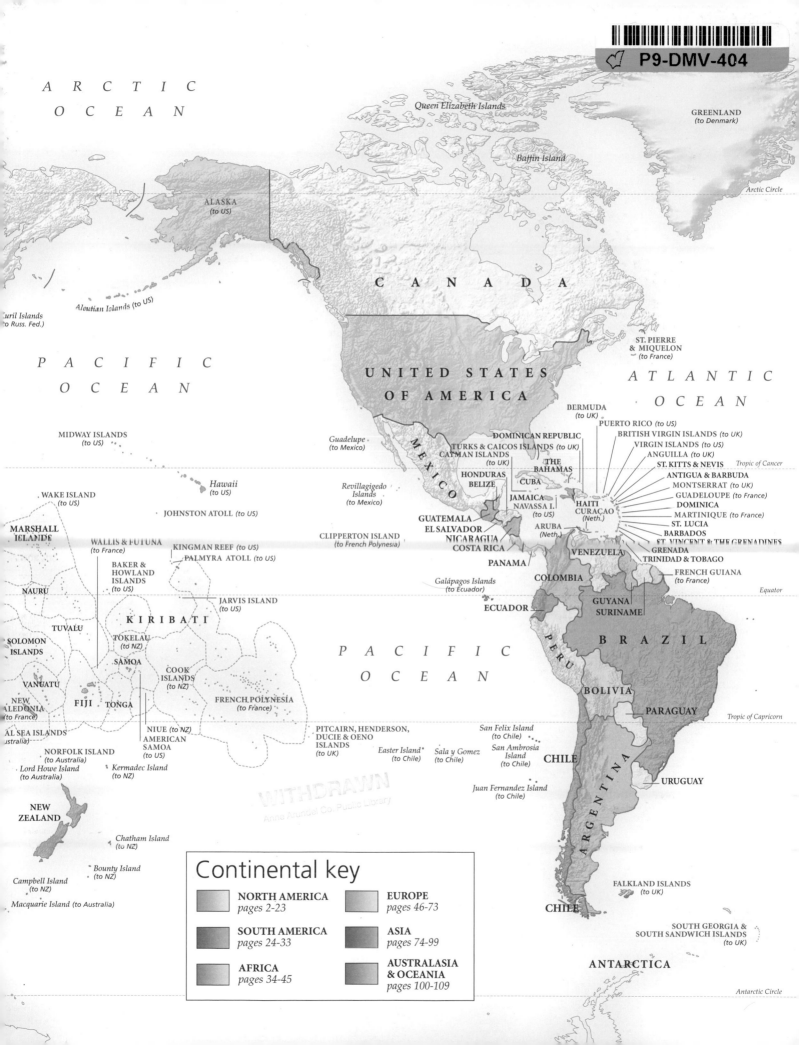

ARCTIC
OCEAN

Queen Elizabeth Islands

GREENLAND
(to Denmark)

Baffin Island

Arctic Circle

ALASKA
(to US)

CANADA

Kuril Islands
(to Russ. Fed.)

Aleutian Islands (to US)

PACIFIC
OCEAN

ST. PIERRE
& MIQUELON
(to France)

UNITED STATES
OF AMERICA

ATLANTIC
OCEAN

BERMUDA
(to UK)

MIDWAY ISLANDS
(to US)

Guadelupe
(to Mexico)

PUERTO RICO (to US)

DOMINICAN REPUBLIC

BRITISH VIRGIN ISLANDS (to UK)
VIRGIN ISLANDS (to US)
ANGUILLA (to UK)
ST. KITTS & NEVIS

TURKS & CAICOS ISLANDS (to UK)
CAYMAN ISLANDS
(to UK)

THE
BAHAMAS

Tropic of Cancer

Hawaii
(to US)

Revillagigedo
Islands
(to Mexico)

HONDURAS
BELIZE

CUBA

ANTIGUA & BARBUDA
MONTSERRAT (to UK)
GUADELOUPE (to France)
DOMINICA
MARTINIQUE (to France)
ST. LUCIA
BARBADOS
ST. VINCENT & THE GRENADINES

WAKE ISLAND
(to US)

JOHNSTON ATOLL (to US)

JAMAICA
NAVASSA I.
(to US)

HAITI
CURAÇAO
(Neth.)

MARSHALL
ISLANDS

WALLIS & FUTUNA
(to France)

KINGMAN REEF (to US)

CLIPPERTON ISLAND
(to French Polynesia)

GUATEMALA
EL SALVADOR
NICARAGUA
COSTA RICA

ARUBA
(Neth.)

GRENADA
TRINIDAD & TOBAGO

PALMYRA ATOLL (to US)

VENEZUELA

NAURU

BAKER &
HOWLAND
ISLANDS
(to US)

PANAMA

FRENCH GUIANA
(to France)

COLOMBIA

Equator

Galápagos Islands
(to Ecuador)

JARVIS ISLAND
(to US)

GUYANA
SURINAME

TUVALU

KIRIBATI

ECUADOR

SOLOMON
ISLANDS

TOKELAU
(to NZ)

BRAZIL

PERU

SAMOA

COOK
ISLANDS
(to NZ)

PACIFIC

VANUATU

FIJI TONGA

FRENCH POLYNESIA
(to France)

OCEAN

BOLIVIA

NEW
CALEDONIA
(to France)

PARAGUAY

Tropic of Capricorn

AL SEA ISLANDS
(Australia)

NIUE (to NZ)
AMERICAN
SAMOA
(to US)

PITCAIRN, HENDERSON,
DUCIE & OENO
ISLANDS
(to UK)

San Felix Island
(to Chile)

NORFOLK ISLAND
(to Australia)

Lord Howe Island
(to Australia)

Kermadec Island
(to NZ)

Easter Island
(to Chile)

Sala y Gomez
(to Chile)

San Ambrosia
Island
(to Chile)

CHILE

ARGENTINA

URUGUAY

WITHDRAWN
Anne Arundel Co. Public Library

Juan Fernandez Island
(to Chile)

NEW
ZEALAND

Chatham Island
(to NZ)

Bounty Island
(to NZ)

Campbell Island
(to NZ)

FALKLAND ISLANDS
(to UK)

Macquarie Island (to Australia)

CHILE

SOUTH GEORGIA &
SOUTH SANDWICH ISLANDS
(to UK)

ANTARCTICA

Continental key

NORTH AMERICA *pages 2-23*		**EUROPE** *pages 46-73*
SOUTH AMERICA *pages 24-33*		**ASIA** *pages 74-99*
AFRICA *pages 34-45*		**AUSTRALASIA & OCEANIA** *pages 100-109*

Antarctic Circle

Children's Illustrated World Atlas

Consultant

Dr Kathleen Baker

Senior Lecturer in Geography, King's College London (retired)
Senior Visiting Fellow, London South Bank University

Written by

Simon Adams • Mary Atkinson • Sarah Phillips • John Woodward

A Dorling Kindersley Book

THIS EDITION

DK DELHI
Senior editor Rupa Rao
Editor Neha Ruth Samuel
Jacket designer Dhirendra Singh
Jackets editorial coordinator Priyanka Sharma
Senior DTP designer Harish Aggarwal
DTP designer Jaypal Chauhan
Managing jackets editor Sreshtha Bhattacharya
Pre-production manager Balwant Singh
Production manager Pankaj Sharma
Managing editor Kingshuk Ghoshal
Managing art editor Govind Mittal

DK LONDON
Senior editor Anna Streiffert Limerick
Senior art editor Spencer Holbrook
US Senior editor Shannon Beatty
US Editor Karyn Gerhard
Senior cartographic editor Simon Mumford
Senior jacket designer Mark Cavanagh
Jacket editor Claire Gell
Jacket design development manager Sophia MTT
Producer, pre-production Andy Hilliard
Producer Gary Batchelor
Managing editor Francesca Baines
Managing art editor Philip Letsu
Publisher Andrew Macintyre
Associate publishing director Liz Wheeler
Art director Karen Self
Design director Philip Ormerod
Publishing director Jonathan Metcalf

FIRST EDITION

Project editors Lucy Hurst, Sadie Smith, Shaila Awan, Amber Tokeley
Art editors Joe Conneally, Sheila Collins, Rebecca Johns, Simon Oon, Andrew Nash
Senior editor Fran Jones
Senior art editor Floyd Sayers
Managing editor Andrew Macintyre
Managing art editor Jane Thomas
Picture research Carolyn Clerkin, Brenda Clynch
DK Pictures Sarah Mills
Production Jenny Jacoby
DTP designer Siu Yin Ho
Senior cartographic editor Simon Mumford
Cartographer Ed Merritt
Digital Cartography Encompass Graphics Limited
Satellite images Rob Stokes
3D globes Planetary Visions Ltd., London

First American Edition, 2003
This edition published in the United States in 2017 by
DK Publishing, 345 Hudson Street, New York, New York 10014

Copyright © 2003, 2008, 2011, 2017 Dorling Kindersley Limited
DK, a Division of Penguin Random House LLC
17 18 19 20 21 10 9 8 7 6 5 4 3 2 1
001—305057—July/2017

A catalog record for this book is available from the Library of Congress.
ISBN: 978-1-4654-6238-1

DK books are available at special discounts when purchased in bulk for sales
promotions, premiums, fund-raising, or educational use. For details, contact:
DK Publishing Special Markets, 345 Hudson Street, New York, New York 10014
SpecialSales@dk.com

Printed and bound in Hong Kong

A WORLD OF IDEAS:
SEE ALL THERE IS TO KNOW

www.dk.com

Contents

Active Planet

EARTH IS A DYNAMIC PLANET that is always changing its form. Heat generated by nuclear reactions deep below the surface creates hugely powerful currents that keep Earth's rocks on the move, triggering earthquakes and volcanic eruptions. Meanwhile, solar energy striking the planet in different ways creates currents in the air, driving the atmospheric turmoil of the weather. This changes with the seasons and from place to place, creating an enormous range of climates and habitats for the most dynamic element of all—life.

DOWN TO THE CORE

Earth formed from iron-rich asteroids that smashed together to build the planet. Early in its history it melted, allowing the heavy iron to sink and create a metallic core. This is surrounded by lighter rock, with the lightest forming Earth's crust. Most of the water on the planet lies in great oceans, and above them is the layer of air that forms the atmosphere.

Lower atmosphere, 10 miles (16 km) thick

Crust, 5–45 miles (8–70 km) thick

Mantle, 1,800 miles (2,900 km) thick

Liquid outer core, 1,400 miles (2,250 km) thick

Solid inner core, 1,515 miles (2,440 km) across

North American Plate

North American Plate

Eurasian Plate

Caribbean Plate

Cocos Plate

Pacific Plate

African Plate

Pacific Plate

South American Plate

Indo-Australian Plate

Nazca Plate

Antarctic Plate

THE PLATES OF EARTH'S CRUST

Heat generated deep within the planet creates currents in the mobile mantle rock beneath the crust. These currents drag some sections of the cool, brittle crust apart while pushing other parts together, fracturing the crust into separate plates. The biggest of these span oceans and continents, but there are many smaller plates. At their boundaries the plates may be diverging (pulling apart), converging (pushing together), or sliding past each other at transform faults.

Key to map

—— Transform fault	—— Divergent boundary
- - - Uncertain boundary	—— Convergent boundary

WHERE MOVING PLATES MEET

The boundaries between the plates are volcanic earthquake zones. The plates move very slowly, pulling apart at divergent boundaries. This allows hot rock below to melt, erupt, and cool to form new crust—especially at the spreading rifts that form mid-ocean ridges. Meanwhile at convergent boundaries, one plate slides beneath another, pushing up mountain ranges and making volcanoes erupt. Other volcanoes erupt over hot spots in the mantle below the crust.

1. Continental crust, much thicker than oceanic crust
2. Broad basin formed near uplifted area
3. Ancient converging boundary, now inactive
4. Mountains created when plate boundary was active
5. Oceanic crust formed from heavy basalt rock
6. Upper mantle, mainly solid but very hot
7. Mantle, solid but mobile owing to heat currents
8. Spreading rift forming a mid-ocean ridge
9. Hot-spot volcano erupting over mantle plume
10. Ocean trench marking convergent plate boundary
11. Volcano erupting over convergent boundary
12. Earthquake zone—one plate grinding under another
13. Plates pulling apart, creating a rift valley

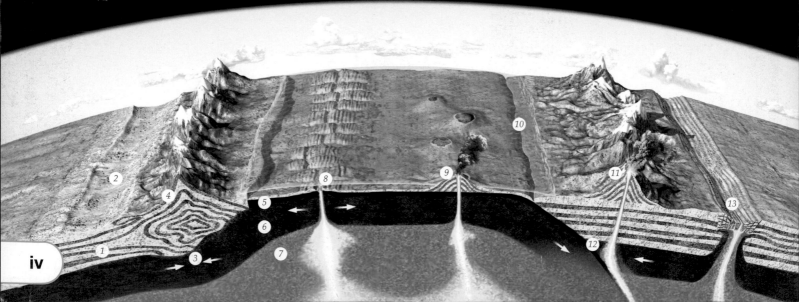

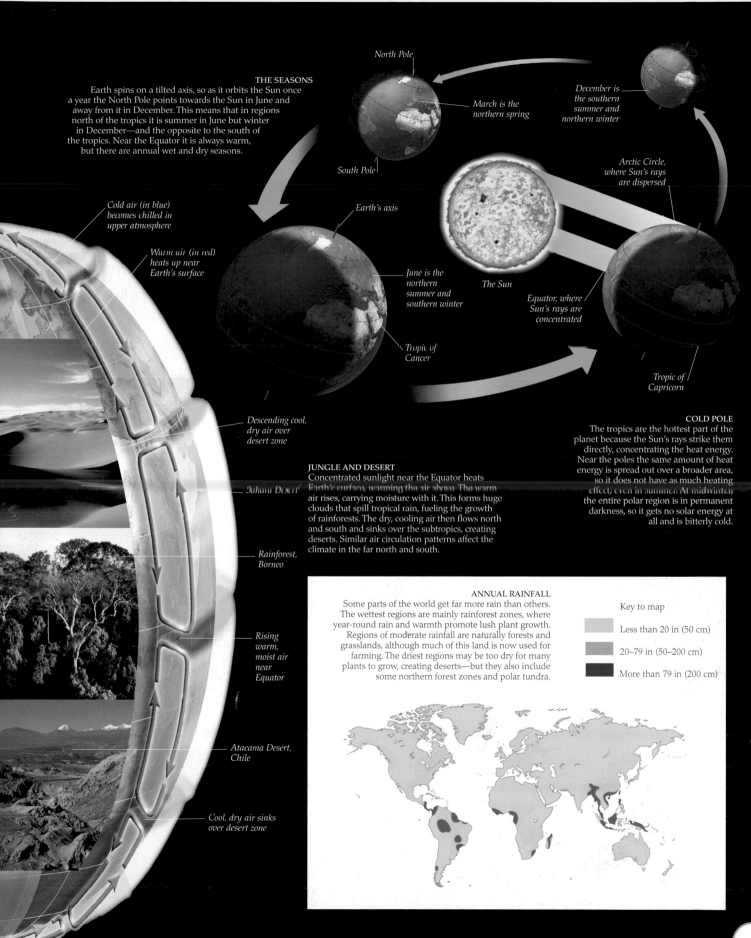

THE SEASONS
Earth spins on a tilted axis, so as it orbits the Sun once a year the North Pole points towards the Sun in June and away from it in December. This means that in regions north of the tropics it is summer in June but winter in December—and the opposite to the south of the tropics. Near the Equator it is always warm, but there are annual wet and dry seasons.

North Pole

March is the northern spring

South Pole

December is the southern summer and northern winter

Arctic Circle, where Sun's rays are dispersed

Earth's axis

Cold air (in blue) becomes chilled in upper atmosphere

Warm air (in red) heats up near Earth's surface

June is the northern summer and southern winter

The Sun

Equator, where Sun's rays are concentrated

Tropic of Cancer

Tropic of Capricorn

Descending cool, dry air over desert zone

JUNGLE AND DESERT
Concentrated sunlight near the Equator heats Earth's surface, warming the air above. The warm air rises, carrying moisture with it. This forms huge clouds that spill tropical rain, fueling the growth of rainforests. The dry, cooling air then flows north and south and sinks over the subtropics, creating deserts. Similar air circulation patterns affect the climate in the far north and south.

COLD POLE
The tropics are the hottest part of the planet because the Sun's rays strike them directly, concentrating the heat energy. Near the poles the same amount of heat energy is spread out over a broader area, so it does not have as much heating effect, even in summer. At midwinter the entire polar region is in permanent darkness, so it gets no solar energy at all and is bitterly cold.

Sahara Desert

Rainforest, Borneo

Rising warm, moist air near Equator

Atacama Desert, Chile

Cool, dry air sinks over desert zone

ANNUAL RAINFALL
Some parts of the world get far more rain than others. The wettest regions are mainly rainforest zones, where year-round rain and warmth promote lush plant growth. Regions of moderate rainfall are naturally forests and grasslands, although much of this land is now used for farming. The driest regions may be too dry for many plants to grow, creating deserts—but they also include some northern forest zones and polar tundra.

Key to map

Less than 20 in (50 cm)

20–79 in (50–200 cm)

More than 79 in (200 cm)

Planet People

THE NUMBER OF PEOPLE ON THE PLANET has quadrupled since 1900. Much of this growth has taken place in the developing world, which is now home to more than 80 percent of the population. Many of these people are very poor and do not experience the living conditions that most citizens of the developed world take for granted. This is changing, however, especially in nations such as China, India, and Brazil. Here, new technology and international trade are fueling rapid economic growth that is transforming how people live. But as more of the planet's people demand more of its scarce resources, there may be some difficult challenges ahead.

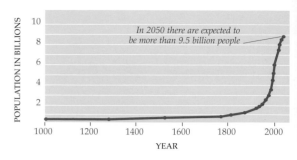

In 2050 there are expected to be more than 9.5 billion people

POPULATION INCREASE
For centuries, the number of people on the planet stayed the same, at roughly 300 million. But since the 1750s, better living conditions and healthcare have allowed more babies to survive, causing a population explosion. Since 1950, the population has soared from 2.5 billion to nearly 7.5 billion today. It will keep growing, but probably not quite so fast.

POPULATION DENSITY
On this map the area of each part of the world is adjusted to reflect the number of people who live there. For example, Japan's population of 127 million is far bigger than that of Australia, with 23 million, so it is shown much larger here despite being a smaller country. More people live in Nigeria—186 million—than in all of Russia. But the nations with the biggest populations by far are India and China, each with far more than 1 billion citizens.

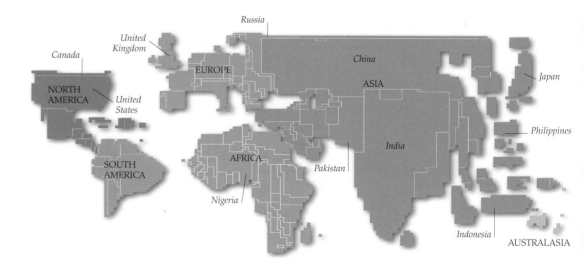

FAMILY SIZE
All over the world, some women have more children than others, but the average varies from continent to continent. European women have 1.6 children on average, so two families may have three children between them. This is far fewer than in Africa, where the population is growing faster despite higher death rates among children. Worldwide the average is 2.5—more than enough to replace both parents.

AFRICA	ASIA	SOUTH AMERICA	NORTH AMERICA	AUSTRALASIA	EUROPE
4.7 children per woman	*2.2 children per woman*	*2.2 children per woman*	*1.9 children per woman*	*2.4 children per woman*	*1.6 children per woman*

BIRTH AND DEATH RATES
If the birth rate is the same as the death rate, the population stays the same. But in most countries, the birth rate is higher. In Niger, west Africa, there are 44.8 births but only 12.1 deaths per 1,000 people, and the population is growing at 3.2 per cent a year. Brazil's population is also growing, with 14.3 births against 6.6 deaths. By contrast, Lithuania has a shrinking population, with 10 births outweighed by 14.5 deaths.

A country with few young people is said to have an aging population. But these school children in Burundi, east Africa, are part of a youthful population, with fewer old people. Both situations can cause problems.

NIGER

BRAZIL

LITHUANIA

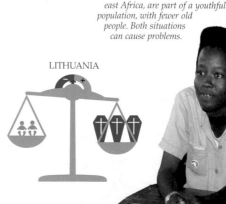

CITY POPULATIONS

As populations grow, people tend to move from the country to a city to find work. Today, one-third of the world's people live in cities, which grow bigger every year. Some are colossal, like Tokyo—the largest city in Asia. The other cities shown here are the most populous on each continent. They are vibrant centers of civilization, but some cities are fringed by sprawling shantytowns, where poor people live in makeshift shacks with no proper services such as clean water.

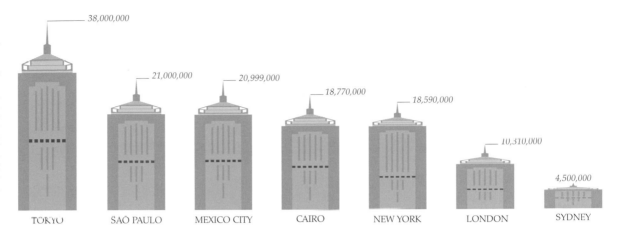

38,000,000 — TOKYO
21,000,000 — SÃO PAULO
20,999,000 — MEXICO CITY
18,770,000 — CAIRO
18,590,000 — NEW YORK
10,310,000 — LONDON
4,500,000 — SYDNEY

LANGUAGES

These are the 10 most common languages worldwide, sized in proportion to the number of native speakers. Chinese outstrips the others because China has such a huge population. But Spanish comes next because it is the main language of many Latin American countries, such as Mexico. English is almost as common, thanks mainly to being the language of the United States. It is also used as an international language for trade.

HINDI ARABIC SPANISH CHINESE ENGLISH PORTUGUESE RUSSIAN JAPANESE BENGALI PUNJABI

Christianity 2.2 billion

Islam 1.6 billion

Hinduism 1 billion

Buddhism 487 million

Chinese traditional 300 million

Indigenous 300 million

African traditional 100 million

Others 97.7 million

Others	
Sikhism	23 million
Juche	19 million
Spiritism	15 million
Judaism	14 million
Baha'i	7 million
Jainism	4.2 million
Shinto	4 million
Cao Đài	4 million
Zoroastrianism	2.6 million
Tenrikyo	2 million
Neo-Paganism	1 million
Unitarian Universalism	800,000
Rastafarianism	600,000
Scientology	500,000

RELIGIONS AND BELIEFS

Almost three-quarters of the world's population are followers of Christianity, Islam, Hinduism, or Buddhism. But many people follow other faiths, particularly in China where the traditional folk religion, Shenism, is practised by nearly one-fifth of the huge population. The "indigenous" and "African traditional religions" data points are both groupings of different, but similar, religions. Others are listed at far right, in order of popularity.

ONLINE ACCESS

Over the last decades, the Internet has become a vital tool for global business, education, and politics, so the more people who can use it, the better. These charts show the percentage of people with Internet access both worldwide and in particular regions. Australia, North America, and Europe lead the field, but the number of Internet users is growing fastest in the Middle East and Africa.

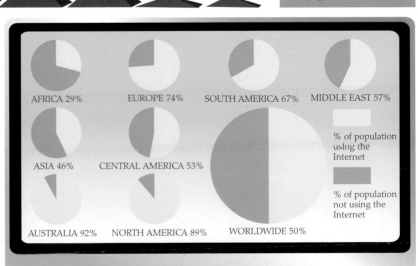

AFRICA 29%
EUROPE 74%
SOUTH AMERICA 67%
MIDDLE EAST 57%
ASIA 46%
CENTRAL AMERICA 53%
AUSTRALIA 92%
NORTH AMERICA 89%
WORLDWIDE 50%

% of population using the Internet

% of population not using the Internet

WEALTH

A country's wealth is often measured in terms of the money it earns in a year divided by its number of inhabitants. This is called its Gross Domestic Product (GDP) per capita. Both Norway and Qatar make lots of money from exporting oil and gas, and since they have small populations their GDP per capita are very high. Burundi in east Africa has only one-twentyfifth of the income of Qatar divided between five times as many people, so its GDP per capita is very low.

Burundi	Bolivia	Lithuania	Japan	Canada	Qatar	Norway
$277	$3,076	$14,147	$32,477	$43,248	$73,653	$74,400

BUSIEST AIRPORTS

Air travel has expanded enormously since the 1950s, when international air travel was a luxury enjoyed by a few wealthy people known as the "jet set." Today, flying is often the most economical way to travel, as well as the quickest. This is reflected in the vast number of passengers who pass through the world's airports as they travel for business or pleasure. The world's busiest airport is Hartsfield-Jackson International Airport in Atlanta, with more than 100 million people arriving and departing each year. The graphics below show the busiest airport in each continent, and number of passengers.

AIRBUS A380
The growth in air travel has led to the development of giant airliners such as the Airbus A380. When it entered service in 2007, this was the world's largest passenger plane, capable of carrying up to 853 people.

N. AMERICA:
Hartsfield-Jackson, Atlanta, USA

101.5 million

ASIA:
Beijing Capital, China

89.9 million

EUROPE:
Heathrow, London, UK

75 million

AUSTRALIA & OCEANIA:
Kingsford Smith, Sydney, Australia

39.9 million

S. AMERICA:
Guarulhos, São Paulo, Brazil

39.2 million

AFRICA:
Tambo, Jo'Burg, South Africa

19.1 million

TRADE

Although air freight is an important element of international trade, about 90 percent of cargo by weight is transported by sea. Altogether, this adds up to around 11 billion tons of freight. Much of this is transported in containers, carried by more than 5,000 container ships. The busiest shipping routes link Europe and North America with the Middle East and Far East, with ports such as Singapore, Shanghai, Dubai, and Rotterdam handling most of the trade.

Traffic in millions of tons

400+	
300–400	
200–300	
100–200	
20–100	
10–20	
5–10	

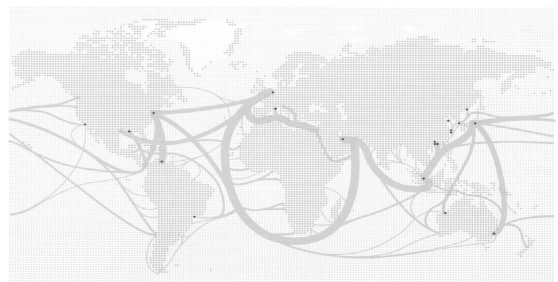

Mapping the World

ABOUT THE ATLAS

This atlas is divided into six continental sections—North America, South America, Africa, Europe, Asia, and Australasia and Oceania. Each country, or group of countries, then has its own map that shows cities, towns, and main geographical features such as rivers, lakes, and mountain ranges. Photographs and text provide detailed information about life in that country—its people, traditions, politics, and economy. Each continental section has a different color border to help you locate that section. There is also a gazetteer and an index to help you access information.

MAP LOCATOR

This map shows, in red, the location of each country, part of a country, or group of countries in relation to the whole planet. There is a locator for each map in the book.

MAP COLORS

The colors shown on the maps are built up from numerous satellite photographs and reflect the true colors of the land, averaged over the seasons. Certain colors give clues to what the land is like—whether it is forested or farmland, mountains or desert.

Land appearing sandy tends to be desert, semi-desert, or scrub.

Mountainous desert looks like this, with shadows on the sandy background color.

Pale green is usually grassland or crop land.

Darker greens usually indicate wooded land or pasture.

White shows land under permanent cover by snow and ice.

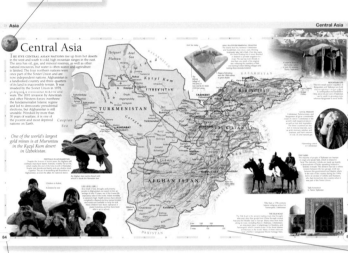

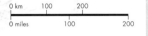

FOREIGN NAMES

Features on the maps are generally labeled in the language of that country. For example, it would be:

Lake on English-speaking countries
Lago on Spanish-speaking countries
Lac on French-speaking countries

However, if a feature is well-known or mentioned in the main text on the page, it will appear there in English so that readers can find it easily.

USING THE GRID REFERENCES

The letters and numbers around the outside of the page form a grid to help you find places on the map. For example, to find Kabul, look up its name in the gazetteer (see pp.112–133), and you'll find the reference 85 J7. The first number is the page, the letter and number refer to the square made by following up or down from J and across from 7 to form J7.

SCALE

Each map features a scale that shows how distances on the map relate to miles and kilometers. The scale guide can be used to see how big a country is. Not all maps in the book are drawn to the same scale.

KEY TO MAP SYMBOLS

BORDERS

— International border: Border between countries which is mutually recognized.

— State border: Border used in some large countries to show internal divisions.

— Disputed border: Border used in practice, but not mutually agreed between two countries.

••••• Claimed border: Border which is not mutually recognized—where territory belonging to one country is claimed by another.

×—×—× Ceasefire line

▪ ▪ ▪ ▪ Undefined boundary

PHYSICAL FEATURES

▲ Mountain

▽ Depression

▲ Volcano

⋈ Pass/Tunnel

DRAINAGE FEATURES

— Major river

— Minor river

------ Seasonal river

—|— Dam

— Canal

| Waterfall

⌐ ⌐ Seasonal lake

MISCELLANEOUS FEATURES

◇ Site of interest

∿∿∿ Ancient wall

COMMUNICATIONS

═══ Highway

═══ Major road

— Minor road

— Rail

✈ Airport

TOWNS & CITIES

◉ More than 500,000

◎ 100,000 – 500,000

○ 50,000 – 100,000

○ Less than 50,000

● National capital

● Internal administrative capital

◉ Polar research station

LATITUDE & LONGITUDE

— Equator

------ Tropics/Circles

NAMES

REGIONS

FRANCE Country

JERSEY Dependent
*(British Crown territory
Dependency)*

KANSAS Administrative
region

Dordogne Cultural region

TOWNS & CITIES

PARIS National capital

SAN JUAN Dependent
territory
capital city

Seattle
Limón Other
Genk towns
San José & cities

NAMES *continued*

PHYSICAL

Andes Landscape
Ardennes features

Balearic Islands Island group

Majorca Island

Lake Baikal Lake/River
/Canal

*PACIFIC
OCEAN*

*Gulf of
Mexico* Sea features

Bay of Campeche

Chile Rise Undersea
feature

OTHER FEATURES

Tropic of Cancer Graticule text

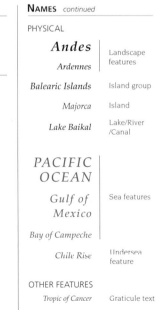

NORTH AMERICA

The North American continent extends from the frozen wastes of Arctic Canada to the Caribbean islands and the tropical jungles of Panama. It is dominated politically by the United States, the richest nation on Earth, yet life in countries such as Mexico and Nicaragua is still a struggle. The data below is arranged in order of each nation's size.

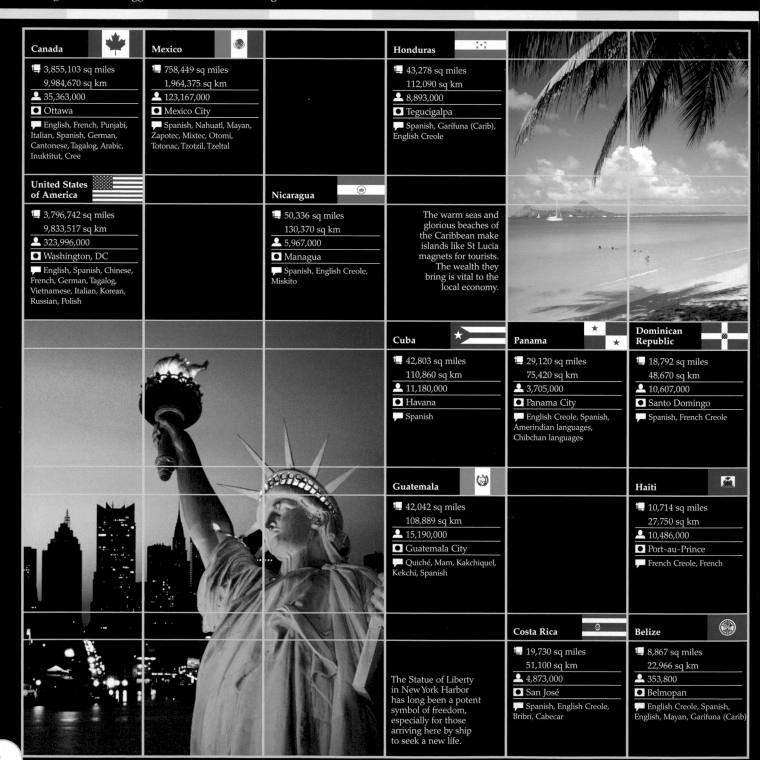

Canada
🏳 3,855,103 sq miles
9,984,670 sq km
👤 35,363,000
🏛 Ottawa
💬 English, French, Punjabi, Italian, Spanish, German, Cantonese, Tagalog, Arabic, Inuktitut, Cree

United States of America
🏳 3,796,742 sq miles
9,833,517 sq km
👤 323,996,000
🏛 Washington, DC
💬 English, Spanish, Chinese, French, German, Tagalog, Vietnamese, Italian, Korean, Russian, Polish

Mexico
🏳 758,449 sq miles
1,964,375 sq km
👤 123,167,000
🏛 Mexico City
💬 Spanish, Nahuatl, Mayan, Zapotec, Mixtec, Otomi, Totonac, Tzotzil, Tzeltal

Nicaragua
🏳 50,336 sq miles
130,370 sq km
👤 5,967,000
🏛 Managua
💬 Spanish, English Creole, Miskito

Honduras
🏳 43,278 sq miles
112,090 sq km
👤 8,893,000
🏛 Tegucigalpa
💬 Spanish, Garífuna (Carib), English Creole

The warm seas and glorious beaches of the Caribbean make islands like St Lucia magnets for tourists. The wealth they bring is vital to the local economy.

Cuba
🏳 42,803 sq miles
110,860 sq km
👤 11,180,000
🏛 Havana
💬 Spanish

Guatemala
🏳 42,042 sq miles
108,889 sq km
👤 15,190,000
🏛 Guatemala City
💬 Quiché, Mam, Kakchiquel, Kekchí, Spanish

Panama
🏳 29,120 sq miles
75,420 sq km
👤 3,705,000
🏛 Panama City
💬 English Creole, Spanish, Amerindian languages, Chibchan languages

Costa Rica
🏳 19,730 sq miles
51,100 sq km
👤 4,873,000
🏛 San José
💬 Spanish, English Creole, Bribri, Cabecar

Dominican Republic
🏳 18,792 sq miles
48,670 sq km
👤 10,607,000
🏛 Santo Domingo
💬 Spanish, French Creole

Haiti
🏳 10,714 sq miles
27,750 sq km
👤 10,486,000
🏛 Port-au-Prince
💬 French Creole, French

Belize
🏳 8,867 sq miles
22,966 sq km
👤 353,800
🏛 Belmopan
💬 English Creole, Spanish, English, Mayan, Garifuna (Carib)

The Statue of Liberty in New York Harbor has long been a potent symbol of freedom, especially for those arriving here by ship to seek a new life.

El Salvador

- 8,124 sq miles
  21,041 sq km
- 6,157,000
- San Salvador
- Spanish

Dominica

- 290 sq miles
  751 sq km
- 73,700
- Roseau
- French Creole, English

The Bahamas

- 5,359 sq miles
  13,880 sq km
- 327,300
- Nassau
- English, English Creole, French Creole

St Lucia

- 238 sq miles
  616 sq km
- 164,500
- Castries
- English, French Creole

Antigua and Barbuda

- 171 sq miles
  443 sq km
- 93,600
- St John's
- English, English Patois

Jamaica

- 4,244 sq miles
  10,991 sq km
- 2,970,000
- Kingston
- English Creole, English

Grenada

- 133 sq miles
  344 sq km
- 111,200
- St George's
- English, English Creole

Much of Canada is still untamed wilderness—a land of huge, dramatic landscapes like this lake high up in the rugged, frost-shattered Rocky Mountains.

Trinidad and Tobago

- 1,980 sq miles
  5,128 sq km
- 1,220,000
- Port-of-Spain
- English Creole, English, Hindi, French, Spanish

Barbados

- 166 sq miles
  430 sq km
- 291,500
- Bridgetown
- Bajan (Barbadian English), English

St Vincent and the Grenadines

- 150 sq miles
  389 sq km
- 102,300
- Kingstown
- English, English Creole

St Kitts and Nevis

- 101 sq miles
  261 sq km
- 52,300
- Basseterre
- English, English Creole

Western Canada and Alaska

CANADA IS A HUGE COUNTRY—its western half stretches from the flat prairies in the east to the towering Rocky Mountains in the west, and from the relatively mild south to the permanently frozen area north of the Arctic Circle. Harsh conditions over much of the region mean that most of the population is concentrated in cities in the south, such as Vancouver, Calgary, and Winnipeg. The Prairies—once a vast expanse of grassland—are now used mainly for growing wheat on huge mechanized farms. Oil and natural gas are found there as well. These natural resources are also important in Alaska, a part of the United States. The majority of Alaska's people moved there to work in these lucrative industries.

FORESTRY
Large parts of western Canada are covered in forests and lumbering is a major part of the local economy. The trees are used to make buildings, furniture, and paper. In the past, whole areas of trees were cleared but now sustainable methods, such as selective cutting and replanting, are practiced.

Felled trees transported down a river near Vancouver

TOTEM POLES
The native peoples of British Columbia use totem poles to record their clan history. Each carved and painted totem describes a real or mythical event and often features animals that the clan has a close connection with, such as the eagle (left).

DOGSLED RACING
The state sport of Alaska is dogsled racing. Here, competitors take part in the annual Iditarod Trail Sled Dog Race, a grueling run across the rugged landscape for drivers and their teams of dogs.

VANCOUVER
This city's vibrant cultural mix is typical of Canada's diversity. Many South Asian, Chinese, as well as other ethnic groups live here and reflect Vancouver's historic role as a destination for migrants. Hosting the 2010 Winter Olympics raised its profile and its bustling economy, mild climate, and cultural links make it an attractive place to live.

Map labels

Near Islands
Rat Islands
Bering Strait
Chukchi Sea
Wevok
Point Lay
Barrow
Kivalina
Wales
Gambell
Saint Lawrence Island
Deering
Colville River
Umiat
Prudhoe Bay
Kaktovik
Brooks Range
Norton Sound
Alakanuk
Grayling
Yukon River
Kokrines
Fort Yukon
Aklavik
Fort McPherson
Inuvik
Paulatuk
Nunivak Island
Pribilof Islands
Kwigillingok
ALASKA (to US)
Fairbanks
Yukon River
Fort Good Hope (Rádeyilikóé)
Kugluktuk (Coppermine)
Andreanof Islands
Aleutian Islands
Atka
Platinum
Kuskokwim Mts
Denali (Mount McKinley) 20,433ft (6194m)
McKinley Park
Alaska Range
Fort Simpson
Great Bear Lake
Echo
Umnak Island
Unalaska Island
Unimak Island
Dutch Harbor
Bristol Bay
Iliamna Lake
Susitna
Anchorage
Hope
Gulkana
YUKON
Mackenzie
NORTHWEST TERRITORIES
Belkofski
Alaska Peninsula
Valdez
Chitina
Mount Logan 19,551ft (5959m)
Shumagin Islands
Kodiak
Cordova
Katalla
Whitehorse
Tungsten
Edzo
Yellowknife
Great S Lake
Kodiak Island
Gulf of Alaska
Yakutat
Fort Providence
Fort Liard
Hay River
Haines
Atlin
Fort Nelson
Gustavus
Juneau
BRITISH COLUMBIA
Fort Vermili
Kake
Fort St. John
ALBERTA
McMu
Alexander Archipelago
Port Alexander
Ketchikan
Ware
Grande Prairie
Athabasca
Prince Rupert
Kitimat
Athabasca
Queen Charlotte Islands
Ocean Falls
Prince George
Edmonton
Mount Robson 12,972ft (3954m)
Le
Queen Charlotte Sound
Mount Waddington 13,176ft (4016m)
Red Deer
Port Hardy
Kamloops
Calgary
Campbell River
Vancouver Island
Nanaimo
Vancouver
Kelowna
Victoria
Lethbridge
Cranbrook
Milk Ri
UNITE
ARCTIC OCEAN
Beaufort Sea
Prince Patrick Island
Mould Bay
Banks Island
Sachs Harbour (Ikaahuk)
Tuktoyaktuk
Amundsen Gulf
Holma
Bering Sea
PACIFIC OCEAN
Rocky Mountains

B C D E F G H

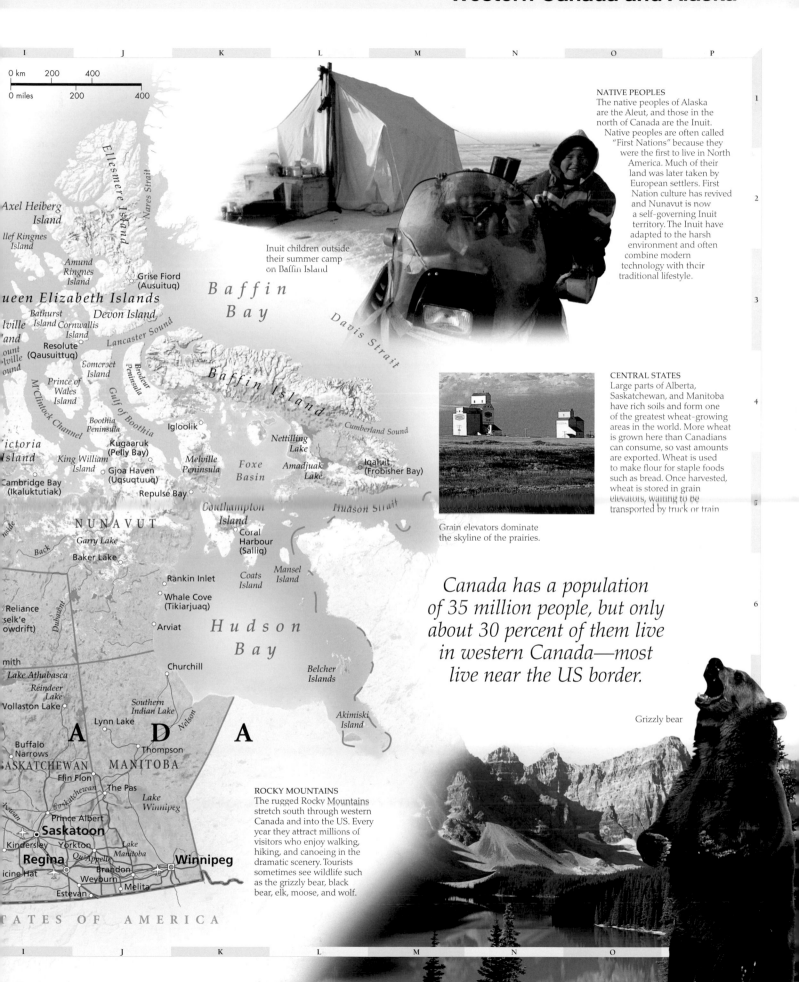

0 km 200 400
0 miles 200 400

NATIVE PEOPLES
The native peoples of Alaska are the Aleut, and those in the north of Canada are the Inuit. Native peoples are often called "First Nations" because they were the first to live in North America. Much of their land was later taken by European settlers. First Nation culture has revived and Nunavut is now a self-governing Inuit territory. The Inuit have adapted to the harsh environment and often combine modern technology with their traditional lifestyle.

Inuit children outside their summer camp on Baffin Island

CENTRAL STATES
Large parts of Alberta, Saskatchewan, and Manitoba have rich soils and form one of the greatest wheat-growing areas in the world. More wheat is grown here than Canadians can consume, so vast amounts are exported. Wheat is used to make flour for staple foods such as bread. Once harvested, wheat is stored in grain elevators, waiting to be transported by truck or train

Grain elevators dominate the skyline of the prairies.

Canada has a population of 35 million people, but only about 30 percent of them live in western Canada—most live near the US border.

Grizzly bear

ROCKY MOUNTAINS
The rugged Rocky Mountains stretch south through western Canada and into the US. Every year they attract millions of visitors who enjoy walking, hiking, and canoeing in the dramatic scenery. Tourists sometimes see wildlife such as the grizzly bear, black bear, elk, moose, and wolf.

Axel Heiberg Island
Ilef Ringnes Island
Amund Ringnes Island
Grise Fiord (Ausuituq)
Ellesmere Island
Nares Strait

Baffin Bay
Davis Strait

Queen Elizabeth Islands
Bathurst Island
Cornwallis Island
Devon Island
Lancaster Sound
Resolute (Qausuittuq)
Somerset Island
Prince of Wales Island
Brodeur Peninsula
Baffin Island

Boothia Peninsula
Igloolik
Cumberland Sound
Kugaaruk (Pelly Bay)
King William Island
Gjoa Haven (Uqsuqtuuq)
Melville Peninsula
Nettilling Lake
Foxe Basin
Amadjuak Lake
Iqaluit (Frobisher Bay)
Cambridge Bay (Ikaluktutiak)
Victoria Island
Repulse Bay
Southampton Island
Coral Harbour (Salliq)
Hudson Strait

NUNAVUT
Garry Lake
Baker Lake
Back
Rankin Inlet
Coats Island
Mansel Island
Whale Cove (Tikiarjuaq)
Arviat

Hudson Bay

Reliance
selk'e
owdrift
Dubawnt
Churchill
Belcher Islands

smith
Lake Athabasca
Reindeer Lake
Wollaston Lake
Southern Indian Lake
Lynn Lake
Nelson
Akimiski Island

A
D
A
Buffalo Narrows
Thompson
SASKATCHEWAN
MANITOBA
Flin Flon
The Pas
Lake Winnipeg
Prince Albert
Saskatoon
Lake Manitoba
Kindersley
Yorkton
Qu'Appelle
Regina
Brandon
Winnipeg
icine Hat
Weyburn
Melita
Estevan

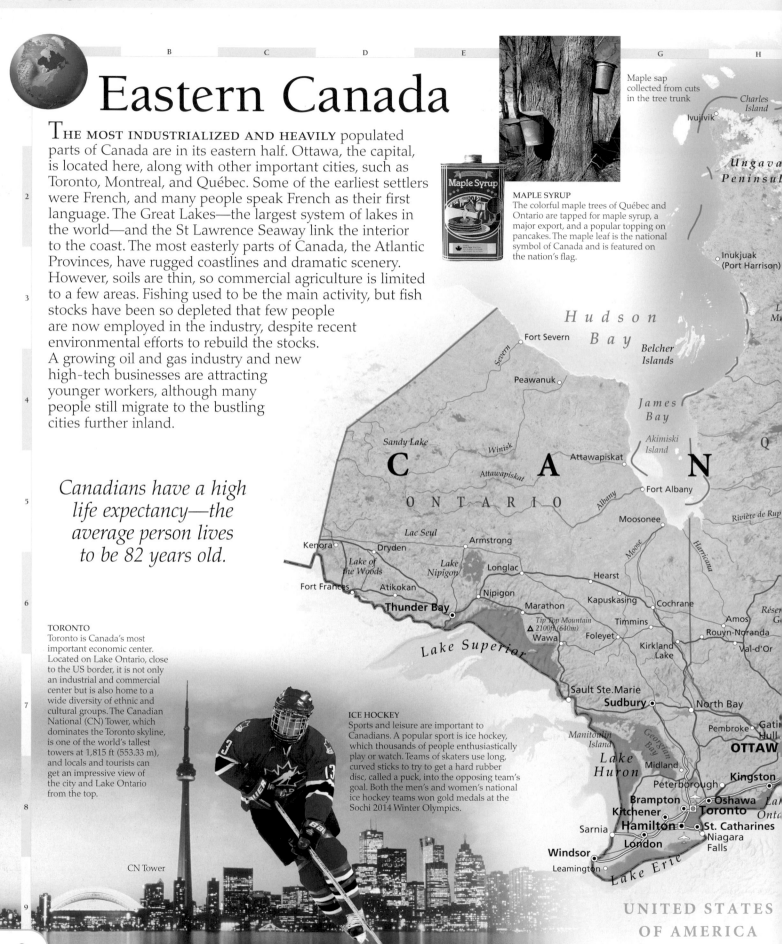

Eastern Canada

THE MOST INDUSTRIALIZED AND HEAVILY populated parts of Canada are in its eastern half. Ottawa, the capital, is located here, along with other important cities, such as Toronto, Montreal, and Québec. Some of the earliest settlers were French, and many people speak French as their first language. The Great Lakes—the largest system of lakes in the world—and the St Lawrence Seaway link the interior to the coast. The most easterly parts of Canada, the Atlantic Provinces, have rugged coastlines and dramatic scenery. However, soils are thin, so commercial agriculture is limited to a few areas. Fishing used to be the main activity, but fish stocks have been so depleted that few people are now employed in the industry, despite recent environmental efforts to rebuild the stocks. A growing oil and gas industry and new high-tech businesses are attracting younger workers, although many people still migrate to the bustling cities further inland.

Canadians have a high life expectancy—the average person lives to be 82 years old.

Maple sap collected from cuts in the tree trunk

MAPLE SYRUP
The colorful maple trees of Québec and Ontario are tapped for maple syrup, a major export, and a popular topping on pancakes. The maple leaf is the national symbol of Canada and is featured on the nation's flag.

TORONTO
Toronto is Canada's most important economic center. Located on Lake Ontario, close to the US border, it is not only an industrial and commercial center but is also home to a wide diversity of ethnic and cultural groups. The Canadian National (CN) Tower, which dominates the Toronto skyline, is one of the world's tallest towers at 1,815 ft (553.33 m), and locals and tourists can get an impressive view of the city and Lake Ontario from the top.

ICE HOCKEY
Sports and leisure are important to Canadians. A popular sport is ice hockey, which thousands of people enthusiastically play or watch. Teams of skaters use long, curved sticks to try to get a hard rubber disc, called a puck, into the opposing team's goal. Both the men's and women's national ice hockey teams won gold medals at the Sochi 2014 Winter Olympics.

CN Tower

Map labels:
Charles Island
Ivujivik
Ungava Peninsula
Inukjuak (Port Harrison)
Hudson Bay
Fort Severn
Belcher Islands
Peawanuk
James Bay
Akimiski Island
Sandy Lake
Winisk
Attawapiskat
Fort Albany
Moosonee
Rivière de Rup
ONTARIO
Lac Seul
Armstrong
Kenora
Dryden
Lake Nipigon
Longlac
Hearst
Lake of the Woods
Hurricana
Fort Frances
Atikokan
Nipigon
Kapuskasing
Cochrane
Amos
Thunder Bay
Marathon
Tip Top Mountain 2100ft (640m)
Timmins
Rouyn-Noranda
Wawa
Foleyet
Kirkland Lake
Val-d'Or
Lake Superior
Sault Ste.Marie
Sudbury
North Bay
Pembroke
Gati Hull
Manitoulin Island
OTTAW
Georgian Bay
Lake Huron
Midland
Kingston
Peterborough
Brampton
Oshawa
Kitchener
Toronto
Ontar
Sarnia
Hamilton
St. Catharines
London
Niagara Falls
Windsor
Leamington
Lake Erie

C   A   N
Q

UNITED STATES OF AMERICA

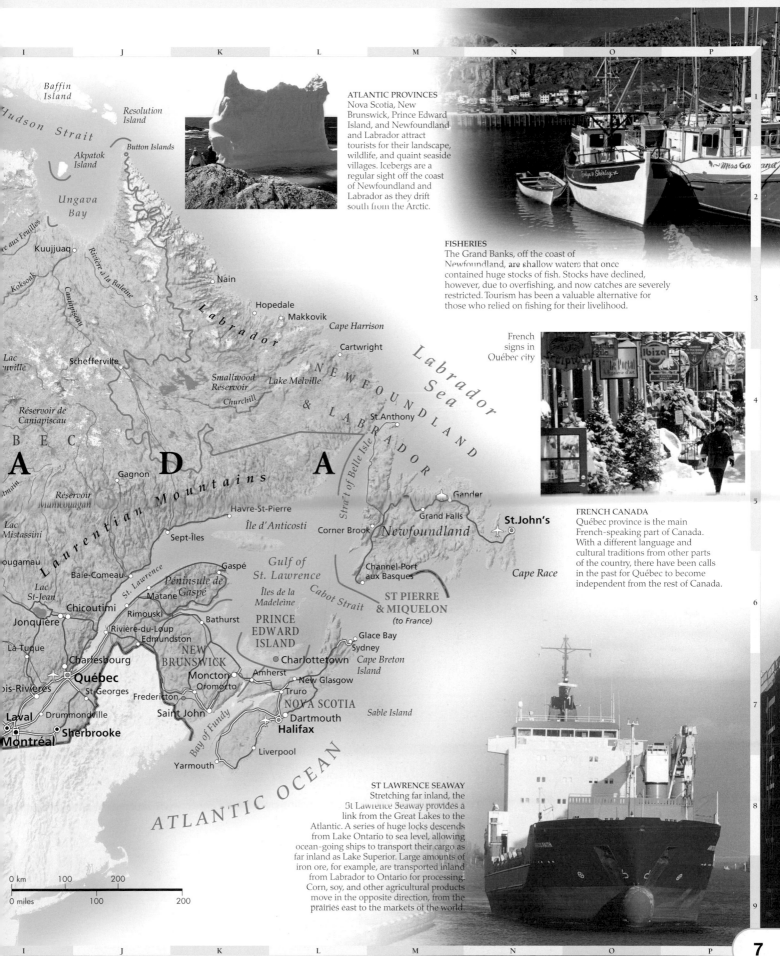

Baffin
Island

Hudson Strait

Resolution
Island

Akpatok
Island

Button Islands

Ungava
Bay

rivière aux Feuilles

Kuujjuaq

Rivière à la Baleine

Koksoak

Caniapiscau

Lac
...nville

Schefferville

Nain

Hopedale

Makkovik

Cape Harrison

Cartwright

ATLANTIC PROVINCES
Nova Scotia, New
Brunswick, Prince Edward
Island, and Newfoundland
and Labrador attract
tourists for their landscape,
wildlife, and quaint seaside
villages. Icebergs are a
regular sight off the coast
of Newfoundland and
Labrador as they drift
south from the Arctic.

FISHERIES
The Grand Banks, off the coast of
Newfoundland, are shallow waters that once
contained huge stocks of fish. Stocks have declined,
however, due to overfishing, and now catches are severely
restricted. Tourism has been a valuable alternative for
those who relied on fishing for their livelihood.

Réservoir de
Caniapiscau

Labrador

Smallwood
Reservoir

Lake Melville

Churchill

NEWFOUNDLAND
& LABRADOR

Labrador
Sea

St. Anthony

French
signs in
Québec city

B E C

Gagnon

A   D   A

Laurentian Mountains

Réservoir
Manicouagan

Lac
Mistassini

...ougamau

Baie-Comeau

Lac
St-Jean

Chicoutimi

Jonquière

La Tuque

Charlesbourg

Québec

...ois-Rivières

St-Georges

Laval

Drummondville

Montréal

Sherbrooke

Havre-St-Pierre

Sept-Îles

St. Lawrence

Matane

Rimouski

Rivière-du-Loup

Edmundston

NEW
BRUNSWICK

Fredericton

Saint John

Bay of Fundy

Yarmouth

Île d'Anticosti

Gaspé

Péninsule de
Gaspé

Gulf of
St. Lawrence

Îles de la
Madeleine

PRINCE
EDWARD
ISLAND

Bathurst

Moncton

Oromocto

Amherst

Charlottetown

New Glasgow

Truro

NOVA SCOTIA

Dartmouth

Halifax

Liverpool

Strait of Belle Isle

Corner Brook

Gander

Grand Falls

Newfoundland

St. John's

Cabot Strait

Channel-Port
aux Basques

ST PIERRE
& MIQUELON
(to France)

Glace Bay

Sydney

Cape Breton
Island

Sable Island

Cape Race

FRENCH CANADA
Québec province is the main
French-speaking part of Canada.
With a different language and
cultural traditions from other parts
of the country, there have been calls
in the past for Québec to become
independent from the rest of Canada.

ATLANTIC OCEAN

0 km   100   200
0 miles   100   200

ST LAWRENCE SEAWAY
Stretching far inland, the
St Lawrence Seaway provides a
link from the Great Lakes to the
Atlantic. A series of huge locks descends
from Lake Ontario to sea level, allowing
ocean-going ships to transport their cargo as
far inland as Lake Superior. Large amounts of
iron ore, for example, are transported inland
from Labrador to Ontario for processing.
Corn, soy, and other agricultural products
move in the opposite direction, from the
prairies east to the markets of the world.

USA: Northeast

THE NORTHEASTERN UNITED STATES is a heavily populated area that is steeped in history. This is traditionally the main immigration point into the States, with the Statue of Liberty lighting the way for those arriving into New York by boat. People from all over the world have settled in this region to live and work, creating a "melting pot" of cultures and ethnic groups. Important historical events, such as the signing of the Declaration of Independence and the Constitution, took place in Philadelphia. These documents set the foundations for American life today. It is also here that the capital and center of government were established. Today, while industry and agriculture are still important, finance and commerce are the driving forces of the economy.

The White House in Washington, D.C. has been home to every president except George Washington, after whom the city is named.

THRIVING CITY
New York is the largest city in the US. Historically it grew because it has a good harbor and sits at the mouth of the Hudson River. Immigrants from overseas flooded into the city in the 19th and 20th centuries, boosting its population and economy. Today, it is the main financial center, not just of the US, but of the world.

Lake Ontario
Hudson River
New York City
Appalachian Mountains

PITTSBURGH
Once a major steel manufacturing center with a polluted environment, Pittsburgh is now a thriving financial center with a large number of corporate headquarters. Bridges span the three rivers that run through the city, connecting the core downtown area (above) to the suburbs.

CENTER OF GOVERNMENT
All three branches of the federal government, the executive, legislative, and judicial, reside in Washington, D.C. The United States Congress (the legislative branch) meets here in the Capitol building. Many of the city's residents work for the government.

Capitol building, the seat of government

Map labels

CANADA

ONTARIO

St. Lawrence
Ogdensburg

Lake Ontario
Oswego
Watertown
Boonville
Adirondack Mountains

Niagara Falls
Lockport
Rochester
Syracuse
Newark
Utica
Mohawk R.
NEW YORK

Niagara Falls
Buffalo
Avon
Dansville
Oneonta

Hamburg
Ithaca
Catskill Mountains

Dunkirk
Binghamton

Erie
Jamestown
Allegheny Plateau
Elmira
Sayre

Warren
Mansfield
Scranton
Middleton

Meadville
Wilcox
Wilkes Barre
Milford

Mercer
PENNSYLVANIA
Lock Haven
Stroudsberg

OHIO
Allegheny River
Du Bois
Milton
Allentow

Butler
State College
Reading
Trenton

Aliquippa
Pittsburgh
Indiana
Altoona
Harrisburg
Philadelphia

Washington
Carlisle
Lancaster

Bedford
York
Wilmington

Uniontown
Hagerstown
Aberdeen
Cherry

Cumberland
Towson
Vineland

WEST
VIRGINIA
Oakland
Baltimore
Columbia
Dover

Annapolis
DELAWARE

VIRGINIA
WASHINGTON D.C.
Cambridge
Ocean City

MARYLAND
Salisbury

Chesapeake Bay

Appalachian Mountains

Lake Erie

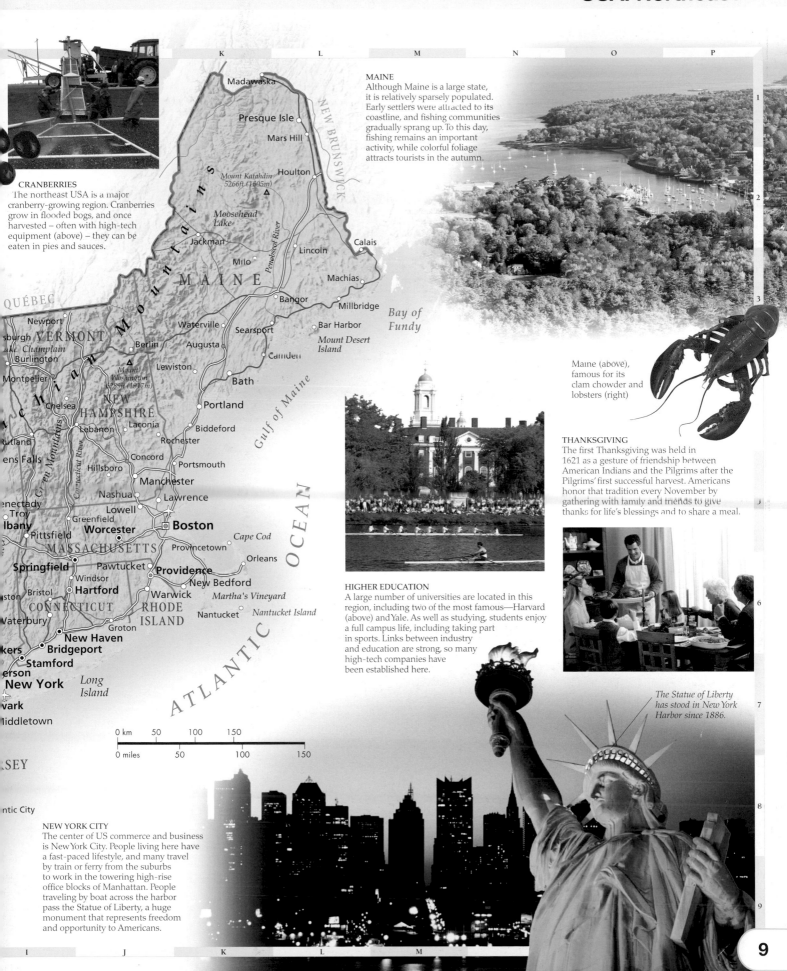

CRANBERRIES
The northeast USA is a major cranberry-growing region. Cranberries grow in flooded bogs, and once harvested – often with high-tech equipment (above) – they can be eaten in pies and sauces.

MAINE
Although Maine is a large state, it is relatively sparsely populated. Early settlers were attracted to its coastline, and fishing communities gradually sprang up. To this day, fishing remains an important activity, while colorful foliage attracts tourists in the autumn.

Maine (above), famous for its clam chowder and lobsters (right)

THANKSGIVING
The first Thanksgiving was held in 1621 as a gesture of friendship between American Indians and the Pilgrims after the Pilgrims' first successful harvest. Americans honor that tradition every November by gathering with family and friends to give thanks for life's blessings and to share a meal.

HIGHER EDUCATION
A large number of universities are located in this region, including two of the most famous—Harvard (above) and Yale. As well as studying, students enjoy a full campus life, including taking part in sports. Links between industry and education are strong, so many high-tech companies have been established here.

The Statue of Liberty has stood in New York Harbor since 1886.

NEW YORK CITY
The center of US commerce and business is New York City. People living here have a fast-paced lifestyle, and many travel by train or ferry from the suburbs to work in the towering high-rise office blocks of Manhattan. People traveling by boat across the harbor pass the Statue of Liberty, a huge monument that represents freedom and opportunity to Americans.

Map labels
Madawaska, Presque Isle, Mars Hill, Houlton, Mount Katahdin 5266ft (1605m), Moosehead Lake, Jackman, Milo, Lincoln, Calais, Machias, Bangor, Millbridge, MAINE, Pennobscot River, Waterville, Searsport, Bar Harbor, Mount Desert Island, Bay of Fundy, NEW BRUNSWICK, QUÉBEC, Newport, VERMONT, Lake Champlain, Burlington, Berlin, Augusta, Camden, Montpelier, Lewiston, Mount Washington 6289ft (1917m), Chelsea, Bath, NEW HAMPSHIRE, Laconia, Portland, Gulf of Maine, Lebanon, Biddeford, Rochester, Green Mountains, Connecticut River, Concord, Portsmouth, Hillsboro, Manchester, Nashua, Lawrence, Lowell, Greenfield, Boston, Troy, Albany, Pittsfield, Worcester, Cape Cod, MASSACHUSETTS, Provincetown, Springfield, Pawtucket, Providence, Orleans, Windsor, New Bedford, Hartford, Warwick, Martha's Vineyard, Bristol, CONNECTICUT, RHODE ISLAND, Nantucket, Nantucket Island, Waterbury, New Haven, Groton, Bridgeport, Stamford, New York, Long Island, Middletown, ATLANTIC OCEAN, Atlantic City, JERSEY

0 km 50 100 150
0 miles 50 100 150

USA: South

THE SOUTHERN STATES of the US have a varied landscape and an interesting mix of people, both culturally and economically. Some areas of the region are poor, especially the Appalachian Mountain communities, while other parts, such as the Florida coast, are wealthy and attract many people from other states and countries. The cultural mix includes people of Latin American origin, African Americans, Cajuns (French Canadians), and European Americans, giving rise to diverse music styles, dialects, pastimes, and food. While coal mining in the Appalachian Mountains has declined in recent years, agriculture is still important, as are tourism and industry. Tourism is particularly important in Florida and in New Orleans near the mouth of the mighty Mississippi River.

COTTON CROPS
Cotton was once the mainstay crop of the south and was grown by African-American slaves. Today, cotton is still important for the economy of the region and is grown in large fields and harvested with huge machinery. Cotton has many uses, primarily as the raw material for textiles.

Cotton pod, or boll

The Mississippi is the largest river in North America and the third largest in the world.

Jazz musician on Bourbon Street, New Orleans

Mississippi River Delta

MUSICAL ORIGINS
The southern US is famous for its music, much of which reflects the cultural mix of the region. New Orleans and other parts of Louisiana are the birthplaces of jazz and Cajun music, while bluegrass and country have origins in Nashville and Memphis. These music styles started here, but quickly spread throughout the country and developed even further in the cities.

Chef holding a skillet of jambalaya, a Cajun dish

CAJUN CULTURE
The Cajuns in this region are French-speaking people who were expelled from Canada in the 18th century. They mixed with other cultures in Louisiana, but their French influence can be seen in the music, food, and place names, such as Lafayette.

FLORIDA EVERGLADES
The increasing population of Florida means that the Everglades, swampy plains inhabited by alligators and other wildlife, are under threat as land is needed for houses and farms. However, the Everglades National Park protects part of this important ecosystem.

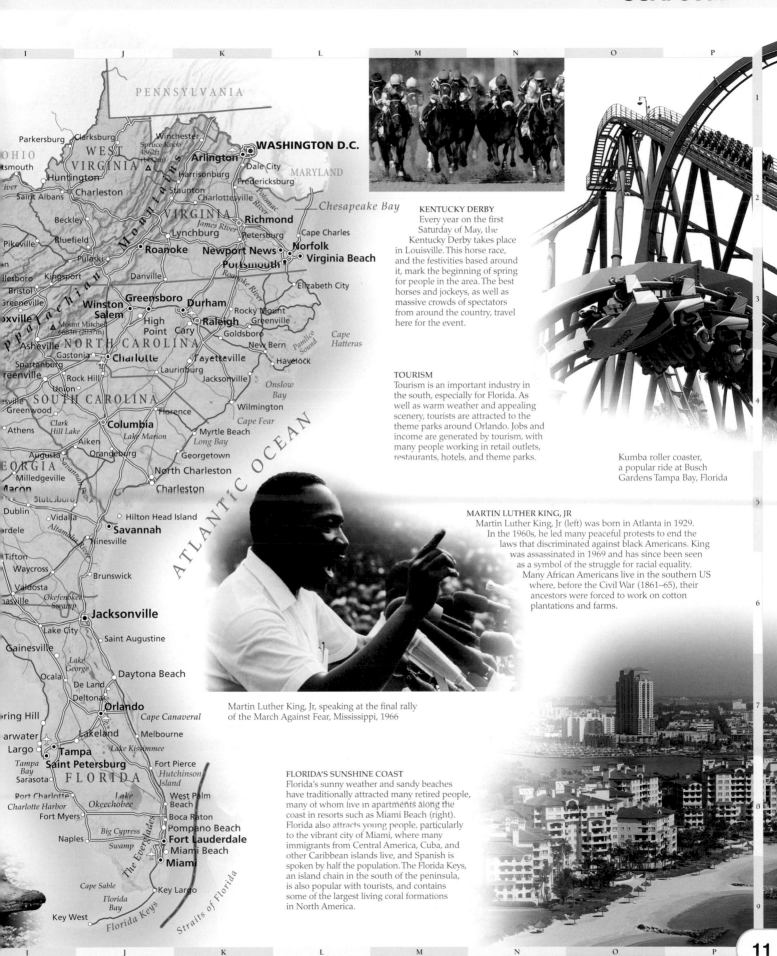

KENTUCKY DERBY
Every year on the first Saturday of May, the Kentucky Derby takes place in Louisville. This horse race, and the festivities based around it, mark the beginning of spring for people in the area. The best horses and jockeys, as well as massive crowds of spectators from around the country, travel here for the event.

TOURISM
Tourism is an important industry in the south, especially for Florida. As well as warm weather and appealing scenery, tourists are attracted to the theme parks around Orlando. Jobs and income are generated by tourism, with many people working in retail outlets, restaurants, hotels, and theme parks.

Kumba roller coaster, a popular ride at Busch Gardens Tampa Bay, Florida

MARTIN LUTHER KING, JR
Martin Luther King, Jr (left) was born in Atlanta in 1929. In the 1960s, he led many peaceful protests to end the laws that discriminated against black Americans. King was assassinated in 1969 and has since been seen as a symbol of the struggle for racial equality. Many African Americans live in the southern US where, before the Civil War (1861–65), their ancestors were forced to work on cotton plantations and farms.

Martin Luther King, Jr, speaking at the final rally of the March Against Fear, Mississippi, 1966

FLORIDA'S SUNSHINE COAST
Florida's sunny weather and sandy beaches have traditionally attracted many retired people, many of whom live in apartments along the coast in resorts such as Miami Beach (right). Florida also attracts young people, particularly to the vibrant city of Miami, where many immigrants from Central America, Cuba, and other Caribbean islands live, and Spanish is spoken by half the population. The Florida Keys, an island chain in the south of the peninsula, is also popular with tourists, and contains some of the largest living coral formations in North America.

USA: Midwest

THE AMERICAN MIDWEST is dominated by the Great Plains, once the home of cattle ranches, cowboys, and American Indian peoples. However, the discovery of gold in South Dakota brought a rush of settlers to the area. This, combined with a decline in buffalo numbers, led to the eventual displacement of the American Indians from the Plains. The area is prone to dramatic weather—tornadoes, freezing blizzards, and blazing hot summers. To the west, vast areas of farmland generate more wheat and corn than anywhere else in the world. East of the Mississippi the landscape varies and, although farming is still important, it is an industrial heartland. The greater Detroit area and other parts of Michigan make up a big manufacturing center, with other hubs in Ohio, Indiana, and Illinois.

BUFFALO ON THE PLAINS
Up to 100 million buffalo once grazed on the Great Plains. They provided local American Indians with food for the family, and skin for clothes and tepees. The Dakota people used buffalo bones to make shields and tools, and the animal's bladder into a bag for carrying water. But over-hunting and the destruction of the buffalo's habitat by early European settlers drastically reduced the number of animals. The buffalo is now a protected species and lives in reserves.

Buffalo herd on a reserve, South Dakota

MOUNT RUSHMORE NATIONAL MEMORIAL
Mount Rushmore, in the Black Hills of South Dakota, was created as a tribute to the American presidency. Four of the United States' greatest presidents—(left to right) Washington, Jefferson, Roosevelt, and Lincoln—were carved into the granite cliff between 1927 and 1941. Teams of workers hung from saddles anchored to the mountain to complete the work, often enduring harsh winds or blazing sun. Today, it is a popular tourist attraction.

Each carved face is about 60 ft (18 m) high.

TORNADO ALLEY
Dramatic tornadoes, or "twisters," regularly tear through the states of Kansas and Oklahoma along a path known as Tornado Alley. Tornadoes occur when warm and cold air masses meet. As the warm air rises it cools, and under the right conditions it can suck in more and more air until a whirling twister develops. The more air that is drawn in, the greater the power of the tornado.

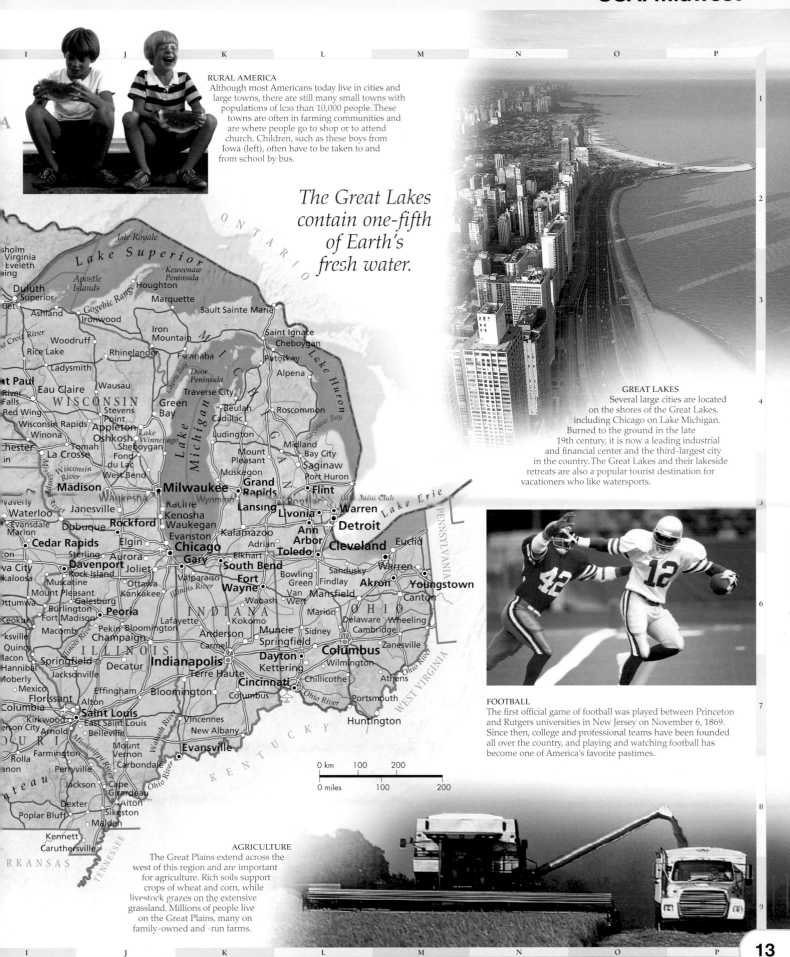

RURAL AMERICA
Although most Americans today live in cities and large towns, there are still many small towns with populations of less than 10,000 people. These towns are often in farming communities and are where people go to shop or to attend church. Children, such as these boys from Iowa (left), often have to be taken to and from school by bus.

The Great Lakes contain one-fifth of Earth's fresh water.

GREAT LAKES
Several large cities are located on the shores of the Great Lakes, including Chicago on Lake Michigan. Burned to the ground in the late 19th century, it is now a leading industrial and financial center and the third-largest city in the country. The Great Lakes and their lakeside retreats are also a popular tourist destination for vacationers who like watersports.

FOOTBALL
The first official game of football was played between Princeton and Rutgers universities in New Jersey on November 6, 1869. Since then, college and professional teams have been founded all over the country, and playing and watching football has become one of America's favorite pastimes.

AGRICULTURE
The Great Plains extend across the west of this region and are important for agriculture. Rich soils support crops of wheat and corn, while livestock grazes on the extensive grassland. Millions of people live on the Great Plains, many on family-owned and -run farms.

0 km 100 200
0 miles 100 200

USA: West

THE ROCKY MOUNTAINS separate the coastal region from the drier inland states. Large and fast-growing cities such as San Francisco, Los Angeles, and San Diego hug the Pacific coast, and have attracted many migrants because of good job opportunities. Inland, blazing desert and towering mountains provide some of the most dramatic landscapes in the country. National parks such as Yellowstone in northwestern Wyoming and Montana and Yosemite in central California protect some of these wilderness areas. Further east, the foothills of the Rockies give way to vast plains grazed by large herds of cattle.

NORTHERN FORESTS
The coastal areas of Oregon and Washington contain large forests. These produce economically important timber, but much land is also left in its natural state and is popular with hikers. Most people here live in large cities like Seattle, and in the fertile inland valleys.

CALIFORNIA AGRICULTURE
California is warm, fertile, and, with irrigation, ideal for agriculture. Grapes are an important crop north of San Francisco in the Napa Valley. Further south, citrus crops such as oranges also flourish. Premium farming land is under threat, however, as the population expands.

The American Indian name for Death Valley is Tomesha, which means "land where the ground is on fire."

LOS ANGELES
This sprawling city— the second largest in the USA— is home to migrants from all over the world, as well as from other states in the country. Sandwiched between the coast and the mountains, the city has massive air pollution problems. This mostly arises from the exhaust fumes from the high number of cars used by commuters on the city's highways.

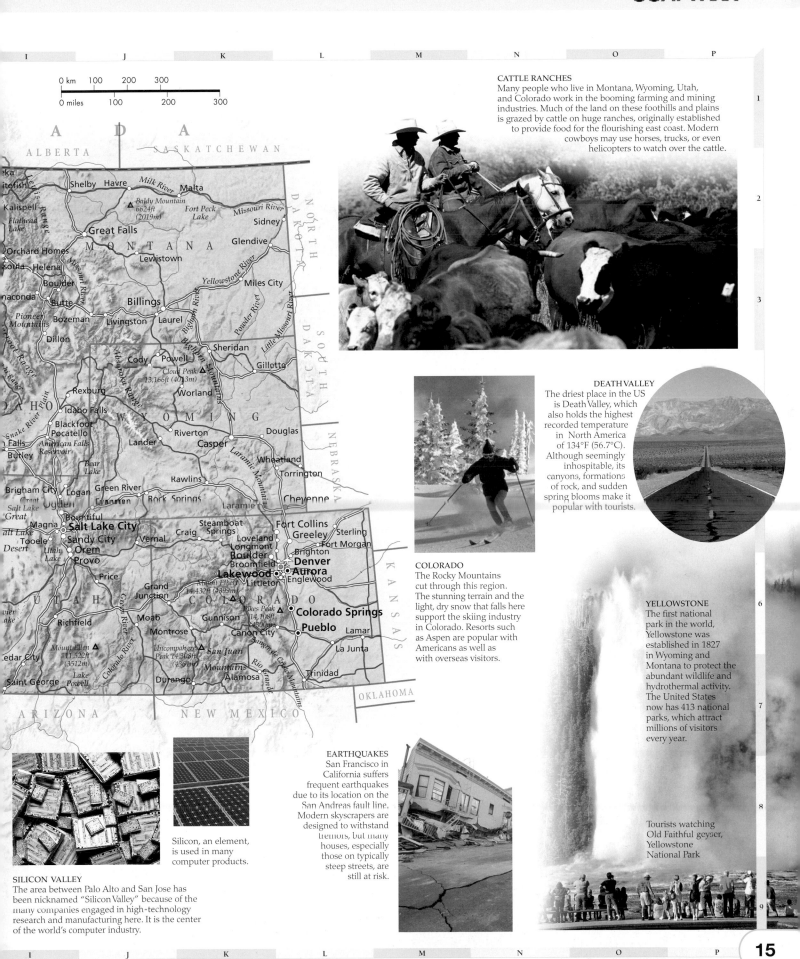

CATTLE RANCHES
Many people who live in Montana, Wyoming, Utah, and Colorado work in the booming farming and mining industries. Much of the land on these foothills and plains is grazed by cattle on huge ranches, originally established to provide food for the flourishing east coast. Modern cowboys may use horses, trucks, or even helicopters to watch over the cattle.

DEATH VALLEY
The driest place in the US is Death Valley, which also holds the highest recorded temperature in North America of 134°F (56.7°C). Although seemingly inhospitable, its canyons, formations of rock, and sudden spring blooms make it popular with tourists.

COLORADO
The Rocky Mountains cut through this region. The stunning terrain and the light, dry snow that falls here support the skiing industry in Colorado. Resorts such as Aspen are popular with Americans as well as with overseas visitors.

YELLOWSTONE
The first national park in the world, Yellowstone was established in 1827 in Wyoming and Montana to protect the abundant wildlife and hydrothermal activity. The United States now has 413 national parks, which attract millions of visitors every year.

Tourists watching Old Faithful geyser, Yellowstone National Park

Silicon, an element, is used in many computer products.

SILICON VALLEY
The area between Palo Alto and San Jose has been nicknamed "Silicon Valley" because of the many companies engaged in high-technology research and manufacturing here. It is the center of the world's computer industry.

EARTHQUAKES
San Francisco in California suffers frequent earthquakes due to its location on the San Andreas fault line. Modern skyscrapers are designed to withstand tremors, but many houses, especially those on typically steep streets, are still at risk.

USA: Southwest

HOT PLACE TO LIVE
The climate across much of the Southwest is hot and dry, with summer temperatures often reaching 100°F (38°C). Although water can be scarce, many people have a swimming pool in their backyard so they can cool off.

THE SOUTHWEST is an area of great contrasts. Much of Oklahoma and Texas consists of flat, rolling grasslands and huge farms, while both Arizona and New Mexico are hot, arid, and mountainous, with vast canyons and river valleys carving their way through the land. Since the discovery of oil in 1901, Texas has become the country's top oil producer with Houston as the center of the billion-dollar industry. Tourism is also important to the Southwest, as visitors flock to see the Grand Canyon, the Painted Desert, and other natural wonders. Buildings here reflect the mix of Latino, American Indian, European American, and modern American cultures.

Suburbs of Phoenix, Arizona

DESERT LIFE
The saguaro cactus can reach up to 50 ft (15 m) tall, grow as many as 40 branches, and live for 200 years. Cacti, yucca, and other plants have all adapted to the hot, dry desert conditions found in the Southwest. So, too, have many animals, including the deadly rattlesnake.

Saguaro cacti in the Sonoran Desert

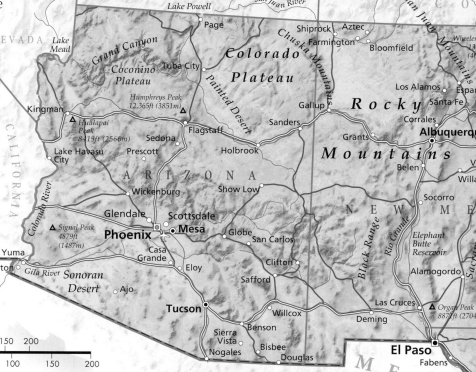

UTAH · COLORADO
NEVADA
Lake Powell
San Juan River
San Juan Mountains
Page
Shiprock Aztec
Farmington
Grand Canyon
Bloomfield
Wheeler
Lake Mead
Coconino Plateau
Tuba City
Colorado Plateau
Chuska Mountains
Gallup
Los Alamos Espan
Santa Fe
Humphreys Peak 12,365ft (3851m)
Painted Desert
Rocky
Corrales
Kingman
Hualapai Peak 8419ft (2566m)
Sedona
Flagstaff
Sanders
Grants
Albuquerqu
Lake Havasu City
Prescott
Holbrook
Mountains
Belen
Willa
Wickenburg
Show Low
Socorro
Signal Peak 4879ft (1487m)
Glendale Scottsdale
Globe
Phoenix Mesa
San Carlos
Clifton
Elephant Butte Reservoir
Casa Grande
Eloy
Safford
Alamogordo
Yuma
Gila River
Black Range
Somerton
Sonoran Desert
Ajo
Rio Grande
Las Cruces
Organ Peak 8871ft (2704m)
Tucson
Willcox
Deming
Sierra Vista Benson
Bisbee
El Paso
Nogales Douglas
Fabens
MEXICO

0 km 50 100 150 200
0 miles 50 100 150 200

THE GRAND CANYON
The Grand Canyon in northern Arizona is one of the natural wonders of the world. This incredibly deep gorge was slowly cut out of the rock, beginning 6 million years ago, by the Colorado River. People can hike around its edge or venture down into the canyon to camp for the night.

AMERICAN-INDIAN CULTURES
American Indians, including Navajo, Hopi, and Apache, used to live across the Southwest but are now concentrated in reservations set up by the US government. The largest of these is in Arizona and New Mexico, and is home to the Navajo people. The Navajo farm the land and produce crafts, like the woven blanket wrapped around these Navajo children.

Kachina doll made by the Hopi

ADOBE HOUSES
Traditional homes of the Pueblo peoples of the Southwest were made from adobe bricks of sun-baked earth and straw covered with plaster. Dwellings had a flat roof and smooth walls. Modern adobe-style buildings can still be seen in the Southwest, but are often made of concrete and then painted to look like adobe. Here, a woman demonstrates baking bread in an adobe oven.

Astronaut leaving the shuttle by means of a manned maneuvering unit (MMU)

NASA
Houston, Texas, is the center of the United States space program. After a rocket has blasted off from Cape Canaveral in Florida, its journey is controlled by the National Aeronautics and Space Administration (NASA) from Houston. Astronauts are also trained at the center and new space technology is developed here.

The Grand Canyon is up to 1 mile (1.6 km) deep, 18 miles (29 km) wide, and stretches for 217 miles (349 km).

SPANISH INFLUENCE
Close to Mexico and Central America, the Southwestern states have long been settled by Hispanic people, whose influence can be seen—and heard—throughout the Southwest. Spanish is widely spoken, and the Roman Catholic religion that the Spanish brought is evident in the churches scattered throughout the region.

OIL FIELDS
The oil industry has provided Texas with much of its wealth. Oil lies deep underground and is brought up to the surface by massive oil jacks, known as nodding donkeys.

Mexico

ONCE HOME TO THE GREAT Aztec and Mayan civilizations and then the focus of Spanish conquistadors who came in search of wealth, Mexico today reflects its colorful past through its culture and architecture. The majority of Mexicans is mestizo (mixed race), of Spanish and native Indian descent. Mexico City, site of the ancient Aztec capital, is today one of the largest cities in the world, with a population of around 21 million. Despite oil and natural gas reserves, and a plentiful supply of labor, large numbers of Mexicans are still poor, especially in the rural areas and the urban slums.

ALONG THE BORDER
In 1994, Mexico signed the North American Free Trade Agreement (NAFTA), which effectively bound its economy to that of the US. A large industrial area has developed along the Mexican border with the US.

DAY OF THE DEAD
One of the biggest festivals in Mexico is the Day of the Dead. It is believed that once a year the souls of the dead can come back and visit their loved ones. In celebration of this, special food is prepared to welcome the souls, and offerings of flowers, candles, and incense are made at the gravesides.

LIFE IN THE CITY
Mexico City is the political, economic, and cultural hub of the country, and is home to some 16 million people. Its site, in a basin surrounded by mountains, means that expansion is difficult. Air pollution from factories and cars cannot escape, so on most days a thick layer of smog builds up over the city. Attempts to deal with the pollution, including banning cars from some parts, have had limited success.

The volcano Popocatépetl is the highest peak around the city.

Mexico City is contained within a ring of mountains.

WORKING ON THE LAND
Agriculture employs 6.5 million people – about one-eighth of Mexico's work force. However, only 12 percent of the land is suitable for farming because it is so mountainous and dry. The peasant communities of the south rely on farming for their food, while communities in the north are more industrialized. Here, the agave plant is being harvested near the town of Tequila.

Map labels

UNITED STATES O

Mexicali
Tijuana
Rosarito
Ensenada
San Luis Río Colorado
Ciudad Juárez
Río Grande
Río Bravo del Norte
Nogales
Agua Prieta
Samalayuca
Cananea
Caborca
Magdalena
Nuevo Casas Grandes
El Sueco
Ojinag
Cumpas
El Sáuz
San Pedro de la Cueva
Río Conchos
Desierto de Altar
Isla Ángel de la Guarda
Hermosillo
Chihuahua
Delicias
Cuauhtémoc
Ciudad Camargo
Isla Guadalupe
Bahía Sebastián Vizcaíno
Isla Tiburón
Empalme
Guaymas
Esperanza
Ciudad Obregón
Navojoa
San Francisco del Oro
Jiméne
Hidalgo del Parral
Santa Barbara
Isla Cedros
Guerrero Negro
Huatabampo
San Blas
Gómez Pa
San Ignacio
Los Mochis
Guasave
Guamúchil
Culiacán
Loreto
Bahía de La Paz
Navolato
Durango
El Dorado
Isla Magdalena
Isla Santa Margarita
La Paz
Tropic of Cancer
Miraflores
Mazatlán
Santa Genoveva 7894ft (2406m)
Escuinapa
Acaponeta
Tuxpan
Tepic
Islas Marías
Puerto Vallarta
Manza

Baja California
Sierra San Pedro Mártir
Gulf of California
Sierra de la Giganta
Sierra Madre Occidental
M
PACIFIC OCEAN

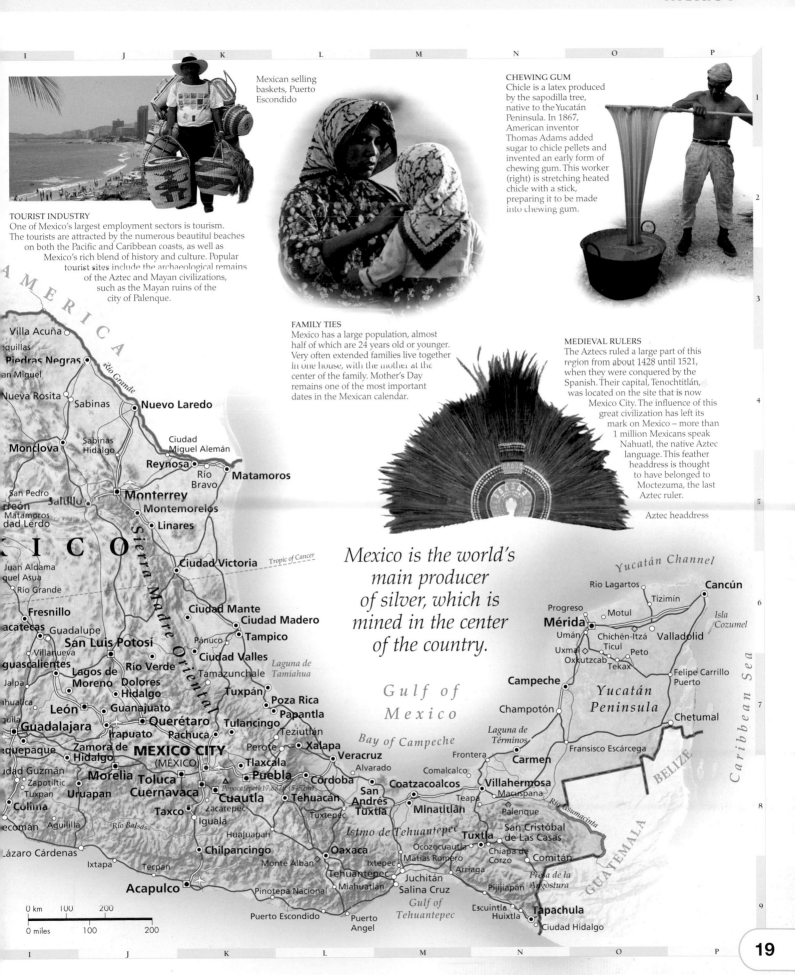

Mexican selling baskets, Puerto Escondido

TOURIST INDUSTRY
One of Mexico's largest employment sectors is tourism. The tourists are attracted by the numerous beautiful beaches on both the Pacific and Caribbean coasts, as well as Mexico's rich blend of history and culture. Popular tourist sites include the archaeological remains of the Aztec and Mayan civilizations, such as the Mayan ruins of the city of Palenque.

CHEWING GUM
Chicle is a latex produced by the sapodilla tree, native to the Yucatán Peninsula. In 1867, American inventor Thomas Adams added sugar to chicle pellets and invented an early form of chewing gum. This worker (right) is stretching heated chicle with a stick, preparing it to be made into chewing gum.

FAMILY TIES
Mexico has a large population, almost half of which are 24 years old or younger. Very often extended families live together in one house, with the mother at the center of the family. Mother's Day remains one of the most important dates in the Mexican calendar.

MEDIEVAL RULERS
The Aztecs ruled a large part of this region from about 1428 until 1521, when they were conquered by the Spanish. Their capital, Tenochtitlán, was located on the site that is now Mexico City. The influence of this great civilization has left its mark on Mexico – more than 1 million Mexicans speak Nahuatl, the native Aztec language. This feather headdress is thought to have belonged to Moctezuma, the last Aztec ruler.

Aztec headdress

Mexico is the world's main producer of silver, which is mined in the center of the country.

19

Central America

VOLCANOES, EARTHQUAKES, and hurricanes threaten the livelihoods of people in the seven countries of Central America. People here have also struggled with poverty and civil war. In more recent years, however, peace and economic recovery have offered hope, and education is now free in all countries. Remains of the ancient Mayan civilization that flourished until the 16th century, when the Spanish invaded, can be seen throughout the region. Large numbers of the native population died after the invasion, mostly from disease. Today, Spanish is the main language of the region.

Lake Nicaragua is the only freshwater lake in the world that contains sharks.

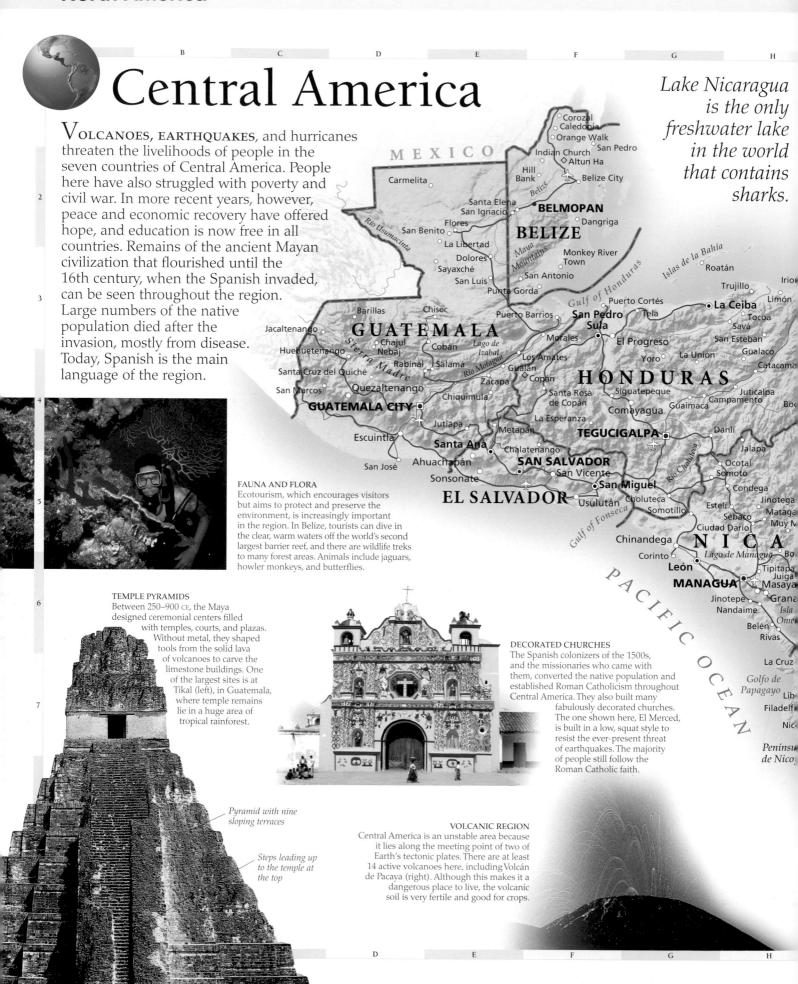

FAUNA AND FLORA
Ecotourism, which encourages visitors but aims to protect and preserve the environment, is increasingly important in the region. In Belize, tourists can dive in the clear, warm waters off the world's second largest barrier reef, and there are wildlife treks to many forest areas. Animals include jaguars, howler monkeys, and butterflies.

TEMPLE PYRAMIDS
Between 250–900 CE, the Maya designed ceremonial centers filled with temples, courts, and plazas. Without metal, they shaped tools from the solid lava of volcanoes to carve the limestone buildings. One of the largest sites is at Tikal (left), in Guatemala, where temple remains lie in a huge area of tropical rainforest.

Pyramid with nine sloping terraces

Steps leading up to the temple at the top

DECORATED CHURCHES
The Spanish colonizers of the 1500s, and the missionaries who came with them, converted the native population and established Roman Catholicism throughout Central America. They also built many fabulously decorated churches. The one shown here, El Merced, is built in a low, squat style to resist the ever-present threat of earthquakes. The majority of people still follow the Roman Catholic faith.

VOLCANIC REGION
Central America is an unstable area because it lies along the meeting point of two of Earth's tectonic plates. There are at least 14 active volcanoes here, including Volcán de Pacaya (right). Although this makes it a dangerous place to live, the volcanic soil is very fertile and good for crops.

Map labels:
MEXICO · Carmelita · Santa Elena · San Ignacio · Flores · San Benito · La Libertad · Dolores · Sayaxché · San Luis · Punta Gorda · Río Usumacinta · Corozal · Caledonia · Orange Walk · San Pedro · Indian Church · Altun Ha · Hill Bank · Belize City · BELMOPAN · BELIZE · Dangriga · Maya Mountains · Monkey River Town · San Antonio · Barillas · Chisec · Jacaltenango · GUATEMALA · Chajul · Nebaj · Cobán · Lago de Izabal · Morales · El Progreso · Islas de la Bahía · Roatán · Trujillo · Irio · Limón · La Ceiba · Tocoa · Savá · San Esteban · Gualaco · Catacamo · Huehuetenango · Rabinal · Salamá · Gualán · Zacapa · Copán · HONDURAS · Yoro · La Unión · Santa Cruz del Quiché · Río Motagua · Chiquimula · Santa Rosa de Copán · Siguatepeque · Campamento · Juticalpa · San Marcos · Quezaltenango · GUATEMALA CITY · Comayagua · Guaimaca · Jutiapa · La Esperanza · Metapán · TEGUCIGALPA · Danlí · Escuintla · Santa Ana · Chalatenango · SAN SALVADOR · San Vicente · Jalapa · Ocotal · Somoto · San José · Ahuachapán · San Miguel · Condega · Sonsonate · EL SALVADOR · Usulután · Choluteca · Somotillo · Estelí · Jinotega · Matag · Sébaco · Muy M · Gulf of Fonseca · Chinandega · Ciudad Darío · NICA · Corinto · Lago de Managua · Bo · León · Tipitapa · Juiga · MANAGUA · Masaya · Jinotepe · Grana · Nandaime · Isla Ome · Belén · Rivas · La Cruz · Golfo de Papagayo · Lib · Filadelfi · Nic · Península de Nico · PACIFIC OCEAN · Puerto Cortés · Tela · San Pedro Sula · Los Amates · Chiquimula · Puerto Barrios · Gulf of Honduras · Sierra Madre · Río Choluteca

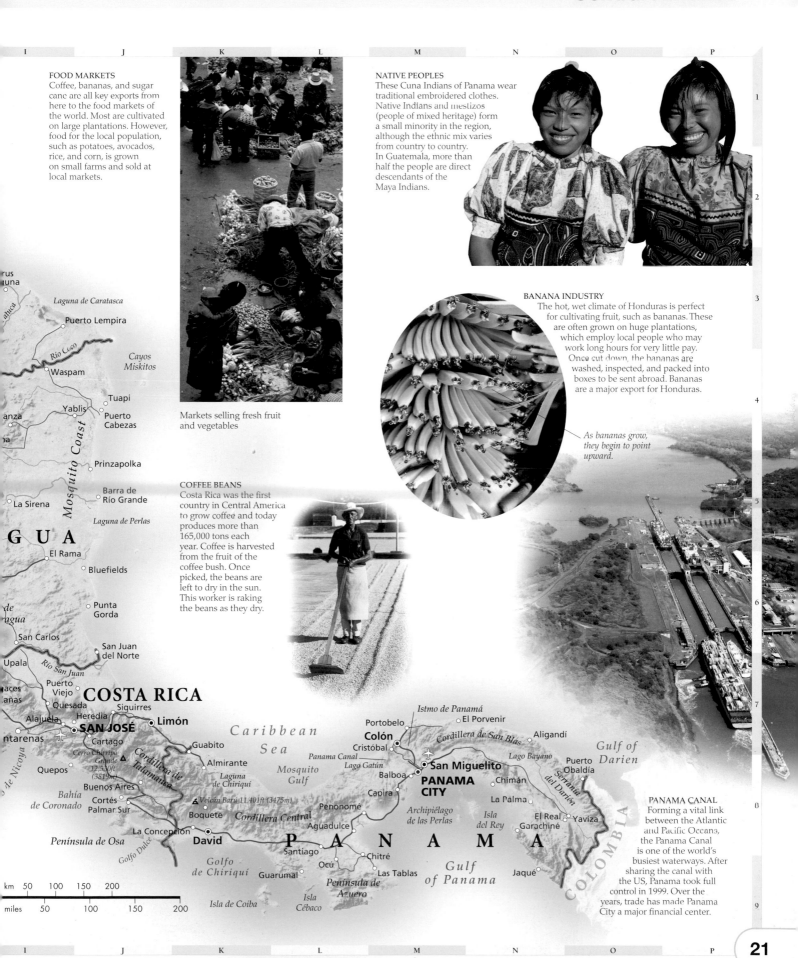

FOOD MARKETS
Coffee, bananas, and sugar cane are all key exports from here to the food markets of the world. Most are cultivated on large plantations. However, food for the local population, such as potatoes, avocados, rice, and corn, is grown on small farms and sold at local markets.

Markets selling fresh fruit and vegetables

NATIVE PEOPLES
These Cuna Indians of Panama wear traditional embroidered clothes. Native Indians and mestizos (people of mixed heritage) form a small minority in the region, although the ethnic mix varies from country to country. In Guatemala, more than half the people are direct descendants of the Maya Indians.

BANANA INDUSTRY
The hot, wet climate of Honduras is perfect for cultivating fruit, such as bananas. These are often grown on huge plantations, which employ local people who may work long hours for very little pay. Once cut down, the bananas are washed, inspected, and packed into boxes to be sent abroad. Bananas are a major export for Honduras.

As bananas grow, they begin to point upward.

COFFEE BEANS
Costa Rica was the first country in Central America to grow coffee and today produces more than 165,000 tons each year. Coffee is harvested from the fruit of the coffee bush. Once picked, the beans are left to dry in the sun. This worker is raking the beans as they dry.

PANAMA CANAL
Forming a vital link between the Atlantic and Pacific Oceans, the Panama Canal is one of the world's busiest waterways. After sharing the canal with the US, Panama took full control in 1999. Over the years, trade has made Panama City a major financial center.

Laguna de Caratasca
Puerto Lempira
Río Coco
Cayos Miskitos
Waspam
Tuapi
Yablis
Puerto Cabezas
Prinzapolka
Barra de Río Grande
La Sirena
Laguna de Perlas
GUA
El Rama
Bluefields
Punta Gorda
San Carlos
Upala
Río San Juan
San Juan del Norte
Puerto Viejo
Quesada
Siquirres
COSTA RICA
Alajuela
Heredia
SAN JOSÉ
Limón
Cartago
Guabito
Cerro Chirripó Grande 12,530ft (3819m)
Quepos
Cordillera de Talamanca
Buenos Aires
Bahía de Coronado
Cortés
Palmar Sur
Almirante
Volcán Barú 11,401ft (3475m)
La Concepción
Boquete
David
Cordillera Central
Península de Osa
Golfo Dulce
Golfo de Chiriquí
Guarumal
Santiago
Ocú
Las Tablas
Península de Azuero
Isla de Coiba
Isla Cébaco

Caribbean Sea
Mosquito Gulf
Laguna de Chiriquí
Portobelo
Istmo de Panamá
El Porvenir
Colón
Cristóbal
Cordillera de San Blas
Aligandí
Panama Canal
Lago Gatún
Lago Bayano
Puerto Obaldía
San Miguelito
Balboa
PANAMA CITY
Chimán
Capira
La Palma
Penonomé
Archipiélago de las Perlas
Isla del Rey
El Real
Garachiné
Yaviza
Aguadulce
P A N A M A
Chitré
Gulf of Panama
Jaqué
Serranía del Darién
COLOMBIA
Gulf of Darien

km 50 100 150 200
miles 50 100 150 200

The Caribbean

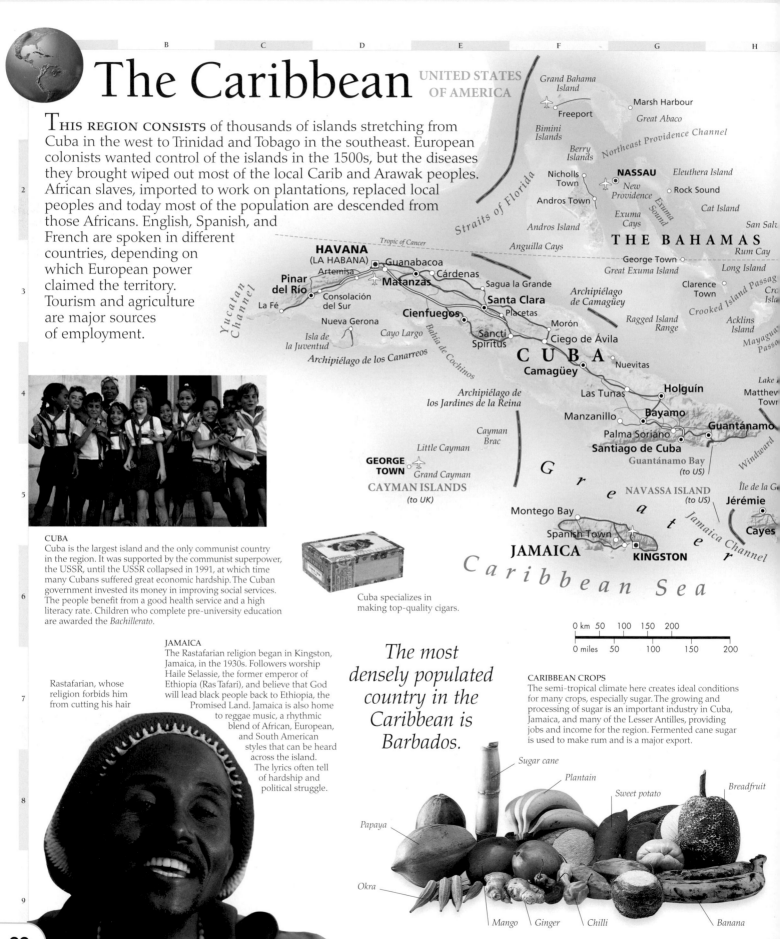

THIS REGION CONSISTS of thousands of islands stretching from Cuba in the west to Trinidad and Tobago in the southeast. European colonists wanted control of the islands in the 1500s, but the diseases they brought wiped out most of the local Carib and Arawak peoples. African slaves, imported to work on plantations, replaced local peoples and today most of the population are descended from those Africans. English, Spanish, and French are spoken in different countries, depending on which European power claimed the territory. Tourism and agriculture are major sources of employment.

UNITED STATES OF AMERICA

Grand Bahama Island
Freeport
Marsh Harbour
Great Abaco
Bimini Islands
Northeast Providence Channel
Berry Islands
Nicholls Town
NASSAU
New Providence
Eleuthera Island
Rock Sound
Cat Island
Andros Town
Exuma Cays
Exuma Sound
San Salv
Andros Island
THE BAHAMAS
Straits of Florida
Tropic of Cancer
Anguilla Cays
George Town
Great Exuma Island
Rum Cay
Long Island

HAVANA (LA HABANA)
Guanabacoa
Artemisa
Cárdenas
Pinar del Río
Matanzas
Sagua la Grande
Consolación del Sur
Santa Clara
Archipiélago de Camagüey
Clarence Town
Crooked Island Passag
Cro Isla
La Fé
Cienfuegos
Placetas
Ragged Island Range
Acklins Island
Nueva Gerona
Cayo Largo
Sancti Spíritus
Morón
Ciego de Ávila
Mayaguan Passa
Isla de la Juventud
Archipiélago de los Canarreos
Bahía de Cochinos
C U B A
Camagüey
Nuevitas
Archipiélago de los Jardines de la Reina
Las Tunas
Holguín
Lake Matthew Tow
Cayman Brac
Manzanillo
Bayamo
Little Cayman
Palma Soriano
Guantánamo
GEORGE TOWN
Grand Cayman
Santiago de Cuba
Guantánamo Bay (to US)
Windward
CAYMAN ISLANDS (to UK)
G
NAVASSA ISLAND (to US)
Île de la G
Jérémie
Montego Bay
Cayes
Spanish Town
JAMAICA
KINGSTON
Jamaica Channel
Caribbean Sea

CUBA
Cuba is the largest island and the only communist country in the region. It was supported by the communist superpower, the USSR, until the USSR collapsed in 1991, at which time many Cubans suffered great economic hardship. The Cuban government invested its money in improving social services. The people benefit from a good health service and a high literacy rate. Children who complete pre-university education are awarded the *Bachillerato*.

Cuba specializes in making top-quality cigars.

JAMAICA
The Rastafarian religion began in Kingston, Jamaica, in the 1930s. Followers worship Haile Selassie, the former emperor of Ethiopia (Ras Tafari), and believe that God will lead black people back to Ethiopia, the Promised Land. Jamaica is also home to reggae music, a rhythmic blend of African, European, and South American styles that can be heard across the island. The lyrics often tell of hardship and political struggle.

Rastafarian, whose religion forbids him from cutting his hair

The most densely populated country in the Caribbean is Barbados.

0 km 50 100 150 200
0 miles 50 100 150 200

CARIBBEAN CROPS
The semi-tropical climate here creates ideal conditions for many crops, especially sugar. The growing and processing of sugar is an important industry in Cuba, Jamaica, and many of the Lesser Antilles, providing jobs and income for the region. Fermented cane sugar is used to make rum and is a major export.

Sugar cane
Plantain
Sweet potato
Breadfruit
Papaya
Okra
Mango
Ginger
Chilli
Banana

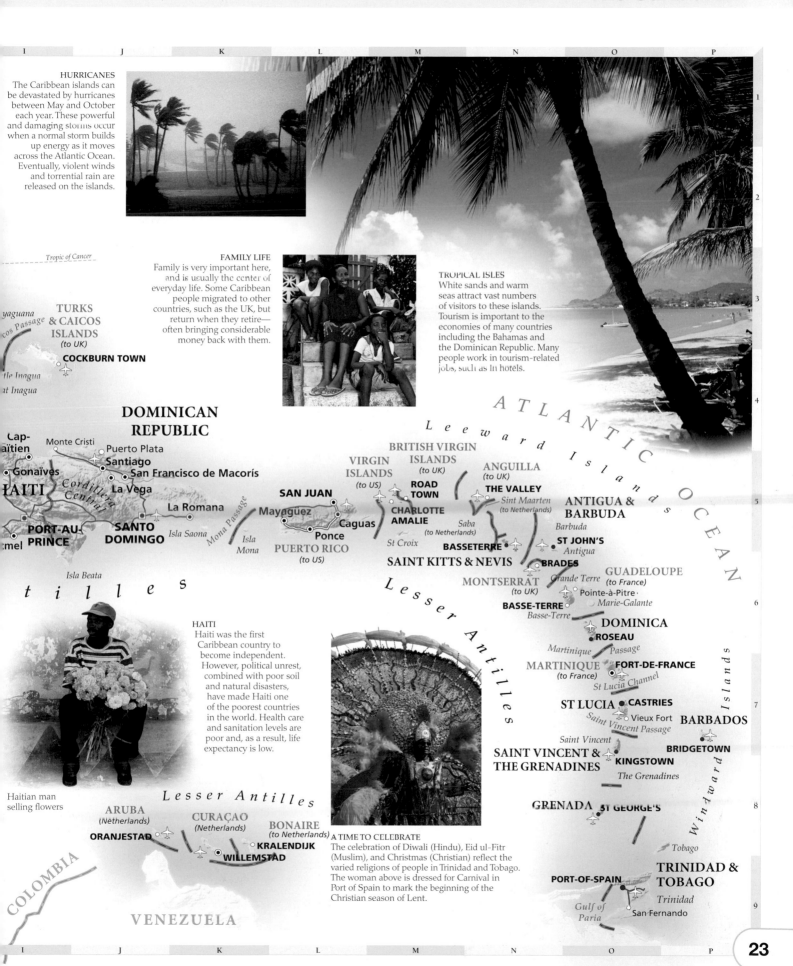

HURRICANES
The Caribbean islands can be devastated by hurricanes between May and October each year. These powerful and damaging storms occur when a normal storm builds up energy as it moves across the Atlantic Ocean. Eventually, violent winds and torrential rain are released on the islands.

Tropic of Cancer

FAMILY LIFE
Family is very important here, and is usually the center of everyday life. Some Caribbean people migrated to other countries, such as the UK, but return when they retire—often bringing considerable money back with them.

TROPICAL ISLES
White sands and warm seas attract vast numbers of visitors to these islands. Tourism is important to the economies of many countries including the Bahamas and the Dominican Republic. Many people work in tourism-related jobs, such as in hotels.

ATLANTIC OCEAN

Leeward Islands

Lesser Antilles

TURKS & CAICOS ISLANDS
(to UK)
✈ **COCKBURN TOWN**

yaguana
cos Passage
tle Inagua
at Inagua

DOMINICAN REPUBLIC

Cap-
aïtien
Monte Cristi
Puerto Plata
✈ **Santiago**
San Francisco de Macorís
Gonaïves
Cordillera Central
La Vega
HAITI
La Romana
SAN JUAN
Mayagüez
Caguas
Ponce
PUERTO RICO
(to US)
Mona Passage
Isla Saona
Isla Mona

PORT-AU-PRINCE
mel
SANTO DOMINGO
Isla Beata

VIRGIN ISLANDS
(to US)
✈ **CHARLOTTE AMALIE**
St Croix

BRITISH VIRGIN ISLANDS
(to UK)
✈ **ROAD TOWN**
Sint Maarten
(to Netherlands)
Saba
(to Netherlands)

ANGUILLA
(to UK)
✈ **THE VALLEY**

ANTIGUA & BARBUDA
Barbuda
✈ **ST JOHN'S**
Antigua

BASSETERRE ✈
SAINT KITTS & NEVIS
✈ **BRADES**
MONTSERRAT
(to UK)
Grande Terre

GUADELOUPE
(to France)
✈ **Pointe-à-Pitre**
Marie-Galante

BASSE-TERRE
Basse-Terre

✈ **DOMINICA**
• **ROSEAU**
Martinique   Passage
MARTINIQUE
(to France)
✈ **FORT-DE-FRANCE**
St Lucia Channel

Windward Islands

t i l l e s

HAITI
Haiti was the first Caribbean country to become independent. However, political unrest, combined with poor soil and natural disasters, have made Haiti one of the poorest countries in the world. Health care and sanitation levels are poor and, as a result, life expectancy is low.

Haitian man selling flowers

Lesser Antilles

ST LUCIA • **CASTRIES**
✈ **Vieux Fort**
Saint Vincent Passage
Saint Vincent
SAINT VINCENT & THE GRENADINES ✈
KINGSTOWN
The Grenadines

BARBADOS
✈ **BRIDGETOWN**

GRENADA ✈ **ST GEORGE'S**
Tobago

ARUBA
(Netherlands)
✈ **ORANJESTAD**

CURAÇAO
(Netherlands)
✈ **WILLEMSTAD**

BONAIRE
(to Netherlands)
• **KRALENDIJK**

A TIME TO CELEBRATE
The celebration of Diwali (Hindu), Eid ul-Fitr (Muslim), and Christmas (Christian) reflect the varied religions of people in Trinidad and Tobago. The woman above is dressed for Carnival in Port of Spain to mark the beginning of the Christian season of Lent.

TRINIDAD & TOBAGO
PORT-OF-SPAIN ✈
Trinidad
• **San Fernando**
Gulf of Paria

COLOMBIA

VENEZUELA

SOUTH AMERICA

Although South America is much poorer than its northern neighbor, it is rich in natural resources. Its mineral wealth led to its invasion by the Portuguese and Spanish in the 1500s, and their languages and culture still shape the lives of the people here. The nations below are listed in order of area, headed by Brazil—the world's fifth largest country.

Brazil
- 3,287,957 sq miles
  8,515,770 sq km
- 205,824,000
- Brasília
- Portuguese, German, Italian, Spanish, Polish, Japanese, Amerindian languages

Venezuela
- 352,144 sq miles
  912,050 sq km
- 30,912,000
- Caracas
- Spanish, Amerindian languages

Latin American culture is world famous, thanks to its infectious music and dance. Here a couple in Buenos Aires, Argentina, demonstrate the art of the tango.

Bolivia
- 424,164 sq miles
  1,098,581 sq km
- 10,970,000
- La Paz
- Aymara, Quechua, Spanish

Chile
- 291,933 sq miles
  756,102 sq km
- 17,650,000
- Santiago
- Spanish, Amerindian languages

Argentina
- 1,073,518 sq miles
  2,780,400 sq km
- 43,887,000
- Buenos Aires
- Spanish, Italian, Amerindian languages

Paraguay
- 157,048 sq miles
  406,752 sq km
- 6,863,000
- Asunción
- Guaraní, Spanish, German

Ecuador
- 109,484 sq miles
  283,561 sq km
- 16,081,000
- Quito
- Spanish, Quechua, other Amerindian languages

Peru
- 496,225 sq miles
  1,285,216 sq km
- 30,741,000
- Lima
- Spanish, Quechua, Aymara

Guyana
- 83,000 sq miles
  214,969 sq km
- 736,000
- Georgetown
- English Creole, Hindi, Tamil, Amerindian languages, English

Uruguay
- 68,037 sq miles
  176,215 sq km
- 3,351,000
- Montevideo
- Spanish

Colombia
- 439,736 sq miles
  1,138,910 sq km
- 47,221,000
- Bogotá
- Spanish, Wayuu, Páez, and other Amerindian languages

Soccer is a national passion in Brazil. Most of these barefoot boys on Ipanema beach, Rio de Janeiro, will be dreaming of playing for Brazil in the World Cup.

Suriname
- 63,251 sq miles
  163,820 sq km
- 585,800
- Paramaribo
- Sranan (creole), Dutch, Javanese, Sarnami Hindi, Saramaccan (creole), Chinese, Carib

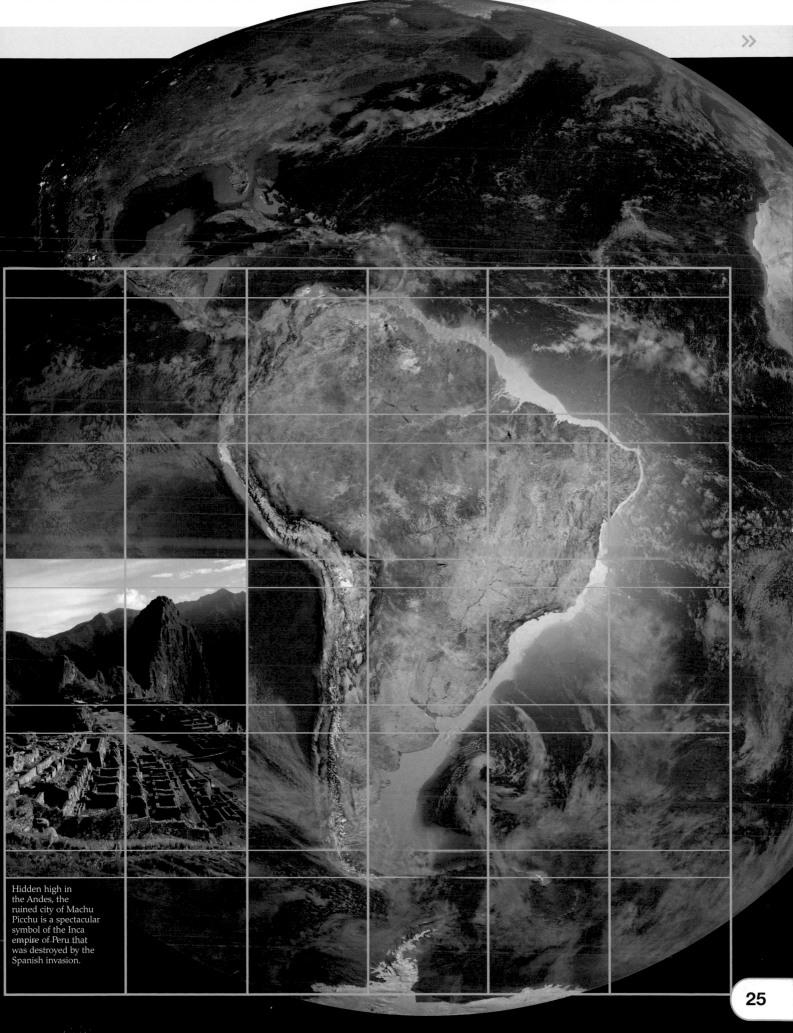

Hidden high in
the Andes, the
ruined city of Machu
Picchu is a spectacular
symbol of the Inca
empire of Peru that
was destroyed by the
Spanish invasion.

Northwest South America

HIGH MOUNTAINS AND PLATEAUS, dense tropical rainforest, and coastal swamps are found in this region. In the 16th century, promises of untold riches attracted the Spanish to the countries here. They found the vast empire of the Incas, which stretched from what is now Peru into northern Colombia. To the north and east, other colonizers—Dutch, English, and French—arrived. Today, although the countries are independent, with the exception of French Guiana, Spanish remains the main language. The population is mainly a mix of native peoples and Europeans, except along the Caribbean coast where descendants of former African slaves live.

ANDES MOUNTAINS
The Andes, the world's longest mountain chain, extends 4,505 miles (7,250 km) down the western edge of South America. Barley, wheat, and potatoes grow well in highland areas, and are cultivated on the terraced hillsides.

FRENCH GUIANA
French Guiana is the only remaining colony in South America, and is governed by France. Tropical forests cover more than four-fifths of its land. In 1968, the European Space Agency established a launch site on the coast at Kourou, which is still used today.

CARACAS
Venezuela's population is growing rapidly and more than 89 per cent of its people now live in cities. The oil industry brings in considerable wealth, but many people are still poor. Although Caracas, Venezuela's capital city, is an important financial center, it has many shantytowns.

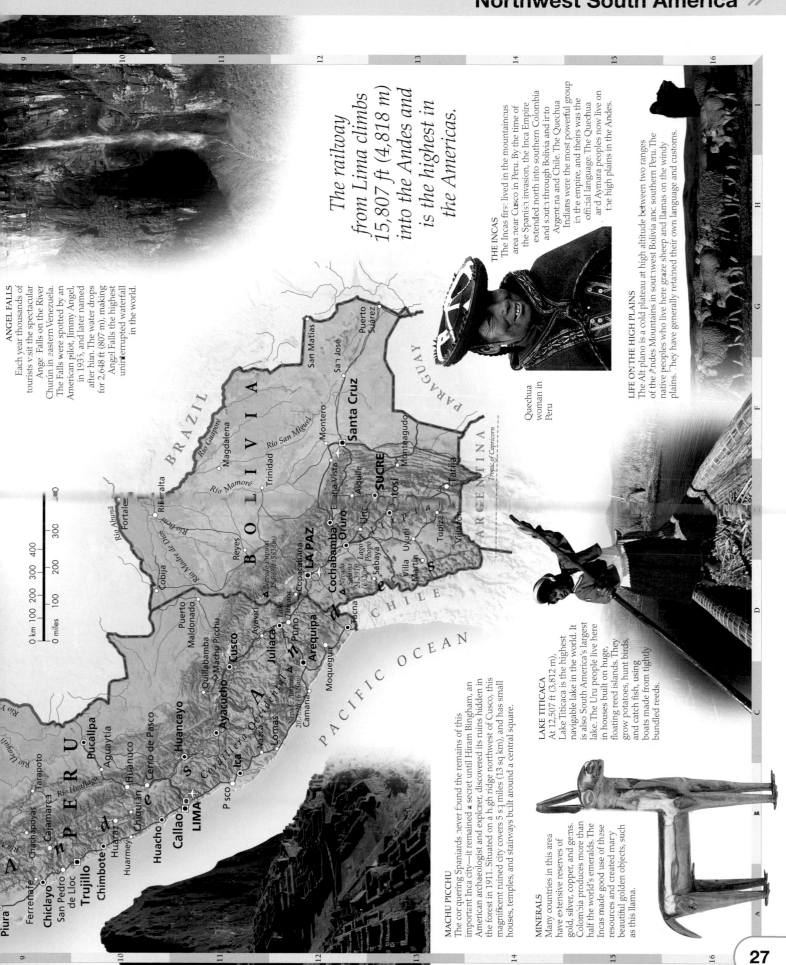

The railway from Lima climbs 15,807 ft (4,818 m) into the Andes and is the highest in the Americas.

ANGEL FALLS
Each year thousands of tourists visit the spectacular Angel Falls on the River Churún in eastern Venezuela. The Falls were spotted by an American pilot, Jimmy Angel, in 1935, and later named after him. The water drops for 2,648 ft (807 m), making Angel Falls the highest uninterrupted waterfall in the world.

THE INCAS
The Incas first lived in the mountainous area near Cusco in Peru. By the time of the Spanish invasion, the Inca Empire extended north into southern Colombia and south through Bolivia and into Argentina and Chile. The Quechua Indians were the most powerful group in the empire, and theirs was the official language. The Quechua and Aymara peoples now live on the high plains in the Andes.

Quechua woman in Peru

LIFE ON THE HIGH PLAINS
The Altiplano is a cold plateau at high altitude between two ranges of the Andes Mountains in southwest Bolivia and southern Peru. The native peoples who live here graze sheep and llamas on the windy plains. They have generally retained their own language and customs.

MACHU PICCHU
The conquering Spaniards never found the remains of this important Inca city—it remained a secret until Hiram Bingham, an American archaeologist and explorer, discovered its ruins hidden in the forest in 1911. Situated on a high ridge northwest of Cusco, this magnificent ruined city covers 5 sq miles (13 sq km), and has small houses, temples, and stairways built around a central square.

MINERALS
Many countries in this area have extensive reserves of gold, silver, copper, and gems. Colombia produces more than half the world's emeralds. The Incas made good use of these resources and created many beautiful golden objects, such as this llama.

LAKE TITICACA
At 12,507 ft (3,812 m), Lake Titicaca is the highest navigable lake in the world. It is also South America's largest lake. The Uru people live here in houses built on huge, floating reed islands. They grow potatoes, hunt birds, and catch fish, using boats made from tightly bundled reeds.

0 km 100 200 300 400
0 miles 100 200 300

Map labels
BRAZIL
BOLIVIA
PARAGUAY
ARGENTINA
CHILE
PERU

Piura
Ferreñafe
Chachapoyas
Chiclayo
Cajamarca
San Pedro de Lloc
Trujillo
Chimbote
Huaraz
Huarmey
Chiquián
Huánuco
Cerro de Pasco
Pucallpa
Aguaytía
Tarapoto
Ica
Nazca
Lomas
Camaná
Moquegua
Arequipa
Callao
LIMA
Huacho
Huancayo
Ayacucho
Cusco
Machu Picchu
Quillabamba
Puerto Maldonado
Juliaca
Puno
Tacna
Avaviri
Luke
Lago Titicaca
Copacabana
LA PAZ
Cochabamba
Oruro
Uncía
Potosí
SUCRE
Sabaya
Villa Martín
Uyuni
Tupiza
Vilazón
Tarija
Monteagudo
Aiquile
Buena Vista
Santa Cruz
Montero
Trinidad
Reyes
Magdalena
Cobija
Riberalta
Fortaleza
Puerto Suárez
San José
San Matías

Río Guaporé
Río San Miguel
Río Mamoré
Río Madre de Dios
Río Abuná
Río Beni
Río Huallaga

Cordillera Occidental
Cordillera Oriental

PACIFIC OCEAN

Tropic of Capricorn

Brazil

THE VIBRANT CULTURE OF BRAZIL—
with its fusion of music and dance—reflects
the rich mix of its ethnic groups. The country
also boasts immense natural resources with
well-developed mining and manufacturing
industries. Brazil grows all its own food
and exports large quantities of coffee,
sugar cane, soya beans, oranges, and
cotton. However, the wealth is not
evenly distributed, with some people
living in luxury while most struggle
with poverty. São Paulo is home to more
than 21 million people, but poverty and
lack of housing means that many live in
shantytowns without running water or
sanitation. Brazil was colonized in the 16th
century by the Portuguese, who established
their language and their Roman Catholic
faith. It remains a deeply Catholic country
with a strong emphasis on family life.

COFFEE
Brazil produces about one-quarter
of the world's coffee, which is
grown on large plantations in the
states of Paraná and São Paulo.
However, because world coffee
prices go up and down so much,
Brazilians are now growing other
crops for export as well.

AMAZON RAINFOREST
Covering more than one-third of
Brazil, the rainforest is home to a
huge variety of animals and plant life.
At one time, more than 5 million
native Indians also lived here, but
now only about 200,000 remain. Over
the years, vast areas of forest have
been cut down to provide timber for
export, to make way for farmland, or
to mine minerals such as gold, silver,
and iron. The Kaxinawa Indians (left)
still cultivate root vegetables as
a food crop.

Brazilian morpho butterfly
with brilliant blue wings
lives in rainforests from
Brazil to Venezuela.

BRASÍLIA
Brasília replaced Rio de Janeiro as Brazil's capital
in 1960 as part of a scheme to develop the interior
of the country. Situated on land that was once
rainforest, the city is laid out in the shape of
an airplane. Government buildings are in the
"cockpit," and residential areas are in the "wings."

SOCCER ENTHUSIASTS
Brazilians are passionate about soccer,
which is played everywhere from beaches
to shantytowns. There is fervent support for the
national team, which has won the World Cup more
times than any other country, most recently in 2002.

PEOPLE OF BRAZIL
Brazilians come from a variety
of different ethnic groups,
including descendants
of the original native
Indians, the Portuguese
colonizers, African
slaves brought over
to work in the sugar
plantations, and
European
migrants.

Map labels: VENEZUELA, COLOMBIA, Guiana Highland, Uraricoera, Boa Vista, Caracaraí, Pico da Neblina 9888ft (3014m), Roraima, Equator, Repres. Balbin, Rio Japurá, Rio Negro, Rio Içá, Rio Iça, Amazon, Tefé, Manaus, Coari, Rio Juruá, Rio Purús, Rio Madeira, Amazon Basin, Rio Javari, Humaitá, Japiim, Feijó, B R, Acre, Rio Abunã, Porto Velho, PERU, Rondônia, Chapada dos Parecis, Guaporé, Vilhen, BOLIVIA

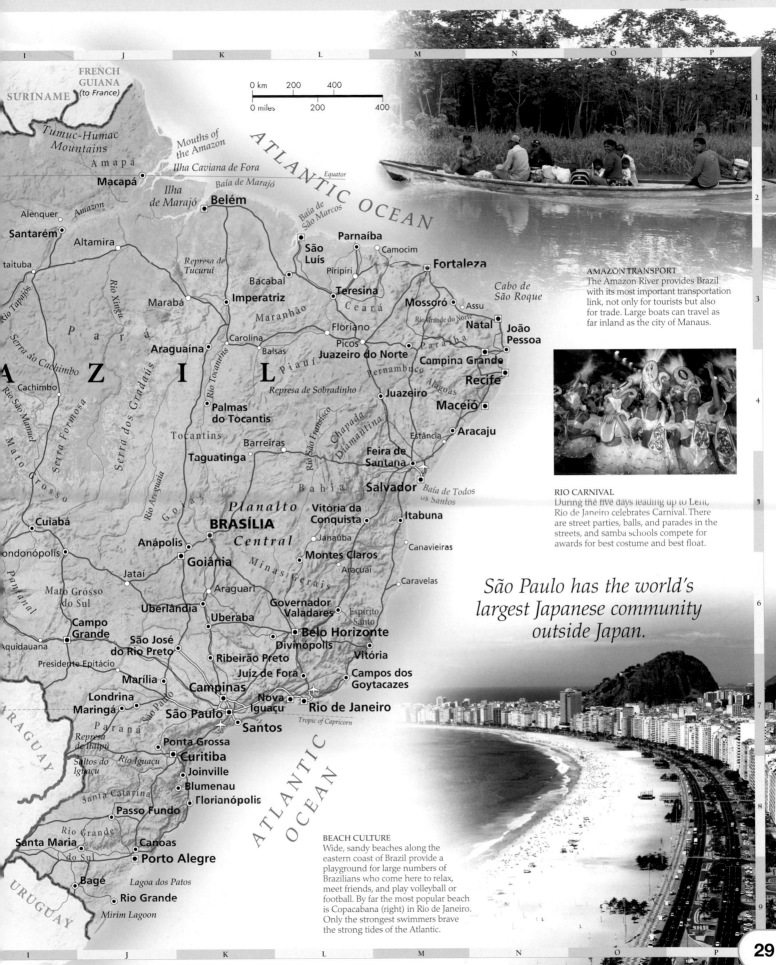

AMAZON TRANSPORT
The Amazon River provides Brazil with its most important transportation link, not only for tourists but also for trade. Large boats can travel as far inland as the city of Manaus.

RIO CARNIVAL
During the five days leading up to Lent, Rio de Janeiro celebrates Carnival. There are street parties, balls, and parades in the streets, and samba schools compete for awards for best costume and best float.

São Paulo has the world's largest Japanese community outside Japan.

BEACH CULTURE
Wide, sandy beaches along the eastern coast of Brazil provide a playground for large numbers of Brazilians who come here to relax, meet friends, and play volleyball or football. By far the most popular beach is Copacabana (right) in Rio de Janeiro. Only the strongest swimmers brave the strong tides of the Atlantic.

Southern South America

TOWERING MOUNTAINS, vast grassy plains, and hot deserts create a very diverse geographical landscape. The four countries in this region—Chile, Paraguay, Uruguay, and Argentina—were once Spanish colonies but gained their independence in the early 1800s. Each country has an elected government but their economies remain fragile. Most of the population speak Spanish and are mestizo—of mixed Spanish and native Indian descent—except for Argentina, where up to 97 percent are descended from Europeans.

A mix of Colonial Spanish, Italian, and Art Deco styles of architecture shows Montevideo's rich history.

URUGUAY'S CAPITAL
The capital of Uruguay, Montevideo, is home to nearly half the country's population. It is also the main port and economic center. This lively capital lies on the east bank of the Río de la Plata, and is a popular holiday resort because of its white sandy beaches.

ITAIPÚ DAM
The enormous Itaipú dam on the Paraná River in Paraguay is one of the world's largest hydroelectric projects. It generates 75 percent of the electricity Paraguay needs as well as large amounts for export.

ATACAMA DESERT
Sandwiched between the high Andes and the sea, the Atacama Desert in northern Chile is one of the hottest and driest areas in the world. Rain hardly ever falls here. This harsh landscape, however, is rich in copper deposits.

CHILEAN EDUCATION
Chile has a relatively high literacy rate (ability to read and write). This may be because between the ages of 6 and 18 schooling is both free and compulsory.

Map Labels

BRAZIL

BOLIVIA

PARAGUAY
Pedro Juan Caballero
Capitán Pablo Lagerenza
Fuerte Olimpo
General Eugenio A. Garay
Mariscal Estigarribia
Concepción
Las Lomitas
ASUNCIÓN
Coronel Oviedo
Villarrica
Caazapá
Yuty
San Juan Bautista
Pilar
Encarnación
Posadas

Río Paraguay
Paraguay
Pilcomayo
Río Bermejo

URUGUAY
Melo
Rivera
Artigas
Tacuarembó
Río Negro
Salto
Paysandú
Trinidad
Florida
Mercedes
MONTEVIDEO
Chuy
Mirim Lagoon

BUENOS AIRES
La Plata
Zárate
Junín
Pergamino
Rufino
Realicó
Gualeguaychú
Gualeguay
Dolores

ARGENTINA / Pampas
Corrientes
Resistencia
Formosa
Goya
Reconquista
Vera
Añatuya
Santa Fe
Paraná
Rosario
Villa María
Río Cuarto
Villa Mercedes
San Luis
Córdoba
Dean Funes
Jesús María
La Rioja
San Fernando del Valle de Catamarca
Frías
Santiago del Estero
San Miguel de Tucumán
Metán
Salta
Cafayate
San Salvador de Jujuy
La Quiaca
San Ramón de la Nueva Orán
Rafaela
Monte Caseros
Concordia
Santo Tomé
Mercedes

Laguna Mar Chiquita
Río Salado

Nevado de Chañi 20,341ft (6,200m)
Cerro Galán 21,653ft (6,600m)
Cerro Ojos del Salado 22,573ft (6,880m)

CHILE / Andes
Arica
Iquique
Lagunas
Tocopilla
Mejillones
Antofagasta
Taltal
Chañaral
Caldera
Copiapó
Vallenar
Domeyko
La Serena
Coquimbo
Ovalle
Illapel
Salamanca
Monte Patria
La Ligua
Viña del Mar
Valparaíso
San Antonio
SANTIAGO
Rancagua
Curicó
Pichilemu
San Rafael
Mendoza
Godoy Cruz
San Juan
La Calera
Calama
Chuquicamata

PERU
Cordillera Occidental
Atacama Desert

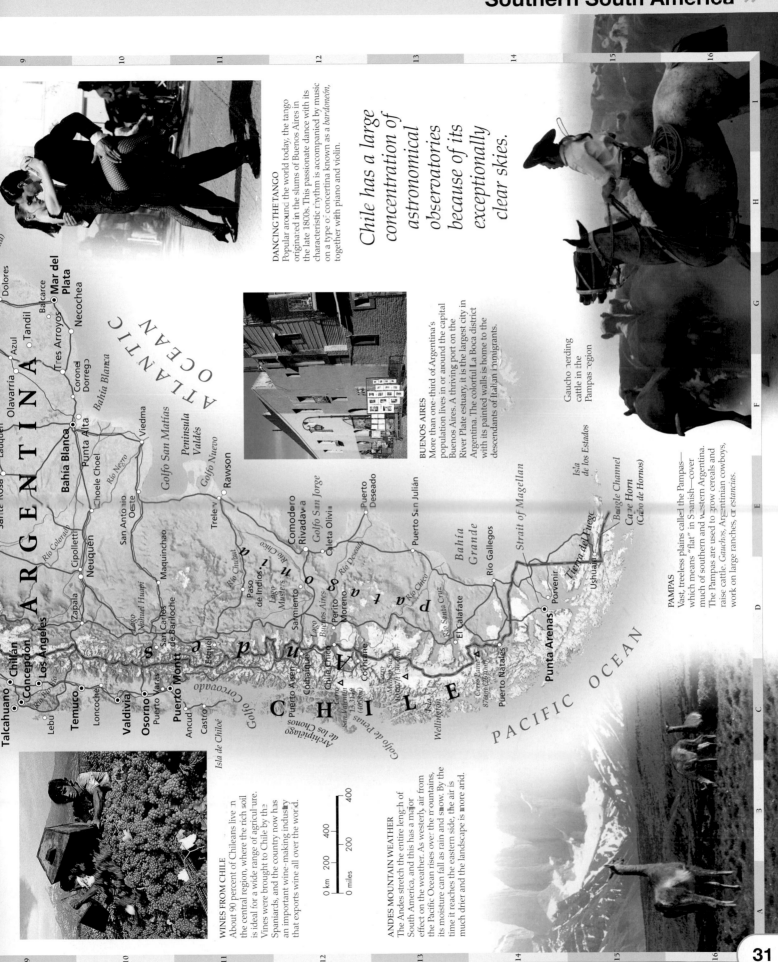

DANCING THE TANGO
Popular around the world today, the tango originated in the slums of Buenos Aires in the late 1800s. This passionate dance with its characteristic rhythm is accompanied by music on a type of concertina known as a *bandoneón*, together with piano and violin.

Chile has a large concentration of astronomical observatories because of its exceptionally clear skies.

BUENOS AIRES
More than one-third of Argentina's population lives in or around the capital Buenos Aires. A thriving port on the River Plate estuary, it is the largest city in Argentina. The colorful La Boca district with its painted walls is home to the descendants of Italian immigrants.

Gaucho herding cattle in the Pampas region

PAMPAS
Vast, treeless plains called the Pampas—which means "flat" in Spanish—cover much of southern and western Argentina. The Pampas are used to grow cereals and raise cattle. *Gauchos*, Argentinian cowboys, work on large ranches, or *estancias*.

WINES FROM CHILE
About 90 percent of Chileans live in the central region, where the rich soil is ideal for a wide range of agriculture. Vines were brought to Chile by the Spaniards, and the country now has an important wine-making industry that exports wine all over the word.

ANDES MOUNTAIN WEATHER
The Andes stretch the entire length of South America, and this has a major effect on the weather. As westerly air from the Pacific Ocean rises over the mountains, its moisture can fall as rain and snow. By the time it reaches the eastern side, the air is much drier and the landscape is more arid.

0 km   200   400
0 miles   200   400

ATLANTIC OCEAN

PACIFIC OCEAN

ARGENTINA

CHILE

Patagonia

Dolores
Balcarce
Mar del Plata
Necochea
Tandil
Azul
Olavarría
Tres Arroyos
Coronel Dorrego
Bahía Blanca
Santa Rosa
Laboulaye
Punta Alta
Viedma
Choele Choel
San Antonio Oeste
Golfo San Matías
Península Valdés
Golfo Nuevo
Rawson
Cipolletti
Neuquén
Zapala
Maquinchao
Trelew
Río Negro
Río Colorado
Lago Nahuel Huapi
Comodoro Rivadavia
Golfo San Jorge
Caleta Olivia
Puerto Deseado
Río Chubut
Paso de Indios
Lago Musters
Sarmiento
Río Chico
Puerto San Julián
Río Deseado
Bahía Grande
Río Gallegos
Isla de los Estados
Strait of Magellan
Beagle Channel
Cape Horn (Cabo de Hornos)
Tierra del Fuego
Ushuaia
Porvenir
Punta Arenas
Puerto Natales
El Calafate
Río Santa Cruz
Perito Moreno
Lago Buenos Aires
Chile Chico
Cochrane
Coyhaique
Puerto Aisén
Cerro San Valentín 13,314ft (4059m)
Monte San Valentín 12,887ft (3910m)
Cerro Darwin 7218ft (2200m)
Isla Wellington
Golfo de Penas
Archipiélago de los Chonos
Golfo Corcovado
Esquel
San Carlos de Bariloche
Loncoche
Ancud
Castro
Isla de Chiloé
Puerto Montt
Osorno
Puerto Varas
Valdivia
Temuco
Los Ángeles
Concepción
Chillán
Talcahuano
Lebu
Río Bío Bío

31

B   C   D   E   F   G   H

Atlantic Ocean

THE WORLD'S SECOND-LARGEST OCEAN, the Atlantic separates the Americas from Europe and Africa. The Atlantic is the world's youngest ocean, starting to form about 180 million years ago, as the continental plates began to separate. This movement continues today, as the oceanic plates that meet at the Mid-Atlantic Ridge continue to pull apart. The Atlantic is a major source of fish but, due to overfishing, stocks are now low. Many shipping routes cross the Atlantic, and pollution is an international problem as ships dump chemicals and waste. There are substantial reserves of oil and gas in the Gulf of Mexico, off the coast of west Africa, and in the north Atlantic.

GREENLAND
The largest island in the world, Greenland is a self-governing part of Denmark. Most Greenlanders live on the southwest coast. Mainly Inuit, with some Danish-Norwegian influences, they make their living by seal hunting, fishing, and fur trapping.

Fishing for halibut

TOURISM
The volcanic islands and black beaches of the eastern Atlantic, especially the Canaries (left), Madeira, and the Azores, are popular with tourists, who are attracted by the scenery and subtropical climate.

NORTH
AMERICA

BERMUD
(to U

Gulf of
Mexico

Hatteras Plain

Greater Antilles

Puerto R
Trench

Caribbean Sea

Guatemala
Basin

Colombian
Basin

Lesser Antil

Panama
Basin

Galápagos Islands
(to Ecuador)

SOUTH

A n d e s

Peru-Chile Trench

Peru Basin

PACIFIC
OCEAN

Chile
Basin

Peru-Chile Trench

Chile Rise

WARM CURRENTS
The Gulf Stream flows up the east coast of North America and across the Atlantic. It brings warm water and a mild climate to northern Europe, which would otherwise be cooler.

Mid-Atlantic
Ridge

Tristan da Cunha island

At the center of the ridge is a valley at least 10 miles (16 km) wide.

UNDERWATER MOUNTAINS
The Mid-Atlantic Ridge is a great underwater mountain chain that runs the entire length of the Atlantic. It was formed by magma that oozed up from the sea bed, cooled to create solid rock, and gradually built up to form a ridge. Some peaks are so high that they break the surface to form volcanic islands, such as the country of Iceland.

ATLANTIC FISHING INDUSTRY
The Atlantic Ocean contains more than half the world's total stock of fish. Herring, anchovy, sardine, cod, flounder, and tuna are among the most important fish found here. However, overfishing, particularly of cod and tuna, has caused a significant decline in numbers.

Humpback whale breaching

WHALES
Many whales live in the Atlantic, migrating from summer feeding grounds in the cold polar regions to warmer waters in the Caribbean for the winter. They give birth and mate again before returning north.

FALKLANDS
Set in the windy south Atlantic off the coast of Argentina, the Falkland Islands belong to the UK but are also claimed by Argentina. Fishing and sheep farming are important. The land is rocky, mountainous, boggy, and almost treeless.

Mineral-rich waters in the Blue Lagoon, Iceland, are said to be beneficial to people's health.

ICELAND
Iceland is situated in the north Atlantic on the Mid-Atlantic Ridge. As a result, it has at least 20 active volcanoes and suffers frequent earthquakes. There are numerous thermal springs with boiling mud lakes and geysers. Water from hot springs (above) is used to provide hot water and heating for much of Iceland's population, most of whom live on the coast. The warm Gulf Stream ensures that the country's ports stay ice-free in winter.

The Atlantic covers one-fifth of Earth's surface.

ICEBERGS
Icebergs in the Atlantic Ocean are formed when icesheets and glaciers reach the sea. Parts break off and start to drift, driven by winds and currents.

Map labels

GREENLAND (to Denmark)
Labrador Sea
Labrador Basin
Reykjanes Basin
Charlie-Gibbs Fracture Zone
ICELAND
REYKJAVIK
Iceland Basin
FAROE ISLANDS (to Denmark)
Denmark Strait
Rockall Bank
British Isles
North Sea
Baltic Sea
EUROPE
Alps
Bay of Biscay
Mediterranean Sea
Newfoundland
Grand Banks of Newfoundland
Newfoundland Basin
Mid-Atlantic Ridge
Azores (to Portugal)
East Azores Fracture Zone
Atlas Mountains
Sohm Plain
Great Meteor Tablemount
Madeira (to Portugal)
Canary Islands (to Spain)
Madeira Plain
Sahara
Sargasso Sea
Cape Verde Plain
Cape Verde Basin
Kane Fracture Zone
PRAIA
CAPE VERDE
Sahel
ATLANTIC
Doldrums Fracture Zone
Sierra Leone Rise
Sierra Leone Basin
AFRICA
OCEAN
Amazon Fan
Guinea Basin
Gulf of Guinea
Demerara Plain
Ceará Plain
Fernando de Noronha (to Brazil)
Pernambuco Plain
Ascension Fracture Zone
ASCENSION ISLAND (to UK)
Angola Basin
MERICA
Brazil Basin
Atlantic Ridge
ST HELENA (to UK)
Zubov Seamount
Vitória Seamount
Ilha da Trindade (to Brazil)
Santos Plateau
Rio Grande Rise
Walvis Ridge
Orange Fan
Cape Basin
Cape of Good Hope
Argentine Basin
TRISTAN DA CUNHA (to UK)
Gough Island (to Tristan da Cunha)
Gough Fracture Zone
Gulf of San Matías
Gulf of San Jorge
Zapiola Ridge
FALKLAND ISLANDS (to UK)
Scotia Sea
SOUTH SANDWICH ISLANDS (to UK)
BOUVET ISLAND (to Norway)
Cape Horn
SOUTH GEORGIA (to UK)
Drake Passage
SOUTHERN OCEAN
East Scotia Basin

AFRICA

Covering one-fifth of the world's land area, Africa has a rapidly growing population. Many of its 53 nations—listed below in order of size—are desperately poor. This is partly due to hostile climates, especially in and around the vast Sahara desert, but also because of a history of political turmoil, ethnic tension or conflict and, in some countries, war. Despite this, African culture is among the most vibrant on Earth.

Algeria
- 919,595 sq miles
  2,381,741 sq km
- 40,264,000
- Algiers
- Arabic, Tamazight (Berber: Kabyle, Shawia, Tamashek), French

Chad
- 495,755 sq miles
  1,284,000 sq km
- 11,852,000
- N'Djamena
- French, Sara, Arabic, Maba

Ethiopia
- 426,373 sq miles
  1,104,300 sq km
- 102,374,000
- Addis Ababa
- Amharic, Tigrinya, Galla, Sidamo, Somali, English, Arabic (Oromu)

Namibia
- 318,261 sq miles
  824,292 sq km
- 2,436,000
- Windhoek
- Ovambo, Kavango, English, Bergdama, German, Afrikaans

South Sudan
- 248,777 sq miles
  644,329 sq km
- 12,531,000
- Juba
- Dinka, Nuer, Zande, Bari, Shilluk, Lotuko, Arabic

Morocco
- 172,414 sq miles
  446,550 sq km
- 33,656,000
- Rabat
- Arabic, Tamazight (Berber), French, Spanish

Congo, Dem Rep of the
- 905,355 sq miles
  2,344,858 sq km
- 81,331,000
- Kinshasa
- Kiswahili, Tshiluba, Kikongo, Lingala, French

Niger
- 489,191 sq miles
  1,267,000 sq km
- 18,639,000
- Niamey
- Hausa, Djerma, Fula, Tuareg, Teda, French

Mauritania
- 397,955 sq miles
  1,030,700 sq km
- 3,677,000
- Nouakchott
- Hassaniyah Arabic, Wolof, French

Mozambique
- 308,642 sq miles
  799,380 sq km
- 25,930,000
- Maputo
- Makua, Xitsonga, Sena, Lomwe, Portuguese

Madagascar
- 226,658 sq miles
  587,041 sq km
- 24,430,000
- Antananarivo
- Malagasy, French

Zimbabwe
- 150,872 sq miles
  390,757 sq km
- 14,547,000
- Harare
- Shona, isiNdebele, English

Congo, Republic of
- 132,946 sq miles
  342,000 sq km
- 4,852,000
- Brazzaville
- Kikongo, Teke, Lingala, French

Angola
- 481,354 sq miles
  1,246,700 sq km
- 20,172,000
- Luanda
- Portuguese, Umbundu, Kimbundu, Kikongo

Egypt
- 386,662 sq miles
  1,001,450 sq km
- 94,667,000
- Cairo
- Arabic, French, English, Berber

Zambia
- 290,587 sq miles
  752,618 sq km
- 15,511,000
- Lusaka
- Bemba, Tongan, Nyanja, Lozi, Lala-Bisa, Nsenga, English

Botswana
- 224,607 sq miles
  581,730 sq km
- 2,209,000
- Gaborone
- Setswana, English, Shona, San, Khoikhoi, isiNdebele

Ivory Coast
- 124,504 sq miles
  322,463 sq km
- 23,740,000
- Yamoussoukro
- Akan, French, Kru, Voltaïque

Sudan
- 718,723 sq miles
  1,861,484 sq km
- 36,730,000
- Khartoum
- Arabic, Nubian, Beja, Fur

Mali
- 478,841 sq miles
  1,240,192 sq km
- 17,467,000
- Bamako
- Bambara, Fula, Senufo, Soninke, French

Tanzania
- 365,755 sq miles
  947,300 sq km
- 52,483,000
- Dodoma
- Kiswahili, Sukuma,Kichagga, Nyamwezi, Hehe, Makonde, Yao, Sandawe, English

Somalia
- 246,201 sq miles
  637,657 sq km
- 10,817,000
- Mogadishu
- Somali, Arabic, English, Italian

Kenya
- 224,081 sq miles
  580,367 sq km
- 46,791,000
- Nairobi
- Kiswahili, English, Kikuyu, Luo, Kalenjin, Kamba

Burkina Faso
- 105,869 sq miles
  274,200 sq km
- 19,513,000
- Ouagadougou
- Mossi, Fulani, French, Tuareg, Diyula, Songhai

Libya
- 679,362 sq miles
  1,759,540 sq km
- 6,542,000
- Tripoli
- Arabic, Tuareg

South Africa
- 470,693 sq miles
  1,219,090 sq km
- 54,301,000
- Pretoria
- English, isiZulu, isiXhosa, Afrikaans, Sepedi, Setswana, Sesotho, Xitsonga, siSwati, Tshivenda, isiNdebele

Nigeria
- 356,669 sq miles
  923,768 sq km
- 186,053,000
- Abuja
- Hausa, English, Yoruba, Igbo

Central African Republic
- 240,535 sq miles
  622,984 sq km
- 5,507,000
- Bangui
- Sango, Banda, Gbaya, French

Cameroon
- 183,568 sq miles
  475,440 sq km
- 24,361,000
- Yaoundé
- Bamileke, Fang, Fula, French, English

Gabon
- 103,347 sq miles
  267,667 sq km
- 1,739,000
- Libreville
- Fang, French, Punu, Sira, Nzebi, Mpongwe

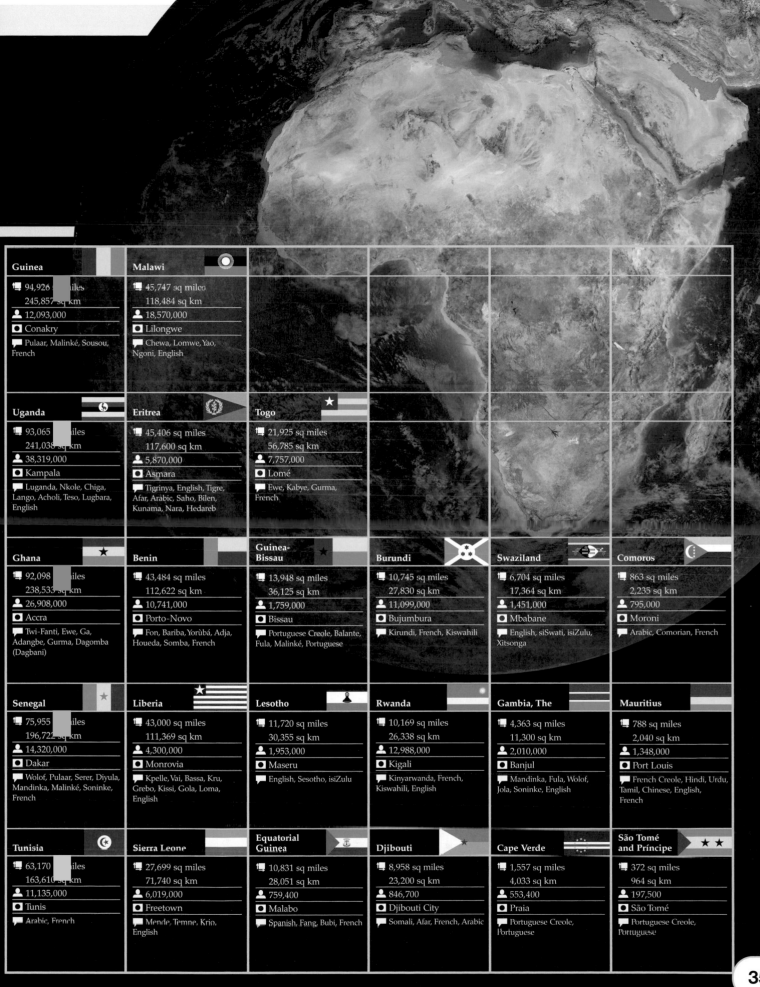

Guinea
- 94,926 sq miles
  245,857 sq km
- 12,093,000
- Conakry
- Pulaar, Malinké, Sousou, French

Malawi
- 45,747 sq miles
  118,484 sq km
- 18,570,000
- Lilongwe
- Chewa, Lomwe, Yao, Ngoni, English

Uganda
- 93,065 sq miles
  241,038 sq km
- 38,319,000
- Kampala
- Luganda, Nkole, Chiga, Lango, Acholi, Teso, Lugbara, English

Eritrea
- 45,406 sq miles
  117,600 sq km
- 5,870,000
- Asmara
- Tigrinya, English, Tigre, Afar, Arabic, Saho, Bilen, Kunama, Nara, Hedareb

Togo
- 21,925 sq miles
  56,785 sq km
- 7,757,000
- Lomé
- Ewe, Kabye, Gurma, French

Ghana
- 92,098 sq miles
  238,533 sq km
- 26,908,000
- Accra
- Twi-Fanti, Ewe, Ga, Adangbe, Gurma, Dagomba (Dagbani)

Benin
- 43,484 sq miles
  112,622 sq km
- 10,741,000
- Porto-Novo
- Fon, Bariba, Yorùbá, Adja, Houeda, Somba, French

Guinea-Bissau
- 13,948 sq miles
  36,125 sq km
- 1,759,000
- Bissau
- Portuguese Creole, Balante, Fula, Malinké, Portuguese

Burundi
- 10,745 sq miles
  27,830 sq km
- 11,099,000
- Bujumbura
- Kirundi, French, Kiswahili

Swaziland
- 6,704 sq miles
  17,364 sq km
- 1,451,000
- Mbabane
- English, siSwati, isiZulu, Xitsonga

Comoros
- 863 sq miles
  2,235 sq km
- 795,000
- Moroni
- Arabic, Comorian, French

Senegal
- 75,955 sq miles
  196,722 sq km
- 14,320,000
- Dakar
- Wolof, Pulaar, Serer, Diyula, Mandinka, Malinké, Soninke, French

Liberia
- 43,000 sq miles
  111,369 sq km
- 4,300,000
- Monrovia
- Kpelle, Vai, Bassa, Kru, Grebo, Kissi, Gola, Loma, English

Lesotho
- 11,720 sq miles
  30,355 sq km
- 1,953,000
- Maseru
- English, Sesotho, isiZulu

Rwanda
- 10,169 sq miles
  26,338 sq km
- 12,988,000
- Kigali
- Kinyarwanda, French, Kiswahili, English

Gambia, The
- 4,363 sq miles
  11,300 sq km
- 2,010,000
- Banjul
- Mandinka, Fula, Wolof, Jola, Soninke, English

Mauritius
- 788 sq miles
  2,040 sq km
- 1,348,000
- Port Louis
- French Creole, Hindi, Urdu, Tamil, Chinese, English, French

Tunisia
- 63,170 sq miles
  163,610 sq km
- 11,135,000
- Tunis
- Arabic, French

Sierra Leone
- 27,699 sq miles
  71,740 sq km
- 6,019,000
- Freetown
- Mende, Temne, Krio, English

Equatorial Guinea
- 10,831 sq miles
  28,051 sq km
- 759,400
- Malabo
- Spanish, Fang, Bubi, French

Djibouti
- 8,958 sq miles
  23,200 sq km
- 846,700
- Djibouti City
- Somali, Afar, French, Arabic

Cape Verde
- 1,557 sq miles
  4,033 sq km
- 553,400
- Praia
- Portuguese Creole, Portuguese

São Tomé and Príncipe
- 372 sq miles
  964 sq km
- 197,500
- São Tomé
- Portuguese Creole, Portuguese

B   C   D   E   F   G   H

Northwest Africa

FOUR COUNTRIES, plus the disputed area of Western Sahara, make up this part of Africa. Algeria, Libya, and Tunisia have rich supplies of oil and natural gas that boost their economies. Morocco relies on tourism, phosphates used for chemicals and fertilizer, and agriculture. In the fertile valleys of the Atlas Mountains, farmers grow grapes, citrus fruit, dates, and olives. The area also attracts tourists to its colorful markets, historical sites, and sandy beaches. The Sahara Desert dominates the region, particularly in Algeria and Libya.

SUN AND SEA
Many tourists visit Tunisia and Morocco each year to enjoy the warm climate and sandy beaches. Tourism provides jobs for the local people and brings much-needed income.

ARAB INFLUENCE
Arab invasions during the 7th and 11th centuries have influenced the culture, religion (Islam), architecture, and language of northwest Africa. Today, Arabic is the main language, and more than 95 percent of the people here are Muslim.

MOROCCAN MARKET
In a souk, or market, craftworkers sell handmade products to tourists. Goods are displayed in booths along the bustling streets.

Muslims going to worship at the Hassan II mosque in Casablanca, Morocco

BERBERS
The Berber people were the original inhabitants of northwest Africa. Most now live in the Atlas Mountains or the desert. Although most Berbers converted to Islam when the Arabs arrived, they kept their own language and way of life. In 2001, Algeria recognized Berber (Tamazight) as an official language.

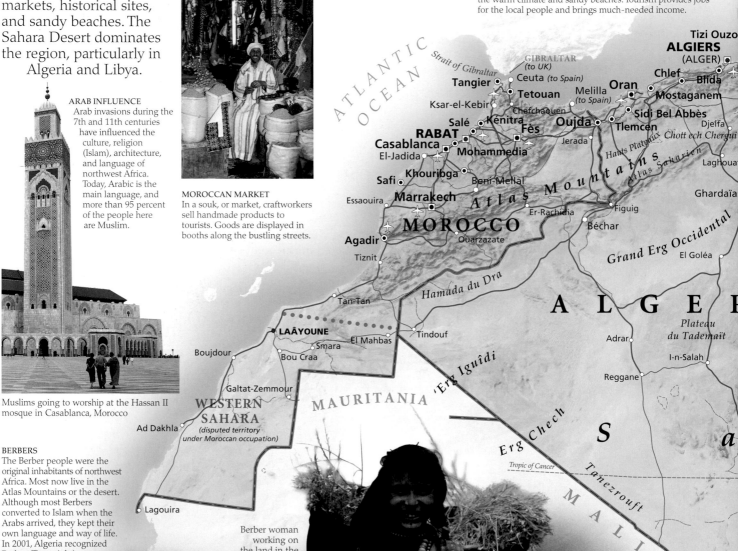

Berber woman working on the land in the Atlas Mountains

ATLANTIC OCEAN

Strait of Gibraltar
GIBRALTAR (to UK)
Tangier ● Ceuta (to Spain)
Tetouan
Ksar-el-Kebir
Chefchaouen
Salé ● Kénitra
RABAT
Casablanca
Mohammedia
El-Jadida
Safi ● Khouribga
Beni-Mellal
Essaouira
Marrakech
Agadir
Tiznit
Ouarzazate
Er-Rachidia

Tizi Ouzo
ALGIERS (ALGER)
Chlef ● Blida
Oran ● Mostaganem
Melilla (to Spain)
Sidi Bel Abbès
Oujda ● Tlemcen ● Djelfa
Jerada Hauts Plateaux Chott ech Chergui
Atlas Saharien Laghouat
Figuig Ghardaïa
Béchar

MOROCCO

Atlas Mountains

Hamada du Dra
Tan-Tan
Tindouf
LAÂYOUNE
Smara ● El Mahbas
Boujdour
Bou Craa
Galtat-Zemmour
WESTERN SAHARA
(disputed territory under Moroccan occupation)
Ad Dakhla

MAURITANIA

'Erg Iguîdi

A L G E
Plateau du Tademaït
Adrar
I-n-Salah
Reggane
El Goléa
Grand Erg Occidental

Lagouira

Erg Chech
Tropic of Cancer
Tanezrouft

M A L I

S   a

A   B   C   D   E   F   G   H

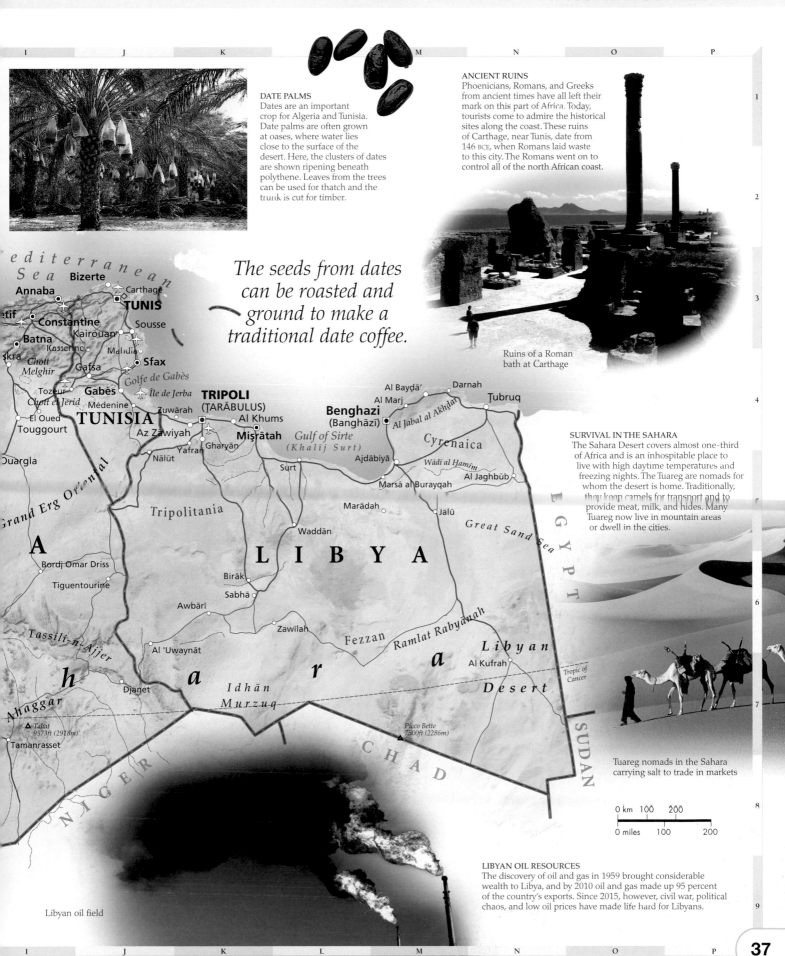

DATE PALMS
Dates are an important crop for Algeria and Tunisia. Date palms are often grown at oases, where water lies close to the surface of the desert. Here, the clusters of dates are shown ripening beneath polythene. Leaves from the trees can be used for thatch and the trunk is cut for timber.

ANCIENT RUINS
Phoenicians, Romans, and Greeks from ancient times have all left their mark on this part of Africa. Today, tourists come to admire the historical sites along the coast. These ruins of Carthage, near Tunis, date from 146 BCE, when Romans laid waste to this city. The Romans went on to control all of the north African coast.

Ruins of a Roman bath at Carthage

The seeds from dates can be roasted and ground to make a traditional date coffee.

SURVIVAL IN THE SAHARA
The Sahara Desert covers almost one-third of Africa and is an inhospitable place to live with high daytime temperatures and freezing nights. The Tuareg are nomads for whom the desert is home. Traditionally, they keep camels for transport and to provide meat, milk, and hides. Many Tuareg now live in mountain areas or dwell in the cities.

Tuareg nomads in the Sahara carrying salt to trade in markets

0 km 100 200
0 miles 100 200

LIBYAN OIL RESOURCES
The discovery of oil and gas in 1959 brought considerable wealth to Libya, and by 2010 oil and gas made up 95 percent of the country's exports. Since 2015, however, civil war, political chaos, and low oil prices have made life hard for Libyans.

Libyan oil field

Map labels:

Mediterranean Sea
Bizerte
Annaba
Carthage
Sétif
TUNIS
Constantine
Sousse
Kairouan
Batna
Kasserine
Mahdia
Skra
Chott Melghir
Gafsa
Sfax
Tozeur
Gabès
Golfe de Gabès
Chott el Jérid
Médenine
Île de Jerba
El Oued
TUNISIA
Zuwārah
TRIPOLI (ṬARĀBULUS)
Al Bayḍā'
Darnah
Ṭubruq
Touggourt
Az Zāwiyah
Al Khums
Benghazi (Banghāzī)
Al Marj
Ouargla
Yafran
Miṣrātah
Al Jabal al Akhḍar
Gharyān
Gulf of Sirte (Khalīj Surt)
Cyrenaica
Nālūt
Surt
Ajdābiyā
Wādī al Hamīm
Marādah
Marsā al Burayqah
Al Jaghbūb
Grand Erg Oriental
Tripolitania
Jalū
Waddān
Great Sand Sea
A
LIBYA
EGYPT
Bordj Omar Driss
Birāk
Tiguentourine
Sabhā
Awbārī
Fezzan
Ramlat Rabyānah
Libyan
Tassili-n-Ajjer
Zawīlah
Al 'Uwaynāt
Al Kufrah
Tropic of Cancer
h
Djanet
Idhān Murzuq
a
r
a
Desert
Ahaggar
Tahat 9573ft (2918m)
Tamanrasset
Picco Bette 7500ft (2286m)
CHAD
SUDAN
NIGER

Northeast Africa

THIS REGION, KNOWN as the Horn of Africa, contains the oldest civilizations in the continent, and some of its poorest countries. The borders that divide the countries today were mostly created by colonial rulers in the last hundred years. Pastoral nomads with their herds of animals often cross these borders in search of pasture. Most people still live in the countryside and farm the land, but many people now live in the cities. Tourism and agriculture are important sources of income for Egypt and Kenya, two of the richest and fastest-growing countries in the region. Elsewhere, tribal rivalries and disputes over land and resources have sometimes erupted into full-scale war and these, together with drought and poverty, have blighted the lives of millions of people in this region.

RIVER NILE
The Nile is the world's longest river. It flows north from Burundi to run along the Tanzania–Rwanda border, then through Sudan, South Sudan, Sudan, and Egypt to the coast. Most of Egypt's population lives around the valley and delta of the Nile, which provides the region's water. The river also provides irrigation for local crops, such as cotton.

SUEZ CANAL
The Suez Canal, opened in 1869, is one of the world's longest and most important artificial waterways. It links the Mediterranean Sea with the Gulf of Suez and the Red Sea, providing a crucial shortcut from Europe to India and east Asia. The tolls from the canal are a great source of income for Egypt.

LOSING FARMLAND
As the population grows in Ethiopia, forests are cut down for firewood, or to cultivate new areas for food crops. The soil, no longer held firm by the trees, is easily blown or washed away, and valuable farmland is lost.

Plowing fields in Ethiopia

ABU SIMBEL
Tourists come to Egypt to see the pyramids at Giza and the temples along the Nile, such as these two built at Abu Simbel, south of Aswan. Tourism brings in money to preserve these historical sites.

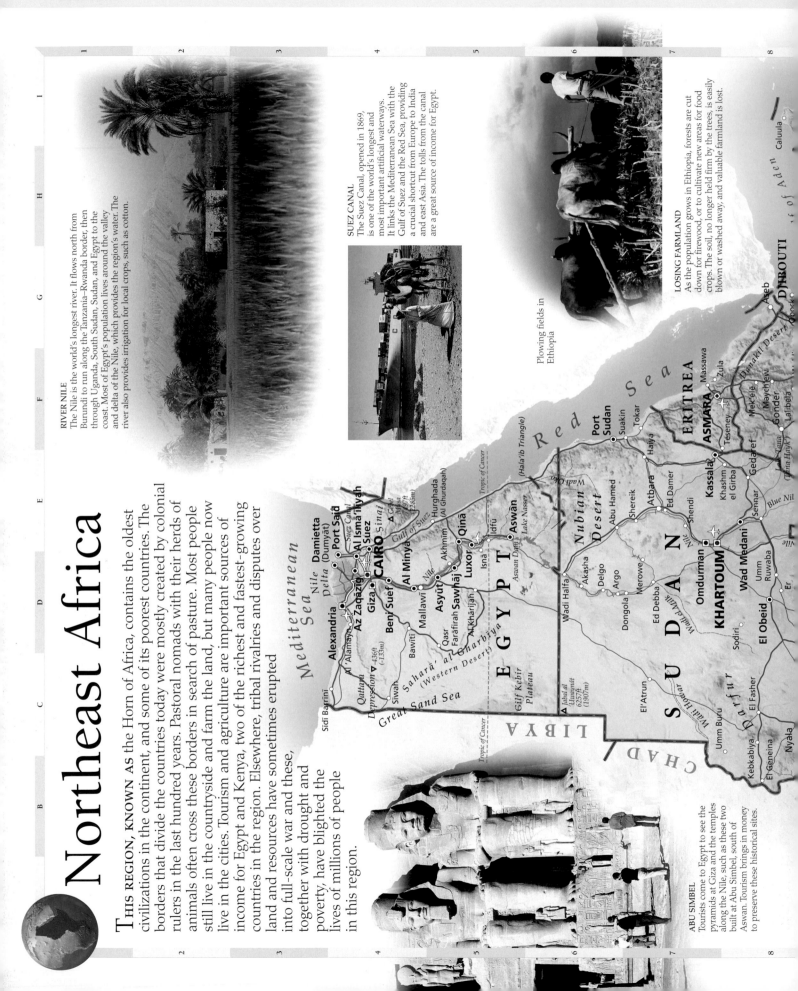

Map labels

INDIAN OCEAN

Puntland

Somaliland

Sinujiif
Doozo Nugaaleed
Garoowe
Gaaiweo

SOMALIA

Hargeysa
Gellinsoor
Dhuusa Marreeb
Gaalkacyo
Beledweyne
Shilabo
Xuddur
Baydhabo
Buulobarde
Jawhar
Doolow
Baardheere

MOGADISHU (MUQDISHO)

Marka
Baraawe

ETHIOPIA

Harer
Jima
Nazret
Ādīs Ābeba (ADDIS ABABA)

Highlands

Great Rift Valley

Dirē Dawa
Mīʼēso
Āwash
Negēlē
Yabēlo
Gorē Agaro

Ogaden
Shebeli
Jubba

Equator

Afmadow
Kismaayo
Bur Gaabo

KENYA

Garissa
Garsen
Malindi

Mombasa
Tanga
Zanzibar

DAR ES SALAAM

Pemba
Mafia

NAIROBI
Nakuru
Nyeri
Meru
Marsabit
Lake Turkana
Lokitaung
Lodwar
Eldoret
Kisumu
Kitale

Kilimanjaro (5895m)
Mt Kenya (5200m)

Moshi
Arusha
Morogoro

Masai Steppe

TANZANIA

DODOMA

Great Rift Valley

SOUTH SUDAN
JUBA
Malakal
Duk Faiwil
Kongor
Bor
Amadi
Maridi
Yambio
Raga
Wau
Toni
Rumbek
Tambura
Sudd
White Nile

DEM. REP. CONGO

Lake Albert
Lake Edward
Lake Kivu

UGANDA
KAMPALA
Arua
Gulu
Lira
Masindi
Entebbe
Jinja
Mbarara
Kabale
Masaka
Bukoba

Lake Victoria

Equator

RWANDA
KIGALI

BURUNDI
BUJUMBURA

Lake Tanganyika
Kigoma
Kasulu
Kipili

Great Rift Valley

ZAMBIA

MALAWI

Lake Nyasa

MOZAMBIQUE

Captions

Water makes up almost one-fifth of the surface area of Uganda.

RELIGIOUS BELIEFS
The Ethiopian Orthodox Union Church has existed since the 4th century CE. It is a branch of the Coptic Church and mixes Christian beliefs, such as Catholic saints, with some traditional African spiritual beliefs.

Coptic cross

TEA IN KENYA
Kenya is an important world producer of tea, which is grown on plantations in the highland areas (such as this one below). High rainfall here ensures a good crop. Coffee is also a valuable export.

Kenyan workers carefully select tea leaves for picking.

CAIRO
The largest city in Africa is Cairo, the capital of Egypt, with a population of more than 18 million. Here, Arab, African, and European influences exist alongside more traditional Egyptian customs.

Busy street bazaar in Cairo

THE DINKA OF SOUTH SUDAN
There are more than 500 tribes in Sudan and South Sudan. They speak more than 100 languages and dialects. Like many tribal people here, the Dinka are nomadic – their cattle graze on the plains east of the Nile. Cattle are central to their lives – young Dinka men officially become adults with an initiation ceremony in which they are given an ox of their own.

Young Dinka man

MOUNTAIN GORILLAS
The Volcanoes National Park in Rwanda is one of the few places where you can still see a mountain gorilla (right) in the wild. These animals are threatened with extinction because of poachers and the destruction of their habitat. Tanzania and Kenya also have many important game reserves, which preserve the wildlife of the savanna.

Scale: 0 km 100 200 300 400 / 0 miles 200 400

West Africa

DRAMATICALLY DIFFERENT CLIMATES and landscapes influence life in west Africa. In the hot, dry north, it is difficult to grow crops. Only oases in the Sahara and seasonal rainfall in the Sahel make growing crops possible. To the south, the climate is warm and wet, and crops such as cocoa and coffee are grown on large plantations. This region also has many valuable minerals. Despite these rich resources, most countries are poor. Since independence from colonial powers, there has been much political unrest, often sparked by poverty and tribal rivalries in the region. West Africa is also divided by religion, with Islam dominant in the north and Christianity in the south.

GAMBIA
In recent years, tourism has become increasingly important to the economy of Gambia. Visitors come to see wildlife along the Gambia River and to visit the Atlantic coast beaches. These safari tourists are admiring a giant termite mound.

PEOPLE OF GHANA
Family ties and a sense of community are important to the people of Ghana, and ceremonies throughout each year mark the events of childbirth, puberty, marriage, and death. About half of Ghanaians are Ashanti people whose ancestors developed one of the richest and most notable civilizations in Africa.

DIAMONDS AND GOLD
West Africa has many valuable minerals, including diamonds, uranium, copper, and gold. In Sierra Leone, where diamonds (left) provide crucial income, the mines were a focus of fighting in the civil war between rebel groups and the government.

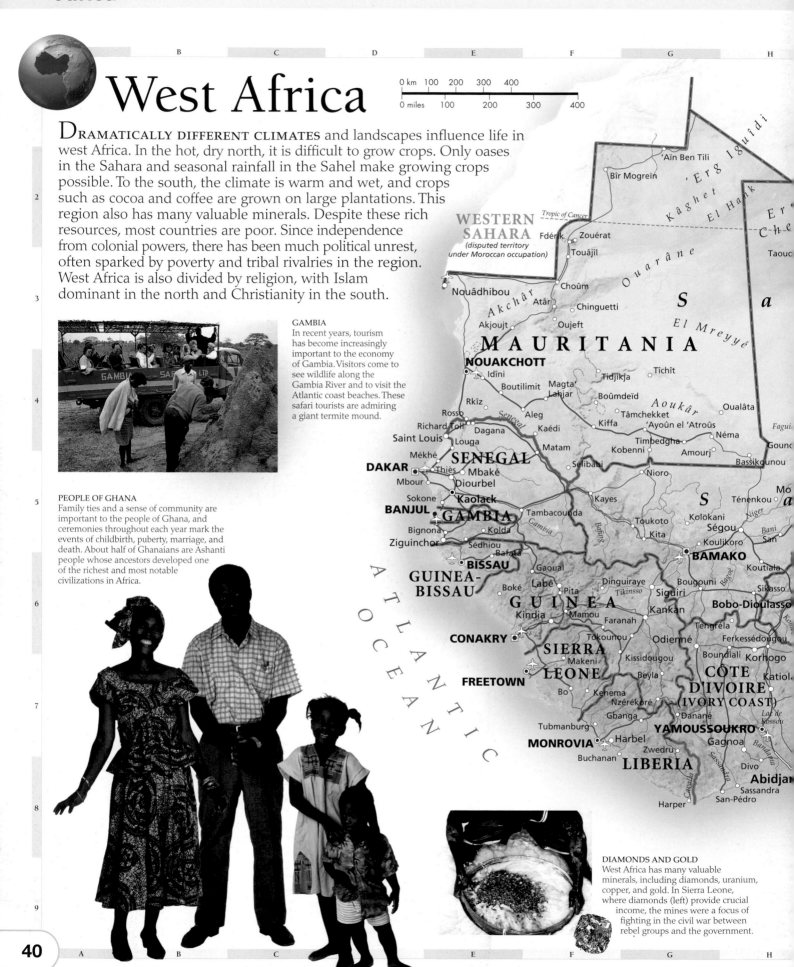

0 km 100 200 300 400
0 miles 100 200 300 400

WESTERN SAHARA (disputed territory under Moroccan occupation)

Tropic of Cancer

'Aïn Ben Tili
Bîr Mogreïn
Fdérik
Zouérat
Touâjîl
'Erg Iguidi
Kâghet
El Hank
Taouc

Nouâdhibou
Choûm
Akchâr
Atâr
Chinguetti
Ouarâne
S
a
Er
Che

Akjoujt
Oujeft
El Mreyyé
Néma
Goun

MAURITANIA

NOUAKCHOTT
Idîni
Boutilimit
Tidjikja
Tîchît

Rkîz
Magta' Lahjar
Boûmdeïd
Aoukâr
Oualâta
Fagui

Rosso
Aleg
Kiffa
Tâmchekket
'Ayoûn el 'Atroûs
Néma
Gound

Richard Toll
Dagana
Kaédi
Timbedgha
Amourj
Bassikounou

Saint Louis
Louga
Matam
Kobenni
Nioro

Mékhé
SENEGAL
Selibabi
S
Ténenkou
Mo
a

DAKAR
Thiès
Mbaké
Diourbel
Kayes
Kolokani
Niger

Mbour
Sokone
Kaolack
Toukoto
Ségou
Bani
San

BANJUL
GAMBIA
Tambacounda
Gambia
Kita
Koulikoro
BAMAKO

Bignona
Kolda
Bafing
Koutiala

Ziguinchor
Sédhiou
Bafatá

BISSAU
Gaoual
Bougouni
Sikasso

GUINEA-BISSAU
Boké
Labé
Dinguiraye
Tikinsso
Siguiri
Bobo-Dioulasso

Pita
Mamou
GUINEA
Kankan
Tengréla

Kindia
Faranah
Odienné
Ferkessédougou

CONAKRY
Tokounou
Boundiali
Korhogo

SIERRA LEONE
Makeni
Kissidougou
Beyla
CÔTE D'IVOIRE (IVORY COAST)
Katiol

FREETOWN
Bo
Kenema
Nzérékoré
Danané
Lac de Kossou

Gbanga
YAMOUSSOUKRO
Gagnoa

Tubmanburg
Harbel
Bandama

MONROVIA
Zwedru
Divo

Buchanan
LIBERIA
Sassandra
Abidja

Harper
San-Pédro

A T L A N T I C   O C E A N

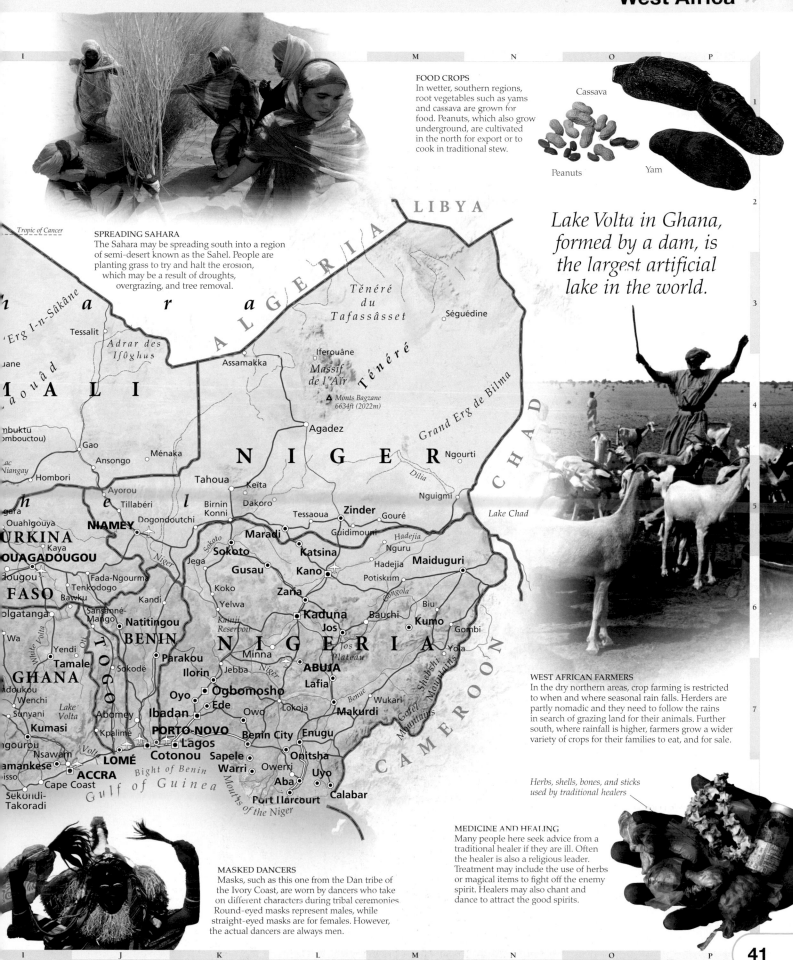

FOOD CROPS
In wetter, southern regions, root vegetables such as yams and cassava are grown for food. Peanuts, which also grow underground, are cultivated in the north for export or to cook in traditional stew.

Cassava

Peanuts

Yam

Lake Volta in Ghana, formed by a dam, is the largest artificial lake in the world.

SPREADING SAHARA
The Sahara may be spreading south into a region of semi-desert known as the Sahel. People are planting grass to try and halt the erosion, which may be a result of droughts, overgrazing, and tree removal.

WEST AFRICAN FARMERS
In the dry northern areas, crop farming is restricted to when and where seasonal rain falls. Herders are partly nomadic and they need to follow the rains in search of grazing land for their animals. Further south, where rainfall is higher, farmers grow a wider variety of crops for their families to eat, and for sale.

Herbs, shells, bones, and sticks used by traditional healers

MEDICINE AND HEALING
Many people here seek advice from a traditional healer if they are ill. Often the healer is also a religious leader. Treatment may include the use of herbs or magical items to fight off the enemy spirit. Healers may also chant and dance to attract the good spirits.

MASKED DANCERS
Masks, such as this one from the Dan tribe of the Ivory Coast, are worn by dancers who take on different characters during tribal ceremonies. Round-eyed masks represent males, while straight-eyed masks are for females. However, the actual dancers are always men.

41

Central Africa

ALL EIGHT COUNTRIES IN central Africa were European colonies with a painful history of slavery. Since the 1960s, independence has brought them mixed success. Rich mineral deposits and the discovery of offshore oil have provided income for Cameroon, Congo, and Gabon, while civil war and repressive governments have damaged other countries in the region. These include Chad and the Central African Republic, two of the world's poorest countries. Although the north is mainly arid, Africa's largest tropical rainforest dominates the south, with the powerful Congo River linking the interior with the coast. The tiny, volcanic country of São Tomé and Príncipe lies off the coast of Gabon.

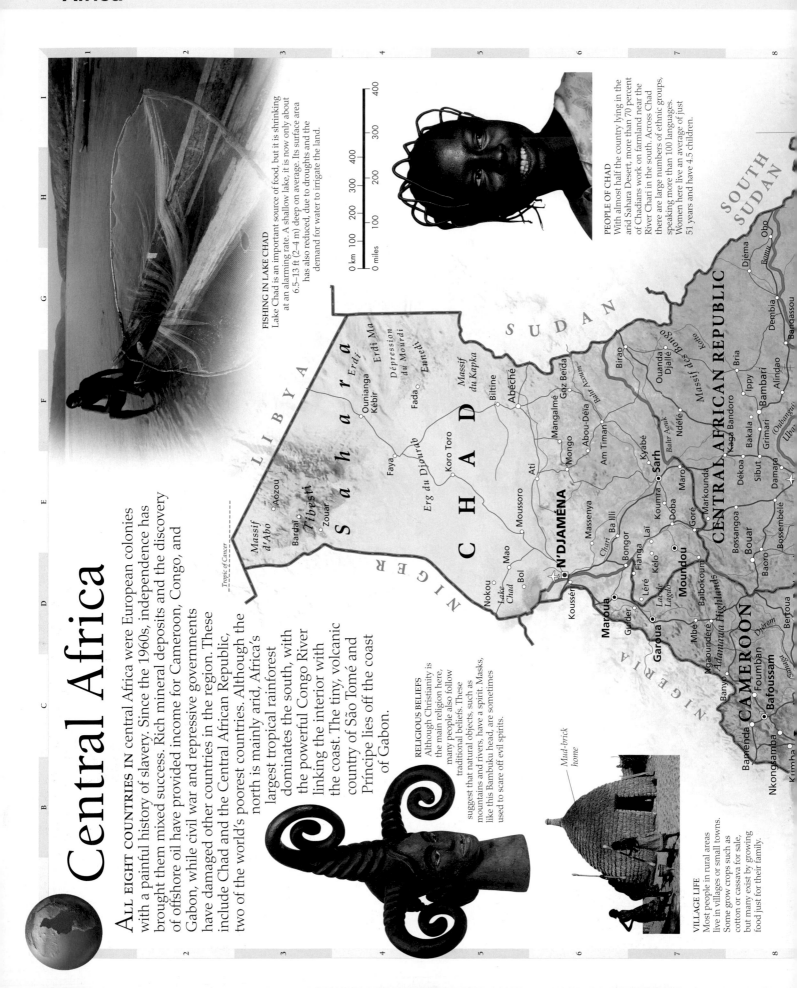

FISHING IN LAKE CHAD
Lake Chad is an important source of food, but it is shrinking at an alarming rate. A shallow lake, it is now only about 6.5–13 ft (2–4 m) deep on average. Its surface area has also reduced, due to droughts and the demand for water to irrigate the land.

PEOPLE OF CHAD
With almost half the country lying in the arid Sahara Desert, more than 70 percent of Chadians work on farmland near the River Chari in the south. Across Chad there are large numbers of ethnic groups, speaking more than 100 languages. Women here live an average of just 51 years and have 4.5 children.

RELIGIOUS BELIEFS
Although Christianity is the main religion here, many people also follow traditional beliefs. These suggest that natural objects, such as mountains and rivers, have a spirit. Masks, like this Bambuku head, are sometimes used to scare off evil spirits.

VILLAGE LIFE
Most people in rural areas live in villages or small towns. Some grow crops such as cotton or cassava for sale, but many exist by growing food just for their family.

Mud-brick home

0 km 100 200 300 400
0 miles 100 200 300 400

Tropic of Cancer

LIBYA

S a h a r a

Massif d'Abo
Aozou
Bardaï
Tibesti
Zouar
Ounianga Kébir
Erdi Ma
Erdi
Fada
Dépression du Mourdi
Ennedi
Massif du Kapka
Bardaï

NIGER

Nokou
Lake Chad
Bol
Mao
Moussoro
Faya
Erg du Djourab
Koro Toro
Ati
N'DJAMÉNA
Massenya
Ba Illi
Bongor
Fianga
Kélo
Léré
Lac
Logone
Moundou
Doba
Goré
Baïbokoum

SUDAN

C H A D

Biltine
Abéché
Mangalmé
Goz Beïda
Mongo
Abou-Déïa
Am Timan
Bahr Azoum
Kyabé
Sarh
Koumra
Maro
Markounda
Bossangoa
Bouar
Baoro
Bossembélé

SOUTH SUDAN

Birao
Ouanda Djallé
Ouandja
Djéma
Kotto
Bria
Ndélé
Kaga Bandoro
Bambari
Ippy
Bakala
Grimari
Sibut
Dékoa
Damara
Bangassou
Dembia
Alindao

CENTRAL AFRICAN REPUBLIC

Kousséri
Maroua
Guider
Garoua
Mbé
Ngaoundéré
Adamaoua Highlands
Banyo
Foumban
Bafoussam
Bamenda
Nkongsamba
Kumba

CAMEROON

NIGERIA

Ubangi
Onbangui

MIGHTY RIVER
The Congo River, also called the Zaire, is a crucial part of the area's transportation system. Dugout canoes and motorized boats take people, goods, and even health clinics from cities to the villages and back. The river is home to many species of fish as well as crocodiles.

The waters of the Congo River have the capacity to provide electrical power for all of Africa.

REFUGEES
There are around 5 million African refugees south of the Sahara – more than 25 percent of the world's total. Conflicts in Chad, the Democratic Republic of the Congo, and the Central African Republic have resulted in huge numbers of Africans leaving their homes.

MINING FOR COPPER
The Democratic Republic of the Congo has vast reserves of copper, and was once one of the world's major exporters. More recently, however, competition from lower-cost producers such as Chile has seen a dramatic downturn in the industry.

Copper

LOGGING IN GABON
Timber provides valuable income for Gabon, with much of the demand for okoumé—a softwood used to make plywood. Hardwoods, such as mahogany and ebony, are also felled. Because logging poses a threat to the future of the forests, the government is now setting up conservation programs, including 13 national parks that together cover at least 10 percent of the country.

43

Southern Africa

FROM THE DRAMATIC Namib and Kalahari deserts in the west, to the tropical forests in the north, southern Africa is a region of contrasts. Oil, diamonds, gold, and other precious metals are all mined here. There are huge inland plains that are home to a variety of wildlife, and large areas devoted to agriculture. But flooding and droughts, together with civil unrest, have hampered development so that, despite an abundance of natural resources, many countries remain poor.

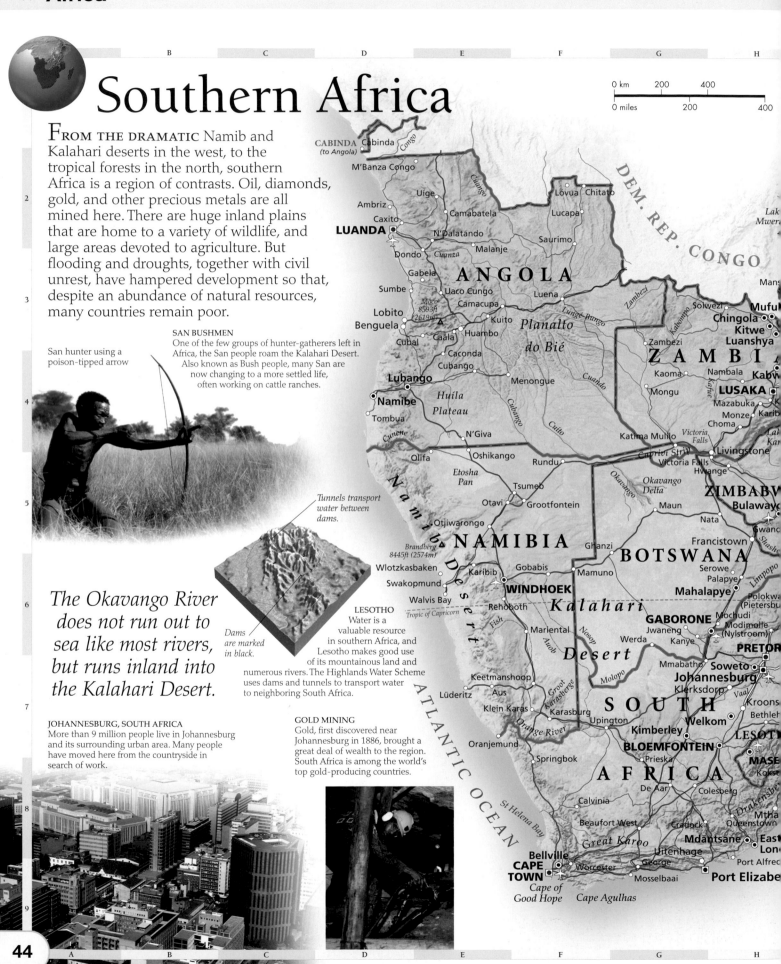

SAN BUSHMEN
One of the few groups of hunter-gatherers left in Africa, the San people roam the Kalahari Desert. Also known as Bush people, many San are now changing to a more settled life, often working on cattle ranches.

San hunter using a poison-tipped arrow

Tunnels transport water between dams.

Dams are marked in black.

The Okavango River does not run out to sea like most rivers, but runs inland into the Kalahari Desert.

LESOTHO
Water is a valuable resource in southern Africa, and Lesotho makes good use of its mountainous land and numerous rivers. The Highlands Water Scheme uses dams and tunnels to transport water to neighboring South Africa.

JOHANNESBURG, SOUTH AFRICA
More than 9 million people live in Johannesburg and its surrounding urban area. Many people have moved here from the countryside in search of work.

GOLD MINING
Gold, first discovered near Johannesburg in 1886, brought a great deal of wealth to the region. South Africa is among the world's top gold-producing countries.

0 km 200 400
0 miles 200 400

CABINDA (to Angola) — Cabinda
Congo
M'Banza Congo
Uige
Ambriz
Caxito
LUANDA
Dondo
Cuanza
Gabela
Sumbe
Uaco Cungo
Lobito
Benguela
Moco 8593ft (2619m)
Cubal
Caála Huambo
Caconda
Cubango
Lubango
Namibe
Huíla Plateau
Tombua
Cunene
N'Giva
Olifa
Oshikango
Camabatela
N'Dalatando
Malanje
Kuito
Camacupa
Planalto do Bié
Menongue
Etosha Pan
Tsumeb
Otavi Grootfontein
Otjiwarongo
Brandberg 8445ft (2574m)
NAMIBIA
Wlotzkasbaken
Swakopmund
Walvis Bay
Rehoboth
Tropic of Capricorn
Mariental
Fish
Keetmanshoop
Aus
Klein Karas
Lüderitz
Karasburg
Orange River
Oranjemund
Springbok
St Helena Bay
CAPE TOWN
Bellville
Worcester
Cape of Good Hope
Cape Agulhas
Mosselbaai
George
Calvinia
Beaufort West
Great Karoo
De Aar
Colesberg
Cradock
Uitenhage
Mdantsane
Lúvua Chitato
Lucapa
Saurimo
Luena
Cuando
Cuito
Cuanza
Cubango
Rundu
Katima Mulilo
Caprivi Strip
Victoria Falls
Okavango Delta
Maun
Nata
Ghanzi
BOTSWANA
Francistown
Serowe
Palapye
Mahalapye
Kalahari Desert
GABORONE
Jwaneng
Kanye
Werda
Mmabatho
Klerksdorp
Kimberley
Prieska
BLOEMFONTEIN
SOUTH AFRICA
Welkom
Kroons
Bethleh
Zambezi
Kaoma
Mongu
Mazabuka
Monze
Choma
Victoria Falls
Livingstone
Hwange
ZIMBABWE
Bulawayo
Gwanc
Shasho
DEM. REP. CONGO
Lak Mwera
Mans
Mufu
Chingola
Kitwe
Luanshya
ZAMBIA
Nambala
Kabw
LUSAKA
Karib
Lak Kar
Solwezi
Kabompo
Kafue
Mochudi
Modimolle (Nylstroom)
PRETOR
Soweto
Johannesburg
Vaal
Polokw (Pietersb)
Limpopo
Mamuno
Gobabis
Karibib
WINDHOEK
Nosop
Auob
Groot Karasberge
Upington
Molopo
LESOT
MASE
Koks
Drakensb
Mtha
Queenstown
East Lon
Port Alfred
Port Elizabe
ATLANTIC OCEAN

44
A B C D E F G H

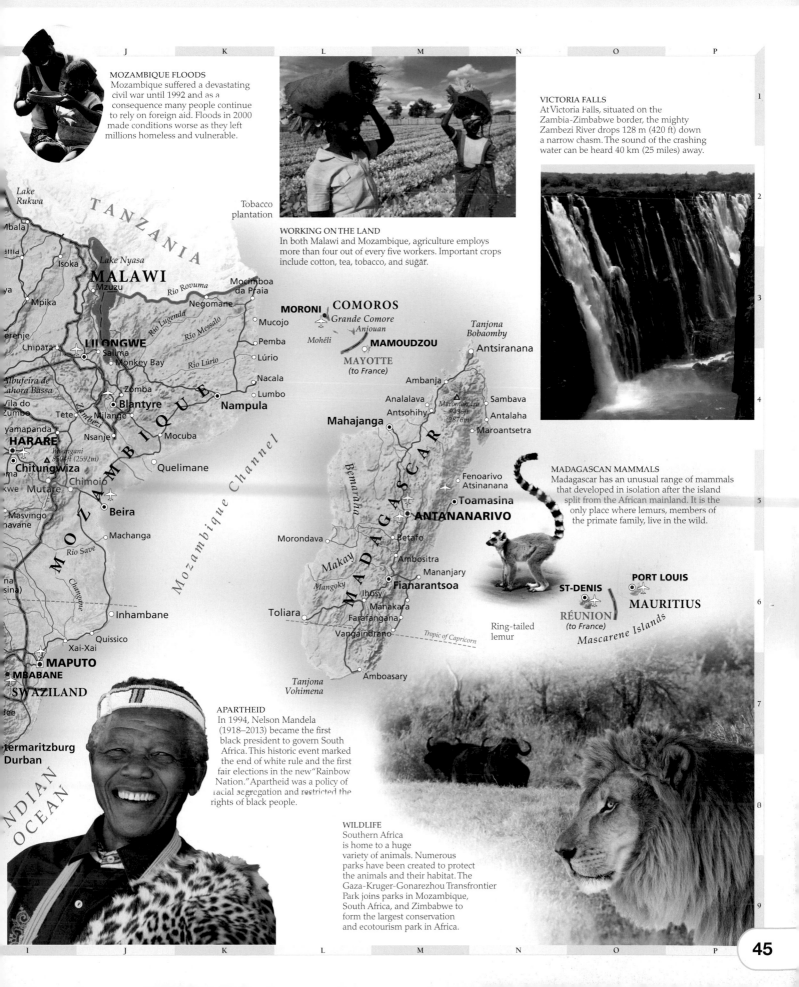

MOZAMBIQUE FLOODS
Mozambique suffered a devastating civil war until 1992 and as a consequence many people continue to rely on foreign aid. Floods in 2000 made conditions worse as they left millions homeless and vulnerable.

Tobacco plantation

WORKING ON THE LAND
In both Malawi and Mozambique, agriculture employs more than four out of every five workers. Important crops include cotton, tea, tobacco, and sugar.

VICTORIA FALLS
At Victoria Falls, situated on the Zambia-Zimbabwe border, the mighty Zambezi River drops 128 m (420 ft) down a narrow chasm. The sound of the crashing water can be heard 40 km (25 miles) away.

MADAGASCAN MAMMALS
Madagascar has an unusual range of mammals that developed in isolation after the island split from the African mainland. It is the only place where lemurs, members of the primate family, live in the wild.

Ring-tailed lemur

APARTHEID
In 1994, Nelson Mandela (1918–2013) became the first black president to govern South Africa. This historic event marked the end of white rule and the first fair elections in the new "Rainbow Nation." Apartheid was a policy of racial segregation and restricted the rights of black people.

WILDLIFE
Southern Africa is home to a huge variety of animals. Numerous parks have been created to protect the animals and their habitat. The Gaza-Kruger-Gonarezhou Transfrontier Park joins parks in Mozambique, South Africa, and Zimbabwe to form the largest conservation and ecotourism park in Africa.

Map labels

Lake Rukwa
TANZANIA
Mbala
Isoka
Lake Nyasa
Mpika
MALAWI
Mzuzu
Rio Rovuma
Negomane
Mocímboa da Praia
Mucojo
erenje
Chipata
LILONGWE
Salima
Monkey Bay
Rio Lugenda
Rio Messalo
Pemba
Lúrio
Rio Lúrio
Nacala
Zomba
Lumbo
Blantyre
Milange
Nampula
Mocuba
Albufeira de Cahora Bassa
Tete
HARARE
Nsanje
Quelimane
Phirangani 8504ft (2592m)
Chitungwiza
Chimoio
Mutare
Beira
Masvingo
Machanga
navane
Rio Save
Inhambane
Changane
Quissico
Xai-Xai
MAPUTO
MBABANE
SWAZILAND
ermaritzburg
Durban
INDIAN OCEAN

MORONI
COMOROS
Grande Comore
Anjouan
Mohéli
MAMOUDZOU
MAYOTTE (to France)
Tanjona Bobaomby
Antsiranana
Ambanja
Analalava
Antsohihy
Maromokotro 9436ft (2876m)
Sambava
Antalaha
Mahajanga
Maroantsetra
Fenoarivo Atsinanana
Bemaraha
Betafo
Toamasina
ANTANANARIVO
Morondava
Makay
MADAGASCAR
Ambositra
Mananjary
Mangoky
Ihosy
Fianarantsoa
Manakara
Toliara
Farafangana
Vangaindrano
Tropic of Capricorn
Amboasary
Tanjona Vohimena

ST-DENIS
RÉUNION (to France)
PORT LOUIS
MAURITIUS
Mascarene Islands

Mozambique Channel
MOZAMBIQUE

EUROPE

Separated from Asia by the ridge of the Ural Mountains, Europe is a continent of very different nations, listed below in order of their land area. Each nation has its own language and culture, but they share a 2,000-year history of civilization that has inspired some of the world's greatest political ideas, works of art, and innovations in technology.

Russia (Russian Federation)
- 6,601,668 sq miles
  17,098,242 sq km
- 142,355,000
- ◘ Moscow
- ▶ Russian, Tatar, Ukrainian, Chuvash, various other national languages

Germany
- 137,847 sq miles
  357,022 sq km
- 80,723,000
- ◘ Berlin
- ▶ German, Turkish

United Kingdom
- 94,058 sq miles
  243,610 sq km
- 64,430,000
- ◘ London
- ▶ English, Welsh, Scottish Gaelic, Irish Gaelic

Iceland
- 39,769 sq miles
  103,000 sq km
- 335,900
- ◘ Reykjavík
- ▶ Icelandic

Serbia
- 29,913 sq miles
  77,474 sq km
- 7,144,000
- ◘ Belgrade
- ▶ Serbian, Hungarian (Magyar)

Bosnia and Herzegovina
- 19,767 sq miles
  51,197 sq km
- 3,862,000
- ◘ Sarajevo
- ▶ Bosnian, Serbian, Croatian

France
- 212,935 sq miles
  551,500 sq km
- 66,836,000
- ◘ Paris
- ▶ French, Provençal, German, Breton, Catalan, Basque

Finland
- 130,559 sq miles
  338,145 sq km
- 5,498,000
- ◘ Helsinki
- ▶ Finnish, Swedish, Sami

Romania
- 92,043 sq miles
  238,391 sq km
- 21,600,000
- ◘ Bucharest
- ▶ Romanian, Hungarian (Magyar), Romany, German

Hungary
- 35,918 sq miles
  93,028 sq km
- 9,875,000
- ◘ Budapest
- ▶ Hungarian (Magyar)

Ireland
- 27,133 sq miles
  70,273 sq km
- 4,952,000
- ◘ Dublin
- ▶ English, Irish Gaelic

Slovakia
- 18,933 sq miles
  49,035 sq km
- 5,446,000
- ◘ Bratislava
- ▶ Slovak, Hungarian (Magyar), Czech

Ukraine
- 233,032 sq miles
  603,550 sq km
- 44,210,000
- ◘ Kiev
- ▶ Ukrainian, Russian, Tatar

Norway
- 125,021 sq miles
  323,802 sq km
- 5,265,000
- ◘ Oslo
- ▶ Norwegian (*Bokmål*, "book language", and *Nynorsk* "new Norsk"), Sami

Belarus
- 180,155 sq miles
  207,600 sq km
- 9,570,000
- ◘ Minsk
- ▶ Belarussian, Russian

Portugal
- 35,556 sq miles
  92,090 sq km
- 10,834,000
- ◘ Lisbon
- ▶ Portuguese

Lithuania
- 25,212 sq miles
  65,300 sq km
- 2,854,000
- ◘ Vilnius
- ▶ Lithuanian, Russian

Estonia
- 17,463 sq miles
  45,228 sq km
- 1,259,000
- ◘ Tallinn
- ▶ Estonian, Russian

Spain
- 195,124 sq miles
  505,370 sq km
- 48,563,000
- ◘ Madrid
- ▶ Spanish, Catalan, Galician, Basque

Poland
- 120,728 sq miles
  312,685 sq km
- 38,523,000
- ◘ Warsaw
- ▶ Polish

Greece
- 50,949 sq miles
  131,957 sq km
- 10,773,000
- ◘ Athens
- ▶ Greek, Turkish, Macedonian, Albanian

Austria
- 32,383 sq miles
  83,871 sq km
- 8,712,000
- ◘ Vienna
- ▶ German, Croatian, Slovenian, Hungarian (Magyar)

Latvia
- 24,938 sq miles
  64,589 sq km
- 1,966,000
- ◘ Riga
- ▶ Latvian, Russian

Denmark
- 16,639 sq miles
  43,094 sq km
- 5,725,000
- ◘ Copenhagen
- ▶ Danish

Sweden
- 173,860 sq miles
  450,295 sq km
- 9,881,000
- ◘ Stockholm
- ▶ Swedish, Finnish, Sami

Italy
- 116,348 sq miles
  301,340 sq km
- 62,008,000
- ◘ Rome
- ▶ Italian, German, French, Rhaeto-Romanic, Sardinian

Bulgaria
- 42,811 sq miles
  110,879 sq km
- 7,145,000
- ◘ Sofia
- ▶ Bulgarian, Turkish, Romany

Czechia
- 30,451 sq miles
  78,867 sq km
- 10,645,000
- ◘ Prague
- ▶ Czech, Slovak, Hungarian (Magyar)

Croatia
- 21,851 sq miles
  56,594 sq km
- 4,314,000
- ◘ Zagreb
- ▶ Croatian

Netherlands
- 16,040 sq miles
  41,543 sq km
- 17,017,000
- ◘ Amsterdam
- ▶ Dutch, Frisian

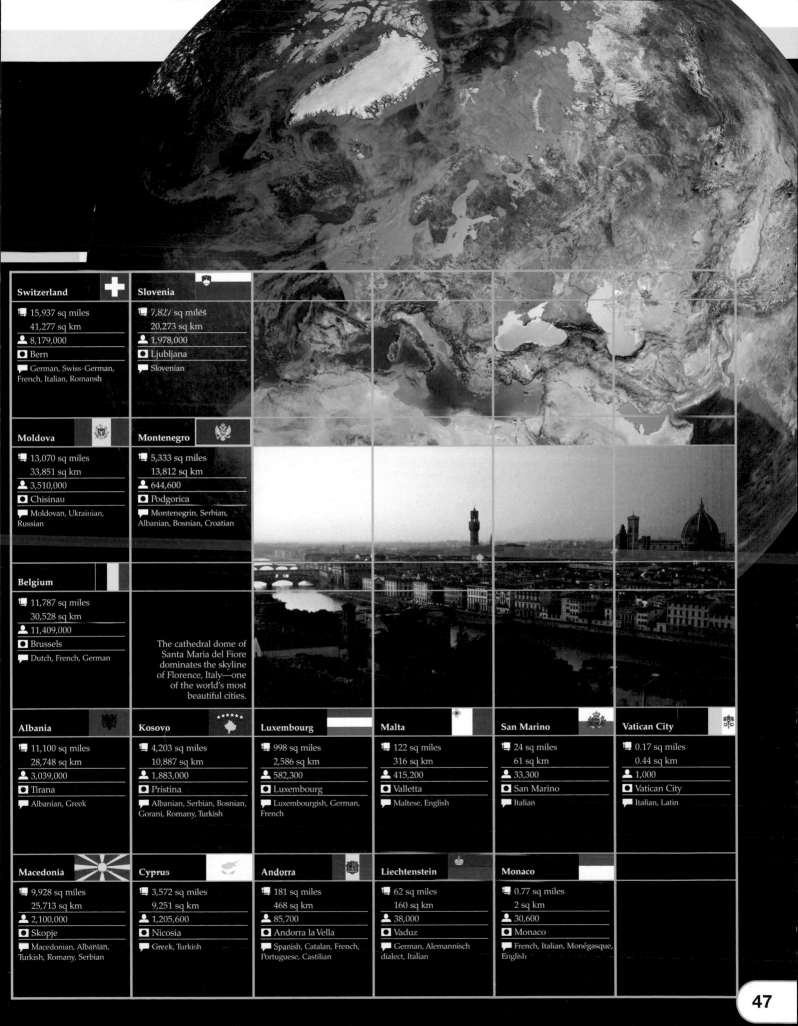

Switzerland
- 15,937 sq miles
  41,277 sq km
- 8,179,000
- Bern
- German, Swiss-German, French, Italian, Romansh

Slovenia
- 7,827 sq miles
  20,273 sq km
- 1,978,000
- Ljubljana
- Slovenian

Moldova
- 13,070 sq miles
  33,851 sq km
- 3,510,000
- Chisinau
- Moldovan, Ukrainian, Russian

Montenegro
- 5,333 sq miles
  13,812 sq km
- 644,600
- Podgorica
- Montenegrin, Serbian, Albanian, Bosnian, Croatian

Belgium
- 11,787 sq miles
  30,528 sq km
- 11,409,000
- Brussels
- Dutch, French, German

The cathedral dome of Santa Maria del Fiore dominates the skyline of Florence, Italy—one of the world's most beautiful cities.

Albania
- 11,100 sq miles
  28,748 sq km
- 3,039,000
- Tirana
- Albanian, Greek

Kosovo
- 4,203 sq miles
  10,887 sq km
- 1,883,000
- Pristina
- Albanian, Serbian, Bosnian, Gorani, Romany, Turkish

Luxembourg
- 998 sq miles
  2,586 sq km
- 582,300
- Luxembourg
- Luxembourgish, German, French

Malta
- 122 sq miles
  316 sq km
- 415,200
- Valletta
- Maltese, English

San Marino
- 24 sq miles
  61 sq km
- 33,300
- San Marino
- Italian

Vatican City
- 0.17 sq miles
  0.44 sq km
- 1,000
- Vatican City
- Italian, Latin

Macedonia
- 9,928 sq miles
  25,713 sq km
- 2,100,000
- Skopje
- Macedonian, Albanian, Turkish, Romany, Serbian

Cyprus
- 3,572 sq miles
  9,251 sq km
- 1,205,600
- Nicosia
- Greek, Turkish

Andorra
- 181 sq miles
  468 sq km
- 85,700
- Andorra la Vella
- Spanish, Catalan, French, Portuguese, Castilian

Liechtenstein
- 62 sq miles
  160 sq km
- 38,000
- Vaduz
- German, Alemannisch dialect, Italian

Monaco
- 0.77 sq miles
  2 sq km
- 30,600
- Monaco
- French, Italian, Monégasque, English

Scandinavia and Finland

THE THREE SCANDINAVIAN countries (Norway, Sweden, and Denmark), along with neighboring Finland, are among the most northerly countries in Europe. Here the winters are long and cold. In the far north, above the Arctic Circle, the Sun remains below the horizon for up to two months a year. Finland is the most densely forested country in Europe, and wood accounts for 30 percent of its exports. All four countries are highly industrialized and are among the wealthiest in the world. In the last few decades, a large number of refugees have found a new home here, and Scandinavia in particular is a lot more ethnically diverse than it used to be.

SKIING
During the winter months, much of Scandinavia is covered with snow, so skiing is a very popular sport.

Sami man in traditional costume

LAPLAND
Northern Sweden and Finland are known as Lapland. Here, the local Sami people survive the cold and inhospitable climate by herding reindeer, which they breed for their meat, milk, and skins.

URBAN POPULATIONS
Scandinavia has a high urban population. Many people live in towns and cities, with less than one-fifth living in the countryside. Since the region is covered in lakes, fjords, and surrounded by sea, many people also live near the water.

Copenhagen in Denmark is the second-largest city in Scandinavia after Stockholm, Sweden.

0 km   100   200
0 miles   100   200

INDUSTRIAL STRENGTH
Manufacturing is an important source of employment and wealth throughout Scandinavia and Finland. Many of the goods produced here, such as machinery, medical and technological equipment, motor vehicles (Sweden), and pharmaceuticals (Denmark), are exported all over the world. In Denmark, many people also work in agriculture, fish processing, and brewing.

THE SAUNA
The sauna, or steam bath, was invented in Finland about 1,000 years ago as a way of cleaning and relaxing the body. After a hot sauna, many Finns cool off by plunging into an icy pool (below) or a snowdrift.

NORWEGIAN FJORDS
The west coast of Norway has thousands of deep inlets, known as fjords, gouged out of the mountains by glaciers during the last ice age and then flooded by the sea. The fjords run inland between high mountains and make a favorite destination for cruise ships bringing tourists to admire the stunning scenery.

BUILDING WITH WOOD
Much of Norway and Sweden, and two-thirds of Finland, is covered by dense forests of birch, pine, spruce, and other trees. Finland has more than 16 times more forested land per person than the European average. Many people in the region work in the forestry industry, producing wood for the construction and furniture industries. This great natural resource is also used to build homes and churches, like this medieval stave church (left) in Norway.

SAVING THE ENVIRONMENT
The people of all four countries are very environmentally conscious and recycle as many household items as they can. Strict national laws protect the environment from industrial waste and pollution, although there is growing concern about the levels of pollution in the Baltic Sea.

The British Isles

FOR SUCH A SMALL GROUP OF ISLANDS, the British Isles has a very rich history. This is evident from its legacy of ancient ruins, medieval castles, dramatic cathedrals, and grand country houses. Once a leading industrial and colonial power, British monarchs ruled an empire that circled the globe. As a result, English is still widely spoken around the world. Today, many traditional industries, such as shipbuilding, mining, and engineering, have declined, and the emphasis is now on banking and insurance, as well as pharmaceuticals. The British Isles consists of two countries: the United Kingdom of Great Britain and Northern Ireland (the UK), and the Republic of Ireland.

Wales has more than 200 castles.

IRELAND
Tourists visit Ireland, attracted by its unspoiled countryside and lively cities, such as Dublin (left). Once part of Britain, Ireland gained independence in 1922. Its economy, the fastest-growing in Europe just before the global banking crisis of 2008, has since seen good recovery.

HORSE BREEDING
Lush pastures and a mild climate have encouraged the breeding of thoroughbred racehorses in Ireland. Stud farms here raise some of the best racehorses in the world.

Irish horse and rider on a training run

SCOTLAND
Scotland and England united as a single country in 1707. Today, however, Scotland is a self-governing part of the UK, with its own parliament and distinct legal and educational systems. Edinburgh, above, is a popular city with a magnificent castle. Each summer, the city hosts an international arts festival.

NORTH SEA ENERGY
Beneath the shallow seas around Britain, there are supplies of oil and natural gas. Oil rigs raise oil and gas to the surface, where it is pumped by pipeline to be refined on the mainland. Production has declined and supplies are now running low, but more distant reserves still wait to be exploited. However, few businesses are willing to take on further costly exploration.

MONEY MATTERS
The City of London is the UK's financial center. Before the banking crash of 2008, more than 500 banks had offices there. Lloyd's Insurance Building (right) is one of the city's most distinctive skyscrapers. Built of steel and glass, its elevators are outside.

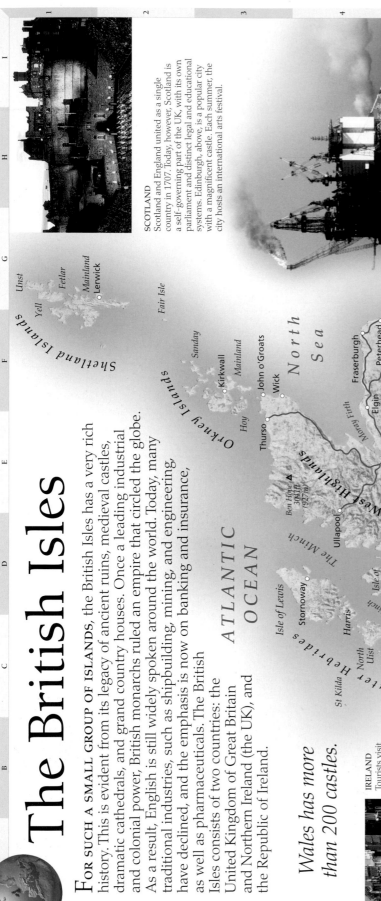

Map labels

Shetland Islands
Unst
Fetlar
Yell
Mainland
Lerwick

Fair Isle

Orkney Islands
Sanday
Kirkwall
Mainland
Hoy

North Sea

ATLANTIC OCEAN

Thurso
Wick
John o'Groats
Elgin
Moray Firth
Fraserburgh
Peterhead
Aberdeen
Montrose
Arbroath
Forfar
Dundee
St Andrews

Ben Hope 3041ft (927m)
North West Highlands
Ullapool
Inverness
Loch Ness
Aviemore
Ben Nevis 4406ft (1343m)
Fort William
Oban
Firth of Lorn

Isle of Lewis
Stornoway
Harris
North Uist
South Uist
Barra
St Kilda
Outer Hebrides

The Minch
The Little Minch
Isle of Skye
Stromeferry
Mallaig
Rhum
Eigg
Coll
Tiree
Isle of Mull
Inner Hebrides
Jura
Islay
Kintyre

SCOTLAND
Grampian Mountains
Dee
Spey
Tay

Perth
Stirling
Dunfermline
Firth of Forth
Edinburgh
Glasgow
Greenock
Paisley
East Kilbride
Hamilton
Clyde
Loch Lomond
Loch Fyne
Isle of Arran
Ayr
Prestwick
Kilmarnock
Southern Uplands
Galashiels
Hawick
Berwick-upon-Tweed
Dumfries
Stranraer

NORTHERN IRELAND
Coleraine
Londonderry
Strabane
Strensaw
Newtownabbey
Belfast
Bangor
Downpatrick
Armagh
Newry
Portadown
Omagh
Enniskillen
Lough Neagh
Lower Lough Erne
Upper Lough Erne
Donegal
Donegal Bay
Sligo
Colloney
Boyle
Castlebar
Cavan
Dundalk

Stranraer
Carlisle
Penrith
Workington
Whitehaven
Barrow-in-Furness
Lake District
Kendal
Lancaster
ISLE OF MAN
DOUGLAS

UNITED KINGDOM
Pennines
Cheviot Hills
Newcastle upon Tyne
Tyne
South Shields
Sunderland
Durham
Hartlepool
Darlington
Tees
Northallerton
Middlesbrough
Whitby
Scarborough
Bridlington
York
Harrogate
Ouse
Ribble
Beverley

LONDON

The capital of the UK is London, a sprawling city on the banks of the River Thames. It is the political and financial center of the country, as well as home to more than 8 million people. One of its most popular attractions is the London Eye— a giant ferris wheel, 443 ft (135 m) high.

Each pod is nearly entirely see-through, giving the occupants a view of the whole city beneath them when it reaches the top.

BRITISH LANDMARKS

Tourism is a major industry in Britain. Visitors come from all over the world to see the many churches, castles, and ancient monuments, such as Stonehenge (above), and to admire the pretty villages. Many also come for the theaters, galleries, and shops in Britain's vibrant cities.

Stonehenge in southern England was built from about 3000 BCE onward.

MULTICULTURAL SOCIETY

Britain once controlled a world empire with colonies in every continent. Many people— from the Indian subcontinent, Africa, and the Caribbean in particular—came here and brought their cultures with them, as well as settling into British life. Today, about one in eight British people are from an ethnic minority background.

WALES

Wales was formally united with England in 1536, but retains its own language and traditions. Welsh is spoken widely in some parts, and public signs appear in both Welsh and English. Coal mining and steel production were important in the south, but have both declined. Rugby is the national game.

Wales playing Scotland at rugby in the Millennium Stadium, Cardiff

The Low Countries

The NETHERLANDS, BELGIUM, AND LUXEMBOURG are known as the Low Countries because the land is so flat and low-lying. In the case of the Netherlands, much of the land is below sea level—*Netherlands* is Dutch for "under lands." The three countries are among the richest in Europe and, while farming still plays an important part, they all have strong, modern economies based on manufacturing and trade. Luxembourg in particular is known as a tax haven and is a major center for international finance. Their location at the mouth of the River Rhine and other major European rivers places the three countries at the heart of western European trade and politics—all three were founder members of the European Economic Community (now the European Union, or EU), established in 1957.

ROTTERDAM, NETHERLANDS
Every year, around 30,000 sea-going ships and 110,000 barges call at the port of Rotterdam. Lying at the mouth of the River Rhine, this port is the largest in the world and is where vast container ships from all over the world load or unload their cargoes. The smaller barges help to transport goods farther inland. With the port's advanced Vessel Traffic Service (VTS) it's possible to track ships on a radar screen up to 37 miles (60 km) off the coast and 25 miles (40 km) inland.

Dutch tulips

CROPS
Fertile soil and good irrigation have helped the Netherlands become a major exporter of agricultural products, with vegetables and tomatoes forming important crops. It is also famous for its bulbs and cut flowers, notably tulips.

Tulips were introduced to the Netherlands from Turkey in 1562. Black tulips were the most valuable.

Land below sea level on main map

RECLAIMING THE LAND
Over the centuries, the Dutch have reclaimed land from the sea. They did this by building huge dykes, or dams, to keep out the sea, and then draining the surface water into canals. Windmills originally pumped out the water, but electric pumps are now used.

DUTCH PEOPLE
The Dutch once ruled a vast empire in Indonesia, the Caribbean, and South America. As a result, many nationalities now live here. Ethnic minorities make up about 15 percent of the people and in some cities, the majority of primary school children have a non-Dutch background.

GERMANY

NETHERLANDS

Delfzijl
Appingedam
Groningen
Haren
Zuidlaren
Vlagtwedde
Emmen
Coevorden
Eemshaven
Loppersum
Zuidborn
Borger
Harkstede
Den Ham
Denekamp
Hengelo
Enschede
Leek
Assen
Beilen
Hoogeveen
Staphorst
Almelo
Rijssen
Goor
Deventer
Schiermonnikoog
Leeuwarden
Heerenveen
Wolvega
Steenwijk
Zwolle
Apeldoorn
Dokkum
Drachten
Joure
Meppel
Emmeloord
Vaassen
Winsum
Sneek
Lelystad
Zeewolde
Menaldum
Harlingen
Flevoland
Baarn
Hilversum
Harderwijk
Hoorn
Almere
Amstelveen
Soest
Purmerend
Zaanstad
AMSTERDAM
Opmeer
Schagen
Alkmaar
Castricum
Haarlem
Leiden
Den Helder
Velsen-Noord
Noordwijk aan Zee

West Frisian Islands (Waddeneilanden)
Schiermonnikoog
Ameland
Terschelling
Vlieland
Texel
Waddenzee
IJsselmeer

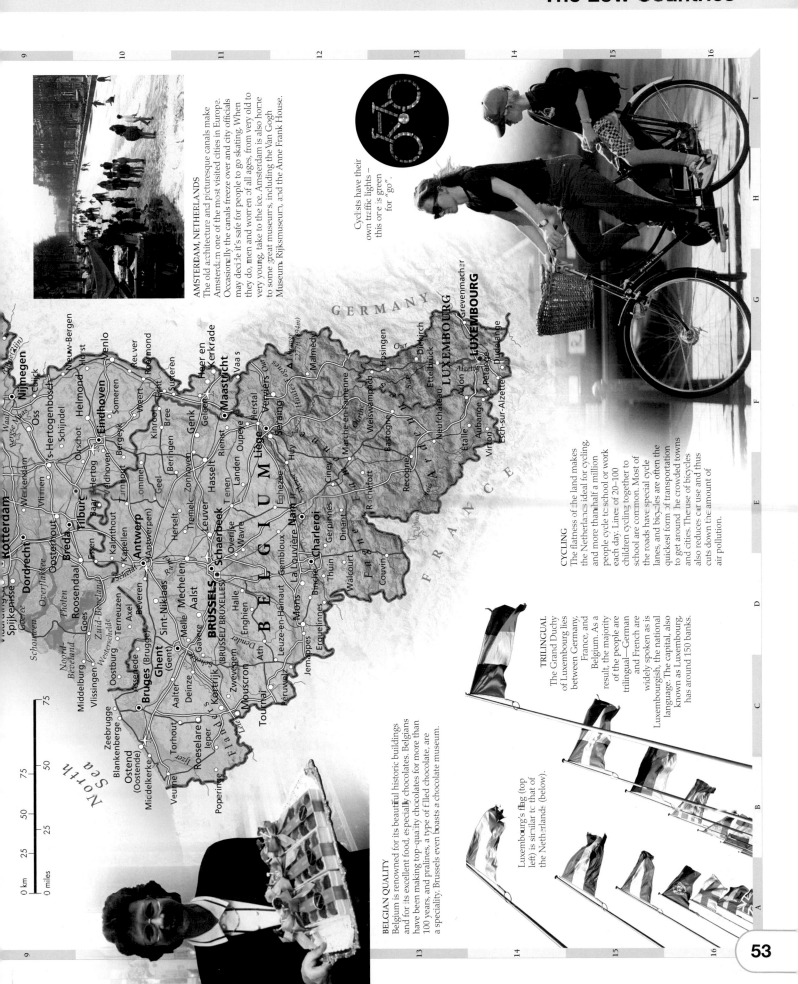

AMSTERDAM, NETHERLANDS
The old architecture and picturesque canals make Amsterdam one of the most visited cities in Europe. Occasionally the canals freeze over and city officials may decide it's safe for people to go skating. When they do, men and women of all ages, from very old to very young, take to the ice. Amsterdam is also home to some great museums, including the Van Gogh Museum Rijksmuseum, and the Anne Frank House.

Cyclists have their own traffic lights – this one is green for "go".

CYCLING
The flatness of the land makes the Netherlands ideal for cycling, and more than half a million people cycle to school or work each day. Lines of 20–100 children cycling together to school are common. Most of the roads have special cycle lanes, and bicycles are often the quickest form of transportation to get around the crowded towns and cities. The use of bicycles also reduces car use and thus cuts down the amount of air pollution.

TRILINGUAL
The Grand Duchy of Luxembourg lies between Germany, France, and Belgium. As a result, the majority of the people are trilingual—German and French are widely spoken as is Luxembourgish, the national language. The capital, also known as Luxembourg, has around 150 banks.

Luxembourg's flag (top left) is similar to that of the Netherlands (below).

BELGIAN QUALITY
Belgium is renowned for its beautiful historic buildings and for its excellent food, especially chocolates. Belgians have been making top-quality chocolates for more than 100 years, and pralines, a type of filled chocolate, are a speciality. Brussels even boasts a chocolate museum.

GERMANY

FRANCE

LUXEMBOURG
LUXEMBOURG

B E L G I U M

BRUSSELS
(BRUSSEL BRUXELLES)

Rotterdam
Dordrecht
Nijmegen
Oss
's-Hertogenbosch
Helmond
Eindhoven
Tilburg
Breda
Antwerp
(Antwerpen)
Ghent
(Gent)
Bruges
(Brugge)
Ostend
(Oostende)
Maastricht
Liège
Namur
Charleroi
Schaerbeek

North Sea
Vlaanderen

0 km
0 miles
25 50 75
25 50 75

France

IN DIRECT CONTRAST TO ITS mainly rural landscape, France is a modern nation with most people now living in towns and cities. While industry makes up the largest section of its economy, tourism also plays a big part—France is the world's most visited country. A land of varied scenery, from gently rolling farmland in the north to a stretch of dry, warm Mediterranean coast in the south, France also shares two mountain ranges—the Pyrenees and the Alps. Each of the 22 regions within France, which includes the island of Corsica, has its own distinct identity and culture. The tiny countries of Andorra and Monaco lie next to France.

Boules, the national game of France, is still played in village squares around the country.

NUCLEAR POWER

Three-quarters of France's electricity is produced by nuclear power plants (above), making the country largely self-sufficient in energy and one of the main producers of nuclear power in Europe. Hydroelectric plants are also an important source of power.

HIGH-SPEED TRAVEL

France has Europe's fastest train, the TGV – *train à grande vitesse* – which travels at up to 186 mph (300 kph) during normal services. In 2007, a modified TGV even set a speed record for conventional trains of 357.2 mph (574.8 kph). The TGV network connects Paris with all the country's major cities, which makes it easier to commute or visit relatives. It also extends to Germany, Italy, Belgium, Switzerland, and through the Channel Tunnel to Britain.

STREETS OF PARIS

Tourists flock to Paris to visit its world-famous museums and art galleries, shop in its elegant stores, and soak up its vibrant atmosphere. Montmartre, which overlooks the city, is famous for its artists. Close by, in the Place du Tertre (above), visitors can have their portrait painted.

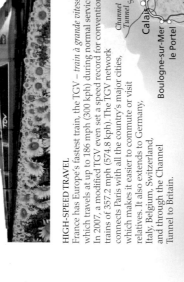

Map of France showing cities and regions including Paris, Strasbourg, Metz, Reims, Rouen, Caen, Rennes, Nantes, Tours, Orléans, Dijon, Besançon, Mulhouse, and neighboring countries Belgium, Luxembourg, Germany, Switzerland, with the English Channel, Atlantic Ocean, Channel Islands (Guernsey, Jersey).

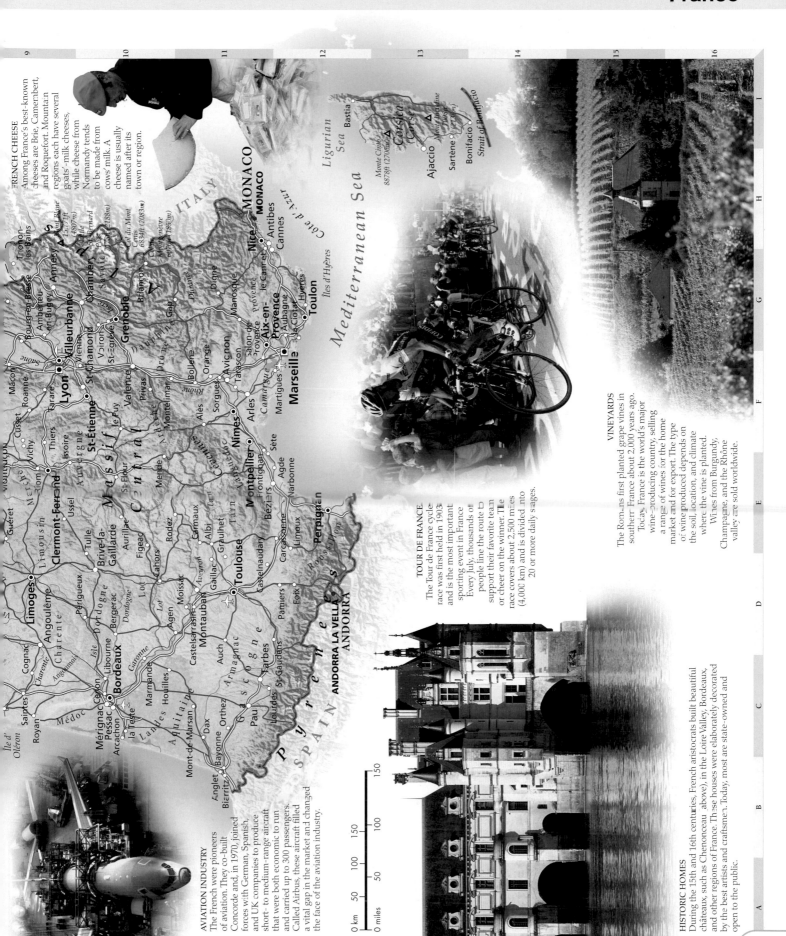

FRENCH CHEESE
Among France's best-known cheeses are Brie, Camembert, and Roquefort. Mountain regions each have several goats'-milk cheeses, while cheese from Normandy tends to be made from cows' milk. A cheese is usually named after its town or region.

AVIATION INDUSTRY
The French were pioneers of aviation. They co-built Concorde and, in 1970, joined forces with German, Spanish, and UK companies to produce short- to medium-range aircraft that were both economic to run and carried up to 300 passengers. Called Airbus, these aircraft filled a vital gap in the market and changed the face of the aviation industry.

TOUR DE FRANCE
The Tour de France cycle race was first held in 1903 and is the most important sporting event in France. Every July, thousands of people line the route to support their favorite team or cheer on the winner. The race covers about 2,500 miles (4,000 km) and is divided into 20 or more daily stages.

VINEYARDS
The Romans first planted grape vines in southern France about 2,000 years ago. Today, France is the world's major wine-producing country, selling a range of wines for the home market and for export. The type of wine produced depends on the soil, location, and climate where the vine is planted. Wines from Burgundy, Champagne, and the Rhône valley are sold worldwide.

HISTORIC HOMES
During the 15th and 16th centuries, French aristocrats built beautiful châteaux, such as Chenonceau (above), in the Loire Valley, Bordeaux, and other regions of France. These houses were elaborately decorated by the best artists and craftsmen. Today, most are state-owned and open to the public.

Mediterranean Sea

Ligurian Sea

Corsica
Corse

Côte d'Azur

MONACO
MONACO

Bastia
Ajaccio
Sartène
Bonifacio
Strait of Bonifacio

Monte Cinto
8878ft (2706m)
Monte Incudine
7008ft (2136m)

Nice
Antibes
Cannes
Toulon
Îles d'Hyères

ITALY

SPAIN

ANDORRA LA VELLA
ANDORRA

0 km 50 100 150
0 miles 50 100 150

Germany and the Alpine States

LYING AT THE VERY HEART OF EUROPE, Germany is one of the world's wealthiest nations. It is also Europe's leading industrial power. To its south lie the Alpine states of Switzerland, Austria, Liechtenstein, and Slovenia. The region is famed for its beautiful Alpine scenery, mountains, and lakes. German is the main language in all but Slovenia. However, each of the five countries has its own distinct history, culture, and national identity. Indeed, since 1815, Switzerland has been recognized as a neutral nation, and has stayed out of all the wars that have affected Europe.

THE JOY OF UNIFICATION
After World War II, Germany was split, with a US-backed capitalist state in the west and a Russian-backed state in the east. Built in 1961, the Berlin Wall was 96 miles (155 km) long and was designed to stop East Germans from leaving for a better life in the West. The wall divided Berlin and separated families, friends, and a nation for 28 years. When Germany was unified (reunited) in 1990, the wall was officially demolished.

Celebrations at the Brandenburg Gate marking the 10th anniversary of the fall of the Berlin Wall

GENEVA
Geneva lies on the shores of Lake Geneva, Europe's largest Alpine lake. This orderly city is a global center for banking and finance. It is also a base for many international organizations, such as the Red Cross.

The Swiss speak German, French, Italian, and Romansh.

GERMAN INDUSTRY
With its coal and iron mines, the Ruhr Valley was once the powerhouse of the German economy. Today's industry ranges from engineering to high-tech goods. Quality assembly and design make Germany the fourth-largest car producer in the world.

FOOD AND DRINK
The annual Munich *Oktoberfest* is Germany's biggest beer festival. Entertainment includes parades and music.

Map labels

Baltic Sea

DENMARK
POLAND
NETHERLANDS
BELGIUM
GERMANY

Sassnitz, Rügen, Bergen, Pomeranian Bay, Greifswald, Stralsund, Wolgast, Anklam, Oderhaff, Wolin, Oder, Frankfurt an der Oder, Eberswalde-Finow, Bad Freienwalde, Neubrandenburg, Pasewalk, Angermünde, Bernau, BERLIN, Guben, Cottbus, Eisenhüttenstadt, Ludwigsfelde, Lübben, Hoyerswerda, Görlitz, Löbau, Zittau, Bautzen, Potsdam, Lübbenau, Finsterwalde, Senftenberg, Spree, Dresden, Pirna

Mecklenburger Bucht, Fehmarn Belt, Fehmarn, Rostock, Warnemünde, Wismar, Demmin, Teterow, Malchin, Waren, Neustrelitz, Neuruppin, Wittstock, Oranienburg, Brandenburg, Riesa, Döbeln, Hainichen, Chemnitz, Zwickau, Gera, Jena, Leipzig, Torgau, Dessau, Dessau, Schönebeck, Magdeburg, Halle-Neustadt, Halle

Kappeln, Kieler Bucht, Kiel, Schleswig, Schleswig-Holstein, Flensburg, Husum, Heide, Rendsburg, Kiel Canal, Neumünster, Itzehoe, Elmshorn, Stade, Rosengarten, Scheessel, Soltau, Uelzen, Salzwedel, Stendal, Wittenberge, Perleberg, Dannenberg, Lüneburg, Lauenburg, Boizenburg, Schwerin, Parchim, Ludwigslust, Güstrow, Elbe, Bernburg, Eisleben, Halberstadt, Seesen, Nordhausen, Erfurt, Weimar, Gotha, Suhl, Hof, Plauen, Mühlberg (Erzgebirge), Coburg, Kronach, Lichtenfels, Schweinfurt

Westerland, North Frisian Islands (Nordfriesische Inseln), Helgoland Bay, Cuxhaven, Norderstedt, Hamburg, Winsen, Celle, Peine, Wolfsburg, Braunschweig, Salzgitter, Goslar, Göttingen, Northeim, Bad Hersfeld, Fulda, Hünfeld, Melsungen, Bad Hersfeld

East Frisian Islands (Ostfriesische Inseln), Norden, Emden, Leer, Weener, Wilhelmshaven, Bremerhaven, Delmenhorst, Bassum, Diepholz, Bremen, Verden, Weser, Minden, Hanover (Hannover), Hildesheim, Hamelin, Kassel, Warburg, Marburg an der Lahn, Giessen, Wetzlar, Hessen

Nordhorn, Rheine, Lingen, Clappenburg, Cloppenburg, Oldenburg, Osnabrück, Münster, Dülmen, Bielefeld, Gütersloh, Paderborn, Herford, Ahlen, Hamm, Siegen, Olpe, Siegen, Marsberg, Neuwied, Offenbach, Frankfurt am Main, Wiesbaden, Mainz, Koblenz, Boppard

Recklinghausen, Essen, Bottrop, Bochum, Duisburg, Krefeld, Düsseldorf, Wuppertal, Solingen, Leverkusen, Cologne (Köln), Aachen, Bonn, Rhine, Eifel, Rheinisches Schiefergebirge

SLOVAKIA

CZECHIA

HUNGARY

CROATIA

VIENNA
(WIEN)

Mistelbach an der Zaya
Hollabrunn
Zwettl
Hauzenberg
Perchtoldsdorf
Bad Vöslau
Tulln
Traiskirchen
Eisenstadt
Neusiedler See

Sankt Pölten
Wiener Neustadt
Mürzzuschlag

Mühlenbach
Murska Sobota
Drava
Maribor
Ptuj
Krško
Novo Mesto

Graz
Mur
Wolfsberg

SLOVENIA
Jadranje
Leoben
Judenburg
Klagenfurt
Velenje
Celje
Trbovlje
Kočevje
Postojna

AUSTRIA

Linz
Wels
Steyr
Enns
Salzburg
Ebensee
Badgastein
Hieflau
Villach
Kranj
Jesenice
Tolmin
LJUBLJANA

Nova Gorica
Koper

Gulf of Venice
Istra

VIENNA, AUSTRIA
Vienna is a city of Baroque buildings, palaces, and famous concert halls. Grand balls with traditional waltzes are still customary. These are a reminder of when the city was the center of the Austro-Hungarian Empire, which controlled large parts of east and central Europe.

The opera ball in Vienna

Danube (Donau)
Hauzenberg
Regenstauf
Schwarzenfeld
Schwandorf
Regensburg
Straubing
Deggendorf
Passau
Ried im Innkreis
Vöcklabruck
Pocking

Landshut
Ingolstadt
Donauwörth
Augsburg
Rosenheim
Kufstein
Schwaz
Innsbruck

Nuremberg (Nürnberg)
Neumarkt
Weissenburg
Aalen
Weißenburg
Heidenheim an der Brenz
Munich (München)
Mindelheim
Kempten
Memmingen
Kaufbeuren

Bavaria (Bayern)

Bregenz
Friedrichshafen
Füssen
LIECHTENSTEIN
VADUZ

Plöcken Pass
4508ft (1374m)

Bolzano

The high and graceful stride of the Lipizzaner horses makes them excel in competitions.

Neunkirchen
Saarbrücken
Heidelberg
Heilbronn
Neustadt an der Weinstrasse
Karlsruhe
Pforzheim
Ludwigsburg
Göppingen
Stuttgart
Reutlingen
Ulm
Neu-Ulm
Sinsheim

Baden-Baden
Kehl
Offenburg
Lahr
Emmendingen
Villingen
Rottweil
Schwenningen
Stockach
Singen
Konstanz
Lake Constance

Freiburg im Breisgau
Bad Krozingen
Müllheim
Lörrach
Basel

Black Forest (Schwarzwald)

Schwäbische Alb

Neckar

Rhine (Rhein)

Schaffhausen
Winterthur
Sankt Gallen
Chur
Klosters

Zürich
Zürichsee
Zug
Schwyz
Davos
St. Moritz

SWITZERLAND

BERN
Luzern
Thun
Thuner See
Brig
Bellinzona
Locarno
Lugano
Lake Maggiore

Berner Alps
Finsteraarhorn 14,022ft (4274m)
Simplon Pass 6578ft (2005m)

La Chaux-de-Fonds
Neuchâtel
Lausanne
Geneva (Genève)
Onex

Lake Neuchâtel
Lake Geneva (Lac Léman)

Matterhorn 14,692ft (4478m)
Great Saint Bernard Pass 8100ft (2469m)
Monte Rosa

FRANCE
ITALY

Rhône

SWISS WATCHES
The Swiss invented the first wristwatch, the first quartz watch, and the first water-resistant watch. With their worldwide reputation for quality and style, timepieces make up the country's third largest export

SLOVENIA
After centuries of rule by overlords, Slovenia became independent in 1991. Although the population is only 2 million, the national culture is strong. The famous Lipizzaner show horses are named after the Slovenian farm where they were first bred.

ALPS
The Alps run from southeast France and spread eastward through Switzerland and northern Italy into Austria and Slovenia. A popular tourist destination, the Alps are famous for dramatic scenery and winter sports.

0 km 100
0 miles 100
50
50

Spain and Portugal

Spanish families tend to eat dinner late, at around 9 pm. So after school, children eat a snack called a merienda.

THE COUNTRIES OF SPAIN AND PORTUGAL share an area of land called the Iberian Peninsula. In the north, this land is cut off from the rest of Europe by the Pyrenees Mountains, while to the south, it is separated from Africa by the Strait of Gibraltar. The region was once ruled by Islamic people from north Africa, known as the Moors. Evidence of their culture can still be seen in buildings in the cities of Andalucía. The Moors were eventually defeated in 1492 and, for a while, Portugal came under Spanish control, as did much of Europe. During the 20th century, both countries were ruled by brutal dictatorships, which were overthrown in the 1970s. They are now modern democracies and popular tourist destinations.

HARVESTING CORK
Cork is made from the outer bark of the evergreen cork oak tree. The bark is carefully stripped off, flattened, laid out in sheets, and then left to dry. The cork is used for many products, such as stoppers for wine bottles, matting, and tiles. Portugal is the world's leading exporter of cork.

LISBON
Portugal's capital city is Lisbon, which is situated at the mouth of the River Tagus on a series of steep hills and valleys. In 1755, two-thirds of the city was completely destroyed by an earthquake and tidal wave but was rebuilt with beautiful squares and public buildings. Many explorers have set sail from Lisbon in their quest to find new lands.

Trams are a feature of Lisbon streets and a popular form of transportation for both the locals and tourists.

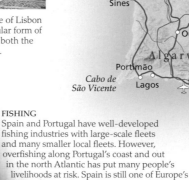

FISHING
Spain and Portugal have well-developed fishing industries with large-scale fleets and many smaller local fleets. However, overfishing along Portugal's coast and out in the north Atlantic has put many people's livelihoods at risk. Spain is still one of Europe's top fishing nations, with catches of fish, molluscs, and crustaceans reaching around 1,100 tons per year.

Map labels

A Coruña (La Coruña), Ferrol, Luarca, Avilés, Gijon (Xixón), Costa V, Villaviciosa, Lla, Pravia, Tineo, Oviedo, Mieres del Cami, Cantáb, Larracha, Betanzos, Vilalba, La Pola, Cabanaquinta, Santa Catalina de Armada, Galicia, Lugo, Cordillera Cantábrica, Cabo Fisterra, Outes, Santiago de Compostela, Ponferrada, León, Santa Uxía de Ribeira, Muros, Lalín, Chantada, Monforte, Astorga, Castilla-León, Pontevedra, O Carballiño, Ourense (Orense), Marín, Ponteareas, Xinzo de Limia, Benavente, Palencia, Vigo, Viana do Castelo, Ponte da Barca, Bragança, Embalse de Ricobayo, Valladolid, Póvoa de Varzim, Braga, Guimarães, Chaves, Zamora, Vila do Conde, Vila Real, Toro, Duero, Matosinhos, Porto (Oporto), Vila Nova de Gaia, Douro, Lamego, Embalse de Almendra, Medina del Campo, Ovar, São João da Madeira, Salamanca, S, Aveiro, Albergaria-a-Velha, Viseu, Ílhavo, Alto da Torre 6539ft (1993m), Ciudad-Rodrigo, Ávila, Coimbra, Guarda, Béjar, Sistema Centr, Figueira da Foz, Serra da Estrela, Covilhã, Sierra de Gredos, Plasencia, Talavera de la Reina, Leiria, PORTUGAL, Castelo Branco, Coria, Tomar, Tagus, Embalse de Alcántara, Cáceres, Embalse de Valdecañas, Entroncamento, Abrantes, Trujillo, Herrera del Duqu, Peniche, Caldas da Rainha, Portalegre, Extremadura, Torres Vedras, Santarém, Sintra, Coruche, Mérida, Villanueva de la Seren, Cascais, LISBON (LISBOA), Estremoz, Elvas, Don Benito, Almada, Barreiro, Évora, Badajoz, Castuera, Puertol, Setúbal, Serra d'Ossa, Almendralejo, Zafra, Villafranca de los Barros, Pozoblanco, Baía de Setúbal, Alcácer do Sal, Guadiana, Jerez de los Caballeros, Azuaga, Sines, Beja, Sierra Morena, Montor, Cortegana, Córdoba, Buja, Ourique, Nerva, Guadalquivir, Palma del Río, Alca, Valverde del Camino, La Algaba, Carmona, Andaluc, Algarve, Lepe, Ecija, Osuna, Lucena, Portimão, Ayamonte, Seville (Sevilla), Cabo de São Vicente, Lagos, Faro, Isla Cristina, Huelva, Dos Hermanas, Archidon, Olhão, Tavira, Las Cabezas de San Juan, Antequera, Gulf of Cadiz (Golfo de Cádiz), Lebrija, Olvera, Ronda, Ma, Ubrique, Coín, Fuengirola, Cádiz, Jerez de la Frontera, Marbella, San Fernando, Estepona, Costa de la Luz, Barbate de Franco, GIBRALTAR (to UK), Algeciras, Costa del, Strait of Gibraltar, Ceuta (to Spain), MOROCCO

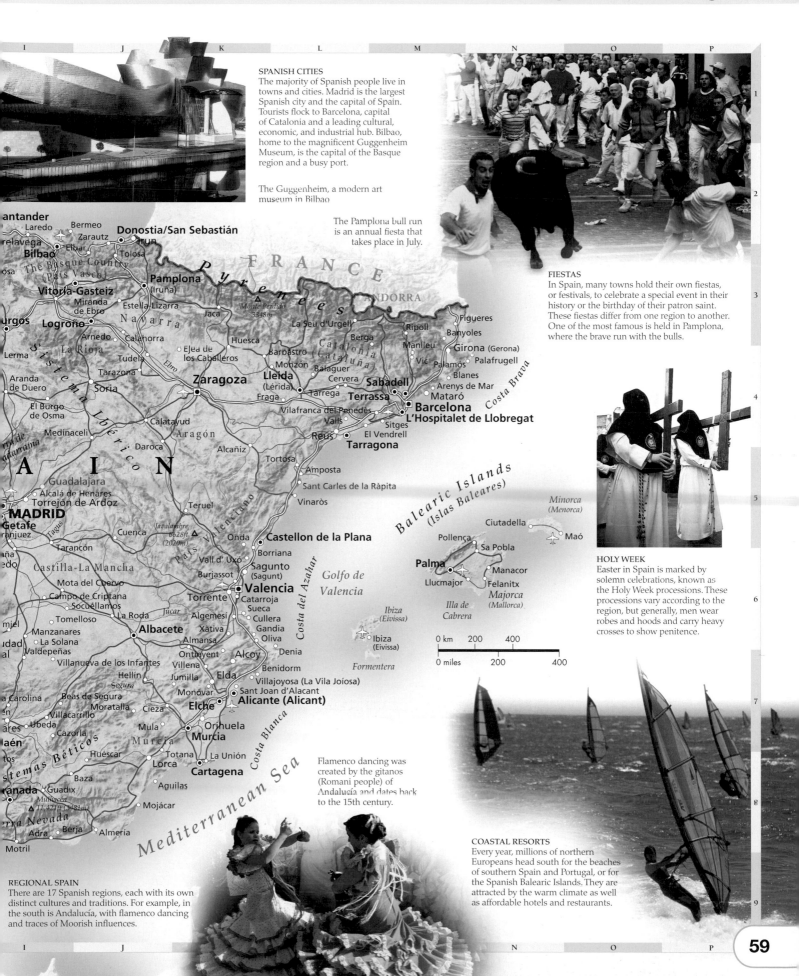

SPANISH CITIES
The majority of Spanish people live in towns and cities. Madrid is the largest Spanish city and the capital of Spain. Tourists flock to Barcelona, capital of Catalonia and a leading cultural, economic, and industrial hub. Bilbao, home to the magnificent Guggenheim Museum, is the capital of the Basque region and a busy port.

The Guggenheim, a modern art museum in Bilbao

The Pamplona bull run is an annual fiesta that takes place in July.

FIESTAS
In Spain, many towns hold their own fiestas, or festivals, to celebrate a special event in their history or the birthday of their patron saint. These fiestas differ from one region to another. One of the most famous is held in Pamplona, where the brave run with the bulls.

HOLY WEEK
Easter in Spain is marked by solemn celebrations, known as the Holy Week processions. These processions vary according to the region, but generally, men wear robes and hoods and carry heavy crosses to show penitence.

COASTAL RESORTS
Every year, millions of northern Europeans head south for the beaches of southern Spain and Portugal, or for the Spanish Balearic Islands. They are attracted by the warm climate as well as affordable hotels and restaurants.

Flamenco dancing was created by the gitanos (Romani people) of Andalucía and dates back to the 15th century.

REGIONAL SPAIN
There are 17 Spanish regions, each with its own distinct cultures and traditions. For example, in the south is Andalucía, with flamenco dancing and traces of Moorish influences.

Santander
Laredo
Bermeo
Zarautz
relavega
Elbar
Tolosa
Irun
Donostia/San Sebastián
Bilbao
The Basque Country
(País Vasco)
Pamplona
(Iruña)
FRANCE
Vitoria-Gasteiz
Miranda de Ebro
Estella-Lizarra
Jaca
Navarra
Monte Perdido
3348m
ANDORRA
Pyrenees
urgos
Logroño
Arnedo
Calahorra
Ejea de los Caballeros
Huesca
La Seu d'Urgell
Berga
Ripoll
Figueres
Banyoles
La Rioja
Lerma
Tudela
Tarazona
Ebro
Barbastro
Monzón
Catalonia
(Cataluña)
Manlleu
Vic
Girona (Gerona)
osa
Aranda de Duero
Soria
Zaragoza
Lleida
(Lérida)
Balaguer
Cervera
Tàrrega
Sabadell
Palamós
Palafrugell
Blanes
Sistema Ibérico
El Burgo de Osma
Fraga
Vilafranca del Penedès
Terrassa
Barcelona
Arenys de Mar
Mataró
Costa Brava
Medinaceli
Calatayud
Aragón
Valls
L'Hospitalet de Llobregat
Sitges
Guadalajara
Daroca
Alcañiz
Reus
El Vendrell
Tarragona
A I N
Alcalá de Henares
Torrejón de Ardoz
Teruel
Tortosa
Amposta
Balearic Islands
(Islas Baleares)
MADRID
Getafe
Javalambre
8628ft
(2020m)
Sant Carles de la Ràpita
Minorca
(Menorca)
anjuez
Tarancón
Cuenca
Vinaròs
Ciutadella
Maó
Castilla-La Mancha
Onda
Castellon de la Plana
Pollença
Sa Pobla
ana
Borriana
Golfo de Valencia
Palma
Manacor
edo
Mota del Cuervo
Vall d' Uxó
Sagunto
(Sagunt)
Burjassot
Llucmajor
Felanitx
Majorca
(Mallorca)
Campo de Criptana
Socuéllamos
Torrente
Valencia
Catarroja
Sueca
Ibiza
(Eivissa)
Illa de Cabrera
miel
La Roda
Júcar
Algemesí
Cullera
udad
Tomelloso
Manzanares
Xàtiva
Gandia
Oliva
Ibiza
(Eivissa)
al
Albacete
Almansa
Denia
La Solana
Valdepeñas
Onthayent
Alcoy
Formentera
Villanueva de los Infantes
Villena
Benidorm
Hellín
Jumilla
Elda
Villajoyosa (La Vila Joíosa)
Segura
Monóvar
Sant Joan d'Alacant
a Carolina
Beas de Segura
Cieza
Elche
Alicante (Alicant)
Moratalla
Villacarrillo
Mula
Orihuela
Ubeda
Cazorla
Murcia
Murcia
Jaén
Huéscar
Totana
La Unión
Sistemas Béticos
Baza
Lorca
Cartagena
anada
Guadix
Aguilas
Sierra Nevada
11,421ft (3481m)
Mojácar
Adra
Berja
Almería
Motril
Mediterranean Sea

0 km 200 400
0 miles 200 400

Italy

THE BOOT-SHAPED COUNTRY of Italy stretches from the mountainous north down to the Mediterranean Sea. For much of its history, Italy consisted of city-states—such as Florence and Venice—and was united only in 1870. Regional differences in Italy are huge, as each region has its own cuisine, customs, and dialect, and is geographically quite distinct. As a result, many Italians identify themselves first by region and then by country. The largest division, however, is between the rich north and the poorer south—a rugged region with several active volcanoes and the occasional severe earthquake. The mainland of Italy includes two tiny independent states—San Marino and Vatican City.

Vatican City has a permanent population of only about 1,000 people, although more than 3,000 come to work in the city-state each day.

Carnival masks

Andrea Bocelli

HOME OF OPERA
The idea of setting drama to music originated in Italy during the 16th century. Since then, Italian composers such as Rossini, Verdi, and Puccini have made opera the most popular musical form in Italy. Many cities have their own opera houses.

CITY OF CANALS
The beautiful city of Venice is made up of 118 islands, 177 canals, and 400 bridges. The only way to get around is to walk or take a boat: a *vaporetto*, *motoscafo*, or *motonave*. The most distinctive boat, however, is the gondola. Each year, in the days before Ash Wednesday, Venice hosts a carnival when the city celebrates with fireworks and everyone wears spectacular masks.

FOOTBALL FANS
Italians are mad about football and fanatically follow the performance of teams such as Juventus, AC Milan, Inter, and Roma. Italian teams frequently win major European competitions, and the national team has won the World Cup four times—in 1934, 1938, 1982, and 2006.

COLOSSEUM
One of Rome's greatest sights is the Colosseum, which opened in 80 CE. Deadly gladiatorial combats and animal fights were staged here before crowds of up to 55,000 people.

The oval-shaped Colosseum stood at 620 ft (189 m) high.

SLOVENIA

CROATIA

AUSTRIA

SWITZERLAND

FRANCE

MONACO

Bremner Pass
4508ft
(1374m)

Mont Blanc
15771ft
(4807m)

Great St.-Bernard
Pass 8100ft
(2469m)

Little St.-Bernard
Pass 7178ft (2188m)

Gran Paradiso
13323ft
(4061m)

Rhône

Trieste

Tarvisio

Monfalcone

Gulf of
Venice

Cortina d'Ampezzo
Dolomites

Gemona del Friuli

Udine

Pordenone

Portogruaro

Venice (Venezia)

Chioggia

Foci del Po

Bressanone

Merano

Bolzano

Trento

Lake Garda

Bassano
del Grappa

Arco

Vicenza

Treviso

Mestre

Padova

Rovigo

Ferrara

Adige

Po

Comacchio

Ravenna

Forlì

Cesena

Rimini

SAN MARINO
SAN MARINO

Pesaro

Fano

Falconara
Marittima

Ancona

Civitanova
Marche

Fermo

Ascoli
Piceno

Giulianova

Teramo

Edolo

Bergamo

Brescia

Sesto San Giovanni

Monza

Como

Lake Como

Lake
Maggiore

Varese

Novara

Vercelli

Rivoli

Turin
(Torino)

Susa

Moncalieri

Piemonte

Savigliano

Mondovì

Cuneo

Ventimiglia

San Remo

Imperia

Finale Ligure

Savona

Appennino Ligure

Gulf of Genoa

Genoa (Genova)

La Spezia

Carrara

Massa

Viareggio

Lucca

Pisa

Livorno

Cecina

Piombino

Portoferraio

Isola
d'Elba

Archipelago Toscano

Grosseto

Orbetello

Lago di
Bolsena

Viterbo

Todi

Terni

Foligno

Lago
Trasimeno

Perugia

Arezzo

Siena

Tus cany
Toscana

Chianti

Prato

Florence
(Firenze)

Arno

Pistoia

Faenza

Imola

Bologna

Modena

Reggio nell'Emilia

Parma

Piacenza

Cremona

Mantova

Pavia

Casteggio

Alessandria

Asti

Milan
(Milano)

Po Valley

Lombardy
(Lombardia)

Aosta

Sansepolcro

Appennino

Umbra
Marchigiano

Marche

Umbria

Gulf of
Venice

Adriatic Sea

Brindisi
Lecce
Maglie
Strait of Otranto

Taranto
Manduria
Gallipoli
Golfo di Taranto
Bari
Molfetta
Barletta
Manfredonia
Andria
Bitonto
Puglia
Matera
San Severo
Foggia
Cerignola
Altamura
Benevento
Potenza
Avellino
Appennino Lucano
Quanto
Torre del Greco
Salerno
Caserta
Laviano
Sala Consilina
Castrovillari
Sapri
Agropoli
Golf of Salerno
Battipaglia
Vesuvio
Naples (Napoli)
Campania
Isernia
Campobasso
Volturno
Gaeta
Golfo di Gaeta
Terracina
Latina
Anzio
Isole Ponziane
ROME (ROMA)

Ciro Marino
Crotone
Rossano
La Sila
Catanzaro
Siderno
Cosenza
Amantea
Lamezia
Reggio di Calabria
Palmi
Strait of Messina
Isola Stromboli
Isola Lipari
Isole Eolie
Isola Vulcano
Messina
Catania
Mount Etna 10,902ft (3340m)
Simeto
Cefalù
Palermo
Alcamo
Caltanissetta
Enna
Gela
Vittoria
Modica
Siracusa
Ragusa
Pozzallo
Agrigento
Sicily (Sicilia)
Trapani
Marsala
Castelvetrano
Strait of Sicily
Malta Channel
Gozo
MALTA
VALLETTA
Malta
Isola di Pantelleria
Isole Pelagie

Ionian Sea

Tyrrhenian Sea

Mediterranean Sea

Sardinia (Sardegna)
Isola Asinara
la Maddalena
Tempio Pausania
Olbia
Porto Torres
Alghero
Ozieri
Siniscola
Sassari
Nuoro
Macomer
Oristano
Vilacidro
Iglesias
Carbonia
Punta La Marmora 6017ft (1834m)
Cagliari
Quartu Sant' Elena

OLIVE HARVEST
Italy is a big producer of olive oil, producing around 330,000 tons, which is second only to Spain in Europe. The oil is produced by first pressing the fruits of the olive tree between steel or stone rollers, then squeezing oil from the pulp using a press. Olive trees flourish in the fertile soils and the mild, frost-free climate of southern Italy.

Olive harvesters gather olives in nets

VATICAN CITY
This tiny state in Rome is the center of the Roman Catholic Church and home to the Pope. As well as St Peter's Basilica and the surrounding buildings and gardens, the Vatican boasts Michelangelo's Sistine Chapel. The state has its own flag, postage stamps, and coins.

Swiss guards, in their red, yellow, and blue striped costumes, stand at the gates into Vatican City.

RENAISSANCE ITALY
Florence (below) sits on either side of the Arno River. During the 15th century, a new movement in art and architecture known as the Renaissance, or rebirth, began in Italy. Painters and sculptors such as Leonardo da Vinci, Michelangelo and Raphael created beautiful works of art using improved techniques of perspective and realism. Many of these can still be seen in the galleries and churches of Florence.

HOME LIFE
Family life is important in Italy, and most people live at home until they marry. This is partly due to lack of cheap housing. Lunch (*pranzo*) is often the main meal of the day.

0 km 50 100
0 miles 50 100

Central Europe

FOUR COUNTRIES LIE at the heart of central Europe—Poland, Czechia (until 2016, the Czech Republic), Slovakia, and Hungary. The region is composed of wide plains broken by gentle hills and the Carpathian mountain range in the south. In the late 1980s, these countries broke away from decades of communist rule and, as new democracies, began to modernize. EU-members since 2004, they have seen a rise in living standards, despite the global economic crisis of 2008 hitting their growing economies.

TRADITIONAL TRADES
The countries of central Europe are heavily industrialized. Vast coal mines, steel works (above), and engineering works dominate the urban landscape. Although some of these sites are old and poorly equipped, these countries are trying to update machinery and introduce measures to improve standards of environmental pollution.

RELIGION
The Roman Catholic Church is very strong throughout central Europe. Attending mass on Sunday and observing religious holidays, such as Christmas and Easter, are important features of family life.

FAMILY FARMS
Poland has one of the largest agricultural sectors in Europe, with more than 12 percent of the workforce employed on the land. Most farms are still small, family-run businesses, growing grains, sugar beet, and potatoes. Large numbers of pigs and other animals are also kept.

GOLDEN PRAGUE
Prague, the capital of Czechia, is one of Europe's most charming and beautiful cities. Unlike many other central European cities, it escaped serious damage in both World Wars, and contains many fine historic buildings, soaring church spires, and grand squares.

Part of Prague's colourful history is preserved in buildings around the Old Town Square.

Map labels

BELARUS

GERMANY

POLAND

Baltic Sea

Gulf of Danzig

Vistula Lagoon

Pomeranian Bay

KALININGRAD (to Russian Federation)

WARSAW (WARSZAWA)

Suwałki, Goldap, Augustów, Kuźnica, Sokółka, Białystok, Łapy, Siemiatycze, Bielsk Podlaski, Biała Podlaska, Międzyrzec Podlaski, Chełm, Krasnystaw, Zamość, Tomaszów Lubelski

Elk, Giżycko, Grajewo, Narew, Zambrów, Bug, Radzyń Podlaski, Włodawa, Lublin

Bartoszyce, Kętrzyn, Pisz, Łomża, Ostrów Mazowiecka, Wyszków, Łuków, Garwolin, Ryki, Puławy, Świdnik, Porjatowa, Wyżyna Lubelska, Stalowa Wola

Górowo, Lidzbark, Dobre Miasto, Szczytno, Nidzica, Mława, Ciechanów, Sierpc, Płońsk, Pułtusk, Góra Kalwaria, Grójec, Skarżysko-Kamienna, Ostrowiec, Świętokrzyski, Sandomierz, Tarnobrzeg

Warmiński, Biskupiec, Olsztyn, Jezioro Śniardwy, Ostrołęka, Mazowiecki, Pruszków, Grójec, Tomaszów Mazowiecki, Piotrków Trybunalski, Starachowice, Kielce, Jędrzejów, Zawiercie

Braniewo, Elbląg, Malbork, Ostróda, Iława, Brodnica, Rypin, Nowy Dwór Mazowiecki, Kutno, Łódź, Zgierz, Bełchatów, Radomsko, Częstochowa, Lubliniec

Rumia, Gdynia, Gdańsk, Tczew, Kwidzyń, Chełmno, Grudziądz, Toruń, Lipno, Włocławek, Płock, Radom

Władysławowo, Wejherowo, Lębork, Kościerzyna, Chojnice, Świecie, Solec Kujawski, Inowrocław, Konin, Koło, Sieradz, Pabianice, Weluń, Kępno, Kluczbork, Opole, Brzeg, Kłobuck

Ustka, Słupsk, Bytów, Szczecinek, Człuchów, Żnin, Mogilno, Gniezno, Września, Pleszew, Kalisz, Ostrów Wielkopolski, Rawicz, Ząbkowice Śląskie

Sławno, Koszalin, Kołobrzeg, Białogard, Świdwin, Piła, Trzcianka, Oborniki, Międzychód, Poznań, Śrem, Leszno, Głogów, Wrocław, Świdnica, Wałbrzych

Darłowo, Szczecin, Goleniów, Nowogard, Stargard Szczeciński, Wałcz, Choszczno, Gorzów Wielkopolski, Sulechów, Nowa Sól, Lubin, Legnica, Jelenia Góra, Świdnica

Świnoujście, Zalew Szczeciński, Pyrzyce, Myślibórz, Sulęcin, Krosno Odrzańskie, Lubsko, Żagań, Szprotawa, Bolesławiec, Zgorzelec, Liberec, Děčín

Słubice, Świebodzin, Zielona Góra, Żary, Oder (Odra)

Ústí nad Labem, Teplice, Chomutov, Most, Lovosice, Karlovy Vary, Turnov

Wisła, Warta, Noteć, Odra

Śnieżka 5259ft (1602m)

Sudety

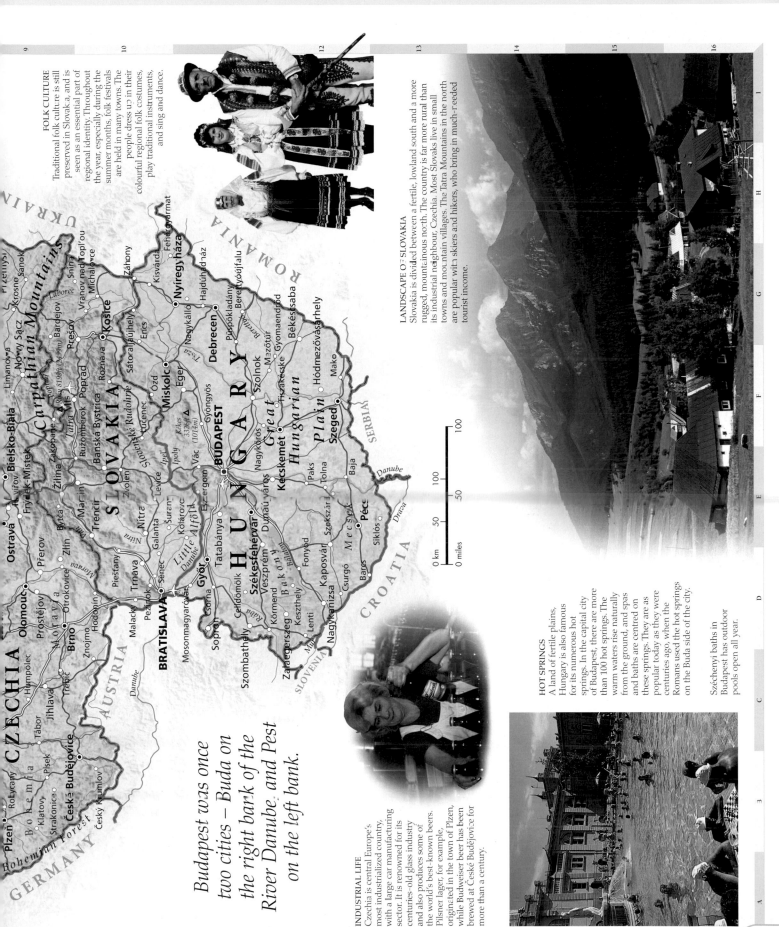

FOLK CULTURE

Traditional folk culture is still preserved in Slovakia, and is seen as an essential part of regional identity. Throughout the year, especially during the summer months, folk festivals are held in many towns. The people dress up in their colourful regional folk costumes, play traditional instruments, and sing and dance.

LANDSCAPE OF SLOVAKIA

Slovakia is divided between a fertile, lowland south and a more rugged, mountainous north. The country is far more rural than its industrial neighbour, Czechia. Most Slovaks live in small towns and mountain villages. The Tatra Mountains in the north are popular with skiers and hikers, who bring in much-needed tourist income.

INDUSTRIAL LIFE

Czechia is central Europe's most industrialized country, with a large car manufacturing sector. It is renowned for its centuries-old glass industry and also produces some of the world's best-known beers. Pilsner lager, for example, originated in the town of Plzen, while Budweiser beer has been brewed at České Budějovice for more than a century.

Budapest was once two cities – Buda on the right bank of the River Danube, and Pest on the left bank.

HOT SPRINGS

A land of fertile plains, Hungary is also famous for its numerous hot springs. In the capital city of Budapest, there are more than 100 hot springs. The warm waters rise naturally from the ground, and spas and baths are centred on these springs. They are as popular today as they were centuries ago, when the Romans used the hot springs on the Buda side of the city.

Széchenyi baths in Budapest has outdoor pools open all year.

Southeast Europe

UNTIL 1991, CROATIA, Bosnia and Herzegovina, Serbia, Montenegro, and Macedonia were all part of Yugoslavia. Ethnic tensions between the Serbs and other peoples in Yugoslavia caused a series of bloody wars that broke up the country. Peace was eventually restored in 1999, but all five countries have suffered intense economic problems as a result. So, too, has Albania since its communist government collapsed. The six nations do, however, have huge potential, with considerable agricultural and mineral resources. In the north, the Danube River is an important trading route for both Croatia and Serbia, while Croatia has a flourishing tourist industry along its beautiful Adriatic coast.

THE ADRIATIC
The long Adriatic coastline of Croatia is one of the most beautiful in Europe. The wooded hillsides, pretty beaches, such as Markarska (right), islands, and historic towns such as Dubrovnik attract tourists from all over Europe. The archipelago is also popular for sailing holidays.

GROWING FOOD
The most fertile area in this region lies along the River Danube in northern Serbia and eastern Croatia. Here, vegetables, fruit, corn, and cereals are grown, as well as grapes for wine-making. Most farms are small-scale family businesses growing a wide range of crops.

The Dalmatian dog is named after the coastal region of Dalmatia in Croatia, its first known home.

SPORTING ACHIEVEMENT
Croatia is a great sporting nation. Former skier Janica Kostelić has won four Olympic gold medals (three in 2002 and one in 2006), making her one of the most successful female Alpine skiers of all time. Other popular sports are football (soccer), tennis, and basketball.

Janica Kostelić

DIFFERENT SCRIPTS
Croatian and Serbian languages are very similar but the people of Croatia, a predominantly Roman Catholic country, write in Roman script, as do Bosnians. Serbians are mainly Eastern Orthodox and write using both Roman and Russian Cyrillic scripts.

Magazine with Cyrillic script

Magazine with Roman script

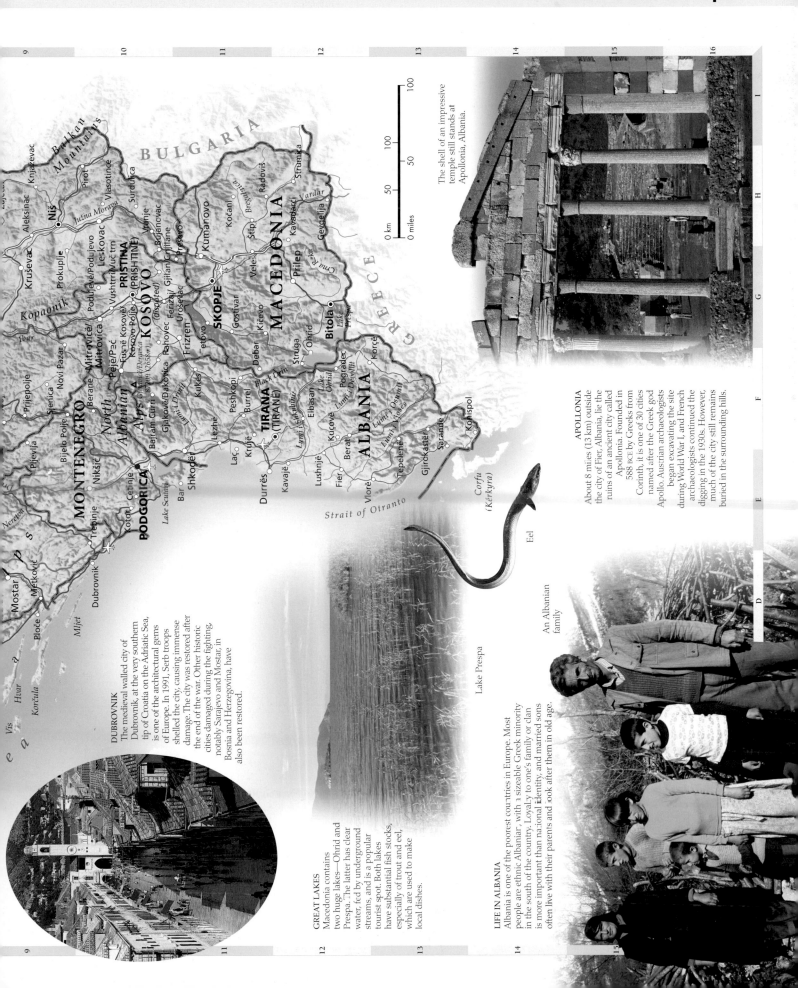

BULGARIA

Balkan Mountains

MONTENEGRO

KOSOVO

PRISTINA
(PRISHTINË)

MACEDONIA

SKOPJE

PODGORICA

ALBANIA

North
Albanian
Alps

TIRANA
(TIRANË)

Bitola

GREECE

Niš
Knjaževac
Aleksinac
Pirot
Prokuplje
Kruševac
Vlasotince
Surdulica
Kopaonik
Podujevo/Podujevë
Leskovac
Ybar
Vuštrri/Vučitrn
Kosovo Polje/
Fushë Kosovë
Vranje
Bujanovac
Preševo
Priepolje
Novi Pazar
Mitrovica/
Mitrovicë
Peja/Peć
Gjilan/Gnjilane
Kumanovo
Kočani
Radoviš
Štip
Bijelo Polje
Berane
Sjenica
Prijepolje
Rahovec/
Orahovac
Ferizaj/
Uroševac
Kičevo
Veles
Vardar
Strumica
Kavadarci
Gjakovë/Đakovica
Prizren
Tetovo
Gostivar
Prilep
Gevgelija
Nikšić
Cetinje
Lumi i Drinit
Kukës
Dibar
Crna Re ka
Struga
Ohrid
Lake
Prespa
Trebinje
Bar
Lake Scutari
Shkodër
Peshkopi
Burrel
Black Drin
Lake
Ohrid
Mostar
Metković
Ploče
Lezhë
Laç
Krujë
Burre
Elbasan
Pogradec
Lumi i Devollit
Korçë
Mljet
Dubrovnik
Durrës
Kavajë
Lumi i Shkumbinit
Lushnjë
Kuçovë
Berati
Lumi i Osumit
Tepelenë
Gjirokastër
Sarandë
Konispol
Fier
Vlorë
Lumi i Vjosës
Korčula
Vis
Hvar
Nereta
Strait of Otranto
Corfu
(Kérkyra)

Djuravica/
Deravica 2658m

0 km ___ 100
0 miles ___ 100
50
50

Eel

Lake Prespa

An Albanian
family

APOLLONIA

About 8 miles (13 km) outside the city of Fier, Albania, lie the ruins of an ancient city called Apollonia. Founded in 588 BCE by Greeks from Corinth, it is one of 30 cities named after the Greek god Apollo. Austrian archaeologists began excavating the site during World War I, and French archaeologists continued the digging in the 1930s. However, much of the city still remains buried in the surrounding hills.

The shell of an impressive temple still stands at Apollonia, Albania.

DUBROVNIK

The medieval walled city of Dubrovnik, at the very southern tip of Croatia on the Adriatic Sea, is one of the architectural gems of Europe. In 1991, Serb troops shelled the city, causing immense damage. The city was restored after the end of the war. Other historic cities damaged during the fighting, notably Sarajevo and Mostar, in Bosnia and Herzegovina, have also been restored.

GREAT LAKES

Macedonia contains two huge lakes—Ohrid and Prespa. The latter has clear water, fed by underground streams, and is a popular tourist spot. Both lakes have substantial fish stocks, especially of trout and eel, which are used to make local dishes.

LIFE IN ALBANIA

Albania is one of the poorest countries in Europe. Most people are ethnic Albanian, with a sizeable Greek minority in the south of the country. Loyalty to one's family or clan is more important than national identity, and married sons often live with their parents and look after them in old age.

Bulgaria and Greece

FOR MORE THAN FOUR CENTURIES Bulgaria and Greece were ruled by the Ottoman Turks. Bulgaria gained independence in 1908, while southern Greece became independent in 1832 and was joined by northern Greece in 1913. After World War II, Bulgaria became a communist state. Both states are now democracies and members of the European Union (EU). Bulgaria remains relatively poor. Greece's economy is struggling, despite the billions of euros lent by the EU since 2010. That's when it was discovered that seemingly wealthy Greece had a huge national deficit (meaning it had spent a lot more than it had collected in taxes). Although they border each other, Bulgaria and Greece are quite different; the Greek mainland is mountainous with only one-third of the land suitable for cultivation. By contrast, Bulgaria is more fertile with a strong agricultural tradition. Tourism is an important source of income to both countries, with visitors flocking to the Black Sea resorts in Bulgaria, to the Greek mainland to see the ancient ruins, and to the Greek islands in search of sandy beaches.

First held in Athens in 1896, the modern Olympic Games were staged there again in 2004.

BULGARIAN AGRICULTURE
Wheat, corn, and other cereals grow in the fertile Danube river valley in the north of the country. Tobacco (right) grows in the Maritsa river valley in the southeast, while grapes for the wine industry flourish on the slopes of the Balkan Mountains. The festival of Kukerov Den, with traditional processions, celebrates the start of the agricultural year.

CITY LIFE
Bulgarians make up about 77 percent of the total population of the country. Most of the rest are Turkish, Macedonian, or Roma. Most people live in apartment blocks in the main towns and cities. They are more likely to use public transportation as not all households have a car.

Trams provide an efficient way for people to get around Bulgaria's capital, Sofia.

ARCHITECTURE
Bulgaria contains many fine old churches, monasteries, and mosques, despite the damage done to the country during World War II. Rila Monastery (above) was founded by a hermit monk who took to the mountains in search of solitude in 927 CE. After a fire in 1833, Rila was rebuilt and the magnificent church now boasts three great domes, a museum, and 1,200 frescoes.

LANGUAGE
The 24 characters in the Greek alphabet date from the 8th century BCE, when the first texts were written in classical Greek. Since then the language has evolved and is now spoken by 13 million people around the world.

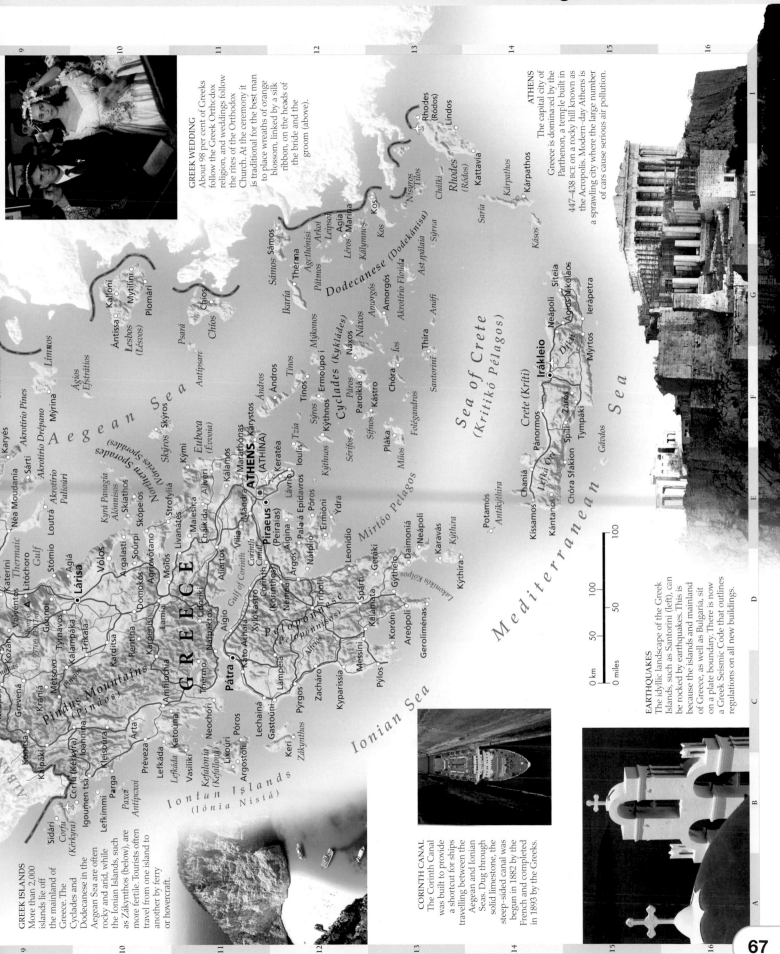

GREEK WEDDING
About 98 per cent of Greeks follow the Greek Orthodox religion, and weddings follow the rites of the Orthodox Church. At the ceremony it is traditional for the best man to place wreaths of orange blossom, linked by a silk ribbon, on the heads of the bride and the groom (above).

ATHENS
The capital city of Greece is dominated by the Parthenon, a temple built in 447–438 BCE on a rocky hill known as the Acropolis. Modern-day Athens is a sprawling city where the large number of cars cause serious air pollution.

GREEK ISLANDS
More than 2,000 islands lie off the mainland of Greece. The Cyclades and Dodecanese in the Aegean Sea are often rocky and arid, while the Ionian Islands, such as Zákynthos (below), are more fertile. Tourists often travel from one island to another by ferry or hovercraft.

CORINTH CANAL
The Corinth Canal was built to provide a shortcut for ships travelling between the Aegean and Ionian Seas. Dug through solid limestone, the steep-sided canal was begun in 1882 by the French and completed in 1893 by the Greeks.

EARTHQUAKES
The idyllic landscape of the Greek Islands, such as Santorini (left), can be rocked by earthquakes. This is because the islands and mainland of Greece, as well as Bulgaria, sit on a plate boundary. There is now a Greek Seismic Code that outlines regulations on all new buildings.

Ukraine, Moldova, & Romania

THROUGHOUT MUCH OF THE LAST CENTURY, Ukraine and Moldova formed part of the Soviet Union (USSR), while Romania was ruled for 20 years by the communist dictator Nicolae Ceausescu. In 1989, Ceausescu was overthrown, while Ukraine and Moldova became independent in 1991. Today, the three countries are still struggling to fully transform themselves into modern democracies, although Romania joined the EU in 2007. Outdated technology, dependency on gas and oil from their powerful neighbor Russia, and economic and environmental problems have slowed their progress. It is also a region of ethnic tensions, highlighted in 2014 when Russia annexed Ukraine's Crimean peninsula, where a large part of the population consists of Russians left behind after the USSR break-up.

CITY LIFE
Romania has many cities and towns with a mix of old and new buildings. Sibiu (left) was founded in the 12th century and, at one time, had 19 guilds—each representing a different craft—within its city walls. Much remains from this colorful history, especially in the painted buildings of the old town.

FOLK CUSTOMS
Despite years of communist rule, folk customs thrived in the rural areas of Romania and Ukraine. In Ukraine, singers perform *dumas*, historical epics that tell of slavery under the Turks. One of the traditional instruments is a bandura (left), a stringed instrument that sounds like a harpsichord.

DRACULA'S CASTLE
Situated in Transylvania, Bran Castle is a favorite tourist destination. This is where author Bram Stoker's fictional blood-drinking Count Dracula lived. The story is probably based on a 15th-century Romanian prince, Vlad Dracula, who reigned for less than 10 years but caused more than 50,000 deaths.

The word Transylvania means "land beyond the forests."

EASTER BREAD
In Romania, Easter is celebrated with a meal of roast lamb served with a bread called *cozonac*. This is made by pounding nuts, raisins, and even cocoa, into the dough.

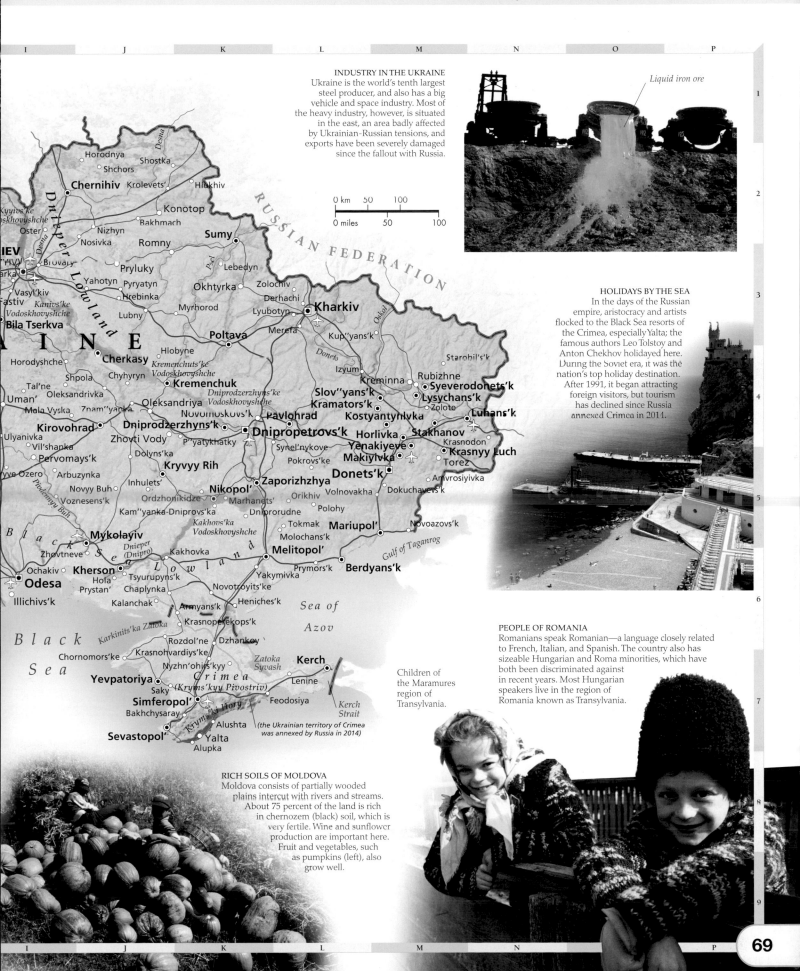

INDUSTRY IN THE UKRAINE
Ukraine is the world's tenth largest steel producer, and also has a big vehicle and space industry. Most of the heavy industry, however, is situated in the east, an area badly affected by Ukrainian-Russian tensions, and exports have been severely damaged since the fallout with Russia.

Liquid iron ore

0 km   50   100
0 miles   50   100

HOLIDAYS BY THE SEA
In the days of the Russian empire, aristocracy and artists flocked to the Black Sea resorts of the Crimea, especially Yalta; the famous authors Leo Tolstoy and Anton Chekhov holidayed here. During the Soviet era, it was the nation's top holiday destination. After 1991, it began attracting foreign visitors, but tourism has declined since Russia annexed Crimea in 2014.

PEOPLE OF ROMANIA
Romanians speak Romanian—a language closely related to French, Italian, and Spanish. The country also has sizeable Hungarian and Roma minorities, which have both been discriminated against in recent years. Most Hungarian speakers live in the region of Romania known as Transylvania.

Children of the Maramures region of Transylvania.

RICH SOILS OF MOLDOVA
Moldova consists of partially wooded plains intercut with rivers and streams. About 75 percent of the land is rich in chernozem (black) soil, which is very fertile. Wine and sunflower production are important here. Fruit and vegetables, such as pumpkins (left), also grow well.

(the Ukrainian territory of Crimea was annexed by Russia in 2014)

Baltic States & Belarus

THE THREE BALTIC STATES, Estonia, Latvia, and Lithuania, all share a stretch of coast on the Baltic Sea lined with sandy beaches. Belarus lies between Poland, Ukraine, and the Russian Federation. Following independence from the Soviet Union in 1991, all these countries faced problems such as price increases, food shortages, and pollution. However, the Baltic States have reformed into hi-tech societies and economies and have been EU members since 2004. Belarus has kept close links with Russia and has been the slowest to reform. This mainly rural country has stayed isolated from the rest of Europe and, with few natural resources, remains one of its poorest nations.

The Estonian flag waved at a pre-independence rally in 1988

SINGING REVOLUTION
Estonia is known for its classical music tradition—most notably its choirs. This love of music was most powerful when people raised their voices during the Singing Revolution in 1988 (right), part of their move toward independence.

TALLINN OLD TOWN
With its colorful buildings, turreted walls, and gabled roofs, Tallinn is one of the best-preserved capital cities in Europe. All the winding, cobbled streets lead to the Town Hall Square (left).

AMBER
Two-thirds of the world's amber, the fossilized resin of pine trees, is washed up from the sea bed along the Baltic coast. Amber is used to make jewelry, among other things.

From the early days of public broadband usage, Estonia has been one of Europe's most connected countries.

RUSSIAN FEDERATION

Gulf of Finland

Narva Bay

Sillamäe
Narva
Narva Reservoir
Kallaste
Lake Peipus
Lake Pskov

ESTONIA

Maardu
Loksa
Kunda
Rakvere
Kohtla-Järve
Palamuse
Aegviidu
Raasiku
Tapa
Rakke
Puurmani
Tartu
Võnnu
Räpina

TALLINN
Keila
Paldiski
Risti
Rapla
Paide
Viljandi
Mõisaküla
Otepää
Põlva
Võru
Valga
Munamägi 1043 ft
Ape

Haapsalu
Vormsi
Kärdla
Hiiumaa
Emmaste
Väinameri
Orissaare
Saaremaa
Kuressaare
Sääre

Lihula
Virtsu
Audru
Pärnu
Sindi
Kilingi-Nõmme
Ruhnu
Ruõge
Tõrva
Jõgeva

Jaagupi
Pärnu Laht
Staicele
Aloja
Buttnieku Ezers
Valmiera
Cēsis
Smiltene
Valka
Rūjiena
Gauja
Alūksne
Balvi
Rugāji

Baltic Sea

Kolkasrags
Kolka
Roja
Mērsrags
Salacgrīva
Ainaži
Gulf of Riga

LATVIA

RIGA
Saulkrasti
Jūrmala
Tukums
Engure
Jelgava
Iecava
Bauska
Aizkraukle
Plaviņas
Madona
Jēkabpils
Līvāni
Gulbene
Jaunpiebalga
Lubāns
Varakļāni
Malta
Rēzekne
Ludza
Kārsava
Viļaka

Mazirbe
Ventspils
Ugāle
Kuldīga
Kandava
Talsi
Saldus
Brocēni
Usmas Ezers
Engures Ezers
Venta
Abava
Dobele
Pasvalys
Nereta
Viesīte
Birži
Viešīte
Spogi
Krāslava
Dagda

Pāvilosta
Liepāja
Durbe
Grobiņa
Mažeikiai
Skuodas
Telšiai
Šiauliai
Radviliškis
Joniškis
Pakruojis
Biržai
Rokiškis
Obeliai
Zarasai
Krāslava
Daugavpils

Rucava
Kretinga
Gargždai
Plungė
Šatai
Kelmė
Naujamiestis
Panevėžys
Subačius
Anykščiai
Utena
Visaginas
Vidzy

Klaipėda
Priekulė
Šilutė
Šilalė
Tauragė
Raseiniai
Jurbarkas
Skaudvilė
Dotnuva
Jonava
Ukmergė
Giedraičiai
Viliya

LITHUANIA

KAUNAS
Nida
Neman
Chernyakhovsk
Marijampolė
Prienai
Kaišiadorys
VILNIUS
Neris
Trakai
Rūdiškės
Merkinė
Šalčininkai

KALININGRAD
(to Russian Federation)
Kaliningrad
Gvardeysk
Gusev
Vilkaviškis
Kalvarija
Alytus
Varėna
Druskininkai
Veisiejai

Pionerskiy
Zelenogradsk
Courland Lagoon
Mamonovo
Bagrationovsk
Primorsk
Zheleznodorozhny

POLAND

Žemaitių Aukštumas
Kuršo
Žemaičių Aukštumas

Western Dvina
Gaiziņkalns 1020 ft (311m)

Vidzy
Viliya
Braslav
Yezyaryshcha
Polatsk/Polotsk
Navapolatsk/Novopolotsk
Yukhavichy
Drysa
Bihosava
Vyerkhnyadzvinsk
Hlybokaye
Vyetryna
Myadzyel
Haranny
Pastavy

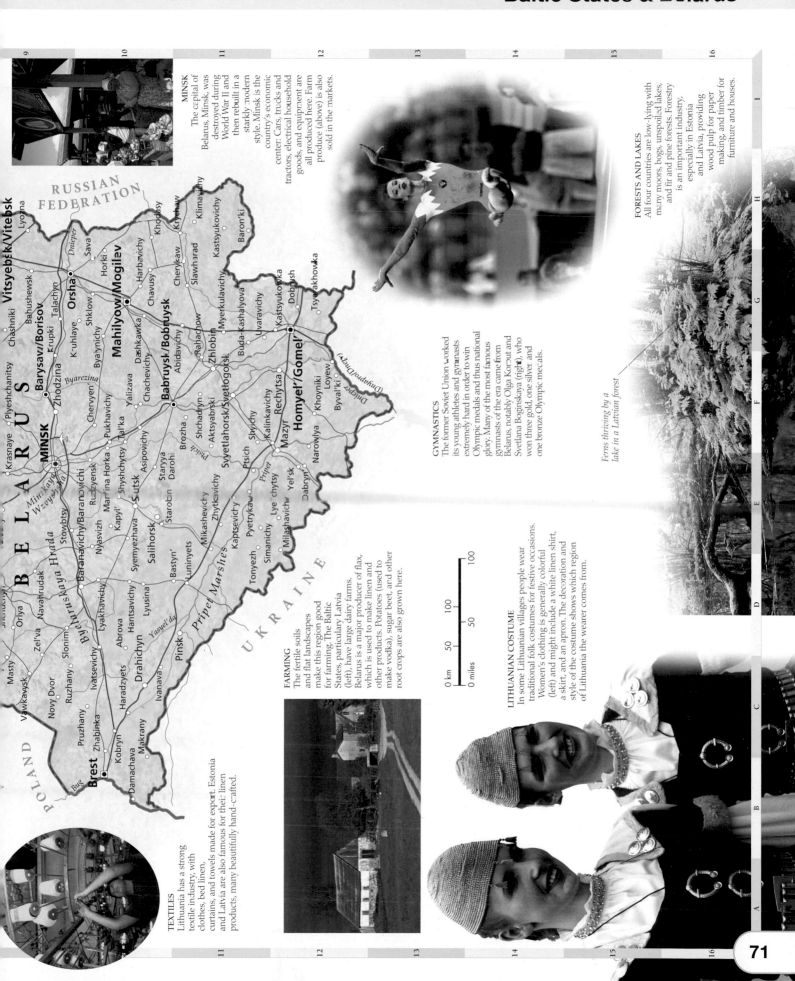

MINSK
The capital of Belarus, Minsk, was destroyed during World War II and then rebuilt in a starkly modern style. Minsk is the country's economic center: Cars, trucks and tractors, electrical household goods, and equipment are all produced here. Farm produce (above) is also sold in the markets.

FORESTS AND LAKES
All four countries are low-lying with many moors, bogs, unspoiled lakes, and fir and pine forests. Forestry is an important industry, especially in Estonia and Latvia, providing wood pulp for paper making, and timber for furniture and houses.

Ferns thriving by a lake in a Latvian forest

GYMNASTICS
The former Soviet Union worked its young athletes and gymnasts extremely hard in order to win Olympic medals and thus national glory. Many of the most famous gymnasts of the era came from Belarus, notably Olga Korbut and Svetlana Boginskaya (right), who won three gold, one silver and one bronze Olympic medals.

FARMING
The fertile soils and flat landscapes make this region good for farming. The Baltic States, particularly Latvia (left), have large dairy farms. Belarus is a major producer of flax, which is used to make linen and other products. Potatoes (used to make vodka), sugar beet, and other root crops are also grown here.

LITHUANIAN COSTUME
In some Lithuanian villages people wear traditional folk costumes for festive occasions. Women's clothing is generally colorful (left) and might include a white linen shirt, a skirt, and an apron. The decoration and style of the costume shows which region of Lithuania the wearer comes from.

TEXTILES
Lithuania has a strong textile industry, with clothes, bed linen, curtains, and towels made for export. Estonia and Latvia are also famous for their linen products, many beautifully hand-crafted.

RUSSIAN FEDERATION

POLAND

BELARUS

UKRAINE

Vitsyebsk/Vitebsk
Lyozna
Chashniki
Plyeshchanitsy
Krasnaye
Bahushewsk
Byarezina
Barysaw/Borisov
Zhodzina
MINSK
Minskaya Wzvyshsha
Maladzyechna
Orlya
Navahrudak
Byelaruskaya Hrada
Baranavichy/Baranovichi
Masty
Vawkavysk
Zel'va
Slonim
Ruzhany
Ivatsevichy
Navy Dvor
Pruzhany
Zhabinka
Brest
Kobryn
Damachava
Makrany
Bug
Pinsk
Pripet Marshes
Yasyel'da
Drahichyn
Ivanava
Lyusina
Hantsavichy
Salihorsk
Syemyezhava
Kapyl'
Nyasvizh
Stowbtsy
Dzyarzhynsk
Lyakhavichy
Abrova
Haradzyets
Lyusina

Lyntupy
Sharkawshchyna
Hlybokaye
Pastavy
Dokshytsy
Lyepyel'
Sianno
Orsha
Talachyn
Barysaw
Krupki
Byalynichy
Mahilyow/Mogilev
Shklow
Horki
Dribin
Klimavichy
Kastsyukovichy
Baron'ki
Khodasy
Krychaw
Cherykaw
Slawharad
Myerkulavichy
Uvaravichy
Dobrush
Kastsyukowka
Tsyerakhowka
Homyel'/Gomel'
Rechytsa
Loyew
Byal'ki
Dnieper (Dnyapro/Dnepr)
Khoyniki
Narowlya
Mazyr
Yel'sk
Dabryn'
Milashavichy
Lyel'chytsy
Simanichy
Tonyezh
Lyel'chytsy
Petrykaw
Kaptsevichy
Zhytkavichy
Mikashevichy
Staratsin
Staryya Darohi
Asipovichy
Byalynkavichy
Shchadryn
Zhlobin
Buda-Kashalyova
Svyetlahorsk/Svetlogorsk
Kalinkavichy
Shatsilki
Ptsich
Lyuban'
Sluch
Lyuninyets
Bastyn'
Luninyets

0 km   50   100
0 miles   50   100

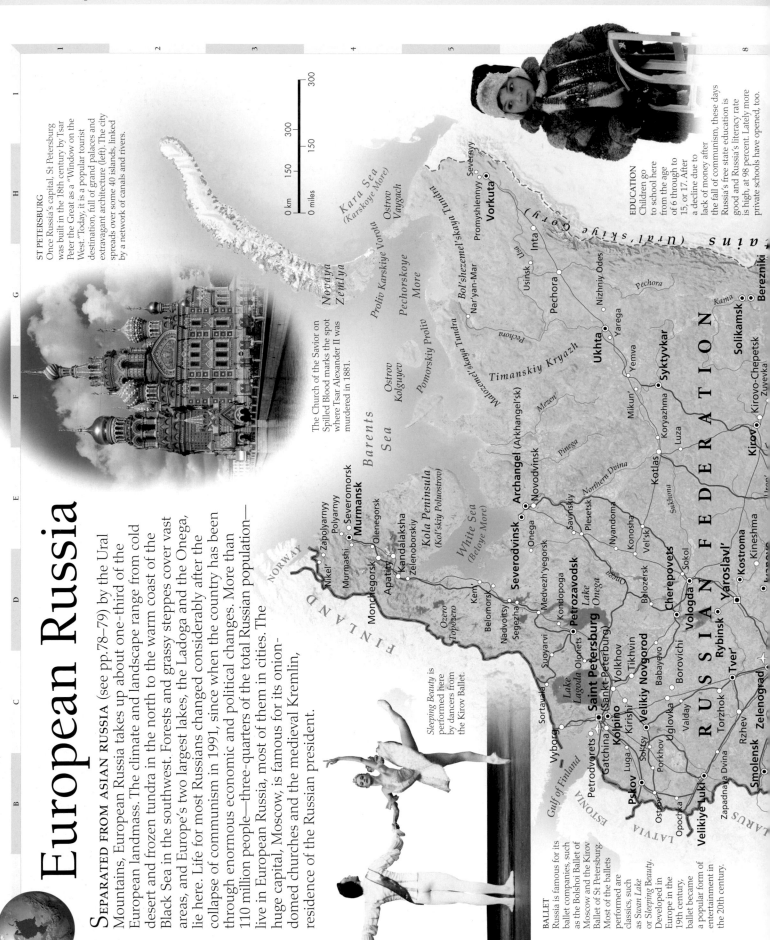

European Russia

SEPARATED FROM ASIAN RUSSIA (see pp.78–79) by the Ural Mountains, European Russia takes up about one-third of the European landmass. The climate and landscape range from cold desert and frozen tundra in the north to the warm coast of the Black Sea in the southwest. Forests and grassy steppes cover vast areas, and Europe's two largest lakes, the Ladoga and the Onega, lie here. Life for most Russians changed considerably after the collapse of communism in 1991, since when the country has been through enormous economic and political changes. More than 110 million people—three-quarters of the total Russian population—live in European Russia, most of them in cities. The huge capital, Moscow, is famous for its onion-domed churches and the medieval Kremlin, residence of the Russian president.

ST PETERSBURG
Once Russia's capital, St Petersburg was built in the 18th century by Tsar Peter the Great as a "Window on the West." Today, it is a popular tourist destination, full of grand palaces and extravagant architecture (left). The city spreads over some 40 islands, linked by a network of canals and rivers.

The Church of the Savior on Spilled Blood marks the spot where Tsar Alexander II was murdered in 1881.

EDUCATION
Children go to school here from the age of 6 through to 15, or 17. After a decline due to lack of money after the fall of communism, these days Russia's free state education is good and Russia's literacy rate is high, at 98 percent. Lately more private schools have opened, too.

BALLET
Russia is famous for its ballet companies, such as the Bolshoi Ballet of Moscow and the Kirov Ballet of St Petersburg. Most of the ballets performed are classics, such as *Swan Lake* or *Sleeping Beauty*. Developed in Europe in the 19th century, ballet became a popular form of entertainment in the 20th century.

Sleeping Beauty is performed here by dancers from the Kirov Ballet.

0 km 150 300
0 miles 150 300

Map labels

Kara Sea (Karskoye More)
Novaya Zemlya
Ostrov Vaygach
Severnyy
Vorkuta
Promyshlennyy
Inta
Usa
Ural Mountains (Ural'skiye Gory)
Usinsk
Nar'yan-Mar
Bol'shezemel'skaya Tundra
Pechora
Nizhniy Odes
Malozemel'skaya Tundra
Pechorskoye More
Proliv Karskiye Vorota
Pomorskiy Proliv
Ostrov Kolguyev
Barents Sea
Pechora
Timanskiy Kryazh
Ukhta
Vorega
Yarega
Yemva
Mikun'
Koryazhma
Luza
Koryazhma
Syktyvkar
Kama
Solikamsk
Berezniki
Mezen
Pinega
Kotlas
Kirovo-Chepetsk
Zuyevka
Kirov
Murmansk
Severomorsk
Olenegorsk
Zapolyarnyy
Polyarnyy
Nikel'
Monchegorsk
Apatity
Kandalaksha
Zelenoborskiy
Kola Peninsula (Kol'skiy Poluostrov)
White Sea (Beloye More)
Kem'
Belomorsk
Onega
Novodvinsk
Archangel (Arkhangel'sk)
Severodvinsk
Savinskiy
Plesetsk
Northern Dvina
Nyandoma
Konosha
Vel'sk
Sukhona
Cherepovets
Sokol
NORWAY
FINLAND
Ozero Topozero
Nadvotsy
Segezha
Medvezh'yegorsk
Kondopoga
Petrozavodsk
Lake Onega
Belozersk
Vologda
Suoyarvi
Olonets
Lake Ladoga
Volkhov
Tikhvin
Babayevo
Onega
Yaroslavl'
Sortavala
Saint Petersburg (Sankt-Peterburg)
Kirishi
Volkhov
Borovichi
Rybinsk
Kostroma
Kineshma
Vyborg
Gulf of Finland
Kolpino
Velikiy Novgorod
Valday
Torzhok
Tver'
Zelenograd
ESTONIA
Petrodvorets
Gatchina
Luga
Soltsy
Uglovka
Rzhev
Pskov
Ostrov
Porkhov
Valday
RUSSIAN FEDERATION
LATVIA
Velikiye Luki
Opochka
Zapadnaya Dvina
Smolensk
BELARUS

RURAL LIFE
Rural life became extremely tough after the collapse of large, state-run farms in the 1990s, and many people lived in poverty. Since then, private-owned, small-scale farms have become more common and productive. Grains—mainly wheat and barley—and sunflower oil are the top agricultural exports.

Icons, common in the Russian Orthodox Church, are religious images painted on wooden panels.

THE TATARS
Russia's largest ethnic minority, the Tatars (below), are an Islamic people descended from the Mongols. Their largest population lives in the Tatarstan Republic, midway between Moscow and the Urals.

The title tsar, or czar, once used for Russian rulers, means "emperor" and comes from the ancient Roman title "Caesar."

THE RUSSIAN CHURCH
The main religion in Russia is the Russian Orthodox Church. Under communism, all religion was banned, and churches and monasteries were left to decay. Today, many of these historic buildings have been restored, and many Russians attend church services regularly.

MOSCOW METRO
Not many underground railways can claim to be tourist attractions, but Moscow's metro can. Built in the 1930s, many of its stations are decorated with beautiful chandeliers, mosaics, paintings, and sculptures. One of the busiest, most efficient metros in the world, it is used by more than 7 million people daily.

POLLUTION
The communists invested heavily in industry, but their outdated methods of production are still affecting the environment. Rivers such as the Volga are badly polluted, and many cities are covered in a permanent and poisonous smog. Chest infections and other diseases related to air pollution are common.

Industrial smog casts a haze over Moscow.

Ural Mts

Belorétsk
Orsk
Novotroitsk
Birsk
Chaykovskiy
Neftekamsk
Naberezhnyye Chelny
Al'met'yevsk
Ufa
Sterlitamak
Salavat
Sibay
Baymak
Saraktash
Oktyabr'skiy
Kazan'
Nizhnekamsk
Kuybyshevskoye
Vodokhranilishche
Bugul'ma
Tol'yatti
Samara
Buguruslan
Buzuluk
Kumertau
Orenburg
Urai
Sol'-Iletsk
Cheboksary
Novocheboksarsk
Kanash
Saransk
Ul'yanovsk
Dimitrovgrad
Syzran'
Chapayevsk
Vol'sk
Balakovo
Kuznetsk
Balashov
Saratov
Krasnyy Kut
Penza
Tambov
Michurinsk
Borisoglebsk
Krasnoarmeysk
Kamyshin
Volzhskiy
Volgograd
Akhtubinsk
Voronezh
Mikhaylovka
Iloviya
Sasovo
Liski
Kantemirovka
Millerovo
Kamensk-Shakhtinskiy
Zimovniki
Astrakhan'
Ryazan'
Novomoskovsk
Tula
Tovarkovskiy
Yefremov
Lipetsk
Gryazi
Shebekino
Rossosh'
Kamensk-Shakhtinskiy
Novocherkassk
Volgodonsk
Sal'sk
Elista
Svetlograd
Prokhladnyy
Groznyy
Khasavyurt
Makhachkala
Kaspiysk
Derbent
Shchëkino
Orël
Yelets
Kursk
Staryy Oskol
Gubkin
Belgorod
Bryansk
Zheleznogorsk
Novoshakhtinsk
Taganrog
Rostov-na-Donu
Starominskaya
Tikhoretsk
Kropotkin
Stavropol'
Cherkessk
Nevinnomyssk
Pyatigorsk
Nal'chik
Vladikavkaz
Novorossiysk
Tuapse
Sochi
Krasnodar
Maykop
Kislovodsk
Buynaksk
El'brus (18,510 ft / 5642m)

UKRAINE
KAZAKHSTAN
GEORGIA
AZERB.
Caucasus

Sea of Azov
Black Sea
Caspian Sea
Caspian Depression
Volga
Don
Donets
Kuma

ASIA

The vast continent of Asia is dominated by two giant nations—China and India, each with more than a billion people and a rich and colorful history. Both are being transformed by rapid economic growth, and so are many other Asian countries, listed below in order of size. Yet in some regions of central Asia life has barely changed in a thousand years.

China
- 🗺 3,705,407 sq miles
  9,596,960 sq km
- 👤 1,373,541,000
- ⬛ Beijing
- 💬 Mandarin, Wu, Cantonese, Hsiang, Min, Hakka, Kan

Iran
- 🗺 636,368 sq miles
  1,648,195 sq km
- 👤 82,801,600
- ⬛ Tehran
- 💬 Farsi, Azeri, Luri, Gilaki, Mazandarani, Kurdish, Turkmen, Arabic, Balochi

Afghanistan
- 🗺 251,826 sq miles
  652,230 sq km
- 👤 33,332,000
- ⬛ Kabul
- 💬 Pashto, Tajik, Dari, Farsi, Uzbek, Turkmen

Iraq
- 🗺 169,234 sq miles
  438,317 sq km
- 👤 38,146,000
- ⬛ Baghdad
- 💬 Arabic, Kurdish, Turkic languages, Armenian, Assyrian

Philippines
- 🗺 115,830 sq miles
  300,000 sq km
- 👤 102,624,000
- ⬛ Manila
- 💬 Filipino, English, Tagalog, Cebuano, Ilocano, Hiligaynon, many other local languages

Nepal
- 🗺 56,827 sq miles
  147,181 sq km
- 👤 29,034,000
- ⬛ Kathmandu
- 💬 Nepali, Maithili, Bhojpuri

India
- 🗺 1,269,212 sq miles
  3,287,263 sq km
- 👤 1,266,884,000
- ⬛ New Delhi
- 💬 Hindi, English, Urdu, Bengali, Marathi, Telugu, Tamil, Bihari, Gujarati, Kannada.

Mongolia
- 🗺 603,905 sq miles
  1,564,116 sq km
- 👤 3,031,000
- ⬛ Ulaanbaatar
- 💬 Khalkha Mongolian, Kazakh, Chinese, Russian

Yemen
- 🗺 203,848 sq miles
  527,968 sq km
- 👤 27,393,000
- ⬛ Sanaak
- 💬 Arabic

Japan
- 🗺 145,913 sq miles
  377,915 sq km
- 👤 126,702,000
- ⬛ Tokyo
- 💬 Japanese, Korean, Chinese

Laos
- 🗺 91,428 sq miles
  236,800 sq km
- 👤 7,019,000
- ⬛ Vientiane
- 💬 Lao, Mon-Khmer, Yao, Vietnamese, Chinese, French

Bangladesh
- 🗺 55,598 sq miles
  143,998 sq km
- 👤 156,187,000
- ⬛ Dhaka
- 💬 Bengali, Urdu, Chakma, Marma (Magh), Garo, Khasi, Santhali, Tripura, Mru

Kazakhstan
- 🗺 1,052,084 sq miles
  2,724,900 sq km
- 👤 18,360,000
- ⬛ Astana
- 💬 Kazakh, Russian, Ukrainian, German, Uzbek, Tatar, Uyghur

Pakistan
- 🗺 307,372 sq miles
  796,095 sq km
- 👤 201,956,000
- ⬛ Islamabad
- 💬 Punjabi, Sindhi, Pashtu, Urdu, Balochi, Brahui

Thailand
- 🗺 198,116 sq miles
  513,120 sq km
- 👤 68,201,000
- ⬛ Bangkok
- 💬 Thai, Chinese, Malay, Khmer, Mon, Karen, Miao

Vietnam
- 🗺 127,880 sq miles
  331,210 sq km
- 👤 95,261,000
- ⬛ Hanoi
- 💬 Vietnamese, Chinese, Thai, Khmer, Muong, Nung, Miao, Yao, Jarai

Kyrgyzstan
- 🗺 77,201 sq miles
  199,951 sq km
- 👤 5,728,000
- ⬛ Bishkek
- 💬 Kyrgyz, Russian, Uzbek, Tatar, Ukrainian

Tajikistan
- 🗺 55,251 sq miles
  143,100 sq km
- 👤 8,331,000
- ⬛ Dushanbe
- 💬 Tajik, Uzbek, Russian

Saudi Arabia
- 🗺 829,995 sq miles
  2,149,690 sq km
- 👤 28,160,000
- ⬛ Riyadh
- 💬 Arabic

Turkey
- 🗺 302,533 sq miles
  783,562 sq km
- 👤 80,275,000
- ⬛ Ankara
- 💬 Turkish, Kurdish, Arabic, Circassian, Armenian, Greek, Georgian, Ladino (Judaeo-Spanish)

Turkmenistan
- 🗺 188,455 sq miles
  488,100 sq km
- 👤 5,291,000
- ⬛ Ashgabat
- 💬 Turkmen, Uzbek, Russian, Kazakh, Tatar

Malaysia
- 🗺 127,354 sq miles
  329,847 sq km
- 👤 30,950,000
- ⬛ Kuala Lumpur
- 💬 Bahasa Malaysia, Malay, Chinese, Tamil, English

Syria
- 🗺 71,498 sq miles
  185,180 sq km
- 👤 17,185,000
- ⬛ Damascus
- 💬 Arabic, French, Kurdish, Armenian, Circassian, Turkic languages, Assyrian, Aramaic

North Korea
- 🗺 46,540 sq miles
  120,538 sq km
- 👤 25,115,000
- ⬛ Pyongyang
- 💬 Korean

Indonesia
- 🗺 735,354 sq miles
  1,904,569 sq km
- 👤 258,316,000
- ⬛ Jakarta
- 💬 Javanese, Sundanese, Madurese, Bahasa Indonesia, Dutch

Myanmar (Burma)
- 🗺 261,227 sq miles
  676,578 sq km
- 👤 56,890,000
- ⬛ Nay Pyi Taw
- 💬 Burmese, Shan, Karen, Rakhine (Arakanese), Chin, Yangbye, Kachin, Mon

Uzbekistan
- 🗺 172,741 sq miles
  447,400 sq km
- 👤 29,474,000
- ⬛ Tashkent
- 💬 Uzbek, Russian, Tajik, Kazakh

Oman
- 🗺 119,498 sq miles
  309,500 sq km
- 👤 3,355,000
- ⬛ Muscat
- 💬 Arabic, Balochi, Farsi, Hindi, Punjabi

Cambodia
- 🗺 69,898 sq miles
  181,035 sq km
- 👤 15,957,000
- ⬛ Phnom Penh
- 💬 Khmer, French, Chinese, Vietnamese, Cham

South Korea
- 🗺 38,502 sq miles
  99,720 sq km
- 👤 50,924,000
- ⬛ Seoul
- 💬 Korean

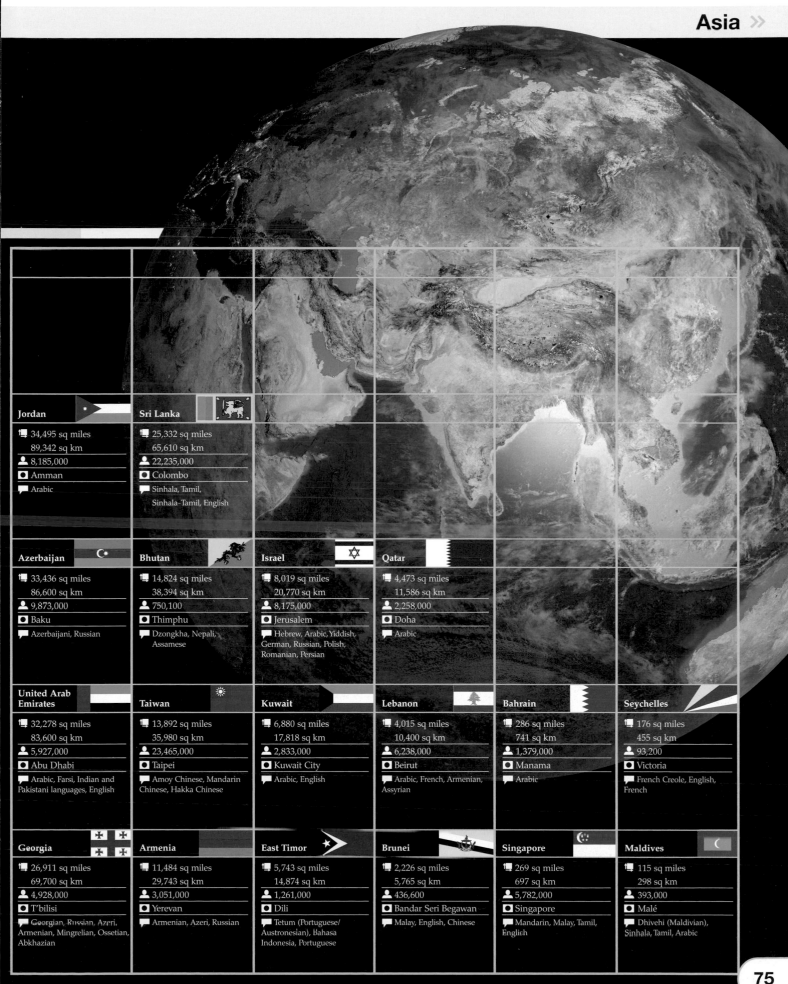

Jordan
- 34,495 sq miles
- 89,342 sq km
- 8,185,000
- Amman
- Arabic

Sri Lanka
- 25,332 sq miles
- 65,610 sq km
- 22,235,000
- Colombo
- Sinhala, Tamil, Sinhala-Tamil, English

Azerbaijan
- 33,436 sq miles
- 86,600 sq km
- 9,873,000
- Baku
- Azerbaijani, Russian

Bhutan
- 14,824 sq miles
- 38,394 sq km
- 750,100
- Thimphu
- Dzongkha, Nepali, Assamese

Israel
- 8,019 sq miles
- 20,770 sq km
- 8,175,000
- Jerusalem
- Hebrew, Arabic, Yiddish, German, Russian, Polish, Romanian, Persian

Qatar
- 4,473 sq miles
- 11,586 sq km
- 2,258,000
- Doha
- Arabic

United Arab Emirates
- 32,278 sq miles
- 83,600 sq km
- 5,927,000
- Abu Dhabi
- Arabic, Farsi, Indian and Pakistani languages, English

Taiwan
- 13,892 sq miles
- 35,980 sq km
- 23,465,000
- Taipei
- Amoy Chinese, Mandarin Chinese, Hakka Chinese

Kuwait
- 6,880 sq miles
- 17,818 sq km
- 2,833,000
- Kuwait City
- Arabic, English

Lebanon
- 4,015 sq miles
- 10,400 sq km
- 6,238,000
- Beirut
- Arabic, French, Armenian, Assyrian

Bahrain
- 286 sq miles
- 741 sq km
- 1,379,000
- Manama
- Arabic

Seychelles
- 176 sq miles
- 455 sq km
- 93,200
- Victoria
- French Creole, English, French

Georgia
- 26,911 sq miles
- 69,700 sq km
- 4,928,000
- T'bilisi
- Georgian, Russian, Azeri, Armenian, Mingrelian, Ossetian, Abkhazian

Armenia
- 11,484 sq miles
- 29,743 sq km
- 3,051,000
- Yerevan
- Armenian, Azeri, Russian

East Timor
- 5,743 sq miles
- 14,874 sq km
- 1,261,000
- Dili
- Tetum (Portuguese/Austronesian), Bahasa Indonesia, Portuguese

Brunei
- 2,226 sq miles
- 5,765 sq km
- 436,600
- Bandar Seri Begawan
- Malay, English, Chinese

Singapore
- 269 sq miles
- 697 sq km
- 5,782,000
- Singapore
- Mandarin, Malay, Tamil, English

Maldives
- 115 sq miles
- 298 sq km
- 393,000
- Malé
- Dhivehi (Maldivian), Sinhala, Tamil, Arabic

Turkey and the Caucasus

TURKEY LIES IN BOTH ASIA and Europe—separated by the Bosphorus—and was once part of the powerful Ottoman Empire. Although the population is 99 percent Muslim, modern Turkey is a country with no official religion. Western Turkey is relatively industrialized, with a tourist industry along the Mediterranean coast that brings in considerable income. Many farmers and herders in the center and east, however, struggle to make a living in the arid environment. To the northeast lie the Caucasus countries of Georgia, Azerbaijan, and Armenia. Once part of the USSR, they are now independent.

ISTANBUL
The different faces of Turkey can be seen in its former capital, Istanbul, which lies on both sides of the Bosphorus waterway. Churches, mosques, and ancient buildings in both European and Islamic styles sit side by side with modern shops and offices. Bridges link the two parts of the city. In 1923, Ankara became the new capital.

TURKISH FOOD
Turkey is self-sufficient in food and grows specialized crops such as eggplants, peppers, figs, and dates. A typical Turkish meal might consist of spiced lamb, often grilled on a skewer with onion and tomato to make a *shish kebab*. This would be served with rice or cracked wheat.

EPHESUS
Tourism is one of Turkey's major industries. As well as beach resorts, the country has many ancient sites. One of these is the old Greek city of Ephesus, which lies 35 miles (56 km) south of modern-day Izmir on the Aegean coast. The city was famous for its Temple of Artemis, which was considered one of the seven wonders of the world.

Visitors to Ephesus admiring the remains of the Library of Celsus

FATHER OF THE TURKS
Mustafa Kemal Atatürk (1881–1938), founder of the modern Turkish state, became its first president in 1923. He introduced many reforms, including more equality for women and better education for all. He also declared that Islam was no longer to be the official religion.

BULGARIA
GREECE
Edirne
Kırklareli
Ekene Çayi
Çorlu
Tekirdağ
İstanbul
Bosphorus (İstanbul Boğazı)
Zonguldak
İnebolu
Cide
Sinop
Gerze
Bartın
Küre Dağları
Bafra
Samsun
Kastamonu
Karabük
Kargı
Devrek
Çerkeş
Canik Dağları
İzmit
Adapazarı
Merzifon
Yalova
Gerede
Bolu
Çankırı
Sea of Marmara (Marmara Denizi)
İznik Gölü
Çorum
Bandırma
Çanakkale
Bilecik
Kızıl Irmak
Alaca
Tokat
Dardanelles (Çanakkale Boğazı)
Bursa
ANKARA
Kalecik
Yıldızeli
Bozüyük
Eskişehir
Balıkesir
Ayvalık
Kırıkkale
Edremit
Kütahya
Polatlı
Hırfanlı Barajı
Boğazlıyan
Şarkışla
Simav
Gediz
Kulu
Akhisar
T   U   R
Manisa
Uşak
Afyon
Cihanbeyli
Lake Tuz (Tuz Gölü)
Nevşehir
İncesu
Bünyan
Gürün
Menemen
Gediz Nehri
Kayseri
İzmir
Akşehir
Aksaray
Ödemiş
Alaşehir
Nazilli
Dinar
Anatolia
Göksun
Aydın
Söke
Büyükmenderes Nehri
Denizli
Beyşehir Gölü
Konya
Niğde
Gün
Milas
Tavas
Burdur
İsparta
Ereğli
Kahramanmaraş
Muğla
Burdur Gölü
Karaman
Bodrum
Taurus Mountains (Toros Dağları)
Ceyhan
Gaziant
Marmaris
Dalaman
Antalya
Manavgat
Tarsus
Adana
Osmaniye
Fethiye
Alanya
Mut
Mersin (İçel)
İskenderun
Kaş
Finike
Silifke
Antakya
Kırıkhan
Antalya Körfezi
Anamur
Mediterranean Sea
TURKISH REPUBLIC OF NORTHERN CYPRUS (recognized only by Turkey)
CYPRUS

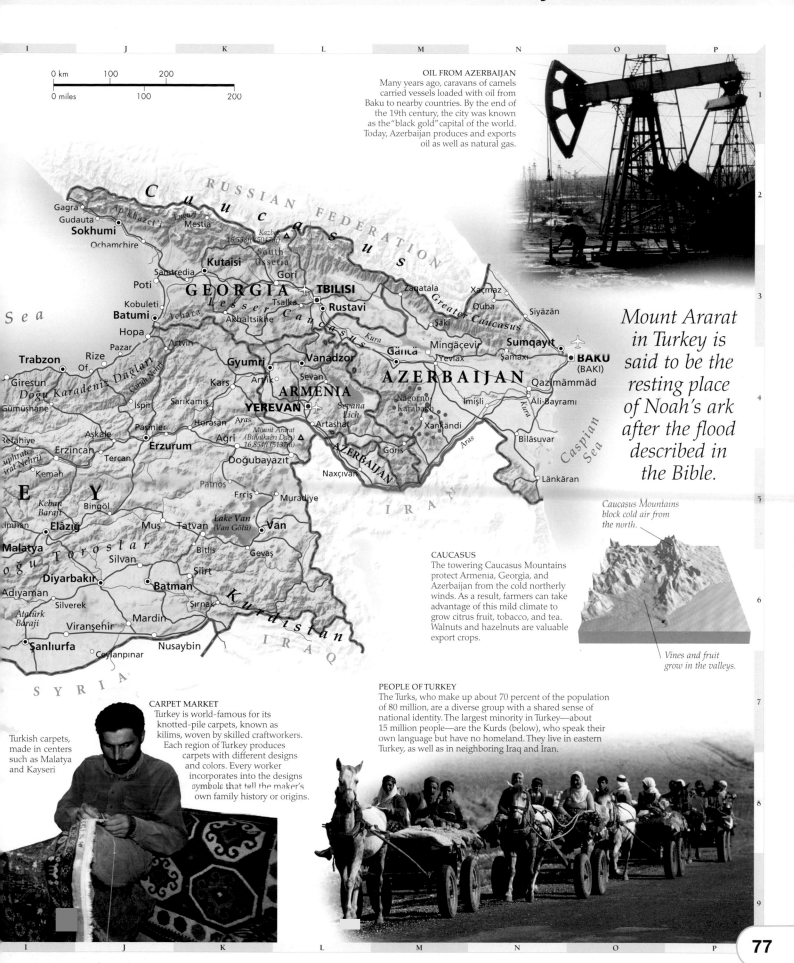

0 km 100 200

0 miles 100 200

OIL FROM AZERBAIJAN
Many years ago, caravans of camels carried vessels loaded with oil from Baku to nearby countries. By the end of the 19th century, the city was known as the "black gold" capital of the world. Today, Azerbaijan produces and exports oil as well as natural gas.

Mount Ararat in Turkey is said to be the resting place of Noah's ark after the flood described in the Bible.

Caucasus Mountains block cold air from the north.

CAUCASUS
The towering Caucasus Mountains protect Armenia, Georgia, and Azerbaijan from the cold northerly winds. As a result, farmers can take advantage of this mild climate to grow citrus fruit, tobacco, and tea. Walnuts and hazelnuts are valuable export crops.

Vines and fruit grow in the valleys.

PEOPLE OF TURKEY
The Turks, who make up about 70 percent of the population of 80 million, are a diverse group with a shared sense of national identity. The largest minority in Turkey—about 15 million people—are the Kurds (below), who speak their own language but have no homeland. They live in eastern Turkey, as well as in neighboring Iraq and Iran.

CARPET MARKET
Turkey is world-famous for its knotted-pile carpets, known as kilims, woven by skilled craftworkers. Each region of Turkey produces carpets with different designs and colors. Every worker incorporates into the designs symbols that tell the maker's own family history or origins.

Turkish carpets, made in centers such as Malatya and Kayseri

Russia and Kazakhstan

THE RUSSIAN FEDERATION is the biggest country in the world, almost twice as big as either the US or China. It extends halfway around the world, crosses two continents, and spans 11 time zones. The vast region of Siberia alone is larger than Canada. Kazakhstan lies to its south and is a large but sparsely populated country. From 1917 to 1991, both countries were part of the Union of Soviet Socialist Republics (USSR), the world's first communist state. When the USSR collapsed, Russia, Kazakhstan, and the 13 other member republics gained independence. Today, Russia and Kazakhstan are both ruled by elected presidents. Both countries have a lot of fertile land, huge mineral deposits, and many other natural resources. However, Russia still has a very low life expectancy rate compared to other industrialized countries.

Lake Baikal is up to 6,365 ft (1,940 m) deep and contains more than 20 percent of the world's freshwater supply.

KAZAKH CULTURE
The majority of people in Kazakhstan are Kazakh Muslims. They were once a nomadic people who traveled around on horseback, herding their sheep. Although about half of the Kazakhs live in rural areas, retaining a strong loyalty to their clans and families, the city of Almaty and the new, modern capital of Astana are growing quickly, due to wealth generated by oil and gas.

Kazakh man hunting with a trained golden eagle

Coal miners in Siberia

NATURAL WEALTH
Siberia contains around a quarter of the world's natural gas reserves and has vast deposits of oil, as well as abundant minerals such as coal and precious metals including gold. However, many of these resources are inaccessible or in remote places, and the extreme winters make it difficult to extract them.

Map labels

0 km 400 800
0 miles 400 800

Franz Josef Land

North Cape (Nordkapp)

ARCTIC

Barents Sea

Murmansk
Kandalaksha
Kola Peninsula
Novaja Zemlya
Kara Sea (Karskoye More)
Ostrov Kolguyev
Ostrov Bely
Diks

FINLAND
Gulf of Finland
LAT.
EST.
Saint Petersburg (Sankt-Peterburg)
Lake Ladoga
Petrozavodsk
Lake Onega
Severodvinsk
Arkhangel'sk
BELARUS
Pskov
Velikiy Novgorod
White Sea
Nar'yan-Mar
Smolensk
Cherepovets
Vel'sk
Severnaya Dvina
Pechora
Ukhta
Vorkuta
MOSCOW (MOSKVA)
Tver'
Vologda
Kotlas
Syktyvkar
Salekhard
Taln
Noril'
UKRAINE
Bryansk
Yaroslavl'
Kineshma
Ob'
Nadym
Igarka
Tula
Vladimir
Nizhniy Novgorod
Yamal Peninsula
Obskaya Guba
Belgorod
Ryazan
Kirov
Glazov
Solikamsk
Nyagan'
Tuz
Yenisey
Voronezh
Tambov
Kazan'
Izhevsk
Perm'
Serov
West Siberian Plain
Penza
Ul'yanovsk
Khanty-Mansiysk
Rostov-na-Donu
Saratov
Naberezhnyye Chelny
Yekaterinburg
Surgut
Nizhnevartovsk
Tol'yatti
Samara
Tyumen'
RUSSIA
Black Sea
Krasnodar
Volgograd
Sterlitamak
Ufa
Chelyabinsk
Tobol'sk
Ob'
Sochi
Stavropol'
Ural Mountains
Magnitogorsk
Orsk
Kostanay
Petropavlovsk
Omsk
Tomsk
Elbrus 18,510ft (5642m)
Nal'chik
Astrakhan'
Orenburg
Ishim
Irtysh
St
Ural
Ural'sk
Rudnyy
Novosibirsk
Krasnoya
Vladikavkaz
Atyrau
Aktobe (Aktyubinsk)
Alga
Kokshetau
Kemerov
Groznyy
Makhachkala
Fort-Shevchenko
Emba
Atbasar
Shchuchinsk
GEORGIA
AZERBAIJAN
Caspian Sea
Aktau
Chelkar
ASTANA
Novokuznetsk
Zhanaozen
KAZAKHSTAN
Temirtau
Pavlodar
Barnaul
Aba
Aral'sk
Novokazalinsk
Saran'
Karagandy
Semey
TURKMENISTAN
Ustyurt Plateau
Aral Sea
Syr Darya
Zhosaly
Zhezkazgan
Kazakh Uplands
Shar
Ridder
Zyryanovsk
Kyzylorda
Ust'-Kamenogorsk
Ozero Zaysan
Kyzyl Kum
Turkistan
Kentau
Balkhash
Ayaguz
Altai Mountain
UZBEKISTAN
Arys
Karatau
Lake Balkhash
Gora Belukha (450
Shymkent
Shu
Taldykorgan
CHINA
Kirghiz Range
Taraz
Tekeli
KYRGYZSTAN
Almaty (Alma-Ata)

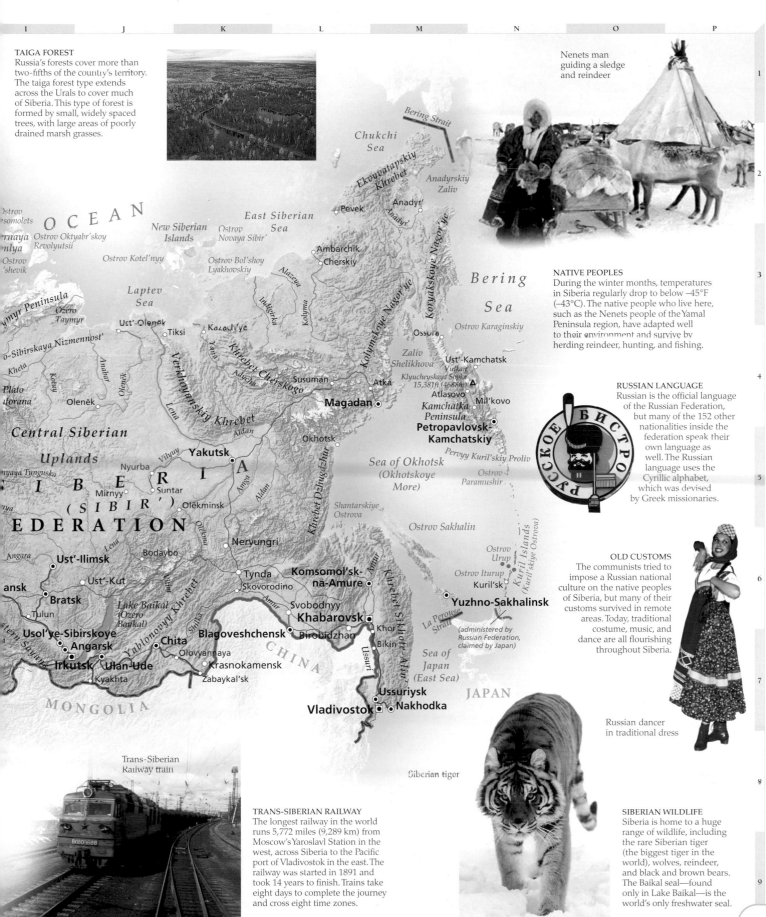

TAIGA FOREST
Russia's forests cover more than two-fifths of the country's territory. The taiga forest type extends across the Urals to cover much of Siberia. This type of forest is formed by small, widely spaced trees, with large areas of poorly drained marsh grasses.

Nenets man guiding a sledge and reindeer

NATIVE PEOPLES
During the winter months, temperatures in Siberia regularly drop to below –45°F (–43°C). The native people who live here, such as the Nenets people of the Yamal Peninsula region, have adapted well to their environment and survive by herding reindeer, hunting, and fishing.

RUSSIAN LANGUAGE
Russian is the official language of the Russian Federation, but many of the 152 other nationalities inside the federation speak their own language as well. The Russian language uses the Cyrillic alphabet, which was devised by Greek missionaries.

OLD CUSTOMS
The communists tried to impose a Russian national culture on the native peoples of Siberia, but many of their customs survived in remote areas. Today, traditional costume, music, and dance are all flourishing throughout Siberia.

Russian dancer in traditional dress

Siberian tiger

Trans-Siberian Railway train

TRANS-SIBERIAN RAILWAY
The longest railway in the world runs 5,772 miles (9,289 km) from Moscow's Yaroslavl Station in the west, across Siberia to the Pacific port of Vladivostok in the east. The railway was started in 1891 and took 14 years to finish. Trains take eight days to complete the journey and cross eight time zones.

SIBERIAN WILDLIFE
Siberia is home to a huge range of wildlife, including the rare Siberian tiger (the biggest tiger in the world), wolves, reindeer, and black and brown bears. The Baikal seal—found only in Lake Baikal—is the world's only freshwater seal.

Map labels:

OCEAN

Ostrov Komsomolets
rnaya nlya
Ostrov 'shevik
Ostrov Oktyabr'skoy Revolyutsii

Chukchi Sea

Bering Strait

East Siberian Sea

New Siberian Islands

Ostrov Novaya Sibir'

Ostrov Kotel'nyy

Ostrov Bol'shoy Lyakhovskiy

Laptev Sea

ymyr Peninsula
Ozero Taymyr

o-Sibirskaya Nizmennost'

Kheta

Ekoyvatapskiy Khrebet

Pevek

Anadyrskiy Zaliv

Anadyr'

Ambarchik
Cherskiy

Alazeya
Indigirka
Kolyma

Koryakskoye Nagor'ye

Bering Sea

Ossora

Ostrov Karaginskiy

Central Siberian Uplands

Plato Iorana

Kotuy
Anabar
Olenëk
Olenëk

Nyaya Tunguska

Ust'-Olenëk
Tiksi
Kazach'ye

Yana
Adycha
Aldan

Khrebet Cherskogo

Verkhoyanskiy Khrebet

Susuman

Atka

Zaliv Shelikhova

Ust'-Kamchatsk

Vulkan Klyucheyskaya Sopka 15,381ft (4688m) △

Atlasovo
Mil'kovo

Magadan

Okhotsk

Kamchatka Peninsula

Petropavlovsk-Kamchatskiy

S I B E R I A

(S I B I R')

Yakutsk
Nyurba
Vilyuy
Anga
Suntar
Lena
Aldan

Mirnyy
Olëkminsk

Pervyy Kuril'skiy Proliv

Sea of Okhotsk (Okhotskoye More)

Ostrov Paramushir

F E D E R A T I O N

Angara

Neryungri

Shantarskiye Ostrova

Ostrov Sakhalin

Ust'-Ilimsk

Bodaybo

Olëkma

Ost rov Urup

Ust'-Kut

ansk

Tynda
Skovorodino

Amur

Kuril Islands (Kuril'skiye Ostrova)

Bratsk
Tulun

Lake Baikal (Ozero Baykal)

Svobodnyy

Khrebet Sikhote Alin

Ostrov Iturup
Kuril'sk

Komsomol'sk-na-Amure

Usol'ye-Sibirskoye
Angarsk
Irkutsk
Ulan-Ude
Kyakhta

Yablonovyy Khrebet

Shilka

Chita

Olovyannaya

Krasnokamensk

Zabaykal'sk

Khabarovsk

Birobidzhan

Blagoveshchensk

Amur

Khor

Bikin

Ussuri

Yuzhno-Sakhalinsk

La Perouse Strait

(administered by Russian Federation, claimed by Japan)

Sea of Japan (East Sea)

JAPAN

C H I N A

stern Sayans

MONGOLIA

Ussuriysk

Vladivostok
Nakhodka

The Near East

ISRAEL, JORDAN, SYRIA, AND LEBANON are the countries collectively known as the Near East. This is a land that is dominated by desert but also has fertile coastal plains. Lack of water is a constant problem here, although Israel has introduced computerized irrigation systems to extend the land suitable for agriculture. The creation of the Jewish state of Israel in 1948, in what was previously Arab-dominated Palestine, has led to almost continuous conflict in the region. Lately, the devastating civil war in Syria has added more tension in the whole Near and Middle East region.

The map on Cyprus's flag is copper-colored because Cyprus means "island of copper."

SYRIAN MARKET
Damascus is one of the oldest inhabited cities in the world. At its center is a massive souk (bazaar), full of stalls and small shops selling everything from carpets, textiles, and jewelery to household goods and fresh produce.

DAILY LIFE
Even during war or conflicts, people try to continue to live as normally as possible, although it might be difficult to get food or go to school. These Palestinian boys enjoy a game of football in the street.

LEBANON REBUILT
Beirut, the capital of Lebanon, was once the commercial and banking center of the Arab world, but was devastated by the civil war that ravaged the country from 1975 to the early 1990s. Today, Beirut has regained some of its former glory. But Lebanon remains unstable, and is still dominated by its two powerful neighbors—Syria and Israel.

CYPRUS
Cyprus became independent from Britain in 1960. However, conflict between Greeks and Turks caused Turkey to invade the island in 1974. Since then, Cyprus has been split between a Turkish Cypriot north and a Greek Cypriot south. Most Cypriots make a living from farming grapes, citrus fruit, and olives, but tourism makes up a big part of the economy.

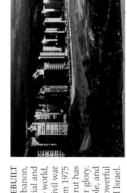

Woman making a lace-item to sell to tourists

Map labels

Tigris

IRAQ

Al Mālikīyah
Al Qāmishlī
Al Jazīrah
Al Ḩasakah
Ash Shadādah
Aş Şuwār
Al Manāşif
Subaykhān
Abū Ḩajdān
Abū Kamāl

Ra's al 'Ayn
Jabal 'Abd al 'Azīz
Buşayrah
Al Mayādīn
Al 'Ashārah

TURKEY

At Tall al Abyaḑ
Ar Raqqah
As Sabkhah
Euphrates
Dayr az Zawr
At Tibnī
Jabal Bishrī
As Suknah

Jarābulus
Euphrates
Manbij
Lake Assad (Buḩayrat al Asad)
Nahr Balīkh
Sabkhat al Jabbūl
Madīnat ath Thawrah

Tudmur (Palmyra)

SYRIA

A'zāz
Al Bāb
Aleppo (Halab)
Abū aḑ Ḑuhūr
Ma'arrat an Nu'mān
Salamiyah
Ar Rāmī

Afrin
Ḩārim
Idlib
Arīḩā
Ḩamāh
Ḩimş (Homs)
Al Qusayr
Al Barīdah

Jibāl as Sāḩilīyah
Mazyaf
Tall Kalakh
Qoubaiyāt
Jebel Liban

Latakia (Al Lādhiqīyah)
Jablah
Bāniyās
Ţarţūs
El Mina
Tripoli
Batroûn

Mediterranean Sea

Agialoúsa (Yenierenköy)
TURKISH REPUBLIC OF NORTHERN CYPRUS (recognized only by Turkey)
Ammóchostos (Gazimağusa) (Famagusta)
Sovereign Base Area (to UK)

Lápithos (Lapta)
Kerýneia (Girne)
Kythréa (Değirmenlik)
Deftera
Lárnaka
CYPRUS

Morfoú (Güzelyurt)
NICOSIA
Sovereign Base Area (to UK)
CYPRUS
Limassol

Pólis
Tróodos
Páfos
Sovereign Base Area (to UK)

Scale bar

100
100
50
50
0 km
0 miles

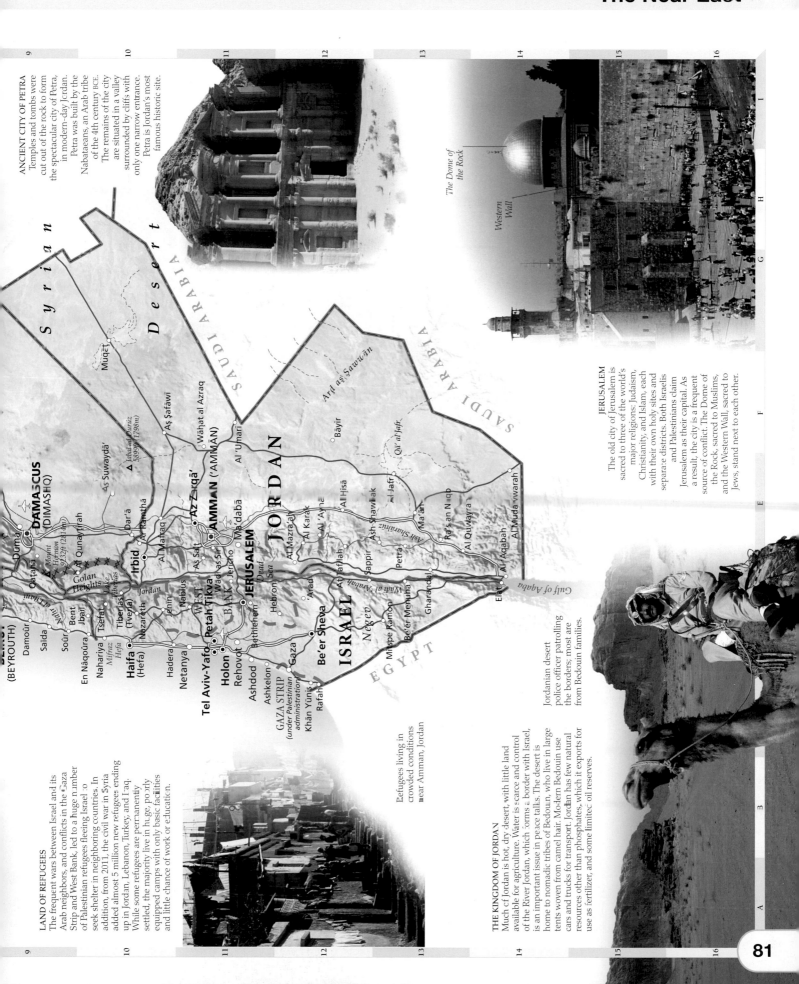

ANCIENT CITY OF PETRA
Temples and tombs were cut out of the rock to form the spectacular city of Petra, in modern-day Jordan. Petra was built by the Nabataeans, an Arab tribe of the 4th century BCE. The remains of the city are situated in a valley surrounded by cliffs with only one narrow entrance. Petra is Jordan's most famous historic site.

The Dome of the Rock

Western Wall

JERUSALEM
The old city of Jerusalem is sacred to three of the world's major religions: Judaism, Christianity, and Islam, each with their own holy sites and separate districts. Both Israelis and Palestinians claim Jerusalem as their capital. As a result, the city is a frequent source of conflict. The Dome of the Rock, sacred to Muslims, and the Western Wall, sacred to Jews, stand next to each other.

Jordanian desert police officer patrolling the borders; most are from Bedouin families.

LAND OF REFUGEES
The frequent wars between Israel and its Arab neighbors, and conflicts in the Gaza Strip and West Bank, led to a huge number of Palestinian refugees fleeing Israel to seek shelter in neighboring countries. In addition, from 2011, the civil war in Syria added almost 5 million new refugees ending up in Jordan, Lebanon, Turkey, and Iraq. While some refugees are permanently settled, the majority live in huge, poorly equipped camps with only basic facilities and little chance of work or education.

Refugees living in crowded conditions near Amman, Jordan

THE KINGDOM OF JORDAN
Much of Jordan is hot, dry desert, with little land available for agriculture. Water is scarce and control of the River Jordan, which forms a border with Israel, is an important issue in peace talks. The desert is home to nomadic tribes of Bedouin, who live in large tents woven from camel hair. Modern Bedouin use cars and trucks for transport. Jordan has few natural resources other than phosphates, which it exports for use as fertilizer, and some limited oil reserves.

The Middle East

THE MIDDLE EAST IS HOME to the world's oldest civilizations, which grew up in the Tigris and Euphrates river valleys of present-day Iraq more than 6,000 years ago. The world's first towns and cities were built here. Since then, many powerful empires have dominated the region, all leaving a wealth of buildings and monuments behind them. Today, the Middle East is at the center of the Islamic world. The population of every country is Arab and speaks Arabic, except Iran, where half the population are Farsi-speaking Persians.

DESERT WARS
Most international boundaries in the Middle East were drawn by the former European colonial powers, and have often caused conflict. Iraq and Iran fought a bitter eight-year war along their common border from 1980. Since then, further conflicts between Iraq and international forces, as well as against the so-called "Islamic State" terrorist organization, have caused much suffering here.

ROLE OF WOMEN
Family life is important throughout the Muslim world. The role of women varies from country to country—traditionally, women stay at home and look after the family, but some now work. In public, many cover their head with a hijab, or whole body with a burqa.

THE IRANIANS
About half the total population of Iran are Persians, who live in the center and north of the country. Large numbers of Azeris live in the northwest, while Kurds live in the west and Baluchis in the southeast. The official language of Iran is Farsi, but many other languages are also spoken.

The Persian language is written in Arabic script

OIL PRODUCTION
The Middle East is the world's major oil producer—Saudi Arabia alone produces more than 12 percent of the world's supply. Oil has brought great wealth to the region, in particular to Saudi Arabia and the Gulf States.

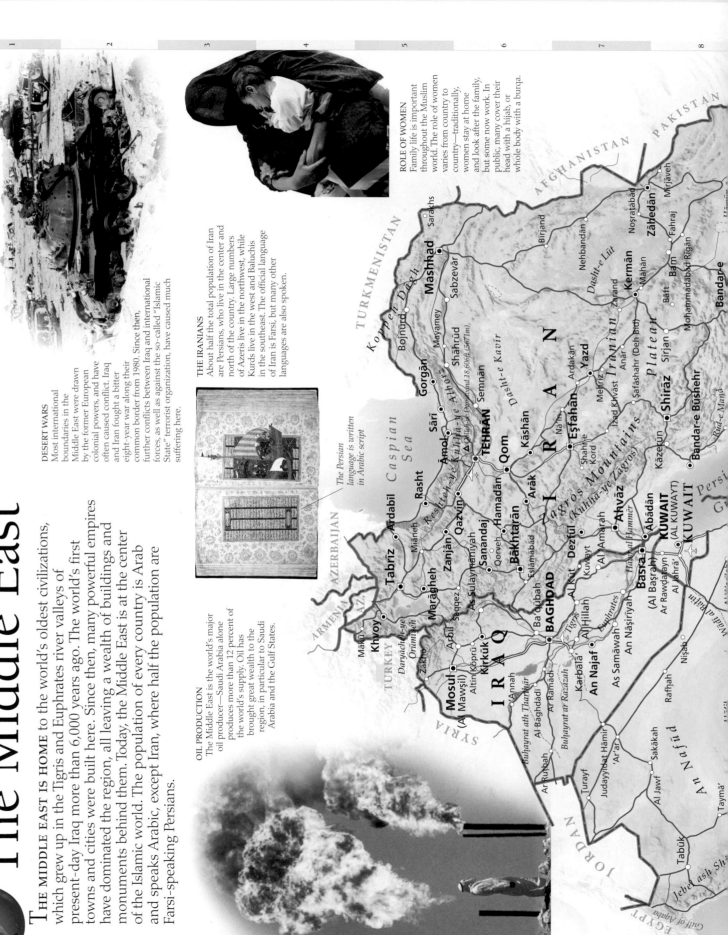

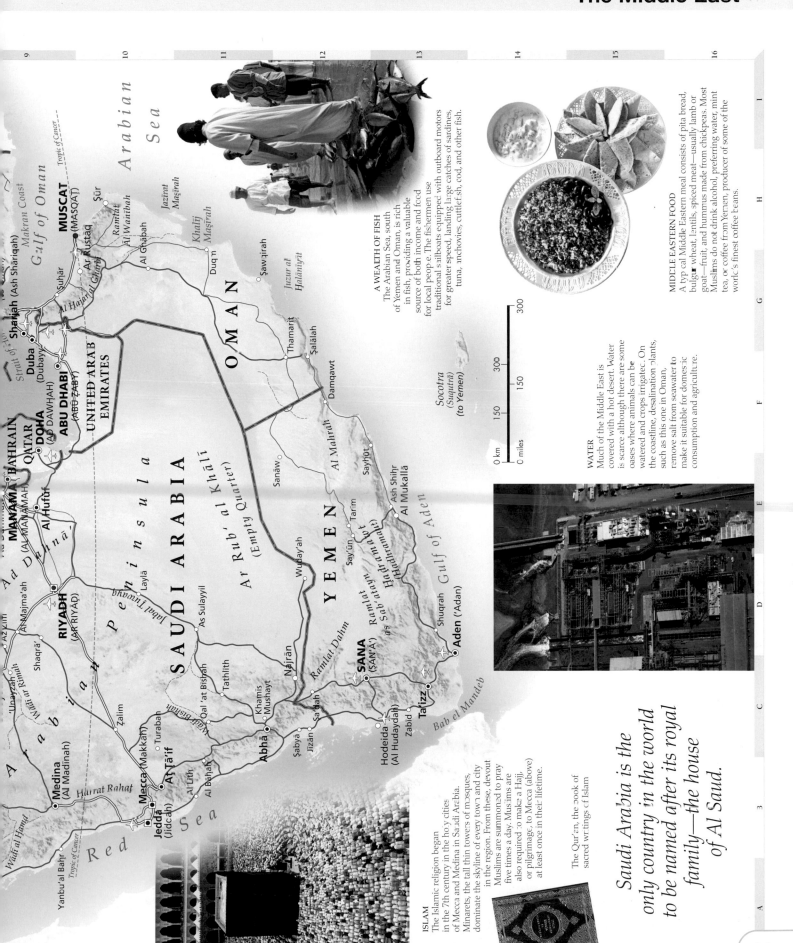

A WEALTH OF FISH
The Arabian Sea, south of Yemen and Oman, is rich in fish, providing a valuable source of both income and food for local people. The fishermen use traditional sailboats equipped with outboard motors for greater speed, landing large catches of sardines, tuna, anchovies, cuttlefish, cod, and other fish.

MIDDLE EASTERN FOOD
A typical Middle Eastern meal consists of pita bread, bulgur wheat, lentils, spiced meat—usually lamb or goat—fruit, and hummus made from chickpeas. Most Muslims do not drink alcohol, preferring water, mint tea, or coffee from Yemen, producer of some of the world's finest coffee beans.

WATER
Much of the Middle East is covered with a hot desert. Water is scarce although there are some oases where animals can be watered and crops irrigated. On the coastline, desalination plants, such as this one in Oman, remove salt from seawater to make it suitable for domestic consumption and agriculture.

ISLAM
The Islamic religion began in the 7th century in the holy cities of Mecca and Medina in Saudi Arabia. Minarets, the tall thin towers of mosques, dominate the skyline of every town and city in the region. From these, devout Muslims are summoned to pray five times a day. Muslims are also required to make a Hajj, or pilgrimage, to Mecca (above) at least once in their lifetime.

The Qur'an, the book of sacred writings of Islam

Saudi Arabia is the only country in the world to be named after its royal family—the house of Al Saud.

Map labels

Arabian Sea
Gulf of Oman
Makran Coast (Ash Shāriqah)
Strait of Hormuz
Tropic of Cancer

MUSCAT (MASQAT)
Ar Rustāq
Şūr
Al Ghābah
Ramlat Al Wahībah
Jazīrat Maşīrah
Khalīj Maşīrah
Şawqirah
Thamarīt
Şalālah
Thamarīt
Damqawt
Al Mahrah
Juzur al Halānīyāt
Socotra (Suquţrā) (to Yemen)

OMAN

Sharjah (Ash Shāriqah)
Şuḩār
Al Hajar al Gharbī
Duba (Dubayy)
ABU DHABI (ABŪ ZABY)
UNITED ARAB EMIRATES
Al Ghābah

BAHRAIN
MANAMA (AL MANĀMAH)
QATAR
DOHA (AD DAWḨAH)
Al Ḩufūf

SAUDI ARABIA

Ad Dahnā'
Arabian Peninsula
Ar Rub' al Khālī (Empty Quarter)
Al Mahrah
Sayḩūt
Ash Shiḩr
Al Mukallā
Gulf of Aden
Bab el Mandeb

Sanāw
Ḩaḑramawt
Ramlat as Sab'atayn
Ramlat Daḩm
Wuḑayʻah
Tarīm
Say'ūn

YEMEN

SANA (ṢAN'Ā')
Ta'izz
Aden ('Adan)
Shuqrah
Zabīd
Hodeida (Al Ḩudaydah)
Sa'dah
Khamīs Mushayt
Najrān
As Sulayyil
Tathlīth
Qal'at Bīshah
Abhā
Şabyā
Jīzān
Al Baḩḩ
Al Lith
Al Birk

Wādī Bīshah
Jabal Tuwayq
Layla
Al Majma'ah
RIYADH (AR RIYĀḌ)
Shaqrā'
Az Zulfī
'Unayzah
Wādī ar Rimah
Zalim
Turabah
At Ţā'if
Mecca (Makkah)
Medina (Al Madīnah)
Ḩurrat Raḩat
Jedda (Jidcah)
Yanbuʻ al Baḩr
Wādī al Ḩamḑ
Tropic of Cancer

Red Sea

Scale
0 km   150   300
0 miles 150 300

Central Asia

THE FIVE CENTRAL ASIAN NATIONS rise up from hot deserts in the west and south to cold, high mountain ranges in the east. The area has oil, gas, and mineral reserves, as well as other natural resources, but water is often scarce and agriculture is limited. The four northern nations were once part of the Soviet Union and are now independent nations. Afghanistan is a landlocked country and three-quarters of its land is inaccessible terrain. It was invaded by the Soviet Union in 1979, prompting a continuous series of civil wars. The 2001 invasion by American and other Western forces overthrew the fundamentalist Islamic regime and led to democratic presidential elections, but Afghanistan is still unstable. Wrecked by more than 30 years of warfare, it is one of the poorest and most deprived nations on Earth.

One of the world's largest gold mines is at Muruntau in the Kyzyl Kum desert in Uzbekistan.

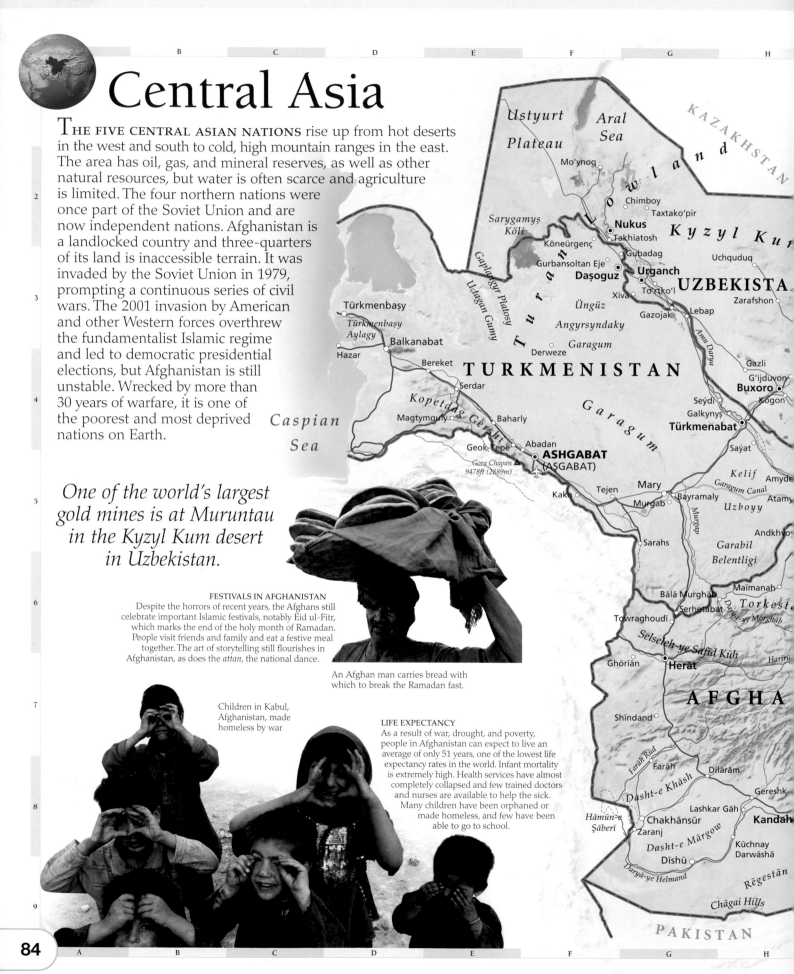

FESTIVALS IN AFGHANISTAN
Despite the horrors of recent years, the Afghans still celebrate important Islamic festivals, notably Eid ul-Fitr, which marks the end of the holy month of Ramadan. People visit friends and family and eat a festive meal together. The art of storytelling still flourishes in Afghanistan, as does the *attan*, the national dance.

An Afghan man carries bread with which to break the Ramadan fast.

Children in Kabul, Afghanistan, made homeless by war

LIFE EXPECTANCY
As a result of war, drought, and poverty, people in Afghanistan can expect to live an average of only 51 years, one of the lowest life expectancy rates in the world. Infant mortality is extremely high. Health services have almost completely collapsed and few trained doctors and nurses are available to help the sick. Many children have been orphaned or made homeless, and few have been able to go to school.

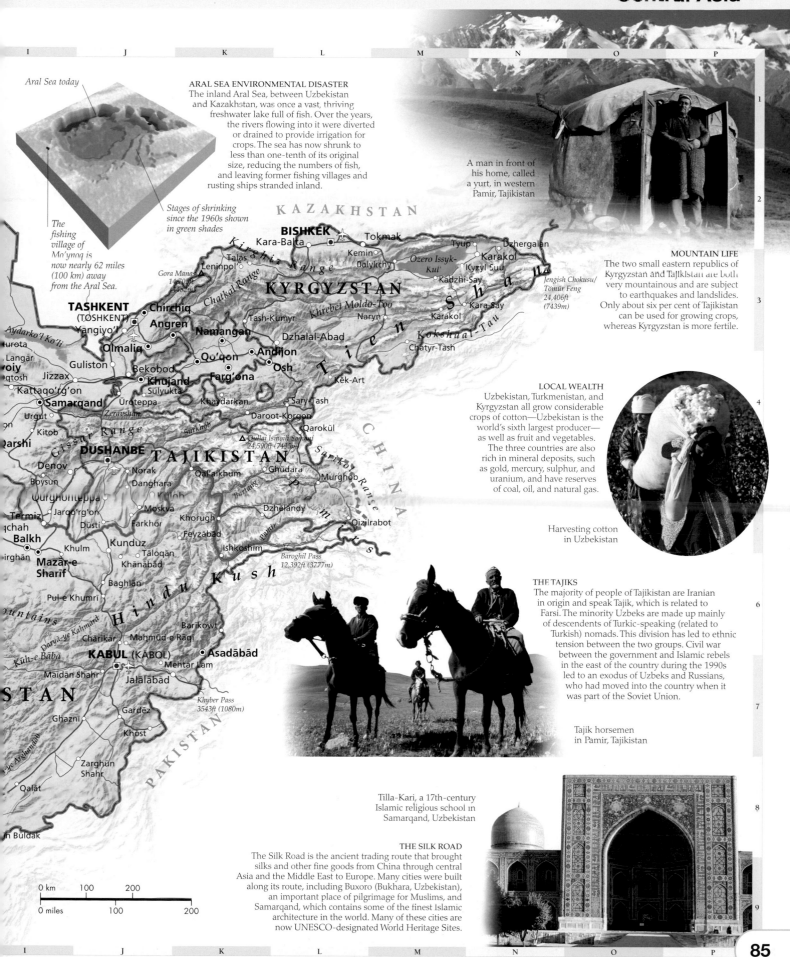

Aral Sea today

ARAL SEA ENVIRONMENTAL DISASTER
The inland Aral Sea, between Uzbekistan and Kazakhstan, was once a vast, thriving freshwater lake full of fish. Over the years, the rivers flowing into it were diverted or drained to provide irrigation for crops. The sea has now shrunk to less than one-tenth of its original size, reducing the numbers of fish, and leaving former fishing villages and rusting ships stranded inland.

The fishing village of Mo'ynoq is now nearly 62 miles (100 km) away from the Aral Sea.

Stages of shrinking since the 1960s shown in green shades

A man in front of his home, called a yurt, in western Pamir, Tajikistan

MOUNTAIN LIFE
The two small eastern republics of Kyrgyzstan and Tajikistan are both very mountainous and are subject to earthquakes and landslides. Only about six per cent of Tajikistan can be used for growing crops, whereas Kyrgyzstan is more fertile.

LOCAL WEALTH
Uzbekistan, Turkmenistan, and Kyrgyzstan all grow considerable crops of cotton—Uzbekistan is the world's sixth largest producer—as well as fruit and vegetables. The three countries are also rich in mineral deposits, such as gold, mercury, sulphur, and uranium, and have reserves of coal, oil, and natural gas.

Harvesting cotton in Uzbekistan

THE TAJIKS
The majority of people of Tajikistan are Iranian in origin and speak Tajik, which is related to Farsi. The minority Uzbeks are made up mainly of descendents of Turkic-speaking (related to Turkish) nomads. This division has led to ethnic tension between the two groups. Civil war between the government and Islamic rebels in the east of the country during the 1990s led to an exodus of Uzbeks and Russians, who had moved into the country when it was part of the Soviet Union.

Tajik horsemen in Pamir, Tajikistan

Tilla-Kari, a 17th-century Islamic religious school in Samarqand, Uzbekistan

THE SILK ROAD
The Silk Road is the ancient trading route that brought silks and other fine goods from China through central Asia and the Middle East to Europe. Many cities were built along its route, including Buxoro (Bukhara, Uzbekistan), an important place of pilgrimage for Muslims, and Samarqand, which contains some of the finest Islamic architecture in the world. Many of these cities are now UNESCO-designated World Heritage Sites.

Map labels

KAZAKHSTAN

BISHKEK
Kara-Balta · Tokmak
Kemin · Tyup · Dzhergalan
Talas · Dolylicchy · Karakol
Leninpol · Ozero Issyk-Kul' · Kyzyl Suu
Gora Manas 14705ft 4482m · Kadzhi-Say
Chatkal Range · Kara-Say

KYRGYZSTAN

Khrebet Moldo-Too
TASHKENT (TOSHKENT)
Chirchiq · Tash-Kumyr · Naryn · Jengish Chokusu/ Tömür Feng 24,406ft (7439m)
Angren · Chatyr-Tash
Yangiyo'l · Dzhalal-Abad · Kara-Say
Namangan · Kök-Art
Olmaliq · Andijon · Kök-Art
Guliston · Qo'qon · Osh
Bekobod · Farg'ona
Jizzax · Khujand · Sary-Tash
Kattaqo'rg'on · Sülyukta · Khaydarkan
Samarqand · Ûroteppa · Daroot-Korgon · Qarokûl
Urgut · Zeravshan · Surkhob
Kitob · Qullai Ismoili Somoni 24,590ft (7495m)
Qarshi · Gissar Range
DUSHANBE · TAJIKISTAN
Denov · Norak · Qal'aikhum · Ghûdara · Murghob
Boysun · Danghara
Qurghonteppa · Moskva · Dzhelandy
Termiz · Jarqo'rg'on · Farkhor · Khorugh · Qizilrabot
ichah · Dûsti · Feyzâbâd · Ishkoshim
Balkh · Kunduz · Tâloqan · Baroghil Pass 12,392ft (3777m)
Khulm · Khânâbâd
Mazar-e Sharif · Baghlân
Pul-e Khumri · Hindu Kush
Barikowt
Chârikâr · Mahmûd-e Râqî
KABUL (KÂBOL) · Asadâbâd
Maidân Shahr · Mehtar Lâm
Jalâlâbâd
Khyber Pass 3543ft (1080m)
Ghaznî · Gardêz
Khôst
Zarghûn Shahr
Qalât

PAKISTAN
CHINA
Pamirs
Tien Shan
Kokshaal-Tau

0 km 100 200
0 miles 100 200

Indian Subcontinent

SEPARATED FROM the rest of Asia by the Himalayas, the Indian subcontinent is home to more than one-fifth of the world's population—almost 1.7 billion people. They have a long and complex history, form many different ethnic groups, speak a wide variety of languages, and worship many different gods. While some people in these countries are wealthy, many others live in poverty. Tensions between and within countries in this region have sometimes erupted in warfare. The Indian subcontinent is often affected by natural disasters, notably cyclones in the Bay of Bengal, and earthquakes and floods in Pakistan. However, India, the most heavily populated nation and once prone to famine, is now more than self-sufficient in food. All but Nepal and Bhutan were once ruled by the British, whose legacy can be seen in the common language of English, in some architecture, the vast railway system, and in sport—most notably cricket.

MONSOON
From May/June to September, warm, moist southerly winds sweep up from the Indian Ocean and the Bay of Bengal across the subcontinent. Once these winds meet dry land, moisture falls as monsoon rainfall. Although this irrigates the land and replenishes the water supply, it can also cause severe flooding.

0 km   150   300
0 miles   150   300

SRI LANKA
In 1983, civil war erupted in Sri Lanka between the Buddhist majority Sinhalese, who dominate the government, and the Hindu minority Tamils, who wanted to establish their own independent state in the north of the island. The civil war, which ended in 2009 when the government defeated the Tamil Tigers, has cost many lives and disrupted the island's economy. Yet Sri Lanka still has one of the highest literacy rates in the world and high levels of health care.

FAMILY LIFE IN PAKISTAN
Pakistanis have strong ties to their extended families, and often many generations live and work together in family-run businesses. Smaller family units, however, are becoming more common in urban areas. Although some women hold prominent positions in public and commercial life, such as Benazir Bhutto who was prime minister twice before she was assassinated in December 2007, most women do not work outside the home.

School child,
Sri Lanka

Hindu Kush
Khyber Pass
3543ft
(1080m)
Mingaora
Mardān
Peshāwar Wāh ISLĀMĀBĀD
Rāwalpindi
Jhelum Jamm
Sargodha Gujrāt Gujrānv
Chaman Toba Kākar Range Lahore Amri
Faisalābād Ludhiā
Quetta Dera Ghāzi Khān Multān Okāra Chandiga
Kālat Sibi Bathinda Haryan
PAKISTAN Bahāwalpur Karr
Baluchistān Jacobābād Rahīmyār Khān NEW DE
Shikārpur Sukkur
Lārkāna Khairpur Bīkāner Alwar
Central Makrān Range Jaisalmer Jaipur
Turbat Nawābshāh Jodhpur
Gwādar Pasni Hyderābād Mīrpur Khās Pāli Beāwar
Karāchi Sind Rājasthān Kota
Sujāwal Udaipur
Mouths of the Indus Rann of Kachchh Pālanpur
Tropic of Cancer Gujarāt Ratlām
Gāndhīdhām Ahmadābād Godhra Vindhya Ra
Gulf of Kachchh
Jāmnagar Rājkot Indore
Porbandar Vadodara Satpura Ra
Bhāvnagar Bhusāwal
Gulf of Khambhāt Sūrat
Damān Manmād
Nāshik Aurangā
Kalyān Godāvari
Mumbai Pune Mahārāshtra
(Bombay) Nānd
Bārāmati
Arabian Solāpur
Sea Gulba
Kolhāpur Rāic
Karnātaka
Belgaum Gadag
Panaji Hubli
Dāvana
Shimoga
Udupi Bangalo
Mangalore Mysore
Kāsaragod
Kannur (Cannanore) Er
Kozhikode (Calicut)
Coimbatore
Ernākulam
Kochi (Cochin)
Kollam (Quilon)
Thiruvananthapuram
(Trivandrum)
Nāgerc

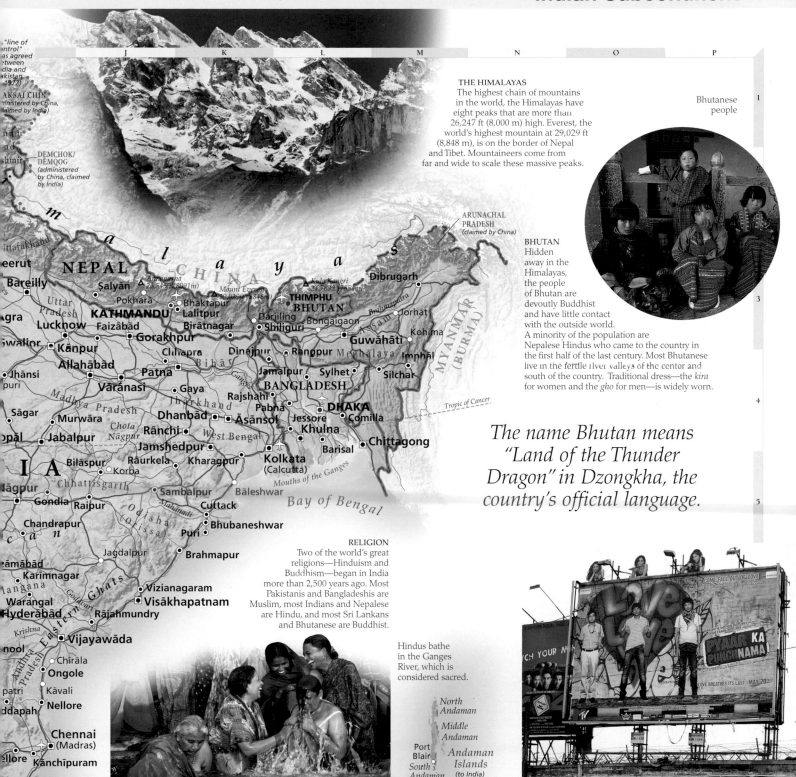

"line of control" as agreed between India and Pakistan (1972)

AKSAI CHIN (administered by China, claimed by India)

DEMCHOK/ DÊMQOG (administered by China, claimed by India)

THE HIMALAYAS
The highest chain of mountains in the world, the Himalayas have eight peaks that are more than 26,247 ft (8,000 m) high. Everest, the world's highest mountain at 29,029 ft (8,848 m), is on the border of Nepal and Tibet. Mountaineers come from far and wide to scale these massive peaks.

Bhutanese people

ARUNACHAL PRADESH (claimed by China)

BHUTAN
Hidden away in the Himalayas, the people of Bhutan are devoutly Buddhist and have little contact with the outside world. A minority of the population are Nepalese Hindus who came to the country in the first half of the last century. Most Bhutanese live in the fertile river valleys of the center and south of the country. Traditional dress—the *kira* for women and the *gho* for men—is widely worn.

The name Bhutan means "Land of the Thunder Dragon" in Dzongkha, the country's official language.

RELIGION
Two of the world's great religions—Hinduism and Buddhism—began in India more than 2,500 years ago. Most Pakistanis and Bangladeshis are Muslim, most Indians and Nepalese are Hindu, and most Sri Lankans and Bhutanese are Buddhist.

Hindus bathe in the Ganges River, which is considered sacred.

North Andaman
Middle Andaman
Port Blair
Andaman Islands (to India)
South Andaman
Little Andaman

BOLLYWOOD
More films are produced in Mumbai (Bombay), India—more than 1,000 a year—than in the whole of the US, turning "Bollywood," as it is known, into a major cultural center. Famous for their musical routines and glamorous stars, Bollywood films generally had historical and social themes. Today, these have expanded to include more contemporary stories as the films have found a fan base in the large Indian diaspora across the world.

TEA IN SRI LANKA
Sri Lanka is the world's largest exporter of tea. The plantations are located mainly in the center of the island and employ women to pick the delicate, green shoots of the bushes.

Car Nicobar
Nicobar Islands (to India)
Katchall Island
Little Nicobar
Great Nicobar
Indira Point
Andaman Sea

INDIAN OCEAN

Western China and Mongolia

CHINA IS A LAND of great geographical diversity and amazing landscapes. More than 90 percent of the population are Han Chinese—descendents of people who settled here more than 5,000 years ago. This region includes western China, Mongolia, and Tibet. Mongolia gained its independence from China in 1911 and is now an independent democracy. Tibet is currently governed by China. Compared with eastern China, this region is sparsely populated and characterized by vast deserts, remote mountains, and extreme temperatures.

DESERT LANDS
The cold, rocky Gobi Desert (right) stretches for more than 380,000 sq miles (1,000,000 sq km) through Mongolia and northeast China. Many dinosaur bones and eggs have been found here, making it one of the richest dinosaur fossil regions in the world.

THE MONGOLIANS
Most of the people living in Mongolia are Khalkh Mongols. About 70 percent of Mongols now live in urban areas, but some still lead traditional lives as nomadic herders. They live in large felt tents, called *yurts*. Smoke from the central iron stove escapes through a chimney in the roof.

In traditional Mongolian khoomi singing, men are able to sing several notes at once.

CHINESE WRITING
The Chinese alphabet is not made up of letters. Instead, separate symbols stand for individual words or parts of words. There are more than 50,000 characters in the Chinese language. The same symbols are used everywhere in China, and no matter what Chinese language or dialect people speak, they can all read the same script.

兒童百科全書

Chinese symbols, whose strokes have to be written in a certain order

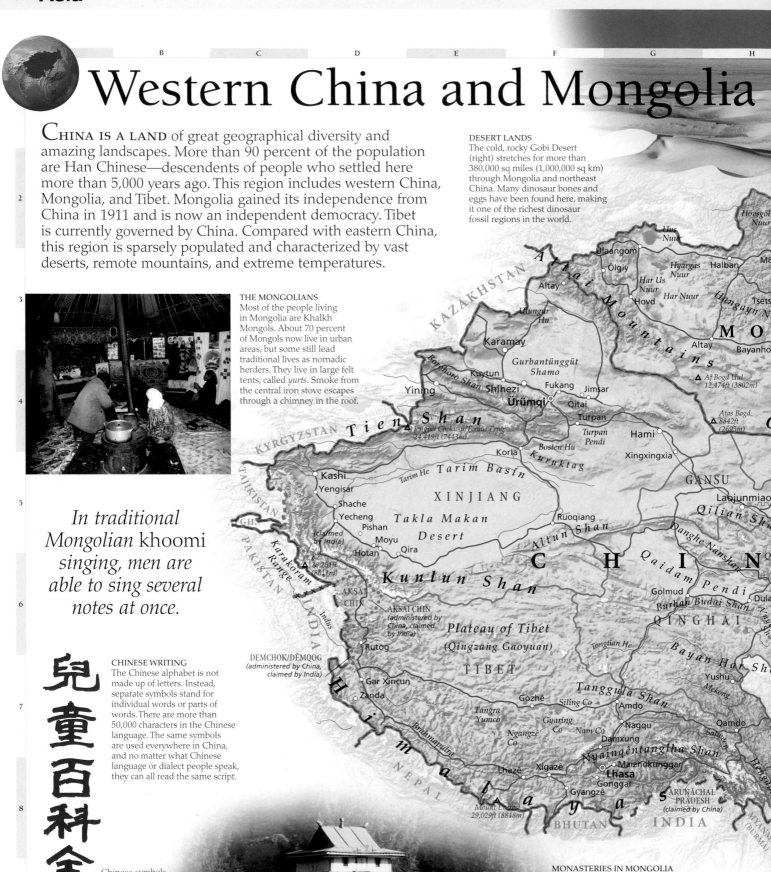

MONASTERIES IN MONGOLIA
Under communism, Mongolians were forbidden to practice their traditional Buddhist faith, which was viewed as superstitious and unscientific. Since the democratic government was set up in 1990, some monasteries have reopened. Many people, however, no longer follow any religion.

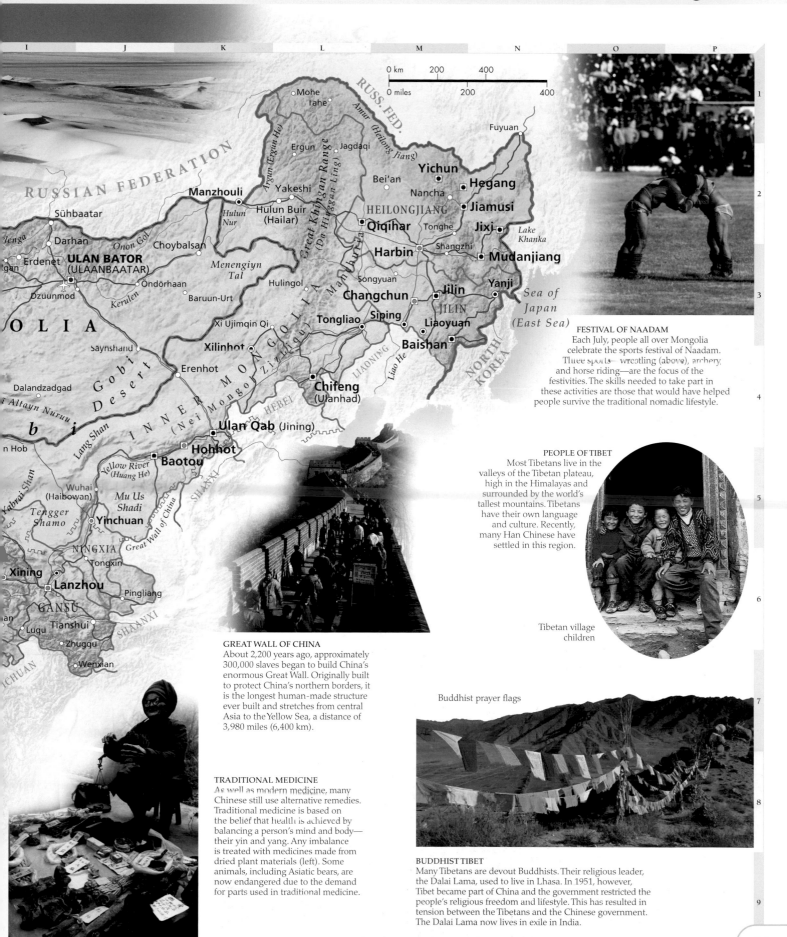

0 km   200   400
0 miles   200   400

RUSSIAN FEDERATION

RUSS. FED.

Amur (Heilong Jiang)

Mohe
Tahe
Fuyuan

Ergun
Jagdaqi

Manzhouli

Argun (Ergun He)

Yakeshi

Bei'an
Nancha

Yichun
Hegang

Sühbaatar

Hulun Buir
(Hailar)

Hulun
Nur

Qiqihar

Tonghe

Jiamusi

HEILONGJIANG

Jixi

Menga
Darhan

Onon Gol

Choybalsan

Harbin

Shangzhi

Lake
Khanka

Erdenet
gan

**ULAN BATOR
(ULAANBAATAR)**

Menengiyn
Tal

Songyuan

Mudanjiang

Dzuunmod

Kerulen

Öndörhaan

Baruun-Urt

Hulingol

Changchun

Jilin

Yanji

*Sea of
Japan
(East Sea)*

Tongliao
Siping

JILIN

Liaoyuan

OLIA

Xi Ujimqin Qi

Xilinhot

Baishan

Saynshand

Liao He

LIAONING

Dalandzadgad

*Gobi
Desert*

Erenhot

i Altayn Nuruu

**Chifeng
(Ulanhad)**

HEBEI

NORTH
KOREA

b
i

**INNER MONGOLIA
(Nei Mongol Zizhiqu)**

n Hob

Lang Shan

Ulan Qab (Jining)

Yabrai Shan

Hohhot
Baotou

Great Wall of China

SHANXI

Wuhai
(Haibowan)

*Yellow River
(Huang He)*

*Mu Us
Shadi*

*Tengger
Shamo*

Yinchuan

Great Wall of China

NINGXIA

Tongxin

Xining

Lanzhou

Pingliang

GANSU

an

Luqu
Tianshui

SHAANXI

Zhuggu

ICHUAN

Wenxian

FESTIVAL OF NAADAM
Each July, people all over Mongolia celebrate the sports festival of Naadam. Three sports—wrestling (above), archery, and horse riding—are the focus of the festivities. The skills needed to take part in these activities are those that would have helped people survive the traditional nomadic lifestyle.

PEOPLE OF TIBET
Most Tibetans live in the valleys of the Tibetan plateau, high in the Himalayas and surrounded by the world's tallest mountains. Tibetans have their own language and culture. Recently, many Han Chinese have settled in this region.

Tibetan village children

GREAT WALL OF CHINA
About 2,200 years ago, approximately 300,000 slaves began to build China's enormous Great Wall. Originally built to protect China's northern borders, it is the longest human-made structure ever built and stretches from central Asia to the Yellow Sea, a distance of 3,980 miles (6,400 km).

Buddhist prayer flags

TRADITIONAL MEDICINE
As well as modern medicine, many Chinese still use alternative remedies. Traditional medicine is based on the belief that health is achieved by balancing a person's mind and body—their yin and yang. Any imbalance is treated with medicines made from dried plant materials (left). Some animals, including Asiatic bears, are now endangered due to the demand for parts used in traditional medicine.

BUDDHIST TIBET
Many Tibetans are devout Buddhists. Their religious leader, the Dalai Lama, used to live in Lhasa. In 1951, however, Tibet became part of China and the government restricted the people's religious freedom and lifestyle. This has resulted in tension between the Tibetans and the Chinese government. The Dalai Lama now lives in exile in India.

Eastern China and Korea

CHINA HAS A LARGE population of almost 1.4 billion, with two-thirds living in eastern China. For thousands of years, powerful emperors ruled China. During this period, Chinese civilization was very advanced, but much of the population lived in poverty. In 1949, after a communist revolution, the People's Republic of China was established. Food, education, and health care became available to more people, but there was also a loss of freedom. Today, Chinese people have more freedom, but the government still has tight control over their lives. The Korean peninsula is divided politically into north and south, and political tensions continue to exist between the two governments. Since 1949, Taiwan has been in dispute with China over who governs the mountainous island of Taiwan.

NEW YEAR CELEBRATIONS
Chinese New Year, also known as the Spring Festival, is the country's most important festival. It is usually held in January or February. Good-luck messages decorate buildings and there are feasts, fireworks, fairs, and processions. People wear red clothes for good luck and give gifts of coins to symbolize wealth.

Chinese New Year parade

HONG KONG
For 100 years, Hong Kong was a British colony. Then, in 1997, it was returned to China. These small islands are some of the most densely populated parts of the world. Most people live and work in high-rise buildings. It has a prosperous economy at the heart of global finance and the people there have one of the world's highest life expectancies.

Skyline of Hong Kong with a Chinese junk in the foreground

SMALL FAMILIES
China's population grows by millions each year. In 1979, to try to control the rising population, the government brought in policies to stop parents from having more than one child. As a result, many Chinese children do not have brothers and sisters, but this might change as a two-child policy was introduced in 2016.

PADDY FIELDS
Rice forms the basis of most Chinese meals. It grows in paddy fields in the southeast of the country. During the growing season, fields are flooded so farmers can grow more rice more quickly. In the drier regions, wheat is grown and used to make noodles, buns, and dumplings. Rice or wheat is combined with local vegetables, meats, and spices to create regional dishes.

NORTH KOREA
North Korea is an independent communist country, but since the break up of the Soviet Union it has lost many of its trading partners and is now very poor. However, the country has a good education system and a high literacy rate. Schooling is free and compulsory for all children for 10 years.

SOUTH KOREA
South Korea is a democratic nation with a thriving electronics and machinery industry. A quarter of the population lives in or near the capital city, Seoul. The Internet developed quickly in South Korea and today almost 90 percent of the population use it, with the highest Internet connection speed in the world.

The majority of the Chinese population lives in just 15 percent of the total land area.

MODERN SHANGHAI
China's largest city is Shanghai. More than 23 million people live in this wealthy east-coast port. International trade has transformed Shanghai's skyline, which is now crowded with high-rise buildings and modern shopping malls. The center of town still has some old western-style buildings that have survived from the days before the revolution.

BEAUTY OF TAIWAN
Taiwan's mountainous countryside is famous for its natural beauty, scenic lakes, and many ornate Buddhist temples. This peaceful environment contrasts sharply with Taiwan's capital city, Taipei, which is one of the fastest growing cities in Asia.

Bicycle factory

CHINESE INDUSTRY
After the revolutionary leader Mao Zedong died in 1976, China's economy opened up. Industry and manufacturing was encouraged and today China plays a big part in the global economy. Many people are moving into cities for better-paid jobs.

Japan

JAPAN IS SITUATED in the north Pacific Ocean off the coast of the Asian continent. It is made up of four main islands and more than 3,000 smaller ones. The Japanese people have a distinctive culture based on traditions built up over thousands of years. They have their own language and script. School children all learn to read and write both in the traditional script and using letters. Social rules in Japan are strict, and respect and politeness are considered very important. Most people bow when greeting one another, for example. Japan is a very modern country, however, with one of the world's most technologically advanced societies. Its economy is based on the development and production of cutting-edge electronics and vehicles, and most families have the latest consumer goods.

RELIGIONS OF JAPAN
Many Japanese people follow a mix of the Shinto and Buddhist religions, attending wedding blessings in Shinto shrines and funerals in Buddhist temples. Buddhism originated in India and arrived in Japan in the 6th century, whereas the Shinto faith is native to Japan. Respect for nature is especially important in the Shinto religion. Many natural locations such as Mount Fuji are considered sacred.

EARTHQUAKES
The islands of Japan are situated in an area where four of Earth's tectonic plates meet. This causes frequent earthquakes. Japanese school children are taught how to keep safe during an earthquake by sheltering in a doorway or under a table.

OVERCROWDING
Most of the country's 127 million people live in cities in the flatter, coastal areas. Tokyo and Osaka are very crowded, and homes here are usually very small and are designed to make the most of the limited space.

FASHION IN JAPAN
On ordinary days, Japanese people usually wear western-style clothes. Most children have a school uniform. On festival days, such as Children's Day, many people prefer to wear the traditional kimono. Women's kimonos are often made of colorful silk, decorated with beautiful designs.

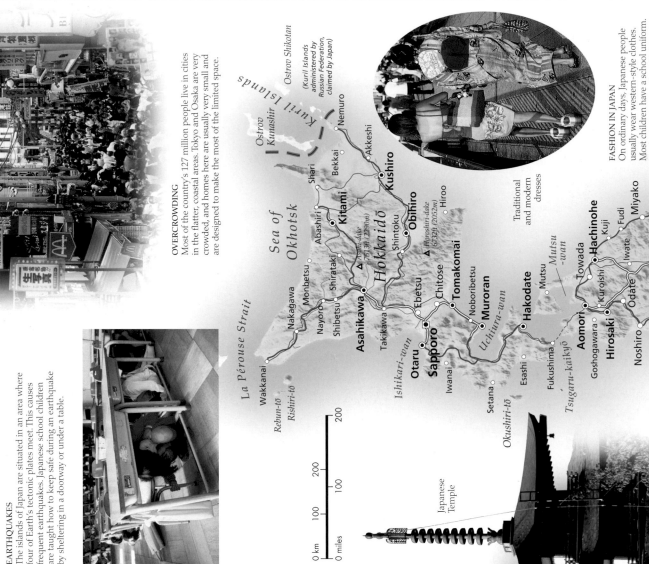

Mount Fuji, a dormant volcano

Japanese Temple

Traditional and modern dresses

Kuril Islands
Ostrov Shikotan
(Kuril Islands administered by Russian Federation, claimed by Japan)
Ostrov Kunashir

Sea of Okhotsk

Nemuro
Akkeshi
Kushiro
Bekkai
Shari
Kitami
Shintoku
Abashiri
Obihiro
△ Asahi-dake (2290m)
Monbetsu
Hokkaidō
△ Hiroshiri-dake (2052m)
Hiroo
Nakagawa
Shirataki
Shibetsu
Nayoro
Tomakomai
Takikawa
Asahikawa
Ebetsu
Chitose
Noboribetsu
Muroran
Otaru
Sapporo
Uchiura-wan
Iwanai
Hakodate
Ishikari-wan
Mutsu -wan
Mutsu
Setana
Esashi
Fukushima
Tsugaru-kaikyō
Aomori
Okushiri-tō
Goshogawara
Towada
Kuroishi
Hachinohe
Kuji
Hirosaki
Odate
Iwate
Fudi
Noshiro
Gojōme
Miyako
Honjō
Morioka
La Pérouse Strait
Rebun-tō
Rishiri-tō
Wakkanai
Yokote
Hanamaki
Kesennuma
Akita
Shinjō
Yuzawa
Shizugawa
Sakata
Tsuruoka
Furukawa
Ishinomaki

Japanese Temple

0 km   100   200
0 miles   100   200

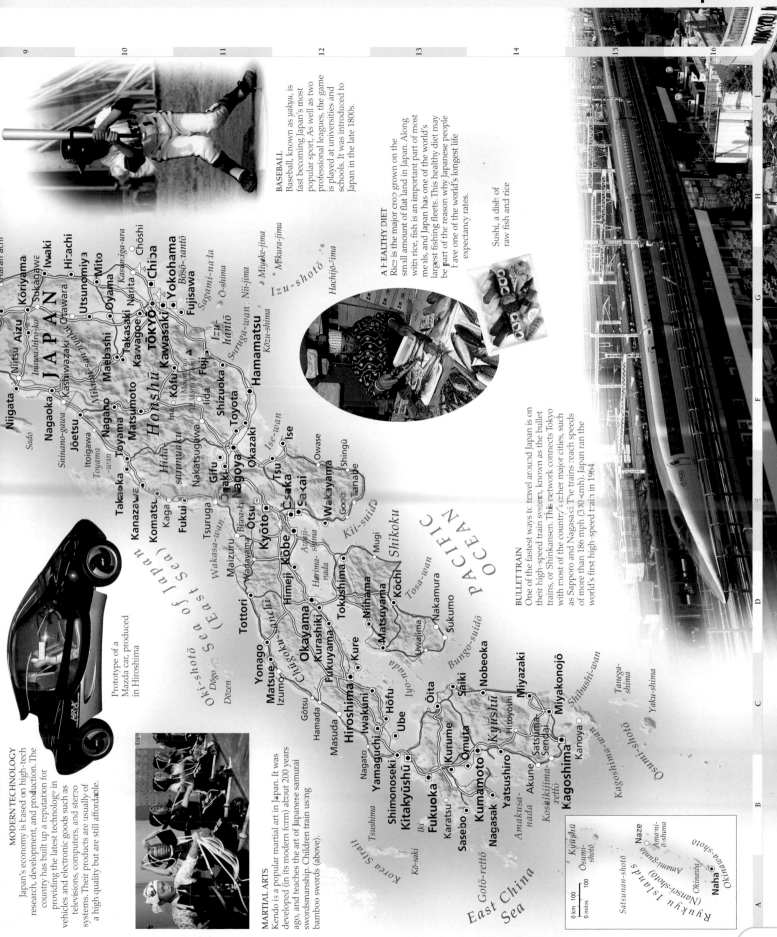

MODERN TECHNOLOGY
Japan's economy is based on high-tech research, development, and production. The country has built up a reputation for providing the latest technology in vehicles and electronic goods such as televisions, computers, and stereo systems. Their products are usually of a high quality but are still affordable.

Prototype of a Mazda car, produced in Hiroshima

MARTIAL ARTS
Kendo is a popular martial art in Japan. It was developed (in its modern form) about 200 years ago, and teaches the art of Japanese samurai swordsmanship. Children train using bamboo swords (above).

BASEBALL
Baseball, known as *yakyu*, is fast becoming Japan's most popular sport. As well as two professional leagues, the game is played at universities and schools. It was introduced to Japan in the late 1800s.

A HEALTHY DIET
Rice is the major crop grown on the small amount of flat land in Japan. Along with rice, fish is an important part of most meals, and Japan has one of the world's largest fishing fleets. This healthy diet may be part of the reason why Japanese people have one of the world's longest life expectancy rates.

Sushi, a dish of raw fish and rice

BULLET TRAIN
One of the fastest ways to travel around Japan is on their high-speed train system, known as the bullet trains, or Shinkansen. This network connects Tokyo with most of the country's other major cities, such as Sapporo and Nagasaki. The trains reach speeds of more than 186 mph (300 kmh). Japan ran the world's first high-speed train in 1964.

Mainland SE Asia

THE PENINSULA of Southeast Asia lies directly to the south of India and China, between the Pacific and Indian Oceans. It is made up of Myanmar (Burma), Thailand, Vietnam, Cambodia, and Laos. Over thousands of years, the influence of people from nearby India, China, and Arabian countries has helped to give this region a diverse mix of cultures and religions. Much of the land here is mountainous, with half the region covered in forest. Most people live in coastal or lowland regions, where they can grow crops such as rice, raise cattle, and catch fish. In recent years, the electronics industry has also become an important part of southeast Asian economies, especially in Thailand.

ORPHANS IN CAMBODIA
A high number of Cambodian children live in orphanages, some because they have lost their parents, others due to poverty.

Cambodian orphanage

GROWING RICE
Rice is the most important crop in Southeast Asia. It grows well in wet lowland areas, such as the Mekong River delta in Vietnam, where the plants can be grown in paddy fields. Most rice is planted and harvested by women.

RURAL LIVING
Most people in Southeast Asia live in rural areas rather than cities, and farming is the most common occupation. The steep, mountainous regions are often unsuitable for growing crops or raising cattle, however, and many farming communities are based in the fertile river valleys and deltas. There are more than 200 villages on and around this lake (right) in Myanmar.

KAREN TRIBE
There are 600,000 tribespeople living in the northeastern hills of Thailand. The Karen are the largest hill tribe. They originated from Myanmar, but moved into Thailand to escape political unrest.

Padaung women, who are part of the Karen tribe, wear distinctive gold neck rings.

(Map of Mainland SE Asia with labels including:)

CHINA — Hengduan Shan

INDIA — Chin Hills, Arakan Yoma

MYANMAR (BURMA) — Kumon Range, Nmai Hka, Irrawaddy, Chindwin, Mogaung, Bhamo, Katha, Banmauk, Mainokwan, Tamu, Falam, Monywa, Shwebo, Sagaing, Amarapura, Mandalay, Kyaukse, Myingyan, Meiktila, Pakokku, Chauk, Yenangyaung, Minbu, Magway, Taungdwingyi, Thayetmyo, Pyay, Paungde, Phyu, Taungup, Myanaung, Letpadan, Hinthada, Myaungmya, Pyechin, Thandwe, Sittwe, Ramree Island, Cheduba Island, Pyinmana, NAY PYI TAW, Taunggyi, Loikaw, Lashio, Pyin-Oo-Lwin, Myitkyina, Mogaung, Shan Plateau, Salween, Pawn, Sittoung, Nyaunglebin, Pyuntaza, Kyaikto, Bago, Yangon, Bay of Bengal

LAOS — Louangphabang, VIENTIANE (VIANGCHAN), Muang Xiang Ngeun, Xaignabouli, Phônsavan, Pakxan, Ban Hin Heup, Xam Nua, Sop Hao, Louangnamtha, Muang Sing, Muang Namo, Muang Namtha, Houayxay, Phôngsali, Nam Ou

THAILAND — Chiang Mai, Chiang Rai, Fang, Phayao, Lampang, Lamphun, Phrae, Nan, Mae Nam Ping, Mae Nam Yom, Nam Nan, Sirikit Reservoir, Korat

VIETNAM — HA NOI, Hai Phong, Ha Long, Câm Pha, Thai Binh, Nam Dinh, Thanh Hoa, Vinh, Dông Hoi, Lang Son, Bac Giang, Ha Dông, Hoa Binh, Viet Tri, Thai Nguyên, Cao Bang, Ha Giang, Lao Cai, Lai Châu, Diên Biên, Hoang Liên Son, Black River, Annamite Mountains, Tuong Duong, Thakhek, Savannakhet, Udon Thani, Loei, Nong Khai, Sakon Nakhon

Gulf of Tonkin

BANGLADESH

Tropic of Cancer

Scale: 0 km 100 200, 0 miles 100 200

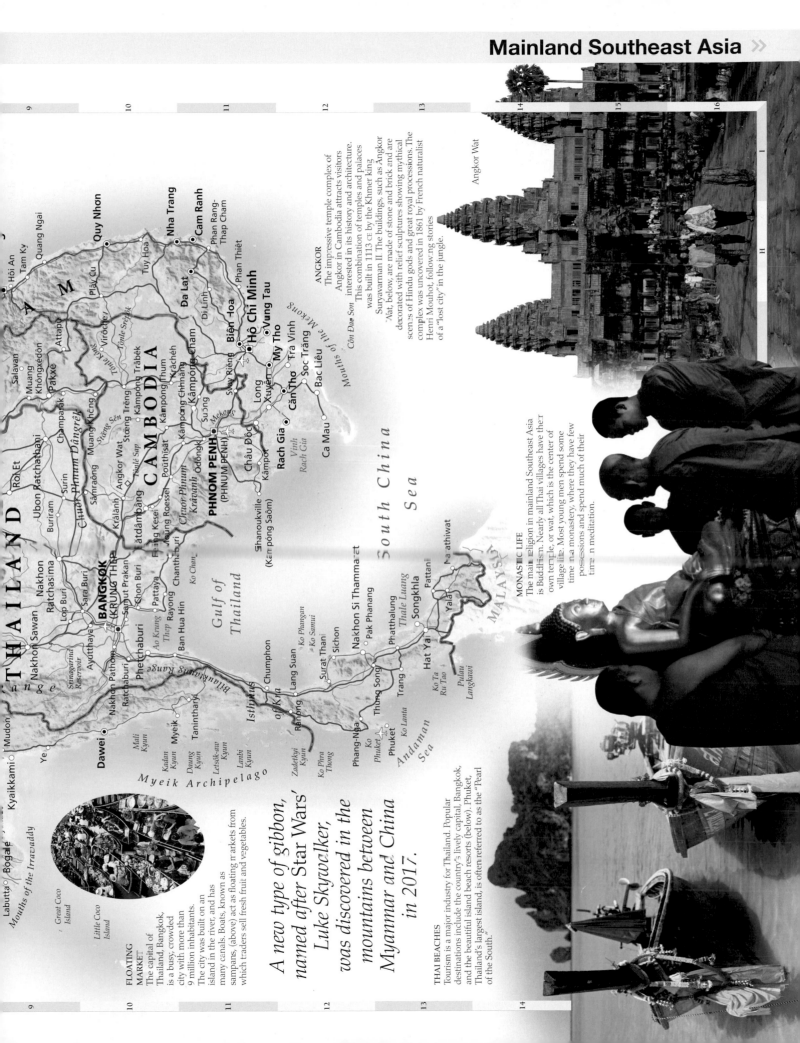

ANGKOR

The impressive temple complex of Angkor in Cambodia attracts visitors interested in its history and architecture. This combination of temples and palaces was built in 1113 CE by the Khmer king Suryavarman II The buildings, such as Angkor Wat, below, are made of stone and brick and are decorated with relief sculptures showing mythical scenes of Hindu gods and great royal processions. The complex was uncovered in 1861 by French naturalist Henri Mouhot, following stories of a "lost city" in the jungle.

Angkor Wat

MONASTIC LIFE

The main religion in mainland Southeast Asia is Buddhism. Nearly all Thai villages have their own temple, or wat, which is the center of village life. Most young men spend some time in a monastery, where they have few possessions and spend much of their time in meditation.

FLOATING MARKET

The capital of Thailand, Bangkok, is a busy, crowded city with more than 9 million inhabitants. The city was built on an island in the river, and has many canals. Boats, known as sampans, (above) act as floating markets from which traders sell fresh fruit and vegetables.

A new type of gibbon, named after Star Wars' Luke Skywalker, was discovered in the mountains between Myanmar and China in 2017.

THAI BEACHES

Tourism is a major industry for Thailand. Popular destinations include the country's lively capital, Bangkok, and the beautiful island beach resorts (below). Phuket, Thailand's largest island, is often referred to as the "Pearl of the South."

Map labels

THAILAND

CAMBODIA

VIETNAM

MALAYSIA

BANGKOK (KRUNG THEP)

PHNOM PENH (PHNUM PENH)

Hồ Chí Minh

South China Sea

Gulf of Thailand

Andaman Sea

Myeik Archipelago

Bilauktaung Range

Isthmus of Kra

Mouths of the Mekong

Mouths of the Irrawaddy

Quy Nhon, Quang Ngai, Tam Ky, Hội An, Pleiku, Tuy Hòa, Nha Trang, Cam Ranh, Phan Rang-Thap Cham, Đà Lạt, Di Linh, Phan Thiết, Biên Hòa, Vung Tau, My Tho, Trà Vinh, Sóc Trăng, Bạc Liêu, Ca Mau, Cần Thơ, Long Xuyên, Rach Gia, Châu Đốc, Kâmpôt, Svay Riêng, Kâmpóng Cham, Kâmpóng Chhnăng, Krâchéh, Stœng Trêng, Kâmpóng Thum, Kâmpóng Trâbêk

Salavan, Muang Khôngxédôn, Pakxe, Champasak, Attapu, Virôchey, Muang Khéng, Stœng Sên, Rôlêt, Ubon Ratchathani, Surin, Buriram, Nakhon Ratchasima, Nakhon Sawan, Lop Buri, Sara Buri, Ayutthaya, Nakhon Pathom, Ratchaburi, Phetchaburi, Ban Hua Hin, Chumphon, Lang Suan, Ranong, Surat Thani, Sichon, Nakhon Si Thammarat, Pak Phanang, Phatthalung, Trang, Thung Song, Songkhla, Hat Yai, Pattani, Yala, Na athiwat

Dawei, Myeik, Taninthary, Ye, Mudon, Kyaikkami, Bogale, Labutta

Kadan Kyun, Daung Kyun, Letsôk-aw Kyun, Lanbi Kyun, Zadetkyi Kyun, Mali Kyun, Ko Phra Thong, Phang-Nga, Phuket, Ko Lanta, Ko Ta Ru Tao, Pulau Langkawi

Great Coco Island, Little Coco Island

Tonle Sap, Stœng Sên, Tonle Srêpók

Srinagarind Reservoir

Ao Krung, Thep Rayong, Pattaya, Chon Buri, Samut Prakan, Samut Songkhram

Krâlánh, Bâtdâmbâng, Siĕmréab, Pouthisat, Angkor Wat, Sāmraōng, Muang Roesssei, Krâvanh, Krâkôr, Chumŭ, Chhuk, Odôngk, Thbông Khmum

Shanoukville (Kâmpóng Saôm)

Maritime SE Asia

To the south of the Asian mainland lies maritime Southeast Asia. It includes Malaysia, Indonesia, East Timor, Singapore, and the Philippines. Part of Malaysia is connected to the mainland, but the rest of the region is made up of more than 20,000 islands that stretch across the Pacific and Indian Oceans. Lying near the Equator, the climate is mostly hot, wet, and humid. Most of the larger islands are mountainous and covered in dense forest, and many people live in villages near rivers or on the coast. Like the rest of Southeast Asia, the population is made up of people from many different cultural backgrounds speaking hundreds of different languages. The most common religion is Islam, except in the Philippines, where most people are Roman Catholic.

GREAT APES
The orangutans are great apes that live only in Borneo and the northern corner of Sumatra. They spend most of their time in the trees, even building tree-top nests in which to sleep. Sadly, the orangutan is endangered because of deforestation.

PEOPLE OF MALAYSIA
Ethnic Malaysians make up 50 percent of the population and are known as bumiputera, meaning "sons of the soil." Most Malaysians are Muslim. Ethnic Chinese form 23 percent of the population.

Sultan of Brunei

THE SULTAN OF BRUNEI
Brunei is ruled by a sultan who lives in the world's largest palace. The sultan is one of the wealthiest men in the world.

Ubadiah Mosque, Malaysia

SINGAPORE
As the financial and industrial center of Southeast Asia, Singapore is one of the wealthiest countries in this region. It has a thriving high-tech industry and a high standard of living. There are strictly enforced laws forbidding littering and other small crimes. The death penalty is imposed for drug smuggling. The government also controls the press and restricts the Internet.

Skyscrapers in Singapore's financial district

KITE FLYING
After the harvest, the people of Malaysia celebrate with the Wau-flying (kite-flying) Festival, where skilled people demonstrate the traditional Malaysian sport.

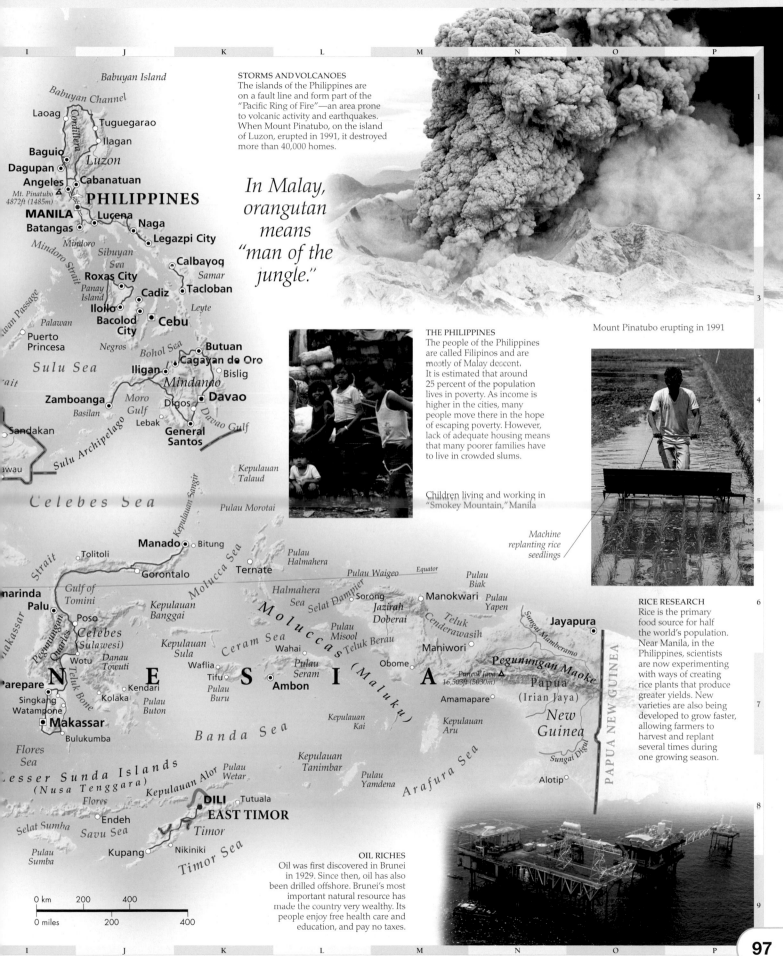

STORMS AND VOLCANOES
The islands of the Philippines are on a fault line and form part of the "Pacific Ring of Fire"—an area prone to volcanic activity and earthquakes. When Mount Pinatubo, on the island of Luzon, erupted in 1991, it destroyed more than 40,000 homes.

In Malay, orangutan means "man of the jungle."

Mount Pinatubo erupting in 1991

THE PHILIPPINES
The people of the Philippines are called Filipinos and are mostly of Malay descent. It is estimated that around 25 percent of the population lives in poverty. As income is higher in the cities, many people move there in the hope of escaping poverty. However, lack of adequate housing means that many poorer families have to live in crowded slums.

Children living and working in "Smokey Mountain," Manila

Machine replanting rice seedlings

RICE RESEARCH
Rice is the primary food source for half the world's population. Near Manila, in the Philippines, scientists are now experimenting with ways of creating rice plants that produce greater yields. New varieties are also being developed to grow faster, allowing farmers to harvest and replant several times during one growing season.

OIL RICHES
Oil was first discovered in Brunei in 1929. Since then, oil has also been drilled offshore. Brunei's most important natural resource has made the country very wealthy. Its people enjoy free health care and education, and pay no taxes.

Babuyan Island
Babuyan Channel
Laoag
Tuguegarao
Cordillera
Ilagan
Baguio
Dagupan
Luzon
Angeles
Cabanatuan
Mt. Pinatubo
4872ft (1485m)
PHILIPPINES
MANILA
Lucena
Naga
Batangas
Legazpi City
Mindoro
Sibuyan Sea
Calbayog
Mindoro Strait
Roxas City
Samar
Panay Island
Cadiz
Tacloban
Iloilo
Leyte
Palawan
Bacolod City
Cebu
Puerto Princesa
Negros
Bohol Sea
Butuan
Cagayan de Oro
Iligan
Bislig
Sulu Sea
Mindanao
Zamboanga
Moro Gulf
Digos
Davao
Basilan
Lebak
Davao Gulf
Sandakan
Sulu Archipelago
General Santos
Kepulauan Talaud
Celebes Sea
Kepulauan Sangir
Pulau Morotai
Manado
Bitung
Molucca Sea
Pulau Halmahera
Tolitoli
Gorontalo
Ternate
Pulau Waigeo
Equator
Strait
Gulf of Tomini
Halmahera Sea
Selat Dampier
Sorong
Pulau Biak
marinda
Palu
Molucca Sea
Jazirah Doberai
Manokwari
Pulau Yapen
Poso
Kepulauan Banggai
Maluku
Teluk Cenderawasih
Maniwori
Sungai Mamberamo
Jayapura
Celebes (Sulawesi)
Kepulauan Sula
Pulau Misool
Teluk Berau
Wotu
Danau Towuti
Ceram Sea
Wahai
Obome
Puncak Jaya
16,503ft (5030m)
Pegunungan Maoke
Parepare
Waflia
Tifu
Pulau Seram
Ambon
Papua (Irian Jaya)
Amamapare
Singkang
Kendari
Pulau Buru
New Guinea
Watampone
Kolaka
Pulau Buton
Kepulauan Kai
Kepulauan Aru
Makassar
Banda Sea
Sungai Digul
Bulukumba
Kepulauan Tanimbar
Flores Sea
Kepulauan Tanimbar
Pulau Yamdena
Arafura Sea
Lesser Sunda Islands
(Nusa Tenggara)
Kepulauan Alor
Pulau Wetar
Flores
DILI
Tutuala
EAST TIMOR
Selat Sumba
Endeh
Timor
Savu Sea
Pulau Sumba
Kupang
Nikiniki
Timor Sea
PAPUA NEW GUINEA
Alotip

0 km   200   400
0 miles   200   400

B   C   D   E   F   G   H

Indian Ocean

THE THIRD LARGEST ocean in the world, the Indian Ocean is bounded by Africa, Asia, Australasia, and the Southern Ocean. The ocean contains some 5,000 islands. Madagascar and Sri Lanka are large, but most of the islands are small and ringed by coral reefs. The people of the Maldives have very mixed origins, incorporating Indian, Sinhalese, Arab, and African heritage, while two-thirds of those living on Mauritius are Indian immigrants and their descendents. Altogether, about one-fifth of the world's population live on this ocean's warm shores. Those along the northern coasts are often threatened by monsoon rain and tropical storms, which can cause severe flooding.

THE MALDIVES
The Maldives is a low-lying archipelago of 1,190 small, coral islands, of which 200 are inhabited. The main industries are fishing—still carried out by traditional pole-and-line methods to conserve stocks—and tourism. Holiday resorts are on separate islands to those inhabited by the locals, so as not to disturb the Maldive peoples' traditional Muslim lifestyles.

CORAL ISLANDS
Coral is a living organism formed in warm water by tiny sea creatures known as polyps. These creatures build limestone skeletons around themselves, which accumulate over thousands of years. As sea levels change, this coral can be exposed as low-lying islands or submerged as reefs.

THE SEYCHELLES
The Seychelles consists of around 155 islands—some are coral islands while others are mountainous and made of granite. Most Seychellois people are Creoles—people of mixed African, Asian, and European ancestry. There are also small Chinese and Indian communities.

Market on the largest Seychelles island, Mahé

ENVIRONMENT
Beautiful shells are for sale on this beach in South Africa. If the trader only collects empty shells, no harm is done, but in many parts of the world, dealers hunt live shellfish, sea turtles, and rare species of starfish and sea urchins. Nations such as the Maldives take great care to protect their environment.

LIMITED TOURISM
The tropical climate, sandy beaches, beautiful coral reefs, and abundant marine life make both the Seychelles and the Maldives ideal tourist destinations. These same features also make them extremely attractive to scuba divers. However, the fragile environment of both island nations means that they have deliberately tried to make them exclusive, attracting only limited numbers of wealthy visitors, instead of pursuing mass tourism.

Mediterranean Sea

Arabia Peninsu

Red Sea

Gulf Ade

Ethiopian Highlands

Horn Afric

Andre Tablemo

AFRICA

Somali

COMOR

MAYOT (to Fran

MADAG

Mozambique Channel

Davie Ridge

Mozambique Plateau

Nata Basi

Africana Seamount

Agulhas Plateau

Agulhas Basin

Prince Edward Island (to South Africa)

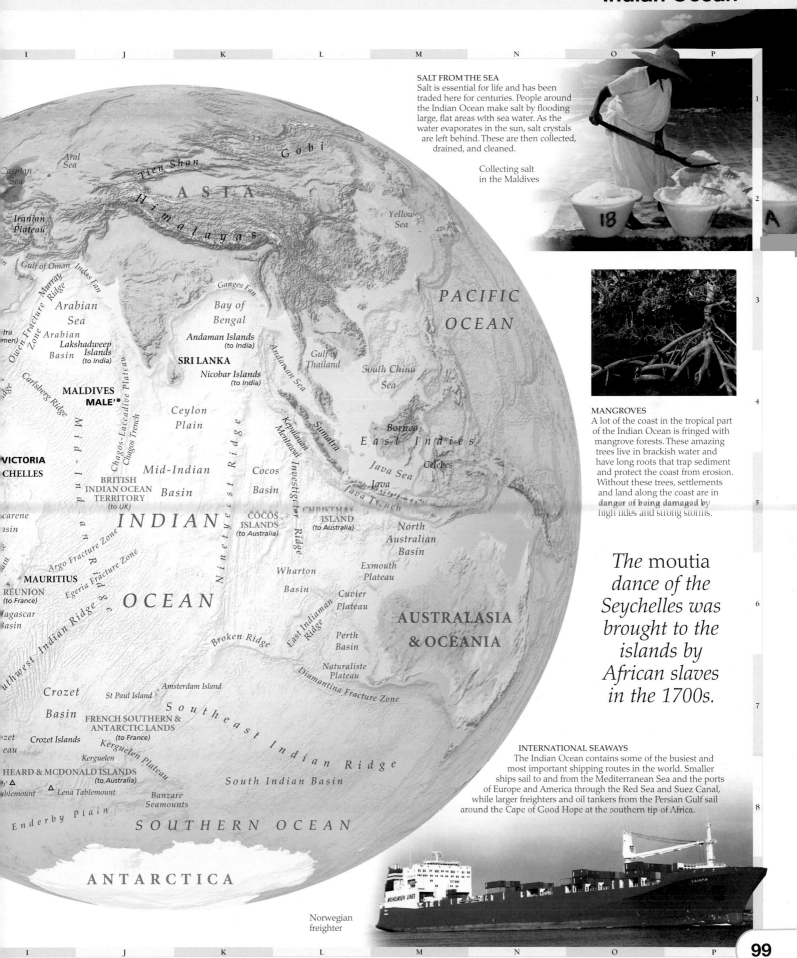

SALT FROM THE SEA
Salt is essential for life and has been traded here for centuries. People around the Indian Ocean make salt by flooding large, flat areas with sea water. As the water evaporates in the sun, salt crystals are left behind. These are then collected, drained, and cleaned.

Collecting salt in the Maldives

MANGROVES
A lot of the coast in the tropical part of the Indian Ocean is fringed with mangrove forests. These amazing trees live in brackish water and have long roots that trap sediment and protect the coast from erosion. Without these trees, settlements and land along the coast are in danger of being damaged by high tides and strong storms.

The moutia dance of the Seychelles was brought to the islands by African slaves in the 1700s.

INTERNATIONAL SEAWAYS
The Indian Ocean contains some of the busiest and most important shipping routes in the world. Smaller ships sail to and from the Mediterranean Sea and the ports of Europe and America through the Red Sea and Suez Canal, while larger freighters and oil tankers from the Persian Gulf sail around the Cape of Good Hope at the southern tip of Africa.

Norwegian freighter

Map labels

Aral Sea
Caspian Sea
Tien Shan
Gobi
ASIA
Himalayas
Iranian Plateau
Yellow Sea
Gulf of Oman
Indus Fan
Murray Ridge
Owen Fracture Zone
Arabian Sea
Ganges Fan
Bay of Bengal
PACIFIC OCEAN
Arabian Basin
Lakshadweep Islands (to India)
Andaman Islands (to India)
SRI LANKA
Carlsberg Ridge
MALDIVES
MALE'
Ceylon Plain
Nicobar Islands (to India)
Andaman Sea
Gulf of Thailand
South China Sea
Chagos-Laccadive Plateau
Chagos Trench
Sumatra
Kepulauan Mentawai
VICTORIA
CHELLES
Mid-Indian Basin
Mid-Indian Ridge
BRITISH INDIAN OCEAN TERRITORY (to UK)
Cocos Basin
Borneo
East Indies
Celebes
Java Sea
Java
Investigator Ridge
Ninetyeast Ridge
INDIAN
COCOS ISLANDS (to Australia)
CHRISTMAS ISLAND (to Australia)
Java Trench
carene Basin
MAURITIUS
Argo Fracture Zone
Egeria Fracture Zone
Wharton Basin
North Australian Basin
RÉUNION (to France)
agascar Basin
OCEAN
Southwest Indian Ridge
Exmouth Plateau
Cuvier Plateau
AUSTRALASIA & OCEANIA
East Indiaman Ridge
Perth Basin
Broken Ridge
Naturaliste Plateau
Diamantina Fracture Zone
Crozet Basin
St Paul Island
Amsterdam Island
Southeast Indian Ridge
FRENCH SOUTHERN & ANTARCTIC LANDS (to France)
Crozet Islands
Kerguelen Plateau
Kerguelen
HEARD & McDONALD ISLANDS (to Australia)
South Indian Basin
Lena Tablemount
Banzare Seamounts
ablemount
Enderby Plain
SOUTHERN OCEAN
ANTARCTICA

AUSTRALASIA & OCEANIA

Unknown to the outside world before the 17th century, Australia is a still a sparsely inhabited land where most people live in cities. At its heart is a great arid desert, in stark contrast to the islands of Oceania where all life revolves around the glittering ocean. The 3,000 named islands are grouped into nations, listed below in order of land area.

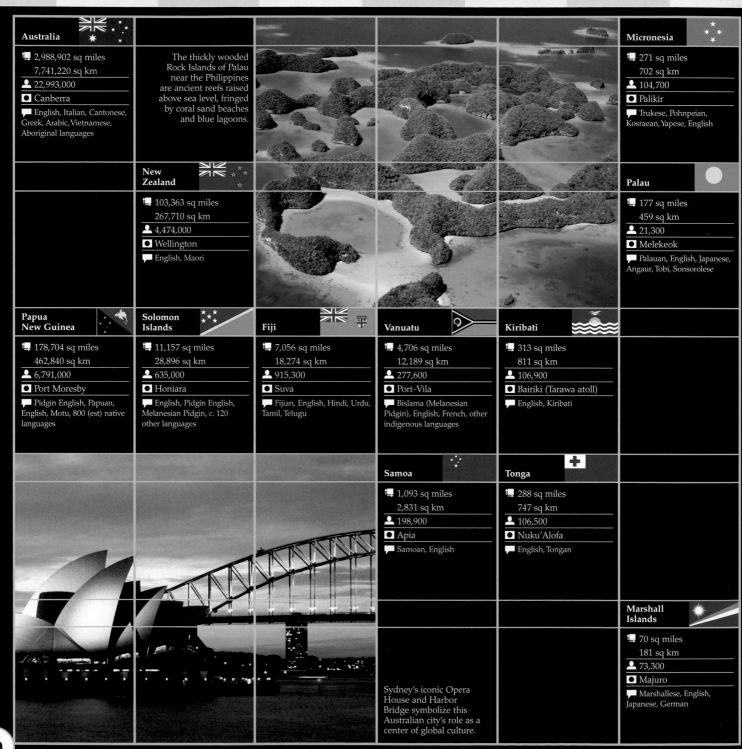

Australia
- 🗺 2,988,902 sq miles
  7,741,220 sq km
- 👤 22,993,000
- ⬛ Canberra
- 💬 English, Italian, Cantonese, Greek, Arabic, Vietnamese, Aboriginal languages

The thickly wooded Rock Islands of Palau near the Philippines are ancient reefs raised above sea level, fringed by coral sand beaches and blue lagoons.

New Zealand
- 🗺 103,363 sq miles
  267,710 sq km
- 👤 4,474,000
- ⬛ Wellington
- 💬 English, Maori

Micronesia
- 🗺 271 sq miles
  702 sq km
- 👤 104,700
- ⬛ Palikir
- 💬 Trukese, Pohnpeian, Kosraean, Yapese, English

Palau
- 🗺 177 sq miles
  459 sq km
- 👤 21,300
- ⬛ Melekeok
- 💬 Palauan, English, Japanese, Angaur, Tobi, Sonsorolese

Papua New Guinea
- 🗺 178,704 sq miles
  462,840 sq km
- 👤 6,791,000
- ⬛ Port Moresby
- 💬 Pidgin English, Papuan, English, Motu, 800 (est) native languages

Solomon Islands
- 🗺 11,157 sq miles
  28,896 sq km
- 👤 635,000
- ⬛ Honiara
- 💬 English, Pidgin English, Melanesian Pidgin, c. 120 other languages

Fiji
- 🗺 7,056 sq miles
  18,274 sq km
- 👤 915,300
- ⬛ Suva
- 💬 Fijian, English, Hindi, Urdu, Tamil, Telugu

Vanuatu
- 🗺 4,706 sq miles
  12,189 sq km
- 👤 277,600
- ⬛ Port-Vila
- 💬 Bislama (Melanesian Pidgin), English, French, other indigenous languages

Kiribati
- 🗺 313 sq miles
  811 sq km
- 👤 106,900
- ⬛ Bairiki (Tarawa atoll)
- 💬 English, Kiribati

Samoa
- 🗺 1,093 sq miles
  2,831 sq km
- 👤 198,900
- ⬛ Apia
- 💬 Samoan, English

Tonga
- 🗺 288 sq miles
  747 sq km
- 👤 106,500
- ⬛ Nuku'Alofa
- 💬 English, Tongan

Marshall Islands
- 🗺 70 sq miles
  181 sq km
- 👤 73,300
- ⬛ Majuro
- 💬 Marshallese, English, Japanese, German

Sydney's iconic Opera House and Harbor Bridge symbolize this Australian city's role as a center of global culture.

The ancestors of today's Pacific Islanders reached their islands by crossing the ocean in giant canoes. Many islanders still rely on the sea for a living.

The colorfully named Champagne Pool is one of many hot springs in Rotorua, New Zealand—one of the most volcanically active countries in the world.

Tuvalu	Nauru
🏝 10 sq miles	🏝 8 sq miles
26 sq km	21 sq km
👤 11,000	👤 9,600
⬤ Fongafale (Funafuti Atol)	⬤ None
💬 Tuvaluan, Kiribati, English	💬 Nauruan, Kiribati, Chinese, Tuvaluan, English

SW Pacific

THE ISLANDS of the southwest Pacific are home to people of many different cultures and languages. The islands are divided into three general groups based on their location and the similarities between their peoples. The Polynesian islands to the east include Tonga, Samoa, the Cook Islands, and Tahiti. Melanesia includes Fiji, the Solomon Islands, and Vanuatu. The smallest group, Micronesia, includes the Marshall, Kiribati, and Caroline Islands. The first Europeans came to the southwest Pacific in the 1600s, several thousand years after Melanesians, Micronesians, and Polynesians first arrived.

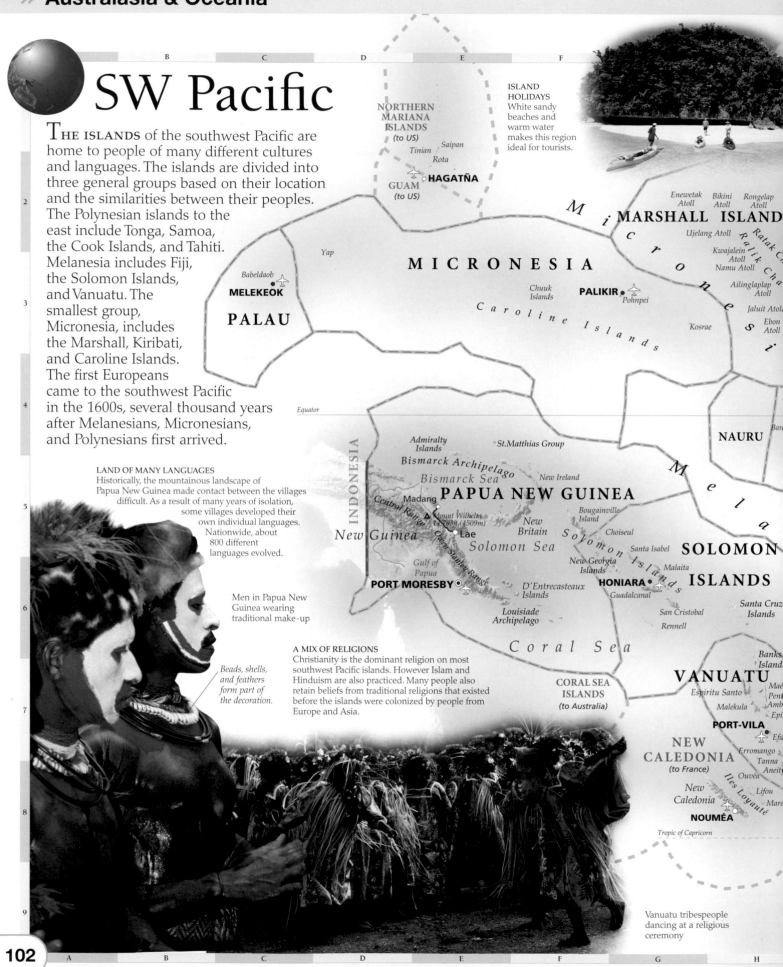

ISLAND HOLIDAYS
White sandy beaches and warm water makes this region ideal for tourists.

LAND OF MANY LANGUAGES
Historically, the mountainous landscape of Papua New Guinea made contact between the villages difficult. As a result of many years of isolation, some villages developed their own individual languages. Nationwide, about 800 different languages evolved.

Men in Papua New Guinea wearing traditional make-up

Beads, shells, and feathers form part of the decoration.

A MIX OF RELIGIONS
Christianity is the dominant religion on most southwest Pacific islands. However Islam and Hinduism are also practiced. Many people also retain beliefs from traditional religions that existed before the islands were colonized by people from Europe and Asia.

Vanuatu tribespeople dancing at a religious ceremony

Map labels

NORTHERN MARIANA ISLANDS (to US)
Tinian
Saipan
Rota
GUAM (to US)
HAGATÑA

MARSHALL ISLAND
Enewetak Atoll
Bikini Atoll
Rongelap Atoll
Ujelang Atoll
Ratak Ch
Kwajalein Atoll
Ratlik Cha
Namu Atoll
Ailinglaplap Atoll
Jaluit Atol
Ebon Atoll

Yap
MICRONESIA
Chuuk Islands
PALIKIR
Pohnpei
Caroline Islands
Kosrae

Babeldaob
MELEKEOK
PALAU

Equator

NAURU

INDONESIA
Admiralty Islands
St.Matthias Group
Bismarck Archipelago
Bismarck Sea
New Ireland
PAPUA NEW GUINEA
Central Range
Madang
Mount Wilhelm 14,793ft (4509m)
New Guinea
Lae
Owen Stanley Range
Bougainville Island
New Britain
Choiseul
Solomon Sea
Santa Isabel
Solomon Islands
Malaita
SOLOMON ISLANDS
New Georgia Islands
Gulf of Papua
PORT MORESBY
D'Entrecasteaux Islands
HONIARA
Guadalcanal
San Cristobal
Santa Cruz Islands
Louisiade Archipelago
Rennell
Coral Sea

CORAL SEA ISLANDS (to Australia)

VANUATU
Banks Island
Espiritu Santo
Maé
Pen
Malekula
Amb
Epi
PORT-VILA
NEW CALEDONIA (to France)
Erromango
Tanna
Aneit
Ouvéa
Lifou
New Caledonia
Iles Loyauté
Mare
NOUMÉA

Tropic of Capricorn

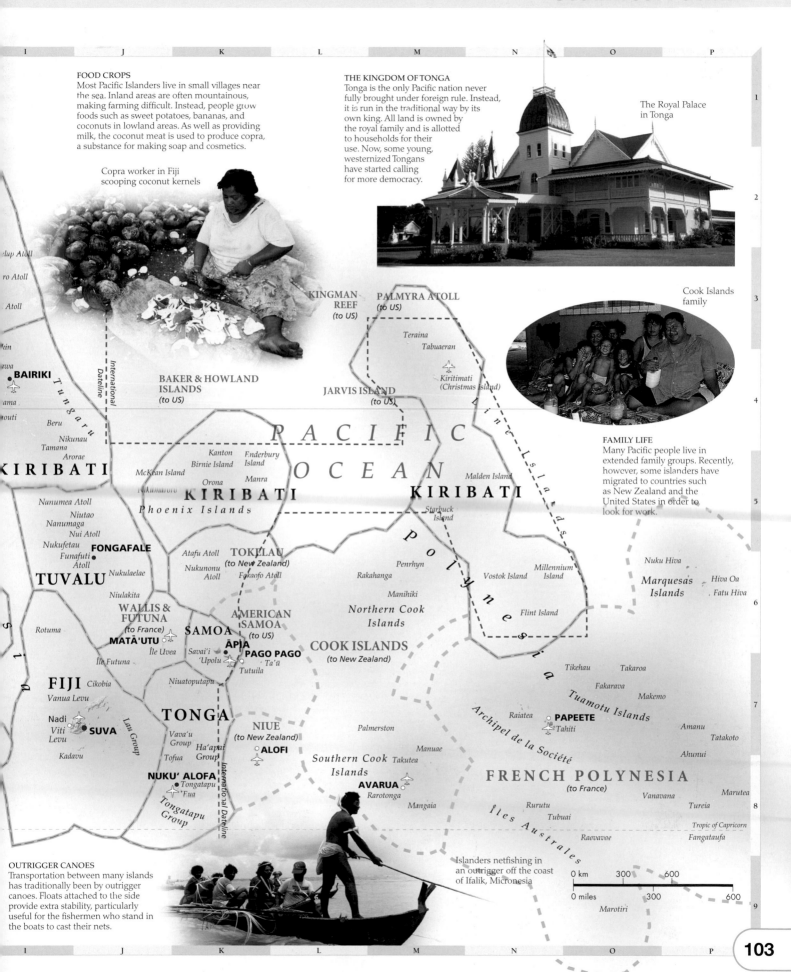

FOOD CROPS
Most Pacific Islanders live in small villages near the sea. Inland areas are often mountainous, making farming difficult. Instead, people grow foods such as sweet potatoes, bananas, and coconuts in lowland areas. As well as providing milk, the coconut meat is used to produce copra, a substance for making soap and cosmetics.

Copra worker in Fiji scooping coconut kernels

THE KINGDOM OF TONGA
Tonga is the only Pacific nation never fully brought under foreign rule. Instead, it is run in the traditional way by its own king. All land is owned by the royal family and is allotted to households for their use. Now, some young, westernized Tongans have started calling for more democracy.

The Royal Palace in Tonga

Cook Islands family

FAMILY LIFE
Many Pacific people live in extended family groups. Recently, however, some islanders have migrated to countries such as New Zealand and the United States in order to look for work.

OUTRIGGER CANOES
Transportation between many islands has traditionally been by outrigger canoes. Floats attached to the side provide extra stability, particularly useful for the fishermen who stand in the boats to cast their nets.

Islanders netfishing in an outrigger off the coast of Ifalik, Micronesia

KINGMAN REEF (to US)
PALMYRA ATOLL (to US)
Teraina
Tabuaeran
Kiritimati (Christmas Island)
BAKER & HOWLAND ISLANDS (to US)
JARVIS ISLAND (to US)

PACIFIC OCEAN

BAIRIKI
International Dateline
Tungaru
Beru
Nikunau
Tamana
Arorae
KIRIBATI
Kanton
Birnie Island
Enderbury Island
McKean Island
Orona
Manra
Nikumaroro
KIRIBATI
Phoenix Islands
Malden Island
Line Islands
KIRIBATI
Starbuck Island
Polynesia

Nunumea Atoll
Niutao
Nanumaga
Nui Atoll
Nukufetau
FONGAFALE
Funafuti Atoll
Nukulaelae
TUVALU
Niulakita
Atafu Atoll
Nukunonu Atoll
TOKELAU (to New Zealand)
Fakaofo Atoll
Penrhyn
Rakahanga
Manihiki
Northern Cook Islands
Vostok Island
Millennium Island
Flint Island
Nuku Hiva
Marquesas Islands
Hiva Oa
Fatu Hiva

WALLIS & FUTUNA (to France)
MATĀ'UTU
Rotuma
Île Futuna
Île Uvea
SAMOA
AMERICAN SAMOA (to US)
ĀPIA
Savai'i
'Upolu
PAGO PAGO
Ta'ū
Tutuila
COOK ISLANDS (to New Zealand)
Tikehau
Takaroa
Fakarava
Makemo
Raiatea
PAPEETE
Tahiti
Amanu
Tatakoto
Ahunui
Tuamotu Islands

FIJI
Cikobia
Vanua Levu
Nadi
Viti Levu
SUVA
Kadavu
Lau Group
Niuatoputapu
TONGA
Vava'u Group
Tofua
Ha'apai Group
ALOFI
NIUE (to New Zealand)
Palmerston
Manuae
Takutea
Southern Cook Islands
AVARUA
Rarotonga
Mangaia
NUKU'ALOFA
Tongatapu
'Eua
Tongatapu Group
International Dateline
Archipel de la Société
FRENCH POLYNESIA (to France)
Rurutu
Tubuai
Îles Australes
Raivavae
Vanavana
Tureia
Marutea
Tropic of Capricorn
Fangataufa
Marotiri

0 km 300 600
0 miles 300 600

Australia

A HUGE, GENERALLY FLAT COUNTRY, Australia has relatively few inhabitants. This is mainly because most of the land is hot, semi-arid desert—known as the outback—unsuitable for towns or farms. In places where there is some vegetation, or the land has been irrigated, sheep and cattle are grazed. Wheat is grown in the fertile south. The first people to live here were the Aboriginals, who arrived from Asia at least 50,000 years ago. Today, most Australians are descendants of European immigrants, with a more recent addition of Asians.

FLYING DOCTOR
For anyone living in the remote Australian outback, the nearest doctor can be many hours away. When emergency help is needed, the Royal Flying Doctor Services can get to the scene to treat a patient or fly them to hospital.

AUSTRALIAN ABORIGINALS
The original inhabitants of Australia had an intimate understanding of their environment. This connection to the land, and its plants and animals, affects every aspect of their culture. When Europeans started arriving in the late 18th century, only the Aboriginals in remote areas escaped contact with the diseases they brought. Today, Aboriginals rarely live off the land, but work in factories or farms.

MINING
Australia has one of the world's most important mining industries, with resources including gold (left), coal, natural gas, iron ore, copper, and opals. However, damage to the environment, and Aboriginal claims over land used for mining, still need to be faced.

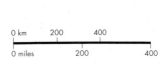

AUSTRALIAN FOOTBALL
A popular sport here is Australian Rules Football. One of the rules is that players can kick or punch the ball but they must not throw it. Many Australians either play the game themselves or support their favorite team. As the name implies, the game originated in Australia, but it now has leagues in other countries, such as Great Britain and the US.

OUTDOOR SPORTS
A warm climate, with easy access to beaches and wilderness areas, has made outdoor activities an important part of modern Australian life. Water sports such as swimming, sailing, and surfing are especially popular. Because of the danger of exposure to strong sunlight, people are told to cover up and always use sunscreen.

Melville Island
Bathurst Island
Die
Darwin
Cape Londonderry
Joseph Bonaparte Gulf
Pine Cr
Bonaparte
Bigge Island
Archipelago
Victoria River
Heywood Islands
Wyndham
Kununurra
Top Spri Roadho
Kimberley Plateau
King Sound
Fitzroy Crossing
Halls Creek
Tanam Deser
Broome
Fitzroy River
INDIAN OCEAN
Eighty Mile Beach
Great Sandy Desert
N
Port Hedland
Barrow Island
Dampier
Marble Bar
Percival Lakes
TE
Exmouth Gulf
Onslow
Fortescue River
WESTERN
Exmouth
Hamersley Range
Ashburton River
Newman
Lake Mackay
Mac
Tropic of Capricorn
Barlee Range
Lake Disappointment
A U S T
Gibson Desert
Lake Amadeus
Bernier Island
Gascoyne River
Uluru (Ayers Rock) △ 2844ft (867m)
Dorre Island
Carnarvon
Robinson Range
Lake Carnegie
Shark Bay
Denham
Lake Wells
Musgra Ranges
Dirk Hartog Island
Murchison River
Meekatharra
A U S T R A L I A
Kalbarri
Mount Magnet
Great Victoria Desert
Geraldton
Lake Carey
Lake Barlee
Lake Moore
Lake Rebecca
Moora
Kalgoorlie
Reid
Coolgardie
Zanthus
Nullarbor Plain
Southern Cross
Gingin
Lake Cowan
Eucla
Perth
Northam
Merredin
Fremantle
Brookton
Norseman
Balladonia
Mandurah
Narrogin
Bunbury
Wagin
Great Australian Bigh
Busselton
Collie
Katanning
Esperance
Manjimup
Augusta
Albany

0 km 200 400
0 miles 200 400

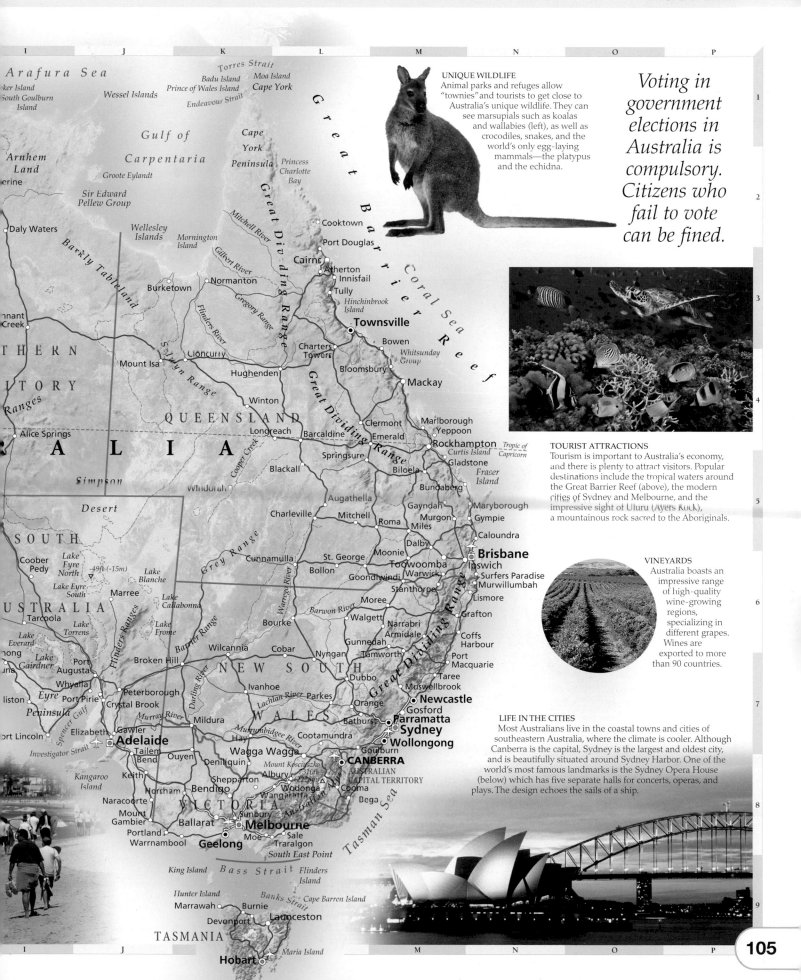

Arafura Sea

Torres Strait
Badu Island
Prince of Wales Island
Moa Island
Cape York
Endeavour Strait

Wessel Islands

Gulf of Carpentaria

Cape York

Cape York Peninsula

Princess Charlotte Bay

Groote Eylandt

Arnhem Land

Sir Edward Pellew Group

Wellesley Islands

Mornington Island

Daly Waters

Barkly Tableland

Burketown

Normanton

Great Dividing Range

Mitchell River

Gilbert River

Gregory Range

Flinders River

Cooktown

Port Douglas

Cairns

Atherton
Innisfail
Tully

Hinchinbrook Island

Townsville

Bowen

Whitsunday Group

Coral Sea

Great Barrier Reef

Charters Towers

Bloomsbury

Mackay

Cloncurry

Mount Isa

Saxby Range

Hughenden

Winton

QUEENSLAND

Clermont

Emerald

Marlborough

Yeppoon

Rockhampton

Curtis Island

Gladstone

Tropic of Capricorn

Fraser Island

Alice Springs

Longreach

Barcaldine

Springsure

Biloela

Bundaberg

TERRITORY

Ranges

Cooper Creek

Simpson

Blackall

Windorah

Desert

Augathella

Maryborough

Gayndah

Murgon

Gympie

SOUTH

Charleville

Mitchell

Roma

Miles

Caloundra

Coober Pedy

Lake Eyre North

-49ft (-15m)

Lake Blanche

Lake Eyre South

Cunnamulla

St. George

Moonie

Dalby

Toowoomba

Warwick

Ipswich

Brisbane

Surfers Paradise

Murwillumbah

Bollon

Goondiwindi

Stanthorpe

Lismore

AUSTRALIA

Marree

Lake Callabonna

Warrego River

Moree

Barwon River

Walgett

Narrabri

Armidale

Grafton

Tarcoola

Lake Frome

Grey Range

Bourke

Coffs Harbour

Lake Everard

Lake Torrens

Flinders Ranges

Barrier Range

Wilcannia

Cobar

Gunnedah

Port Macquarie

Lake Gairdner

Broken Hill

Nyngan

Tamworth

NEW SOUTH

Port Augusta

Whyalla

Peterborough

Darling River

Ivanhoe

Dubbo

Muswellbrook

Taree

Eyre Peninsula

Port Pirie

Crystal Brook

Parkes

Orange

Newcastle

Gosford

Great Dividing Range

Elizabeth

Peterborough

Lachlan River

Bathurst

Parramatta

Sydney

Port Lincoln

Gawler

Murray River

Mildura

Hay

Murrumbidgee River

Cootamundra

WALES

Goulburn

Wollongong

Investigator Strait

Adelaide

Tailem Bend

Ouyen

Deniliquin

Wagga Wagga

Mount Kosciuszko 7310ft 2228m

Cooma

CANBERRA

AUSTRALIAN CAPITAL TERRITORY

Kangaroo Island

Keith

Shepparton

Albury

Wodonga

Wangaratta

Bega

Tasman Sea

Naracoorte

Northam

Bendigo

VICTORIA

Sunbury

Tasman Sea

Mount Gambier

Ballarat

Melbourne

Moe

Sale

Traralgon

Portland

Warrnambool

Geelong

South East Point

King Island

Bass Strait

Flinders Island

Hunter Island

Banks Strait

Cape Barren Island

Marrawah

Burnie

TASMANIA

Devonport

Launceston

Maria Island

Hobart

UNIQUE WILDLIFE
Animal parks and refuges allow "townies" and tourists to get close to Australia's unique wildlife. They can see marsupials such as koalas and wallabies (left), as well as crocodiles, snakes, and the world's only egg-laying mammals—the platypus and the echidna.

Voting in government elections in Australia is compulsory. Citizens who fail to vote can be fined.

TOURIST ATTRACTIONS
Tourism is important to Australia's economy, and there is plenty to attract visitors. Popular destinations include the tropical waters around the Great Barrier Reef (above), the modern cities of Sydney and Melbourne, and the impressive sight of Uluru (Ayers Rock), a mountainous rock sacred to the Aboriginals.

VINEYARDS
Australia boasts an impressive range of high-quality wine-growing regions, specializing in different grapes. Wines are exported to more than 90 countries.

LIFE IN THE CITIES
Most Australians live in the coastal towns and cities of southeastern Australia, where the climate is cooler. Although Canberra is the capital, Sydney is the largest and oldest city, and is beautifully situated around Sydney Harbor. One of the world's most famous landmarks is the Sydney Opera House (below) which has five separate halls for concerts, operas, and plays. The design echoes the sails of a ship.

New Zealand

MADE UP OF TWO MAIN ISLANDS and several smaller ones, New Zealand is one of the most isolated countries in the world. Located in the southern Pacific, the country has a mild climate, with warm summers and cool, wet winters. Both main islands have mountains, short, swift-flowing rivers, forests, and fertile farmland. Until the Europeans arrived, most of the landscape was covered in dense forest, known as native bush. Today, although forests remain, much has been cleared for farming. Most New Zealanders live on North Island, which is warmer and less mountainous. Although New Zealanders are of mainly British descent, the Maoris – a people of Polynesian origin – were the first to arrive about 1,000 years ago. Today, non-Maori Polynesians and Asians are adding to the ethnic mix. The country has a liberal, clean, green image and a high standard of living.

AUCKLAND
With its safe harbor and nearby scenic islands, Auckland is known as the "city of sails." It boasts more pleasure boats per person than anywhere else in the world. The water that separates the bigger islands is home to dolphins, families of blue penguins, and the occasional whale.

Greenstone (jade) carving, an example of Maori art

MAORI CULTURE
Maoris make up almost 14 per cent of the population, with most living on North Island. Before the coming of the *Pakeha* (white man), Maori history was passed on orally to succeeding generations. This included many legends and *waiata* (songs). Their carvings in wood (left) and stone (right) were another way they recorded and remembered events. In recent years, interest in Maori culture has increased, and school children are now taught the Maori language.

In 1893, New Zealand was the first country to give women the vote.

PACIFIC OCEAN

East Cape
Ruatoria
Gisborne
Poverty Bay
Mahia Peninsula
Wairoa
Hawke Bay
Napier
Hastings
Havelock North
Waipawa
Waipukurau
Dannevirke
Woodville

Bay of Plenty
Whakatane
Opotiki
Kawerau
Murupara
Waiouru

Tauranga
Katikati
Matamata
Rotorua
Lake Rotorua
Lake Rotoiti

Mayor Island
Whitianga
Whangamata
Coromandel
Thames
Paeroa
Morrinsville
Cambridge
Tokoroa
Taihape

Coromandel
Coville Channel
Great Barrier Island

Little Barrier Island
Hauraki Gulf

Manurewa
Papakura
Pukekohe
Huntly
Hamilton
Otorohanga
Te Kuiti
Taumarunui

Lake Taupo
Taupo
Turangi
▲ Mount Ruapehu (2797m)

Kaikohe
Hikurangi
Whangarei
Kerikeri
Paihia
Kaitaia
Okaihau
Ruawai
Wellsford
Warkworth
Helensville
Waiuku
Takapuna
Auckland

North
Island

Kaipara Harbour
Wairoa

Hokianga Harbour
Ninety Mile Beach
Cape Reinga
Three Kings Islands
North Cape
Te Kao
Great Exhibition Bay

Kaikohe

Rakaumangai Ranges
Kaweroa

Tasman Sea

North Taranaki Bight
Waitara
New Plymouth
Cape Egmont
Mount Taranaki (Mount Egmont) 8261ft (2518m) ▲
Stratford
Hawera
Patea
Wanganui
Marton
Feilding
Rangitikei
South Taranaki Bight

Ohura
Raetihi
Ruatahuna

0 km | 50 | 100
0 miles | 50 | 100

FILM INDUSTRY
New Zealand has a well-established film industry. Today, thanks to the acclaimed films based on J.R.R. Tolkien's trilogy *The Lord of the Rings* (above) and *The Hobbit*, the country has become increasingly popular with international studios for location work. The country offers an unusually wide range of scenery as well as technical experts.

AN AGRICULTURAL NATION
Agriculture is of prime importance, and accounts for more than half of national export earnings. Orchards produce a vast range of fruit from apples (above) to kiwi fruit (below). Cereals and other crops, such as sunflowers, add color and variety to the landscape. Traditional sheep and cattle farming has expanded to include deer, goats, and even ostriches.

UNIQUE WILDLIFE
New Zealand has many unique and endangered animal species, especially birds. There were no mammal predators before humans introduced them, so many animal species have few means of defense, and some birds such as the kiwi cannot fly. Conservation schemes are now in place to protect endangered species.

Flightless Kiwi bird

GREEN ENERGY
Most of the country's electricity comes from hydroelectric power. It is generated by river water gushing through turbines inside dams at power stations. New Zealand also has geothermal energy, using heat from inside Earth.

VOLCANIC ACTIVITY
A fault line runs through New Zealand, where two major tectonic plates meet. It has caused devastating earthquakes, but has also helped to create breathtaking scenery. This includes South Island's Southern Alps, and many smaller volcanic mountains, hot springs, and geysers on North Island.

Lady Knox geyser, North Island

ADVENTURE SPORTS PARADISE
New Zealand offers a huge range of adventure sports and outdoor activities, from white-water rafting (below) to bungee jumping. The latter originated in Queenstown on South Island. The town is billed as the country's top adventure tourism destination because its surrounding lakes, mountains, and rivers, and its mostly dry climate, are ideal for outdoor pursuits.

Map labels

NEW ZEALAND

North Island area:
Masterton, Porirua, Lower Hutt, **WELLINGTON**, Cape Palliser, Cape Campbell

Cook Strait

South Island:
Golden Bay, Motueka, Nelson, Richmond, Picton, Blenheim, Seddon, Tasman Mountains, Mount Owen 6175ft (1883m), Tapawera, Clarence, Kaikoura, Karamea Bight, Seddonville, Westport, Cape Foulwind, Reefton, Lake Brunner, Runanga, Greymouth, Hokitika, Ross, Otira, Arthur's Pass 3038ft (926m), Rakaia, Harper Springs, Springs Junction, Waiau, Pegasus Bay, Rangiora, Kaiapoi, **Christchurch**, Lyttelton, Banks Peninsula, Lake Ellesmere, Oxford, Darfield, Canterbury Plains, Ashburton, Mayfield, Hinds, Geraldine, Temuka, Timaru, Canterbury Bight, Fairlie, Studholme, Waimate, Oamaru, Abut Head, Whataroa, Fox Glacier, Aoraki (Mt Cook) 12,283ft (3744m), Haast, Lake Pukaki, Mount Cook, Lake Tekapo, Waitaki, Hampden, Otago Peninsula, **Dunedin**, Mosgiel, Balclutha, Milton, Cromwell, Alexandra, Taieri, Clutha, Lake Wanaka, Lake Hawea, Wanaka, Queenstown, Lake Wakatipu, Lumsden, Mataura, Gore, Tokanui, Mataura, Eyre Mts, Te Anau, Lake Te Anau, Lake Manapouri, Winton, Invercargill, Riverton, Toetoes Bay, Ruapuke, Foveaux Strait, Codfish Island, Halfmoon Bay, Stewart Island, Muttonbird Islands, South West Cape, Milford Sound, George Sound, Caswell Sound, Resolution Island, West Cape, Ta Waewae Bay, Waiau, Livingstone Mts, Manapouri, Fiordland

Southern Alps, South Island

Pacific Ocean

THE LARGEST OCEAN ON EARTH, the Pacific covers one-third of Earth's surface. The island nations of Japan, Indonesia, Australia, New Zealand, and many others are completely surrounded by this enormous ocean, which stretches from the Arctic in the north to the Southern Ocean in the south. The Pacific is also the world's deepest ocean – its greatest known depth is in the Mariana Trench, off Guam, which plunges steeply for 36,198 ft (11,033 m). Within the Pacific, there are many smaller seas that lie near land. These include the Tasman Sea, the South China Sea, and the Bering Sea. There are more than 30,000 islands in the Pacific. Most are too small or barren to be inhabited, but others are home to people of many different cultures and religions. The native island peoples fall into three main groups—Polynesians, Melanesians, and Micronesians. Although the word *pacific* means "peaceful," strong currents, tropical storms, and tsunamis can all make this ocean far from peaceful.

HAWAII
This chain of eight volcanic islands and 124 islets forms the 50th state of the United States, and was admitted to the union in 1959. The dramatic landscape and palm-fringed beaches make Hawaii a popular destination for tourists. Today, native Hawaiians are a minority in their own land.

Hawaiian conch shells, once blown to sound a warning

Marine iguana on black volcanic rocks, Galápagos Islands

TSUNAMI
Earthquakes beneath the sea may cause giant waves called tsunamis. These can travel great distances across the ocean, building into a huge wall of water as they approach the coast. They can leave immense damage in their wake.

GALÁPAGOS ISLANDS
When British naturalist Charles Darwin (1809–1882) went to the Galápagos Islands, he found many unusual animals. He also noticed differences between animals of the same species living elsewhere. This led him to believe that, over time, animals adapt, or evolve, to suit their habitats.

SURFING
The Hawaiian sport of surfing ranks as the oldest sport in the USA. It was first practiced by the nobility as a form of religious ceremony until the 1820s when missionaries, who thought it immoral, tried to ban it. Today, surfing is one of the most popular watersports and can be seen all over the world, from Australia to the UK.

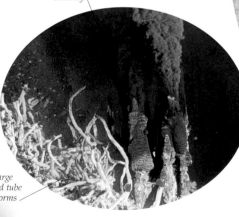

Black smoker chimney

Large red tube worms

DEEP-SEA VENTS
Underwater exploration has revealed some amazing places deep in the Pacific. Large vents, formed by solidified minerals, act as chimneys for super-hot steam and gas that stream up from the sea bed. These vents are known as black smokers. Scientists have found a host of new creatures living in this hostile environment.

ASIA

Sea of Japan (East Sea)

Yellow Sea

Japan

East China Sea

Shikoku Basin

Izu Trench

Ryukyu Trench

Taiwan

Philippine Sea

NORTHERN MARIANA ISLANDS (to US)

Mariana Trench

South China Basin

Philippine Basin

GUAM (to US)

Philippines

South China Sea

PALAU

Challenger Deep 35,827ft (1

Caroline Islan

MICRO

Celebes Sea

Borneo

Celebes

Me

East Indies

Java Sea

Banda Sea

New Guinea

Java

Timor

Timor Sea

Arafura Sea

Torres Strait

Great Ba Reef

INDIAN OCEAN

AUSTRALASIA & OCEANIA

Great Australian Bight

South

Bass S

Australian

Tasma

Basin

The Pacific is larger than Earth's entire land surface.

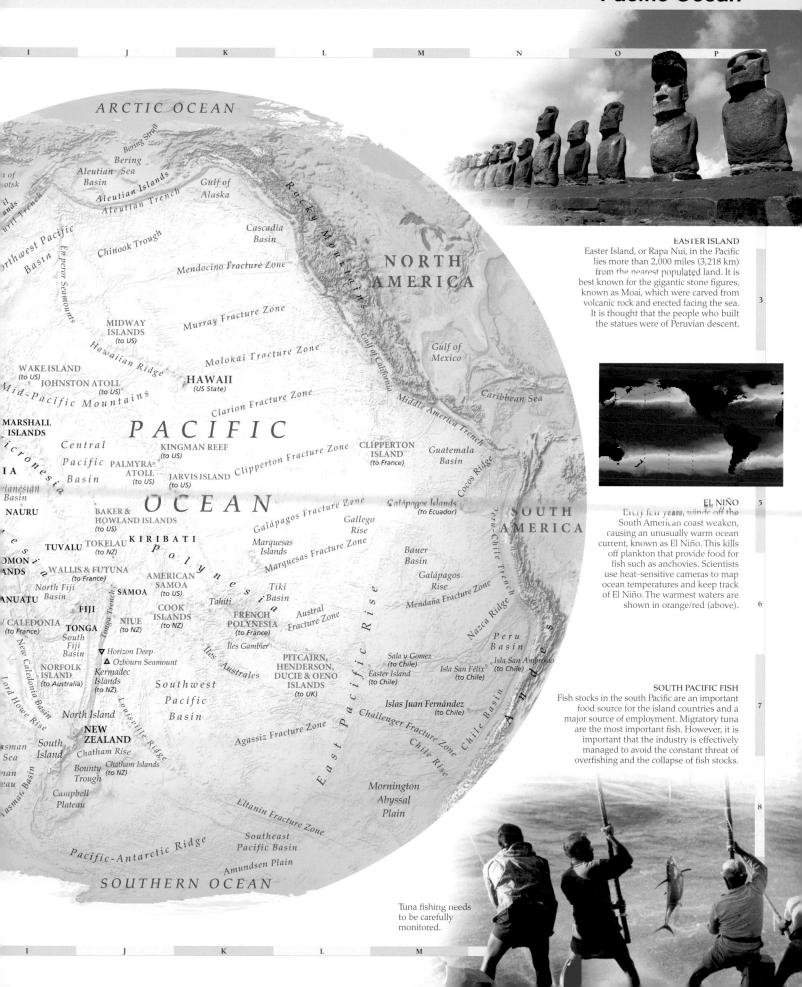

I J K L M N O P

ARCTIC OCEAN

Bering Strait

Bering
Sea

Aleutian Islands

Aleutian Trench

Gulf of
Alaska

Rocky Mountains

Cascadia
Basin

NORTH
AMERICA

Aleutian
Basin

Kuril Trench

a of
otsk
nds

Northwest Pacific
Basin

Emperor Seamounts

Chinook Trough

Mendocino Fracture Zone

Murray Fracture Zone

Gulf of California

MIDWAY
ISLANDS
(to US)

Hawaiian Ridge

Molokai Fracture Zone

Gulf of
Mexico

WAKE ISLAND
(to US)

JOHNSTON ATOLL
(to US)

HAWAII
(US State)

Clarion Fracture Zone

Middle America Trench

Caribbean Sea

Mid-Pacific Mountains

PACIFIC

MARSHALL
ISLANDS

Central
Pacific
Basin

KINGMAN REEF
(to US)

PALMYRA
ATOLL

JARVIS ISLAND
(to US)

Clipperton Fracture Zone

CLIPPERTON
ISLAND
(to France)

Guatemala
Basin

Micronesia

IA

OCEAN

NAURU

BAKER &
HOWLAND ISLANDS
(to US)

Galápagos Fracture Zone

Galápagos Islands
(to Ecuador)

SOUTH
AMERICA

Melanesian
Basin

Gallego
Rise

nesia

TUVALU

TOKELAU
(to NZ)

KIRIBATI

Marquesas
Islands

Marquesas Fracture Zone

Bauer
Basin

Peru-Chile Trench

Cocos Ridge

OMON
NDS

WALLIS & FUTUNA
(to France)

Polynesia

Galápagos
Rise

ANUATU

North Fiji
Basin

AMERICAN
SAMOA
(to US)

SAMOA

Tahiti

Tiki
Basin

Mendaña Fracture Zone

Nazca Ridge

CALEDONIA
(to France)

FIJI

TONGA

NIUE
(to NZ)

COOK
ISLANDS
(to NZ)

FRENCH
POLYNESIA
(to France)

Austral
Fracture Zone

Peru
Basin

Tonga Trench

South
Fiji
Basin

Îles Gambier

East Pacific Rise

Sala y Gomez
(to Chile)

Isla San Félix
(to Chile)

Isla San Ambrosio
(to Chile)

NORFOLK
ISLAND
(to Australia)

▽ Horizon Deep
△ Ozbourn Seamount

Kermadec
Islands
(to NZ)

Îles Australes

PITCAIRN,
HENDERSON,
DUCIE & OENO
ISLANDS
(to UK)

Easter Island
(to Chile)

Lord Howe Rise

Southwest
Pacific
Basin

Islas Juan Fernández
(to Chile)

Andes

Chile Basin

New Caledonia Basin

North Island

Louisville Ridge

Challenger Fracture Zone

Chile Rise

asman
Sea

South
Island

NEW
ZEALAND

Agassiz Fracture Zone

Chile Fracture Zone

an
eau

Chatham Rise

Bounty
Trough

Chatham Islands
(to NZ)

Mornington
Abyssal
Plain

asmat Basin

Campbell
Plateau

Eltanin Fracture Zone

Southeast
Pacific Basin

Pacific-Antarctic Ridge

Amundsen Plain

SOUTHERN OCEAN

I J K L M

Antarctica

THE FROZEN CONTINENT OF ANTARCTICA is covered by a vast icecap, many thousands of years old, and is surrounded by the freezing seas of the Southern Ocean. It is the only continent with no permanent inhabitants—the only people who come here are scientists or tourists. Although the land is rich in oil and minerals, mining is prohibited under the laws of the Antarctic Treaty. This treaty, agreed by 53 countries, made Antarctica a "continent for science" to be used for peaceful purposes only.

DAY TRIPPERS
Tourists visit Antarctica in summer. There are no resorts, so visitors generally stay on small cruise ships. When they come ashore, people have to wear insulated clothing and goggles to protect their eyes from glare off the ice.

OZONE HOLE
High in the atmosphere, ozone (a gas) forms a natural shield that protects us from the Sun's ultraviolet rays. Scientists at both poles have found holes in the ozone layer, caused by chemicals known as CFCs, once used in aerosols, fridges, and plastic packaging.

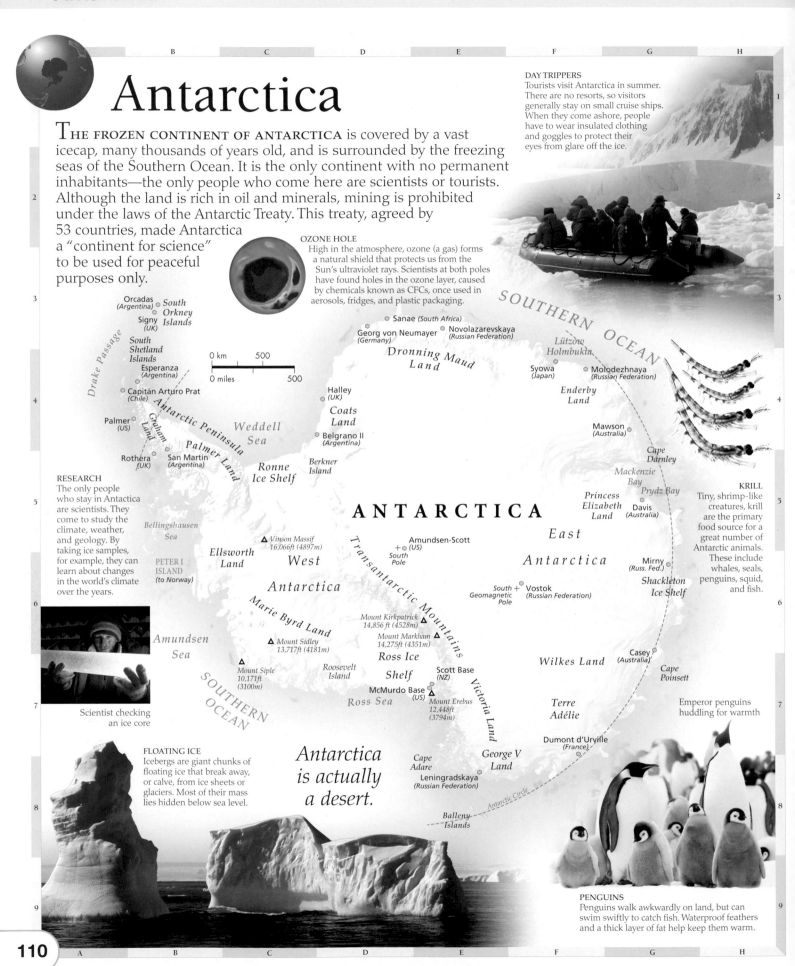

RESEARCH
The only people who stay in Antarctica are scientists. They come to study the climate, weather, and geology. By taking ice samples, for example, they can learn about changes in the world's climate over the years.

Scientist checking an ice core

FLOATING ICE
Icebergs are giant chunks of floating ice that break away, or calve, from ice sheets or glaciers. Most of their mass lies hidden below sea level.

KRILL
Tiny, shrimp-like creatures, krill are the primary food source for a great number of Antarctic animals. These include whales, seals, penguins, squid, and fish.

Emperor penguins huddling for warmth

PENGUINS
Penguins walk awkwardly on land, but can swim swiftly to catch fish. Waterproof feathers and a thick layer of fat help keep them warm.

Antarctica is actually a desert.

Map labels:
SOUTHERN OCEAN
Orcadas (Argentina)
South Orkney Islands
Signy (UK)
South Shetland Islands
Esperanza (Argentina)
Capitán Arturo Prat (Chile)
Palmer (US)
Rothera (UK)
San Martin (Argentina)
Drake Passage
Antarctic Peninsula
Graham Land
Palmer Land
Weddell Sea
Ronne Ice Shelf
Sanae (South Africa)
Georg von Neumayer (Germany)
Novolazarevskaya (Russian Federation)
Dronning Maud Land
Halley (UK)
Coats Land
Belgrano II (Argentina)
Berkner Island
Lützow Holmbukta
Syowa (Japan)
Molodezhnaya (Russian Federation)
Enderby Land
Mawson (Australia)
Cape Darnley
Mackenzie Bay
Prydz Bay
Princess Elizabeth Land
Davis (Australia)
East Antarctica
Bellingshausen Sea
PETER I ISLAND (to Norway)
Ellsworth Land
West Antarctica
Vinson Massif 16,066ft (4897m)
ANTARCTICA
Amundsen-Scott (US)
South Pole
Transantarctic Mountains
South Geomagnetic Pole
Vostok (Russian Federation)
Mirny (Russ. Fed.)
Shackleton Ice Shelf
Amundsen Sea
Marie Byrd Land
Mount Sidley 13,717ft (4181m)
Mount Siple 10,171ft (3100m)
Mount Kirkpatrick 14,856 ft (4528m)
Mount Markham 14,275ft (4351m)
Ross Ice Shelf
Roosevelt Island
Scott Base (NZ)
McMurdo Base (US)
Mount Erebus 12,448ft (3794m)
Victoria Land
Wilkes Land
Casey (Australia)
Cape Poinsett
Terre Adélie
SOUTHERN OCEAN
Ross Sea
Cape Adare
Leningradskaya (Russian Federation)
George V Land
Dumont d'Urville (France)
Antarctic Circle
Balleny Islands

0 km 500
0 miles 500

Arctic Ocean

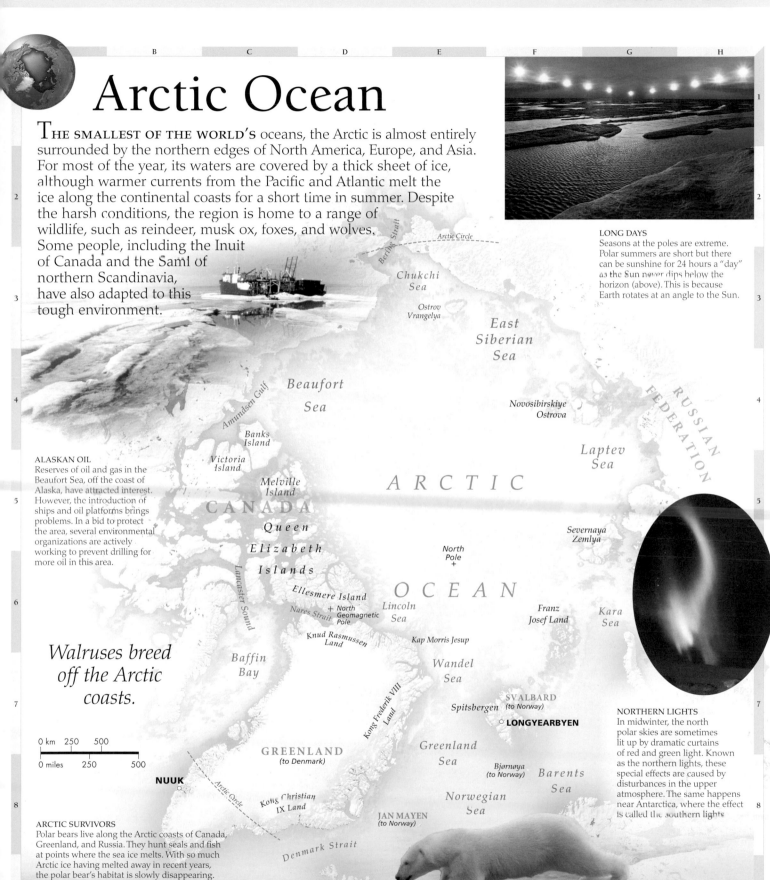

THE SMALLEST OF THE WORLD'S oceans, the Arctic is almost entirely surrounded by the northern edges of North America, Europe, and Asia. For most of the year, its waters are covered by a thick sheet of ice, although warmer currents from the Pacific and Atlantic melt the ice along the continental coasts for a short time in summer. Despite the harsh conditions, the region is home to a range of wildlife, such as reindeer, musk ox, foxes, and wolves. Some people, including the Inuit of Canada and the Sami of northern Scandinavia, have also adapted to this tough environment.

LONG DAYS
Seasons at the poles are extreme. Polar summers are short but there can be sunshine for 24 hours a "day" as the Sun never dips below the horizon (above). This is because Earth rotates at an angle to the Sun.

ALASKAN OIL
Reserves of oil and gas in the Beaufort Sea, off the coast of Alaska, have attracted interest. However, the introduction of ships and oil platforms brings problems. In a bid to protect the area, several environmental organizations are actively working to prevent drilling for more oil in this area.

Walruses breed off the Arctic coasts.

0 km 250 500
0 miles 250 500

NORTHERN LIGHTS
In midwinter, the north polar skies are sometimes lit up by dramatic curtains of red and green light. Known as the northern lights, these special effects are caused by disturbances in the upper atmosphere. The same happens near Antarctica, where the effect is called the southern lights.

ARCTIC SURVIVORS
Polar bears live along the Arctic coasts of Canada, Greenland, and Russia. They hunt seals and fish at points where the sea ice melts. With so much Arctic ice having melted away in recent years, the polar bear's habitat is slowly disappearing. An insulating layer of fat, called blubber, helps the bears survive the cold. Their white fur also provides essential camouflage on the ice.

Bering Strait
Arctic Circle
Chukchi Sea
Ostrov Vrangelya
East Siberian Sea
Novosibirskiye Ostrova
Laptev Sea
RUSSIAN FEDERATION
Beaufort Sea
Amundsen Gulf
Banks Island
Victoria Island
Melville Island
CANADA
Queen Elizabeth Islands
A R C T I C
Severnaya Zemlya
Lancaster Sound
Ellesmere Island
Nares Strait
North Geomagnetic Pole
Lincoln Sea
North Pole +
O C E A N
Franz Josef Land
Kara Sea
Knud Rasmussen Land
Kap Morris Jesup
Baffin Bay
Wandel Sea
SVALBARD (to Norway)
Spitsbergen
○ LONGYEARBYEN
Kong Frederik VIII Land
Greenland Sea
GREENLAND (to Denmark)
Bjørnøya (to Norway)
Barents Sea
NUUK
Arctic Circle
Kong Christian IX Land
Norwegian Sea
JAN MAYEN (to Norway)
Denmark Strait
ICELAND
REYKJAVÍK

Gazetteer

HOW TO USE THE GAZETTEER

This gazetteer is a selection of the names in *Children's Illustrated World Atlas*, and helps you find places on the maps. For example, to find the city of Lisbon in Portugal, look up its name in the gazetteer. The entry reads:

Lisbon *Capital* Portugal 58 E6

The first number, 58, tells you that Lisbon appears on the map on page 58. The second number, E6, shows that it is in square E6. Turn to page 58. Trace down from the letter E along the top of the grid (or up from the letter E on the bottom of the grid), and then across from the number 6 on the side of the grid. You will find Lisbon in the area where the letter and number meet.

A

Aachen *Town* Germany 56 B7
Aalborg *Town* Denmark 49 B11
Aalen *Town* Germany 57 E9
Aalst *Town* Belgium 53 D11
Aalter *Town* Belgium 53 C10
Äänekoski *Town* Finland 48 G8
Aarhus *Town* Denmark 49 C12
Aba *Town* Nigeria 41 L8
Aba *Town* Democratic Republic of the Congo 42 I8
Ābādān *Town* Iran 82 E7
Abakan *Town* Russian Federation 78 H7
Abbeville *Town* France 54 E5
Abéché *Town* Chad 42 F6
Abengourou *Town* Côte d'Ivoire 41 I8
Aberdeen *Town* South Dakota, US 12 G4
Aberdeen *Town* Maryland, US 9 H8
Aberdeen *Town* Scotland, UK 50 F5
Aberystwyth *Town* Wales, UK 51 E10
Abhā *Town* Saudi Arabia 83 C11
Abidjan *Town* Côte d'Ivoire 40 H8
Abilene *Town* Texas, US 17 K5
Åbo *see* Turku
Abomey *Town* Benin 41 J7
Abrantes *Town* Portugal 58 F6
Abu Dhabi *Capital* United Arab Emirates 83 F9
Abu Hamed *Town* Sudan 38 E6
Abuja *Capital* Nigeria 41 L7
Abū Kamāl *Town* Syria 80 I7
Abū Ẓaby *see* Abu Dhabi
Acapulco *Town* Mexico 19 J9
Acarigua *Town* Venezuela 26 D5
Accra *Capital* Ghana 41 I8
Aconcagua, Cerro *Mountain* Argentina 30 D7
A Coruña *Town* Spain 58 E2
Adamawa Highlands *Mountain range* Cameroon 42 D8
'Adan *see* Aden
Adana *Town* Turkey 76 G6
Adapazari *Town* Turkey 76 E4
Ad Dahnā' *Desert* Saudi Arabia 83 E9
Ad Dakhla *Town* Western Sahara 36 C7
Ad Dammān *Town* Saudi Arabia 83 E9
Ad Dawḥah *see* Doha
Addis Ababa *Capital* Ethiopia 39 F9
Adelaide *Town* South Australia, Australia 105 J7

Aden *Town* Yemen 83 D13
Aden, Gulf of Indian Ocean 83 E13
Adirondack Mountains New York, US 8 H4
Ādīs Ābeba *see* Addis Ababa
Adiyaman *Town* Turkey 76 H6
Adrar *Town* Algeria 36 G6
Aegean Sea Greece 67 F9
Afghanistan *Country* 84 H7
Afmadow *Town* Somalia 39 G11
Afyon *Town* Turkey 76 E5
Agadez *Town* Niger 41 L4
Agadir *Town* Morocco 36 E5
Agen *Town* France 55 D10
Agialoúsa *Town* Cyprus 80 B7
Āgra *Town* India 87 I3
Ağrı *Town* Turkey 77 K4
Agrigento *Town* Sicily, Italy 61 E13
Agropoli *Town* Italy 61 F10
Agua Prieta *Town* Mexico 18 F3
Aguascalientes *Town* Mexico 19 I7
Aguaytía *Town* Peru 27 B10
Aguilas *Town* Spain 59 J8
Aguililla *Town* Mexico 19 I8
Ahaggar *Mountain range* Algeria 37 I7
Ahlen *Town* Germany 56 C7
Ahmadābād *Town* India 86 G4
Ahuachapán *Town* El Salvador 20 E5
Ahvāz *Town* Iran 82 E7
Aiken *Town* South Carolina, US 11 J4
Ailigandí *Town* Panama 21 N7
'Aïn Ben Tili *Town* Mauritania 40 G2
Aiquile *Town* Bolivia 27 E12
Aïr, Massif de l' *Mountain range* Niger 41 L4
Aix-en-Provence *Town* France 55 G11
Aizu *Town* Japan 93 G9
Ajaccio *Town* France 55 I13
Ajo *Town* Arizona, US 16 E5
Akchâr *Desert* Mauritania 40 E3
Akhalts'ikhe *Town* Georgia 77 K3
Akhisar *Town* Turkey 76 C5
Akhtubinsk *Town* Russian Federation 73 D11
Akita *Town* Japan 92 F8
Akjoujt *Town* Mauritania 40 E3
Akkeshi *Town* Japan 92 H5
Akron *Town* Ohio, US 13 M6
Akrotírion *Town* Cyprus 80 A8
Aksai Chin *Administrative region* China 88 D6
Aksaray *Town* Turkey 76 F5
Akşehir *Town* Turkey 76 E5
Aktau *Town* Kazakhstan 78 D6
Aktobe *Town* Kazakhstan 78 E6
Aktsyabrski *Town* Belarus 71 F11
Akula *Town* Democratic Republic of the Congo 43 F9
Akune *Town* Japan 93 B14
Alabama *State* US 10 G5
Alabama River Alabama, US 10 G6
Al 'Amārah *Town* Iraq 82 D7
Alamo *Town* Nevada, US 14 H7
Alamogordo *Town* New Mexico, US 16 H5
Åland *Island group* Finland 49 F9
Alanya *Town* Turkey 76 E7
Al 'Aqabah *Town* Jordan 81 D14
Alaşehir *Town* Turkey 76 D5
Alaska *Province* Canada 4 E5
Alaska, Gulf of Alaska, US 4 E6
Alaska Range *Mountain Range* Alaska, US 4 E5
Albacete *Town* Spain 59 J6
Alba Iulia *Town* Romania 68 E6
Albania *Country* 65 F12
Albany *River* Ontario, Canada 6 F5
Albany *Town* Western Australia, Australia 104 E7
Albany *Town* Georgia, US 10 H6
Albany *Town* New York, US 9 I5
Al Bāridah *Town* Syria 80 F8
Al Baṣrah *Town* Iraq 82 D7
Alberta *Province* Canada 4 H7
Albert, Lake Democratic Republic of the Congo 43 I9
Albuquerque *Town* New Mexico, US 16 H4
Alcañiz *Town* Spain 59 K5
Alcoy *Town* Spain 59 K7
Alderney *Island* Channel Islands, UK 51 G13

Aleksin *Town* Russian Federation 73 C9
Alençon *Town* France 54 D7
Alenquer *Town* Brazil 29 I2
Aleppo *Town* Syria 80 E6montserrat
Alessandria *Town* Italy 60 C5
Aleutian Islands *Island Group* Alaska, US 4 B5
Alexander Archipelago *Island* British Colombia, Canada 4 E7
Alexandria *Town* Louisiana, US 10 E6
Alexandria *Town* Egypt 38 D4
Alexandria *Town* Romania 68 F7
Alexandroúpoli *Town* Greece 66 G8
Alga *Town* Kazakhstan 78 E6
Algarve *Region* Spain 58 E8
Algeciras *Town* Spain 58 G9
Alger *see* Algiers
Algeria *Country* 36 H5
Al Ghābah *Town* Oman 83 G10
Al Ghurdaqah *see* Hurghada
Algiers *Capital* Algeria 36 H3
Algona *Town* Iowa, US 12 H5
Al Ḥasakah *Town* Syria 80 H5
Al Ḥillah *Town* Iraq 82 D7
Al Hudaydah *see* Hodeida
Al Hufūf *Town* Saudi Arabia 83 E9
Alíartos *Town* Greece 67 E11
Alicante *Town* Spain 59 L7
Alice Springs *Town* Northern Territory, Australia 105 I4
Aliquippa *Town* Pennsylvania, US 8 E7
Al Ismā'īlīya *Town* Egypt 38 E4
Al Jafr *Town* Jordan 81 E13
Al Jaghbūb *Town* Libya 37 N5
Al Jahrā' *Town* Kuwait 82 D8
Al Jawf *Town* Saudi Arabia 82 B8
Al Jazīrah *Physical region* Syria/Iraq 80 I5
Al Karak *Town* Jordan 81 E12
Al Khārijah *Town* Egypt 38 D5
Al Khums *Town* Libya 37 K4
Alkmaar *Town* Netherlands 52 E7
Al Kufrah *Town* Libya 37 N7
Al Kūt *Town* Iraq 82 D7
Al Kuwayt *see* Kuwait
Allahābād *Town* India 87 I4
Allegheny Plateau Pennsylvania/New York, US 8 F6
Allentown *Town* Pennsylvania, US 9 H7
Al Līth *Town* Saudi Arabia 83 B11
Alma-Ata *see* Almaty
Al Madīnah *see* Medina
Al Mafraq *Town* Jordan 81 E10
Al Majma'ah *Town* Saudi Arabia 83 D9
Al Mālikīyah *Town* Syria 80 I4
Al Manāmah *see* Manama
Almansa *Town* Spain 59 K7
Al Marj *Town* Libya 37 M4
Almaty *Town* Kazakhstan 78 G8
Al Mawṣil *see* Mosul
Al Mayādīn *Town* Syria 80 H6
Almelo *Town* Netherlands 52 G8
Almere *Town* Netherlands 52 F8
Almería *Town* Spain 59 J8
Al'met'yevsk *Town* Russian Federation 73 F9
Al Minyā *Town* Egypt 38 D4
Almirante *Town* Panama 21 K8
Al Mukallā *Town* Yemen 83 E13
Alofi *Capital* Niue 103 K7
Alotip *Town* Indonesia 97 N8
Alpena *Town* Michigan, US 13 L4
Alpine *Town* Texas, US 17 I7
Alps *Mountain range* Central Europe 57 D12
Al Qāmishlī *Town* Syria 80 I4
Al Qunayṭirah *Town* Syria 81 D9
Altai Mountains *Mountain range* Mongolia/Russian Federation 88 F4
Altamaha River Georgia, US 11 I5
Altamira *Town* Brazil 29 J2
Altamura *Town* Italy 61 H10
Altar, Desierto de *Desert* Mexico 18 D2
Altay *Town* China 88 F3
Altay *Town* Mongolia 88 H3
Altin Köprü *Town* Iraq 82 C6
Altiplano *Physical region* Bolivia 27 E13
Altoona *Town* Pennsylvania, US 9 F7
Altun Ha *Ancient site* Belize 20 F2
Altun Shan *Mountain range* China 88 G5

Al 'Umarī *Town* Jordan 81 F11
Al 'Uwaynāt *Town* Libya 37 J6
Alupka *Town* Ukraine 69 K7
Alva *Town* Oklahoma, US 17 L3
Al Wajh *Town* Saudi Arabia 83 A9
Alwar *Town* India 86 H3
Al Wari'ah *Town* Saudi Arabia 82 D8
Alytus *Town* Lithuania 70 D8
Amamapare *Town* Indonesia 97 N7
Amantea *Town* Italy 61 G12
Amapura *Town* Myanmar 94 B6
Amarillo *Town* Texas, US 17 J4
Amazon *River* Brazil 29 J2
Amazon Basin Brazil 28 G3
Ambanja *Town* Madagascar 45 M4
Ambarchik *Town* Russian Federation 78 L3
Ambato *Town* Ecuador 26 A8
Amboasary *Town* Madagascar 45 L7
Ambon *Town* Indonesia 97 K7
American Samoa *Dependent territory* US, Pacific Ocean 103 K6
Amersfoort *Town* Netherlands 52 F8
Amfilochía *Town* Greece 67 C10
Amherst *Town* Nova Scotia, Canada 7 K7
Amiens *Town* France 54 E6
Amman *Capital* Jordan 81 E11
'Ammān *see* Amman
Ammóchostos *Town* Cyprus 80 B8
Āmol *Town* Iran 82 F5
Amos *Town* Québec, Canada 6 H6
Amritsar *Town* India 86 H2
Amstelveen *Town* Netherlands 52 F8
Amsterdam *Capital* Netherlands 52 E8
Am Timan *Town* Chad 42 F6
Amundsen Gulf Canada 4 H4
Amundsen-Scott *Research station* Antarctica 110 E6
Amundsen Sea Southern Ocean 110 B7
Amuntai *Town* Indonesia 96 H7
Amur *River* China 89 L2
Amyderýa *River* Uzbekistan 84 G4
Anadyr' *Town* Russian Federation 78 M2
Anamur *Town* Turkey 76 F7
Anápolis *Town* Brazil 29 K5
Anatolia *Plateau* Turkey 76 E6
Anchorage *Town* Alaska, Canada 4 E5
Andalucía *Region* Spain 58 H8
Andaman Islands *Island group* India 87 M8
Andaman Sea Indian Ocean 87 M8
Anderson *Town* Indiana, US 13 K6
Andes *Mountain range* South America 26–27, 30–31
Andijon *Town* Uzbekistan 85 K4
Andkhvoy *Town* Afghanistan 84 H5
Andorra *Country* 55 D12
Andorra la Vella *Capital* Andorra 55 D12
Andreanof Islands *Island Group* Alaska, US 4 A4
Andrews *Town* Texas, US 17 J5
Andria *Town* Italy 61 H10
Andros Island The Bahamas 22 F2
Andros Town The Bahamas 22 F2
Angarsk *Town* Russian Federation 79 I7
Angeles *Town* Philippines 97 I2
Angel Falls *Waterfall* Venezuela 26 F6
Ångermanälven *River* Sweden 48 E7
Angers *Town* France 54 C7
Angkor Wat *Ancient site* Cambodia 95 F10
Anglesey *Island* Wales, UK 51 E9
Angola *Country* 44 E3
Angola Basin *Undersea feature* Atlantic Ocean 33 M6
Angoulême *Town* France 55 D9
Angren *Town* Uzbekistan 85 J3
Anguilla *Dependent territory* UK, Atlantic Ocean 23 N5
Anhui *Administrative region* China 91 J5
Ankara *Capital* Turkey 76 F4
Annaba *Town* Algeria 37 I3
An Nafūd *Desert* Saudi Arabia 82 B8
'Annah *Town* Iraq 82 C6
An Najaf *Town* Iraq 82 C7
Annamite Mountains *Mountain range* Laos 94 F8
Annapolis *Town* Maryland, US 8 G8
Ann Arbor *Town* Michigan, US 13 L5

» Barisan, Pegunungan – Brecon Beacons

Barisan, Pegunungan *Mountain range* Indonesia 96 D7
Barkly Tableland *Plateau* Northern Territory, Australia 105 J3
Bârlad *Town* Romania 68 G6
Barlee Range *Mountain range* Western Australia, Australia 104 E4
Barletta *Town* Italy 61 H10
Barnaul *Town* Russian Federation 78 H6
Barnstaple *Town* England, UK 51 E11
Baron'ki *Town* Belarus 71 H11
Barquisimeto *Town* Venezuela 26 D5
Barrancabermeja *Town* Colombia 26 C5
Barranquilla *Town* Colombia 26 B4
Barreiras *Town* Brazil 29 L4
Barreiro *Town* Portugal 58 E7
Barrow-in-Furness *Town* England, UK 50 F8
Barstow *Town* California, US 14 H8
Bartlesville *Town* Okahoma, US 17 M3
Bartoszyce *Town* Poland 62 F5
Barysaw *Town* Belarus 71 F9 *see also* Borisov
Basarabeasca *Town* Moldova 68 H6
Basel *Town* Switzerland 57 C11
Basque Country, The *Region* Spain 59 I3
Basra *see* Al Başrah
Bassano del Grappa *Town* Italy 60 E5
Basse-Terre *Island* Guadeloupe 23 N6
Basse-Terre *Capital* Guadeloupe 23 N6
Basseterre *Capital* Saint Kitts & Nevis 23 N6
Bassikounou *Town* Mauritania 40 H5
Bass Strait Australia 105 K9
Bata *Town* Equatorial Guinea 43 C9
Batangas *Town* Philippines 97 I2
Bătdâmbâng *Town* Cambodia 95 E10
Bath *Town* England, UK 51 F11
Bath *Town* Maine, US 8 K4
Bathinda *Town* India 86 H2
Bathurst *Town* New South Wales, Australia 105 L7
Batman *Town* Turkey 77 J6
Batna *Town* Algeria 37 I3
Baton Rouge *Town* Louisiana, US 10 E6
Batticaloa *Town* Sri Lanka 87 J9
Batumi *Town* Georgia 77 J3
Batu Pahat *Town* Malaysia 96 E5
Bauchi *Town* Nigeria 41 L6
Bauska *Town* Latvia 70 E6
Bavaria *Region* Germany 57 E10
Bayamo *Town* Cuba 22 G4
Bayan Har Shan *Mountain range* China 88 H7
Bay City *Town* Michigan, US 13 L5
Baydhabo *Town* Somalia 39 H10
Bayeux *Town* France 54 D6
Bāyir *Town* Jordan 81 F12
Baykal, Ozero *see* Lake Baikal
Bayreuth *Town* Germany 56 E8
Baytown *Town* Texas, US 17 N7
Beaufort Sea Arctic Ocean 111 L4
Beaumont *Town* Texas, US 17 N6
Beauvais *Town* France 54 E6
Beāwar *Town* India 86 H3
Béchar *Town* Algeria 36 G5
Bedford *Town* England, UK 51 H10
Bedford *Town* Pennsylvania, US 8 F8
Be'er Sheva *Town* Israel 81 D12
Bei'an *Town* China 89 M2
Beihai *Town* China 90 H9
Beijing *Capital* China 91 J3
Beilen *Town* Netherlands 52 G7
Beira *Town* Mozambique 45 J5
Beirut *Capital* Lebanon 81 D9
Beja *Town* Portugal 58 F7
Békéscsaba *Town* Hungary 63 G12
Bekobod *Town* Uzbekistan 85 J4
Belarus *Country* 71 E9
Bełchatów *Town* Poland 62 E7
Belcher Islands *Island group* Canada 6 G3
Beledweyne *Town* Somalia 39 H10
Belém *Town* Brazil 29 K2
Belén *Town* Nicaragua 20 H6
Belfast *Town* Northern Ireland, UK 50 D7
Belfield *Town* North Dakota, US 12 E3
Belfort *Town* France 54 H8
Belgaum *Town* India 86 G6
Belgium *Country* 53 D11
Belgorod *Town* Russian Federation 73 B10
Belgrade *Capital* Serbia 64 G7
Belgrano II *Research station* Antarctica 110 D4
Belize *Country* 20 F2
Belize City *Town* Belize 20 F2
Belle Isle, Strait of Québec, Canada 7 M5
Bellevue *Town* Washington, US 14 G2
Bellingham *Town* Washington, US 14 G1
Bello *Town* Colombia 26 C6
Bellville *Town* South Africa 44 F9
Belmopan *Capital* Belize 20 F2
Belogradchik *Town* Bulgaria 66 D5
Belo Horizonte *Town* Brazil 29 L6
Belomorsk *Town* Russian Federation 72 D6
Beloretsk *Town* Russian Federation 73 G10
Bemaraha *Mountain range* Madagascar 45 L5
Benavente *Town* Spain 58 G4
Bend *Town* Oregon, US 14 G3
Bendigo *Town* Victoria, Australia 105 K8
Benevento *Town* Italy 61 F10
Bengal, Bay of Indian Ocean 87 L5
Bengbu *Town* China 91 J5
Benghazi *Town* Libya 37 M4
Bengkulu *Town* Indonesia 96 E7
Benguela *Town* Angola 44 D3
Benidorm *Town* Spain 59 K7
Beni-Mellal *Town* Morocco 36 F4
Benin *Country* 41 J7
Benin, Bight of *Coastal feature* Nigeria 41 J8
Benin City *Town* Nigeria 41 K8
Beni Suef *Town* Egypt 38 D4
Ben Nevis *Mountain* Scotland, UK 50 E5
Benson *Town* Arizona, US 16 F6
Bent Jbaïl *Town* Lebanon 81 D10
Benton *Town* Arkansas, US 10 E4
Benue *River* Nigeria 41 L7
Benue *River* Nigeria 41 L7
Beograd *see* Belgrade
Berat *Town* Albania 65 F12
Berbera *Town* Somalia 39 H9
Berbérati *Town* Cameroon 42 D8
Berdyans'k *Town* Ukraine 69 L6
Berdychiv *Town* Ukraine 68 H3
Berezhany *Town* Ukraine 68 F3
Berezniki *Town* Russian Federation 72 G8
Bergamo *Town* Italy 60 D5
Bergen *Town* Norway 49 A9
Bergen *Town* Germany 56 F4
Bergerac *Town* France 55 D10
Bering Sea Russian Federation 79 N3
Bering Strait Russian Federation/US 79 M2
Berkeley *Town* California, US 14 F6
Berlin *Capital* Germany 56 G6
Berlin *Town* New Hampshire, US 9 J3
Bermuda *Dependent territory* UK, Atlantic Ocean 32 H3
Bern *Capital* Switzerland 57 C11
Berner Alps *Mountain range* Switzerland 57 C12
Bertoua *Town* Cameroon 42 D8
Besançon *Town* France 54 G8
Betafo *Town* Madagascar 45 M5
Bethlehem *Town* Israel 81 D11
Béticos, Sistemas *Mountain range* Spain 59 I8
Bétou *Town* Congo 43 E9
Beveren *Town* Belgium 53 D10
Beyrouth *see* Beirut
Béziers *Town* France 55 E11
Bhaktapur *Town* Nepal 87 J3
Bhāvnagar *Town* India 86 G5
Bhopāl *Town* India 86 H4
Bhubaneshwar *Town* India 87 K5
Bhusāwal *Town* India 86 H5
Bhutan *Country* 87 L3
Biała Podlaska *Town* Poland 62 H7
Białystok *Town* Poland 62 H6
Biarritz *Town* France 55 B11
Bicaz *Town* Romania 68 G5
Biel *Town* Switzerland 57 C11
Bielefeld *Town* Germany 56 D6
Bielsko-Biała *Town* Poland 63 E9
Biên Hoa *Town* Vietnam 95 G11
Bié, Planalto do *Plateau* Angola 44 F3
Bighorn Mountains Wyoming, US 15 K3
Bighorn River Montana, US 15 K3
Bignona *Town* Senegal 40 E5
Big Sioux River South Dakota, US 12 G4
Bihać *Town* Bosnia & Herzegovina 64 C7
Bijelo Polje *Town* Montenegro 65 F9
Bīkāner *Town* India 86 G3
Bikin *Town* Russian Federation 78 M7
Bikini Atoll Marshall Islands 102 H2
Bilāspur *Town* India 87 J5
Biläsuvar *Town* Azerbaijan 77 N4
Bila Tserkva *Town* Ukraine 69 I3
Bilauktaung Range *Mountain range* Thailand 95 D11
Bilbao *Town* Spain 59 I3
Billings *Town* Montana, US 15 J3
Bilma, Grand Erg de *Desert* Niger 41 M4
Biloxi *Town* Mississippi, US 10 F6
Binghamton *Town* New York, US 8 G6
Bingöl *Town* Turkey 77 J5
Bintulu *Town* Malaysia 96 G5
Binzhou *Town* China 91 K4
Birāk *Town* Libya 37 K6
Birao *Town* Central African Republic 42 G7
Birātnagar *Town* Nepal 87 K3
Bīrjand *Town* Iran 82 H6
Birkenfeld *Town* Germany 57 C9
Birkenhead *Town* England, UK 51 F9
Birmingham *Town* England, UK 50 G10
Birmingham *Town* Alabama, US 10 G5
Birnin Konni *Town* Niger 41 K5
Birobidzhan *Town* Russian Federation 79 L7
Birsk *Town* Russian Federation 73 G9
Biržai *Town* Lithuania 70 E6
Biscay, Bay of Atlantic Ocean 33 L2
Bishkek *Capital* Kyrgyzstan 85 L2
Biskra *Town* Algeria 37 I4
Bislig *Town* Philippines 97 K4
Bismarck *Town* North Dakota, US 12 F3
Bismarck Archipelago *Island chain* Papua New Guinea 102 E5
Bismarck Sea Pacific Ocean 102 E5
Bissau *Capital* Guinea-Bissau 40 E6
Bistripa *Town* Romania 68 F5
Bitlis *Town* Turkey 77 K5
Bitola *Town* Macedonia 65 G12
Bitonto *Town* Italy 61 H10
Bitterroot Range *Mountain range* Idaho, US 15 I2
Bitung *Town* Indonesia 97 K6
Bizerte *Town* Tunisia 37 J3
Bjørnøya Norway 111 N8
Black Forest *Region* Germany 57 C10
Black Hills *Mountain range* South Dakota, US 12 E4
Blackpool *Town* England, UK 50 F8
Black Range *Mountain range* New Mexico, US 16 G5
Black Rock Desert Nevada, US 14 G5
Black Sea Asia/Europe 69 I6
Black Sea Lowland Ukraine 69 J6
Black Volta *River* Ghana 41 I6
Blagoevgrad *Town* Bulgaria 66 E7
Blagoveshchensk *Town* Russian Federation 79 L7
Blanca, Bahía *Bay* Argentina 31 F10
Blanca, Costa *Coastal region* Spain 59 K7
Blanes *Town* Spain 59 M4
Blantyre *Town* Malawi 45 J4
Blida *Town* Algeria 36 H3
Bloemfontein *Capital* South Africa 44 H7
Bloomfield *Town* New Mexico, US 16 G3
Bloomington *Town* Indiana, US 12 H4
Bloomington *Town* Minnesota, US 13 K7
Bloomsbury *Town* Queensland, Australia 105 M4
Bluefields *Town* Nicaragua 21 J6
Blue Nile *River* Sudan 38 E8
Blumenau *Town* Brazil 29 K8
Bo *Town* Sierra Leone 40 F7
Boa Vista *Town* Brazil 28 H1
Bobo-Dioulasso *Town* Burkina Faso 40 H6
Bobruysk *Town* Belarus 71 F10 *see also* Babruysk
Bocay *Town* Nicaragua 20 H4
Bocholt *Town* Germany 56 C6
Bochum *Town* Germany 56 C7
Bodaybo *Town* Russian Federation 78 J6
Boden *Town* Sweden 48 F6
Bodrum *Town* Turkey 76 C6
Bogale *Town* Myanmar 95 B9
Bogor *Town* Indonesia 96 F8
Bogotá *Capital* Colombia 26 C6
Bo Hai *Gulf* China 91 K3
Bohemia *Region* Czechia 63 B9
Bohemian Forest *Region* Germany 57 F10
Bohol Sea Philippines 97 J4
Boise *Town* Idaho, US 14 H4
Boise City *Town* Okahoma, US 17 J3
Bojnūrd *Town* Iran 82 G5
Boké *Town* Guinea 40 E6
Bolesławiec *Town* Poland 62 C7
Bolgatanga *Town* Ghana 41 I6
Bolivia *Country* 27 E11
Bologna *Town* Italy 60 E6
Bolton *Town* England, UK 51 F9
Bolu *Town* Turkey 76 E4
Bolzano *Town* Italy 60 E4
Boma *Town* Democratic Republic of the Congo 43 D11
Bombay *see* Mumbai
Bonaire *Dependent territory* Netherlands, Atlantic Ocean 23 K8
Bonaparte Archipelago *Island group* Australia 104 F2
Bondoukou *Town* Côte d'Ivoire 41 I7
Bone, Teluk *Bay* Indonesia 97 I7
Bongaigaon *Town* India 87 L3
Bongo, Massif des *Mountain range* Central African Republic 42 G7
Bonifacio *Town* Corsica, France 55 I13
Bonifacio, Strait of Mediterranean Sea 61 B9
Bonn *Town* Germany 56 C8
Boppard *Town* Germany 56 C8
Borås *Town* Sweden 49 D11
Bordeaux *Town* France 55 D10
Bordj Omar Driss *Town* Algeria 37 I6
Børgefjellet *Mountain range* Norway 48 D6
Borgholm *Town* Sweden 49 E11
Borisoglebsk *Town* Russian Federation 73 D10
Borisov *Town* Belarus 71 F9 *see also* Barysaw
Borneo *Island* Indonesia 96 G6
Bornholm *Island* Denmark 49 D13
Borovan *Town* Bulgaria 66 E5
Borovichi *Town* Russian Federation 72 C7
Boryslav *Town* Ukraine 68 E3
Bose *Town* China 90 H8
Bosnia & Herzegovina *Country* 64 D8
Bosporus *River* Turkey 76 D3
Bossembélé *Town* Central African Republic 42 E8
Bossier City *Town* Louisiana, US 10 D5
Boston *Town* Massachusetts, US 9 K5
Bothnia, Gulf of Finland 48 F7
Botoşani *Town* Romania 68 G5
Botou *Town* China 91 J3
Botswana *Country* 44 G6
Bouar *Town* Central African Republic 42 E8
Bou Craa *Town* Western Sahara 36 D6
Bougouni *Town* Mali 40 G6
Boujdour *Town* Western Sahara 36 C6
Boulder *Town* Colorado, US 15 K5
Boulogne-sur-Mer *Town* France 54 E5
Boundiali *Town* Côte d'Ivoire 40 H7
Bourges *Town* France 54 E8
Bourke *Town* New South Wales, Australia 105 L6
Bournemouth *Town* England, UK 51 G12
Bouvet Island *Dependent territory* Norway, Atlantic Ocean 33 L8
Boysun *Town* Uzbekistan 85 I5
Bozeman *Town* Montana, US 15 J3
Brades *Capital* Montserrat 23 N6
Bradford *Town* England, UK 50 G8
Brahmapur *Town* India 87 K5
Brahmaputra *River* Asia 87 L3
Brăila *Town* Romania 68 G7
Brampton *Town* Ontario, Canada 6 G8
Brandenburg *Town* Germany 56 F6
Brasília *Capital* Brazil 29 K5
Braşov *Town* Romania 68 F6
Bratislava *Capital* Slovakia 63 D10
Bratsk *Town* Russian Federation 79 I6
Braunschweig *Town* Germany 56 E6
Brava, Costa *Coastal region* Spain 59 N4
Brawley *Town* California, US 14 H8
Brazil *Country* 28 G4
Brazzaville *Capital* Congo 43 D11
Brecon Beacons *Hills* Wales, UK 51 F10

» Chārīkār – Dalain Hob

Chārīkār *Town* Afghanistan 85 J6
Charity *Town* Guyana 26 G5
Charleroi *Town* Belgium 53 E12
Charlesbourg *Town* Québec, Canada 7 I7
Charleston *Town* West Virginia, US 11 I2
Charleston *Town* South Carolina, US 11 J5
Charleville-Mézières *Town* France 54 G6
Charlotte *Town* North Carolina, US 11 J4
Charlotte Amalie *Capital* Virgin Islands 23 M5
Charlottetown *Town* Prince Edward Island, Canada 7 L6
Charters Towers *Town* Queensland, Australia 105 L3
Châteaubriant *Town* France 54 D7
Châteauroux *Town* France 54 E8
Châtellerault *Town* France 54 D8
Chatham Islands *Island group* New Zealand 109 J8
Chattahoochee River Alabama/Georgia, US 10 H5
Chattanooga *Town* Tennessee, US 10 H4
Chatyr-Tash *Town* Kyrgyzstan 85 M4
Châu Đốc *Town* Cambodia 95 F11
Chauk *Town* Myanmar 94 B7
Chaykovskiy *Town* Russian Federation 73 F9
Cheb *Town* Czechia 62 A8
Cheboksary *Town* Russian Federation 73 E9
Chech, Erg *Desert* Algeria 36 F7
Chefchaouen *Town* Morocco 36 F4
Chelkar *Town* Kazakhstan 78 E6
Chełm *Town* Poland 62 H7
Chelsea *Town* Vermont, US 9 J4
Cheltenham *Town* England, UK 51 G10
Chelyabinsk *Town* Russian Federation 78 F5
Chemnitz *Town* Germany 56 F7
Chengde *Town* China 91 J2
Chengdu *Town* China 90 G6
Chennai *Town* India 87 I7
Chenzhou *Town* China 91 I7
Chepelare *Town* Bulgaria 66 F7
Cherepovets *Town* Russian Federation 72 D7
Cherkasy *Town* Ukraine 69 J4
Cherkessk *Town* Russian Federation 73 C11
Chernihiv *Town* Ukraine 69 I2
Chernivtsi *Town* Ukraine 68 G4
Chernyakhovsk *Town* Kaliningrad 70 C7
Cherry Hill *Town* New Jersey, US 8 H8
Cherskiy *Town* Russian Federation 78 L3
Cherskogo, Khrebet *Mountain range* Russian Federation 79 K4
Cherykaw *Town* Belarus 71 G11
Chesapeake Bay *Coastal feature* US 8 G9
Chester *Town* England, UK 51 F9
Chetumal *Town* Mexico 19 O7
Cheviot Hills Scotland, UK 50 F7
Cheyenne *Town* Wyoming, US 15 L5
Chhapra *Town* India 87 J3
Chiang Mai *Town* Thailand 94 D8
Chiang Rai *Town* Thailand 94 D7
Chiba *Town* Japan 93 G10
Chibougamau *Town* Québec, Canada 6 H6
Chicago *Town* Illinois, US 13 J6
Chichén-Itzá *Ancient site* Mexico 19 O6
Chickasha *Town* Oklahoma, US 17 L4
Chiclayo *Town* Peru 27 A9
Chicoutimi *Town* Québec, Canada 7 I6
Chieti *Town* Italy 60 F8
Chifeng *Town* China 89 L4
Chihuahua *Town* Mexico 18 G4
Childress *Town* Texas, US 17 K4
Chile *Country* 30 D6
Chillán *Town* Chile 31 C9
Chilpancingo *Town* Mexico 19 K8
Chimán *Town* Panama 21 N8
Chimbote *Town* Peru 27 B10
Chimoio *Town* Mozambique 45 I5
China *Country* 88 H6/91 J6
Chinandega *Town* Nicaragua 20 G5
Chingola *Town* Zambia 44 H3
Chin Hills *Mountain range* Myanmar 94 A6
Chioggia *Town* Italy 60 E5
Chíos *Town* Greece 67 G11
Chipata *Town* Zambia 45 I3
Chiquián *Town* Peru 27 B10
Chīrāla *Town* India 87 I7
Chirchiq *Town* Uzbekistan 85 J3
Chirripó Grande, Cerro *Mountain* Costa Rica 21 J8
Chişinău *Capital* Moldova 68 H6
Chita *Town* Russian Federation 79 J7
Chitato *Town* Angola 44 F2
Chitose *Town* Japan 92 F5
Chittagong *Town* Bangladesh 87 L4
Chitungwiza *Town* Zimbabwe 45 I5
Chlef *Town* Algeria 36 H3
Choele Choel *Town* Argentina 31 E10
Ch'ok'ē *Mountain range* Ethiopia 38 F8
Cholet *Town* France 54 D8
Choluteca *Town* Honduras 20 G5
Chomutov *Town* Czechia 62 B8
Chon Buri *Town* Thailand 95 D10
Ch'ŏngjin *Town* North Korea 91 M2
Chŏngju *Town* North Korea 91 L3
Chongqing *Town* China 90 H6
Chŏnju *Town* South Korea 91 M4
Chóra Sfakíon *Town* Greece 67 E14
Chornomors'ke *Town* Ukraine 69 J7
Chorzów *Town* Poland 62 E8
Chōshi *Town* Japan 93 H10
Choûm *Town* Mauritania 40 F3
Choybalsan *Town* Mongolia 89 K3
Christchurch *Town* New Zealand 107 E11
Christmas Island *Dependent territory* Australia, Indian Ocean 99 L5
Chukchi Sea Arctic Ocean 111 M3
Chula Vista *Town* California, US 14 G9
Chulucanas *Town* Peru 27 B9
Chuncheon *Town* South Korea 91 M3
Churchill *Town* Manitoba, Canada 5 J7
Chusovoy *Town* Russian Federation 72 G8
Chuy *Town* Uruguay 30 H8
Ciechanów *Town* Poland 62 F6
Ciego de Ávila *Town* Cuba 22 F4
Cienfuegos *Town* Cuba 22 E3
Cilacap *Town* Indonesia 96 F8
Cincinnati *Town* Ohio, US 13 L7
Cirebon *Town* Indonesia 96 F7
Cirò Marino *Town* Italy 61 H12
Citrus Heights *Town* California, US 14 G6
Ciudad Bolívar *Town* Venezuela 26 F5
Ciudad Camargo *Town* Mexico 18 H4
Ciudad del Este *Town* Paraguay 30 H5
Ciudad Guayana *Town* Venezuela 26 F5
Ciudad Guzmán *Town* Mexico 19 I8
Ciudad Hidalgo *Town* Mexico 19 N9
Ciudad Juárez *Town* Mexico 18 G2
Ciudad Lerdo *Town* Mexico 19 I5
Ciudad Madero *Town* Mexico 19 K6
Ciudad Mante *Town* Mexico 19 K6
Ciudad Obregón *Town* Mexico 18 F5
Ciudad Ojeda *Town* Colombia 26 C5
Ciudad Real *Town* Spain 59 I6
Ciudad-Rodrigo *Town* Spain 58 G5
Ciudad Valles *Town* Mexico 19 K6
Ciudad Victoria *Town* Mexico 19 K6
Civitanova Marche *Town* Italy 60 F7
Civitavecchia *Town* Italy 60 D8
Clarence Town *Town* The Bahamas 22 H3
Clarksburg *Town* West Virginia, US 11 J1
Clarksville *Town* Tennessee, US 10 G3
Clearwater *Town* Florida, US 11 I7
Clermont-Ferrand *Town* France 55 E9
Cleveland *Town* Ohio, US 13 M6
Clinton *Town* Mississippi, US 10 F5
Clipperton Island *Dependent territory* France, Pacific Ocean 109 M4
Cloppenburg *Town* Germany 56 C6
Clovis *Town* New Mexico, US 17 I4
Cluj-Napoca *Town* Romania 68 E5
Clyde *River* Scotland, UK 50 F6
Coari *Town* Brazil 28 H3
Coast Mountains Alaska/ British Colombia 4 F7
Coast Ranges *Mountain Range* California/ Oregon, US 14 F3
Coatzacoalcos *Town* Mexico 19 M8
Cobán *Town* Guatemala 20 E3
Cobija *Town* Bolivia 27 D10
Coburg *Town* Germany 56 E8
Cochabamba *Town* Bolivia 27 E12
Cochin *Town* India 86 H8 *see also* Kochi
Cochrane *Town* Chile 31 C12
Cochrane *Town* Ontario, Canada 6 G6
Cockburn Town *Capital* Turks & Caicos Islands 23 I4
Coconino Plateau Arizona, US 16 E3
Cocos Islands *Dependent territory* Australia, Indian Ocean 99 K5
Cod, Cape *Coastal feature* Massachusetts, US 9 K5
Cognac *Town* France 55 D9
Coihaique *Town* Chile 31 C12
Coimbatore *Town* Sri Lanka 86 H8
Coimbra *Town* Portugal 58 E5
Colby *Town* Kansas, US 12 E7
Colchester *Town* England, UK 51 I10
Colima *Town* Mexico 19 I8
College Station *Town* Texas, US 17 M6
Colmar *Town* France 54 H7
Cologne *Town* Germany 56 C7
Colombia *Country* 26 C7
Colombo *Capital* Sri Lanka 87 I9
Colón *Town* Panama 21 M7
Colorado *State* US 15 K6
Colorado City *Town* Texas, US 17 K5
Colorado Plateau Arizona, US 16 F3
Colorado, Río *River* Argentina 31 E9
Colorado River Mexico/US 15 J6
Colorado Springs *Town* Colorado, US 15 L6
Columbia *Town* Tennessee, US 10 H3
Columbia *Town* South Carolina, US 11 J4
Columbia *Town* Maryland, US 8 G8
Columbia *Town* Missouri, US 13 I7
Columbia Plateau Idaho/Oregon, US 14 H4
Columbia River Oregon/Washington, US 14 G3
Columbus *Town* Ohio, US 13 L7
Columbus *Town* Nebraska, US 12 G6
Columbus *Town* Georgia, US 10 H5
Comacchio *Town* Italy 60 E6
Comayagua *Town* Honduras 20 G4
Comilla *Town* Bangladesh 87 L4
Comitán *Town* Mexico 19 N9
Como *Town* Italy 60 C4
Comodoro Rivadavia *Town* Argentina 31 E12
Como, Lake Italy 60 D4
Comoros *Country* 45 L3
Conakry *Capital* Guinea 40 E7
Concarneau *Town* France 54 B7
Concepción *Town* Chile 31 C9
Concepción *Town* Paraguay 30 G5
Conchos, Río *River* Mexico 18 H4
Concord *Town* New Hampshire, US 9 J5
Concordia *Town* Argentina 30 G7
Congo *Country* 43 E9
Congo *River* Democratic Republic of the Congo/Congo 43 G9
Congo Basin *Drainage basin* Central Africa 43 F10
Congo, Democratic Republic of the *Country* 43 G10
Connaught *Cultural region* Ireland 50 B8
Connecticut *State* US 9 J6
Connecticut River US 9 J5
Consolación del Sur *Town* Cuba 22 D3
Constanpa *Town* Romania 68 H7
Constantine *Town* Algeria 37 I3
Coober Pedy *Town* South Australia, Australia 105 I6
Cookeville *Town* Tennessee, US 10 H3
Cook Islands *Dependent territory* New Zealand, Pacific Ocean 103 M7
Cook, Mount *see* Aoraki
Cook Strait New Zealand 107 F9
Cooktown *Town* Queensland, Australia 105 L2
Cooma *Town* New South Wales, Australia 105 L8
Coon Rapids *Town* Minnesota, US 12 H4
Coos Bay *Town* Oregon, US 14 F4
Copán *Ancient site* Honduras 20 F4
Copenhagen *Capital* Denmark 49 C12
Copiapó *Town* Chile 30 C6
Coquimbo *Town* Chile 30 C7
Coral Sea Pacific Ocean 102 F6
Coral Sea Islands *Dependent territory* Australia, Coral Sea 102 F7
Corcovado, Golfo *Gulf* Chile 31 C11
Cordele *Town* Georgia, US 11 I5
Córdoba *Town* Spain 58 H7
Córdoba *Town* Argentina 30 E7
Córdoba *Town* Mexico 19 L8
Corfu *Island* Greece 67 B9
Corfu *Town* Greece 67 B9
Corinth *Town* Mississippi, US 10 G4
Corinth *Town* Greece 67 D11
Corinth Canal Greece 67 E11
Cork *Town* Ireland 51 B10
Çorlu *Town* Turkey 76 C3
Corner Brook *Town* Québec, Canada 7 L5
Coro *Town* Venezuela 26 D4
Coromandel *Town* New Zealand 106 G5
Corozal *Town* Belize 20 F1
Corpus Christi *Town* Texas, US 17 M8
Corrientes *Town* Argentina 30 G6
Corse *see* Corsica
Corsica *Island* France 55 I13
Cortés *Town* Costa Rica 21 J8
Cortina d'Ampezzo *Town* Italy 60 F4
Çorum *Town* Turkey 76 G4
Corvallis *Town* Oregon, US 14 F3
Cosenza *Town* Italy 61 G12
Costa Rica *Country* 21 J7
Côte d'Ivoire *Country* 40 G7
Cotonou *Town* Benin 41 J8
Cotswold Hills England, UK 51 G10
Cottbus *Town* Germany 56 G7
Council Bluffs *Town* Iowa, US 12 G6
Couvin *Town* Belgium 53 E13
Coventry *Town* England, UK 51 G10
Craiova *Town* Romania 68 E7
Crawley *Town* England, UK 51 H11
Cremona *Town* Italy 60 D5
Crescent City *Town* California, US 14 F4
Crestview *Town* Florida, US 10 G6
Crete *Island* Greece 67 F14
Crete, Sea of Greece 67 F13
Créteil *Town* France 54 E6
Crewe *Town* England, UK 51 F9
Crimea *Peninsula* Ukraine 69 K7
Cristuru Secuiesc *Town* Romania 68 F6
Croatia *Country* 64 C6
Crookston *Town* Minnesota, US 12 G2
Crotone *Town* Italy 61 H12
Croydon *Town* England, UK 51 H11
Crozet Islands *Island group* Indian Ocean 99 I7
Cuauhtémoc *Town* Mexico 18 G4
Cuautla *Town* Mexico 19 K8
Cuba *Country* 22 F4
Cúcuta *Town* Colombia 26 C5
Cuddapah *Town* India 87 I7
Cuenca *Town* Ecuador 26 A8
Cuernavaca *Town* Mexico 19 K8
Cuiabá *Town* Brazil 29 I5
Cuito *River* Angola 44 F4
Cukai *Town* Malaysia 96 E5
Culiacán *Town* Mexico 18 G6
Cullera *Town* Spain 59 K6
Cumaná *Town* Venezuela 26 E5
Cumberland *Town* Maryland, US 8 F8
Cumberland Plateau Tennessee, US 10 H3
Cuneo *Town* Italy 60 B6
Curaçao *Dependent territory* Netherlands, Atlantic Ocean 23 K8
Curicó *Town* Chile 30 C8
Curitiba *Town* Brazil 29 K7
Cusco *Town* Peru 27 D11
Cuttack *Town* India 87 K5
Cuxhaven *Town* Germany 56 D5
Cyclades *Island group* Greece 67 F12
Cyprus *Country* 80 A8
Cyrenaica *Cultural region* Libya 37 M4
Czechia *Country* 63 C9
Czech Republic *see* Czechia
Częstochowa *Town* Poland 62 E8
Człuchów *Town* Poland 62 D5

D

Dabeiba *Town* Colombia 26 B5
Daegu *Town* South Korea 91 M4
Daejeon *Town* South Korea 91 M4
Dagupan *Town* Philippines 97 I2
Dakar *Capital* Senegal 40 D5
Dalain Hob *Town* China 89 I5

Gniezno *Town* Poland 62 D6
Gobi *Desert* Mongolia 89 I4
Godāvari *River* India 86 H5
Godhra *Town* India 86 G4
Godoy Cruz *Town* Argentina 30 D8
Goes *Town* Netherlands 53 D10
Goiânia *Town* Brazil 29 K6
Göksun *Town* Turkey 76 H6
Golan Heights *Mountain range* Syria 81 D10
Goldsboro *Town* North Carolina, US 11 K3
Goleniów *Town* Poland 62 C5
Golmud *Town* China 88 G6
Goma *Town* Democratic Republic of
   the Congo 43 H10
Gombi *Town* Nigeria 41 M6
Gomel' *Town* Belarus 71 G12 *see also* Homyel'
Gómez Palacio *Town* Mexico 18 H5
Gonaïves *Town* Haiti 23 J5
Gonder *Town* Ethiopia 38 F8
Gondia *Town* India 87 I5
Good Hope, Cape of *Coastal feature*
   South Africa 44 F9
Goor *Town* Netherlands 52 G8
Göppingen *Town* Germany 57 D9
Gorakhpur *Town* Pakistan 87 J3
Goraāde *Town* Bosnia & Herzegovina 65 E9
Gorē *Town* Ethiopia 39 F9
Gorgan *Town* Iran 82 F5
Gori *Town* Georgia 77 L3
Görlitz *Town* Germany 56 G7
Gorontalo *Town* Indonesia 97 J6
Gorzów Wielkopolski *Town* Poland 62 C6
Gosford *Town* New South Wales,
   Australia 105 M7
Goshogawara *Town* Japan 92 F7
Göteborg *see* Gothenburg
Gotel Mountains *Nigeria* 41 M7
Gotha *Town* Germany 56 E7
Gothenburg *Town* Sweden 49 C11
Gotland *Island* Sweden 49 E11
Gōtsu *Town* Japan 93 C12
Göttingen *Town* Germany 56 D7
Gouda *Town* Netherlands 53 E9
Governador Valadares *Town* Brazil 29 L6
Gradaús, Serra dos *Mountain range*
   Brazil 29 J4
Grafton *Town* New South Wales,
   Australia 105 N6
Grafton *Town* North Dakota, US 12 G2
Grampian Mountains *Scotland, UK* 50 E5
Granada *Town* Spain 59 I8
Granada *Town* Nicaragua 20 H6
Gran Chaco *Plain* Paraguay 30 G4
Grand Bahama Island *The Bahamas* 22 F1
Grand Canyon *Arizona, US* 16 E3
Grand Cayman *Island* West Indies 22 E5
Grande, Bahía *Bay* Argentina 31 E13
Grand Erg Occidental *Desert* Algeria 36 G5
Grand Erg Oriental *Desert* Algeria 37 I5
Grande, Rio *River* Mexico/US 16 G5
Grand Forks *Town* North Dakota, US 12 G2
Grand Rapids *Town* Minnesota, US 12 H3
Grand Rapids *Town* Michigan, US 13 K5
Grand-Santi *Town* French Guiana 26 H6
Grants Pass *Town* Oregon, US 14 F4
Grayling *Town* Alaska, US 4 D4
Graz *Town* Austria 57 H11
Great Australian Bight *Sea feature*
   Australia 104 G7
Great Barrier Island *New Zealand* 106 G4
Great Barrier Reef *Coral reef* Australia 105 L3
Great Basin *Nevada, US* 14 H6
Great Bear Lake *Northwest Territories,*
   Canada 4 H5
Great Dividing Range *Mountain range*
   Queensland/New South Wales,
   Australia 105 L4
Greater Antilles *Island group*
   Caribbean Sea 22 G5
Greater Caucasus *Mountain range*
   Asia/Europe 77 M3
Great Falls *Town* Montana, US 15 J2
Great Hungarian Plain *Hungary* 63 F12
Great Inagua *Island* The Bahamas 23 I4
Great Karoo *Plateau* South Africa 44 F8
Great Khingan Range *Mountain range*
   China 89 L3

Great Rift Valley *Africa* 39 F12
Great Sand Sea *Desert* Egypt 38 C4
Great Sandy Desert *Western Australia,*
   Australia 104 G4
Great Slave Lake *Northwest Territories,*
   Canada 4 H6
Great Victoria Desert *Western Australia/*
   South Australia, Australia 104 G6
Great Wall of China *Ancient monument*
   China 89 J5
Great Yarmouth *Town* England, UK 51 I9
Greece *Country* 67 D11
Greeley *Town* Colorado, US 15 L5
Green Bay *Town* Wisconsin, US 13 J4
Greenfield *Town* Massachusetts, US 9 J5
Greeneville *Town* Tennessee, US 11 I3
Greenland *Dependent territory* Denmark,
   Atlantic Ocean 111 C8
Greenland Sea *Arctic Ocean* 111 M7
Green Mountains *Vermont, US* 9 I5
Greenock *Town* Scotland, UK 50 E6
Greensboro *Town* North Carolina, US 11 J3
Greenville *Town* Mississippi, US 10 I5
Greenville *Town* South Carolina, US 11 I4
Greifswald *Town* Germany 56 F4
Grenada *Country* 23 O8
Grenadines, The *Island group* St Vincent &
   The Grenadines 23 O8
Grenoble *Town* France 55 G10
Gresham *Town* Oregon, US 14 F3
Grevenmacher *Town* Luxembourg 53 G13
Greymouth *Town* New Zealand 107 D10
Grey Range *Mountain range* New South
   Wales/Queensland, Australia 105 K6
Griffin *Town* Georgia, US 10 H5
Grimsby *Town* England, UK 51 H9
Grise Fiord *Town* Nunavut, Canada 5 J3
Grodno *Town* Belarus 70 C8 *see also* Hrodna
Grójec *Town* Poland 62 F7
Groningen *Town* Netherlands 52 G6
Grootfontein *Town* Namibia 44 F5
Grosseto *Town* Italy 60 D8
Groznyy *Town* Russian Federation 73 D14
Gubkin *Town* Russian Federation 73 C10
Grudziądz *Town* Poland 62 E5
Gryazi *Town* Russian Federation 73 C10
Guadalajara *Town* Spain 59 I5
Guadalajara *Town* Mexico 19 I7
Guadalcanal *Island* Solomon Islands 102 G6
Guadalupe *Town* Mexico 19 I6
Guadeloupe *Dependent territory* France,
   Atlantic Ocean 23 O6
Guaimaca *Town* Honduras 20 G4
Gualeguaychú *Town* Argentina 30 G8
Guam *Dependent territory* US, Pacific Ocean
   102 D2
Guamúchil *Town* Mexico 18 G5
Guanabacoa *Town* Cuba 22 D3
Guanajuato *Town* Mexico 19 J7
Guanare *Town* Venezuela 26 D5
Guangdong *Administrative region* China 91 J8
Guangxi *Administrative region* China 90 H8
Guangyuan *Town* China 90 H5
Guangzhou *Town* China 91 I8
Guantánamo *Town* Cuba 22 H4
Guantánamo Bay *Territory* US, Cuba 22 H5
Guasave *Town* Mexico 18 G5
Guatemala *Country* 20 D3
Guatemala City *Capital* Guatemala 20 D4
Guayaquil *Town* Ecuador 26 A8
Guaymas *Town* Mexico 18 E4
Guéret *Town* France 55 E9
Guernsey *British Crown Dependency* Channel
   Islands 51 F13
Guerrero Negro *Town* Mexico 18 D4
Guiana Highlands *Mountain range* Colombia/
   Venezuela/Brazil 26 F7
Guider *Town* Cameroon 42 D7
Guildford *Town* England, UK 51 G11
Guilin *Town* China 91 I7
Guinea *Country* 40 F6
Guinea-Bissau *Country* 40 E6
Guinea, Gulf of *Atlantic Ocean* 33 M5
Gulyang *Town* China 90 H7
Guizhou *Administrative region* China 90 G7
Gujrānwāla *Town* Pakistan 86 H2
Gujrāt *Town* Pakistan 86 H2

Gulbarga *Town* India 86 H6
Gulbene *Town* Latvia 70 G6
Gulf, The *Middle East* 82 E6
   see also Persian Gulf
Guliston *Town* Uzbekistan 85 J4
Gulu *Town* Uganda 39 E10
Gümüşhane *Town* Turkey 76 H4
Güney Doğu Toroslar *Mountain range*
   Turkey 76 H6
Gusau *Town* Nigeria 41 K6
Güstrow *Town* Germany 56 F5
Gütersloh *Town* Germany 56 D6
Guwāhāti *Town* India 87 L3
Guyana *Country* 26 G6
Gwādar *Town* Pakistan 86 D3
Gwalior *Town* India 87 I3
Gwangju *Town* South Korea 91 M4
Gyomaendrőd *Town* Hungary 63 G11
Gyöngyös *Town* Hungary 63 F11
Győr *Town* Hungary 63 D11
Gyumri *Town* Armenia 77 K

H

Haarlem *Town* Netherlands 52 E8
Haast *Town* New Zealand 107 B11
Hachinohe *Town* Japan 92 G7
Hadera *Town* Israel 81 D10
Ha Đông *Town* Vietnam 94 G7
Haeju *Town* North Korea 91 L3
Hagåtña *Capital* Guam 102 E2
Hagerstown *Town* Maryland, US 8 F8
Ha Giang *Town* Vietnam 94 G6
Hague, The *Capital* Netherlands 52 D8
Haicheng *Town* China 91 L2
Haifa *Town* Israel 81 D10
Haikou *Town* China 91 I9
Ḥā'il *Town* Saudi Arabia 82 C8
Hainan *Administrative region* China 90 H9
Hainan Dao *Island* China 91 I9
Hai Phong *Town* Vietnam 94 G7
Haiti *Country* 23 J5
Hajdúhadház *Town* Hungary 63 G11
Hakodate *Town* Japan 92 F6
Halab *see* Aleppo
Halifax *Town* Nova Scotia, Canada 7 L7
Halle *Town* Germany 56 F7
Halle *Town* Belgium 53 D11
Halle-Neustadt *Town* Germany 56 F7
Halley *Research station* Antarctica 110 D4
Halmstad *Town* Sweden 49 C11
Ha Long *Town* Vietnam 94 G7
Hamadān *Town* Iran 82 E6
Ḥamāh *Town* Syria 80 E7
Hamamatsu *Town* Japan 93 F11
Hamar *Town* Norway 49 C9
Hamburg *Town* Germany 56 E5
Hamburg *Town* New York, US 9 F5
Hamersley Range *Mountain range* Western
   Australia, Australia 104 F4
Hamhŭng *Town* North Korea 91 M3
Hami *Town* China 88 G4
Hamilton *Town* Scotland, UK 50 E6
Hamilton *Town* New Zealand 106 G6
Hamilton *Town* Ontario, Canada 6 G8
Hamm *Town* Germany 56 C7
Hanamaki *Town* Japan 92 G8
Handan *Town* China 91 J4
Ha Negev *see* Negev
Hangzhou *Town* China 91 K6
Hanover *Town* Germany 56 D6
Hannover *see* Hanover
Ha Nôi *Capital* Vietnam 94 F7
Hantsavichy *Town* Belarus 71 D10
Hanzhong *Town* China 90 H5
Haradok *Town* Belarus 70 H8
Harare *Capital* Zimbabwe 45 I4
Harbel *Town* Liberia 40 F8
Harbin *Town* China 89 M3
Hardangervidda *Plateau* Norway 49 B9
Hardenberg *Town* Netherlands 52 G7
Hārer *Town* Ethiopia 39 G9
Hargeysa *Town* Somalia 39 H9
Ḥārim *Town* Syria 80 D6
Harlingen *Town* Texas, US 17 M9
Harlow *Town* England, UK 51 H10

Harper *Town* Liberia 40 G8
Harrisburg *Town* Pennsylvania, US 9 G7
Harrogate *Town* England, UK 50 G6
Hârşova *Town* Romania 68 G7
Hartford *Town* Connecticut, US 9 J6
Hartlepool *Town* England, UK 50 G7
Hasselt *Town* Belgium 53 E11
Hastings *Town* New Zealand 106 H8
Hastings *Town* England, UK 50 H11
Hapeg *Town* Romania 68 E6
Hatteras, Cape *Coastal feature* North Carolina,
   US 11 L3
Hat Yai *Town* Thailand 95 D13
Haugesund *Town* Norway 49 A10
Havana *Capital* Cuba 22 D3
Havant *Town* England, UK 51 G11
Havelock *Town* North Carolina, US 11 L4
Hawaiian Ridge *Undersea feature* Pacific
   Ocean 109 J4
Hawera *Town* New Zealand 106 F8
Haysyn *Town* Ukraine 68 H4
Hazar *Town* Turkmenistan 84 D4
Heard & McDonald Islands *Dependent*
   territory Australia, Indian Ocean 99 I8
Hearst *Town* Ontario, Canada 6 F6
Hebei *Administrative region* China 91 J3
Hebron *Town* Israel 81 D11
Heerlen *Town* Netherlands 53 F11
Hefa *see* Haifa
Hefei *Town* China 91 J5
Hegang *Town* China 89 M2
Heidelberg *Town* Germany 57 D9
Heidenheim an der Brenz *Town*
   Germany 57 E10
Heilbronn *Town* Germany 57 D9
Heilong Jiang *see* Amur
Heilongjiang *Administrative region*
   China 89 M2
Heimdal *Sweden* 48 D7
Hekimhan *Town* Turkey 76 H5
Helena *Town* Montana, US 15 I3
Helmond *Town* Netherlands 53 F10
Helsingborg *Town* Sweden 49 C12
Helsinki *Capital* Finland 49 G9
Henan *Administrative region* China 91 I5
Henan *Town* Qinghai, China 89 I6
Hengduan Shan *Mountain range* China 90 E7
Hengelo *Town* Netherlands 52 G8
Hengyang *Town* China 91 I7
Henzada *Town* Myanmar 94 B8
Herāt *Town* Afghanistan 84 G7
Herford *Town* Germany 56 D6
Hermosillo *Town* Mexico 18 E4
Hexian *Town* China 91 I8
Hidalgo del Parral *Town* Mexico 18 H5
Hida-sanmyaku *Mountain range* Japan 93 E10
High Point *Town* North Carolina, US 11 J3
Hikurangi *Town* New Zealand 106 F4
Hildesheim *Town* Germany 56 D6
Hillsboro *Town* New Hampshire, US 9 J5
Hilversum *Town* Netherlands 52 E8
Himalayas *Mountain range* Asia 87 I2
Himeji *Town* Japan 93 D12
Ḥimş *Town* Syria 80 E8
Hîncești *Town* Moldova 68 H5
Hindu Kush *Mountain range* Afghanistan/
   Pakistan 85 J6
Hinthada *Town* Myanmar 94 B8
Hirosaki *Town* Japan 92 F7
Hiroshima *Town* Japan 93 C12
Hitachi *Town* Japan 93 G9
Hitoyoshi *Town* Japan 93 C14
Hjørring *Town* Denmark 49 B11
Hlobyne *Town* Ukraine 69 J4
Illybokaye *Town* Belarus 70 F8
Hô Chi Minh *Town* Vietnam 95 G11
Hodeida *Town* Yemen 83 C12
Hódmezővásárhely *Town* Hungary 63 F12
Hodonín *Town* Czechia 63 D10
Hof *Town* Germany 56 F8
Hōfu *Town* Japan 93 C12
Hohhot *Town* China 89 K5
Hokkaidō *Island* Japan 92 G5
Holguín *Town* Cuba 22 G4
Hollabrunn *Town* Austria 57 H10

K

Junín *Town* Argentina 30 F8
Jura *Mountain range* Switzerland 57 C11
Jūrmala *Town* Latvia 70 E5
Juruá, Rio *River* Brazil 28 G3
Jutiapa *Town* Guatemala 20 E4
Juticalpa *Town* Honduras 20 H4
Jutland *Peninsula* Denmark 49 B12
Jwaneng *Town* Botswana 44 G6
Jylland *see* Jutland
Jyväskylä *Town* Finland 48 G8

K

K2 *Mountain* Pakistan/China 86 H1
Kabale *Town* Uganda 39 D11
Kabinda *Town* Democratic Republic of the Congo 43 G11
Kabul *Capital* Afghanistan 85 J7
Kabwe *Town* Zambia 44 H4
Kachchh, Rann of *Salt marsh* India 86 G4
Kadoma *Town* Zimbabwe 44 H4
Kaduna *Town* Nigeria 41 L6
Kadzhi-Say *Town* Kyrgyzstan 85 M3
Kaga *Town* Japan 93 E10
Kagoshima *Town* Japan 93 C14
Kahramanmaraş *Town* Turkey 76 H6
Kaifeng *Town* China 91 J4
Kaikoura *Town* New Zealand 107 F10
Kaili *Town* China 90 H7
Kairouan *Town* Tunisia 37 J3
Kaiserslautern *Town* Germany 57 C9
Kaiyuan *Town* China 90 F8
Kajaani *Town* Finland 48 H7
Kalahari Desert *Namibia* 44 F6
Kalamariá *Town* Greece 66 E8
Kalámata *Town* Greece 67 D12
Kalamazoo *Town* Michigan, US 13 K5
Kalasin *Town* Thailand 95 F9
Kālat *Town* Pakistan 86 F2
Kalbarri *Town* Western Australia, Australia 104 D5
Kalemie *Town* Democratic Republic of the Congo 43 I11
Kalgoorlie *Town* Western Australia, Australia 104 F6
Kalima *Town* Democratic Republic of the Congo 43 H10
Kalimantan *Region* Indonesia 96 G6
Kaliningrad *Administrative region* Russian Federation 70 B7
Kaliningrad *Town* Kaliningrad 70 B6
Kalisz *Town* Poland 62 E7
Kalmar *Town* Sweden 49 E12
Kaluga *Town* Russian Federation 73 C9
Kalyān *Town* India 86 G5
Kamarang *Town* Guyana 26 F6
Kamchatka Peninsula *Russian Federation* 79 M4
Kamensk-Shakhtinskiy *Town* Russian Federation 73 C11
Kamina *Town* Democratic Republic of the Congo 43 G12
Kamloops *Town* British Colombia, Canada 4 G8
Kampala *Capital* Uganda 39 E11
Kâmpóng Cham *Town* Cambodia 95 G11
Kâmpóng Thum *Town* Cambodia 95 F10
Kam"yanets'-Podil's'kyy *Town* Ukraine 68 G4
Kamyshin *Town* Russian Federation 73 D11
Kananga *Town* Democratic Republic of the Congo 43 F11
Kanash *Town* Russian Federation 73 E9
Kanazawa *Town* Japan 93 E10
Kānchīpuram *Town* India 87 I7
Kandahār *Town* Afghanistan 84 H8
Kandalaksha *Town* Russian Federation 72 D5
Kandi *Town* Benin 41 J6
Kandy *Town* Sri Lanka 87 I9
Kanjiža *Town* Serbia 64 G6
Kankan *Town* Guinea 40 G6
Kannur *Town* India 86 H8 *see also* Cannanore
Kano *Town* Nigeria 41 L6
Kanoya *Town* Japan 93 C14
Kānpur *Town* India 87 I3

Kansas *State* US 12 F7
Kansas City *Town* Kansas, US 12 H7
Kansas River *Kansas*, US 12 G7
Kansk *Town* Russian Federation 79 I6
Kaolack *Town* Senegal 40 E5
Kaoma *Town* Zambia 44 G4
Kaposvár *Town* Hungary 63 E12
Kara-Balta *Town* Kyrgyzstan 85 L3
Karabük *Town* Turkey 76 F3
Karāchi *Town* Pakistan 86 F4
Karagandy *Town* Kazakhstan 78 G7
Karakol *Town* Kyrgyzstan 85 M3
Karakoram Range *Mountain range* Pakistan/India 86 H1
Karaman *Town* Turkey 76 F6
Karamay *Town* China 88 F4
Kara Sea *Arctic Ocean* 111 O6
Karatau *Town* Kazakhstan 78 F7
Karatsu *Town* Japan 93 B13
Karbalā' *Town* Iraq 82 C7
Kardítsa *Town* Greece 67 D10
Kärdla *Town* Estonia 70 F3
Kargi *Town* Turkey 76 G3
Karibib *Town* Namibia 44 E6
Karigasniemi *Town* Finland 48 G4
Karimata, Selat *Strait* Indonesia 96 F7
Karīmnagar *Town* India 87 I6
Karin *Town* Somalia 38 H8
Karlovac *Town* Croatia 64 C6
Karlovy Vary *Town* Czechia 62 B8
Karlskrona *Town* Sweden 49 D12
Karlsruhe *Town* Germany 57 C9
Karlstad *Town* Sweden 49 D10
Karnāl *Town* India 86 H3
Karnobat *Town* Bulgaria 66 H6
Kars *Town* Turkey 77 K4
Kárystos *Town* Greece 67 F11
Kaş *Town* Turkey 76 D7
Kasai *River* Democratic Republic of the Congo 43 E11
Kāsaragod *Town* India 86 H7
Kāshān *Town* Iran 82 E6
Kashi *Town* China 88 D5
Kashiwazaki *Town* Japan 93 F9
Kasongo *Town* Democratic Republic of the Congo 43 H11
Kasongo-Lunda *Town* Democratic Republic of the Congo 43 E11
Kaspiysk *Town* Russian Federation 73 D14
Kassala *Town* Sudan 38 F7
Kassel *Town* Germany 56 D7
Kasserine *Town* Tunisia 37 J4
Kastamonu *Town* Turkey 76 F3
Kasulu *Town* Tanzania 39 D12
Katahdin, Mount *Maine*, US 9 L2
Katha *Town* Myanmar 94 C5
Katherine *Town* Northern Territory, Australia 105 I2
Kathmandu *Capital* Nepal 87 J3
Katikati *Town* New Zealand 106 G6
Katiola *Town* Côte d'Ivoire 40 H7
Katowice *Town* Poland 62 E8
Katsina *Town* Nigeria 41 L6
Kattaqo'rg'on *Town* Uzbekistan 85 I4
Kattegat *Sea* Denmark/Sweden 49 C12
Kaunas *Town* Lithuania 70 D7
Kavála *Town* Greece 66 F8
Kāvali *Town* India 87 I7
Kavarna *Town* Bulgaria 66 I5
Kawagoe *Town* Japan 93 G10
Kawasaki *Town* Japan 93 G10
Kayan *Town* Myanmar 94 C8
Kayseri *Town* Turkey 76 G5
Kazach'ye *Town* Russian Federation 78 K4
Kazakhstan *Country* 78 E6
Kazakh Uplands *Kazakhstan* 78 F7
Kazan' *Town* Russian Federation 73 E9
Kazanlŭk *Town* Bulgaria 66 F6
Kāzerūn *Town* Iran 82 F8
Kecskemét *Town* Hungary 63 F11
Kediri *Town* Indonesia 96 G8
Kędzierzyn-Koźle *Town* Poland 62 E8
Keith *Town* South Australia, Australia 105 J8
Kēk-Art *Town* Kyrgyzstan 85 L4
Kelowna *Town* British Colombia, Canada 4 G9
Kelso *Town* Washington, US 14 F3

Keluang *Town* Malaysia 96 E5
Kemah *Town* Turkey 76 H5
Kemerovo *Town* Russian Federation 78 H6
Kemi *Town* Finland 48 G6
Kemijärvi *Town* Finland 48 G5
Kempten *Town* Germany 57 E10
Kendal *Town* England, UK 50 F8
Kengtung *Town* Myanmar 94 D6
Kénitra *Town* Morocco 36 F4
Kenora *Town* Ontario, Canada 6 D5
Kenosha *Town* Wisconsin, US 13 J5
Kentau *Town* Kazakhstan 78 F7
Kentucky *State* US 10 G3
Kenya *Country* 39 F11
Kerch *Town* Ukraine 69 L7
Kerkrade *Town* Netherlands 53 F11
Kérkyra *see* Corfu
Kermadec Islands *Island group* New Zealand 109 J7
Kermān *Town* Iran 82 G7
Kesennuma *Town* Japan 92 G8
Kettering *Town* Ohio, US 13 L7
Key Largo *Town* Florida, US 11 J9
Key West *Town* Florida, US 11 J9
Khabarovsk *Town* Russian Federation 78 D4
Khairpur *Town* Pakistan 86 G3
Khanthabouli *Town* Laos 95 F9
Khanty-Mansiysk *Town* Russian Federation 78 G5
Kharagpur *Town* India 87 K4
Kharkiv *Town* Ukraine 69 L3
Khartoum *Capital* Sudan 38 E7
Khasavyurt *Town* Russian Federation 73 D14
Khaskovo *Town* Bulgaria 66 F7
Khaydarkan *Town* Kyrgyzstan 85 K4
Kherson *Town* Ukraine 69 J6
Khmel'nyts'kyy *Town* Ukraine 68 G3
Khon Kaen *Town* Thailand 95 E9
Khōst *Town* Afghanistan 85 J7
Khouribga *Town* Morocco 36 E4
Khujand *Town* Tajikistan 85 J4
Khulna *Town* Bangladesh 87 I4
Khust *Town* Ukraine 68 E4
Khvoy *Town* Iran 82 D5
Khyber Pass *Afghanistan/Pakistan* 86 G1
Kidderminster *Town* England, UK 51 F10
Kiel *Town* Germany 56 E4
Kielce *Town* Poland 62 F8
Kiev *Capital* Ukraine 69 I3
Kigali *Capital* Rwanda 39 D12
Kigoma *Town* Tanzania 39 D12
Kii-suidō *Bay* Japan 93 E12
Kikinda *Town* Serbia 64 G6
Kikwit *Town* Democratic Republic of the Congo 43 E11
Kilis *Town* Turkey 76 H7
Killarney *Town* Ireland 51 B10
Killeen *Town* Texas, US 17 L6
Kilmarnock *Town* Scotland, UK 50 E6
Kimberley *Town* South Africa 44 G7
Kimberley Plateau *Western Australia*, Australia 104 G3
Kimch'aek *Town* North Korea 91 M2
Kindia *Town* Guinea 40 E6
Kineshma *Town* Russian Federation 72 D8
Kingman Reef *Dependent territory* US, Pacific Ocean 103 L3
Kingston *Town* Jamaica 22 G6
Kingston *Town* Ontario, Canada 6 H8
Kingston upon Hull *Town* England, UK 50 H6
Kingstown *Capital* St Vincent & The Grenadines 23 O8
Kinshasa *Capital* Democratic Republic of the Congo 43 D11
Kipushi *Town* Democratic Republic of the Congo 43 H13
Kirghiz Range *Mountain range* Kyrgyzstan 85 K3
Kiribati *Country* 103 L5
Kirikhan *Town* Turkey 76 H7
Kirikkale *Town* Turkey 76 F4
Kirishi *Town* Russian Federation 72 C7
Kirkenes *Town* Norway 48 H3
Kirkland Lake *Town* Ontario, Canada 6 G6

Kirklareli *Town* Turkey 76 C3
Kirkūk *Town* Iraq 82 D6
Kirkwall *Town* Scotland, UK 50 F3
Kirov *Town* Russian Federation 72 F8
Kirovo-Chepetsk *Town* Russian Federation 72 F8
Kirovohrad *Town* Ukraine 69 J4
Kiruna *Town* Sweden 48 F5
Kisangani *Town* Democratic Republic of the Congo 43 H9
Kislovodsk *Town* Russian Federation 73 C11
Kismaayo *Town* Somalia 39 G11
Kissidougou *Town* Guinea 40 G7
Kissimmee, Lake *Florida*, US 11 J7
Kisumu *Town* Kenya 39 E11
Kitakyūshū *Town* Japan 93 B13
Kitami *Town* Japan 92 G4
Kitchener *Town* Ontario, Canada 6 G8
Kitwe *Town* Zambia 44 H3
Kivalo *Ridge* Finland 48 G6
Kivertsi *Town* Ukraine 68 G2
Kivu, Lake *Democratic Republic of the Congo* 43 H10
Kladno *Town* Czechia 62 B8
Klagenfurt *Town* Austria 57 G11
Klaipėda *Town* Lithuania 70 C6
Klamath Falls *Town* Oregon, US 14 F4
Klang *Town* Malaysia 96 D5
Klarälven *River* Sweden 49 D9
Klerksdorp *Town* South Africa 44 H7
Klintsy *Town* Russian Federation 73 B9
Ključ *Town* Bosnia & Herzegovina 64 D7
Klosters *Town* Switzerland 57 D11
Knin *Town* Croatia 64 C8
Knoxville *Town* Tennessee, US 11 I3
Kōbe *Town* Japan 93 E12
København *see* Copenhagen
Koblenz *Town* Germany 56 C8
Kočani *Town* Macedonia 65 H11
Kočevje *Town* Slovenia 57 H12
Kochi *Town* India 86 H8 *see also* Cochin
Kōchi *Town* Japan 93 D13
Kodiak *Town* Alaska, US 4 D6
Kōfu *Town* Japan 93 F10
Kohīma *Town* India 87 M3
Kohtla-Järve *Town* Estonia 70 H4
Koko *Town* Nigeria 41 K6
Kokshetau *Town* Kazakhstan 78 F6
Kola Peninsula *Russian Federation* 72 E5
Kolari *Town* Finland 48 F5
Kolda *Town* Senegal 40 E5
Kolhāpur *Town* India 86 G5
Kolkatta *Town* India 87 K4
Kollam *Town* India 86 H9 *see also* Quilon
Köln *see* Cologne
Kołobrzeg *Town* Poland 62 C5
Kolomna *Town* Russian Federation 73 C9
Kolpino *Town* Russian Federation 72 C7
Kol'skiy Poluostrov *see* Kola Peninsula
Kolwezi *Town* Democratic Republic of the Congo 43 G13
Komatsu *Town* Japan 93 E10
Komsomol'sk-na-Amure *Town* Russian Federation 79 L6
Konin *Town* Poland 62 E7
Konispol *Town* Albania 65 F13
Konotop *Town* Ukraine 69 J2
Konstanz *Town* Germany 57 D10
Konya *Town* Turkey 76 F6
Kopaonik *Mountain range* Serbia 65 G9
Koper *Town* Slovenia 57 G12
Korat Plateau *Thailand* 94 F8
Korba *Town* India 87 J5
Korçë *Town* Albania 65 F12
Korea Bay *China/North Korea* 91 L3
Korea Strait *Japan/South Korea* 91 M4
Korhogo *Town* Côte d'Ivoire 40 I7
Kórinthos *see* Corinth
Kōriyama *Town* Japan 93 G9
Korla *Town* China 88 F5
Korosten' *Town* Ukraine 68 H2
Kortrijk *Town* Belgium 53 C11
Kos *Town* Greece 67 H13
Kościerzyna *Town* Poland 62 E5
Košice *Town* Slovakia 63 G10
Koson *Town* Uzbekistan 85 I4

Q

Quincy *Town* Missouri, US 13 I7
Quito *Capital* Ecuador 26 B7
Qŭrghonteppa *Town* Tajikistan 85 J5
Quy Nhơn *Town* Vietnam 95 H10
Quzhou *Town* China 91 K6

R

Rabat *Capital* Morocco 36 E4
Rabinal *Town* Guatemala 20 E4
Rabyānah, Ramlat *Desert* Libya 37 M6
Race, Cape *Coastal feature* Newfoundland &
   Labrador, Canada 7 N6
Rach Gia *Town* Vietnam 95 F12
Racine *Town* Wisconsin, US 13 J5
Radom *Town* Poland 62 G7
Rafaela *Town* Argentina 30 F7
Rafah *Town* Israel 81 C12
Ragusa *Town* Sicily, Italy 61 F14
Rahīmyār Khān *Town* Pakistan 86 G3
Rāichūr *Town* India 86 H6
Raipur *Town* India 87 J5
Rājahmundry *Town* India 87 J6
Rājkot *Town* India 86 G4
Rajshahi *Town* Bangladesh 87 K4
Raleigh *Town* North Carolina, US 11 K3
Ralik Chain *Island chain* Marshall Islands
   102 H2
Râmnicu Vâlcea *Town* Romania 68 E7
Rancagua *Town* Chile 30 D8
Rānchi *Town* India 87 J4
Randers *Denmark* 49 B12
Rangoon *see* Yangon
Rangpur *Town* Pakistan 87 L3
Rankin Inlet *Town* Nunavut, Canada 5 J6
Rapid City *Town* South Dakota, US 12 E4
Ra's al 'Ayn *Town* Syria 80 G4
Rasht *Town* Iran 82 E5
Ratak Chain *Island chain* Marshall Islands
   102 H2
Rathkeale *Town* Ireland 51 B10
Rat Islands *Island Group* Alaska, US 4 A4
Ratlām *Town* India 86 H4
Raton *Town* New Mexico, US 17 I3
Rättvik *Town* Sweden 49 D9
Raukumara Range *Mountain range*
   New Zealand 106 I7
Rauma *Town* Finland 49 F9
Rāurkela *Town* India 87 J5
Ravenna *Town* Italy 60 E6
Rāwalpindi *Town* Pakistan 86 G1
Rawicz *Town* Poland 62 D7
Rawlins *Town* Wyoming, US 15 K5
Rawson *Town* Argentina 31 F11
Razgrad *Town* Bulgaria 66 G5
Reading *Town* Pennsylvania, US 9 H7
Reading *Town* England, UK 51 G11
Realicó *Town* Argentina 30 E8
Rechytsa *Town* Belarus 71 F11
Recife *Town* Brazil 29 N4
Recklinghausen *Town* Germany 56 C7
Recogne *Town* Belgium 53 E13
Reconquista *Town* Argentina 30 G6
Red Deer *Town* Alberta, Canada 4 H8
Redding *Town* California, US 14 F5
Red River *US* 17 K4
Red Sea *Africa/Asia* 83 B9
Reefton *Town* New Zealand 107 D10
Regensburg *Town* Germany 57 F9
Reggane *Town* Algeria 36 G6
Reggio di Calabria *Town* Italy 61 G13
Reggio nell' Emilia *Town* Italy 60 D6
Regina *Town* Saskatchewan,
   Canada 5 I9
Rehovot *Town* Israel 81 D11
Reims *Town* France 54 F6
Rengat *Town* Indonesia 96 E6
Rennes *Town* France 54 C7
Reno *Town* Nevada, US 14 G5
Renqiu *Town* Hebei, China 91 J3
Republika Srpska *Administrative region*
   Bosnia & Herzegovina 64 D7
Repulse Bay *Town* Nunavut, Canada 5 K5
Resistencia *Town* Argentina 30 G6
Reşipa *Town* Romania 68 D6

Resolute *Town* Nunavut, Canada 5 J3
Réunion *Dependent territory* France,
   Indian Ocean 45 O6
Reus *Town* Spain 59 L4
Reutlingen *Town* Germany 57 D10
Reyes *Town* Bolivia 27 E11
Reykjavík *Capital* Iceland 111 D9
Reynosa *Town* Mexico 19 K5
Rēzekne *Town* Latvia 70 G7
Rheine *Town* Germany 56 C6
Rhine *River* Europe 56 C8
Rho *Town* Italy 60 C5
Rhode Island *State* US 9 J6
Rhodes *Town* Greece 67 I13
Rhodope Mountains *Mountain range*
   Bulgaria 66 G7
Rhône *River* France 55 F11
Ribeirão Preto *Town* Brazil 29 K7
Rîbnița *Town* Moldova 68 H5
Richmond *Town* Kentucky, US 10 H2
Richmond *Town* Virginia, US 11 K2
Ridder *Town* Kazakhstan 78 H7
Ried im Innkreis *Town* Austria 57 G10
Rīga *Capital* Latvia 70 E5
Riga, Gulf of *Latvia* 70 E5
Rijeka *Town* Croatia 64 B6
Rimini *Town* Italy 60 E7
Rimouski *Town* Québec, Canada 7 J6
Riobamba *Town* Ecuador 26 A8
Río Bravo *Town* Mexico 19 K5
Río Cuarto *Town* Argentina 30 E8
Rio de Janeiro *Town* Brazil 29 L7
Río Gallegos *Town* Argentina 31 E14
Rio Grande *Town* Brazil 29 J9
Ríohacha *Town* Colombia 26 C4
Rio Lagartos *Town* Mexico 19 O6
Río Verde *Town* Mexico 19 J7
Rivera *Town* Uruguay 30 H7
River Falls *Town* Wisconsin, US 13 I4
Riverside *Town* California, US 13 J5
Riverton *Town* Wyoming, US 15 K4
Rivne *Town* Ukraine 68 G2
Rivoli *Town* Italy 60 B5
Riyadh *Capital* Saudi Arabia 83 D9
Road Town *Capital* British Virgin Islands
   23 M5
Rize *Town* Turkey 77 J3
Roanoke *Town* Virginia, US 11 J3
Roatán *Town* Honduras 20 G3
Robinson Range *Mountain range* Western
   Australia, Australia 104 F5
Robstown *Town* Texas, US 17 L8
Rochefort *Town* Belgium 53 E12
Rochefort *Town* France 55 D9
Rochester *Town* New York, US 8 F5
Rochester *Town* Minnesota, US 13 I4
Rockford *Town* Illinois, US 13 J5
Rockhampton *Town* Queensland,
   Australia 105 M4
Rock Hill *Town* South Carolina, US 11 J4
Rock Sound *Town* The Bahamas 22 G2
Rocky Mountains *Canada/US* 4, 14
Ródos *see* Rhodes
Roeselare *Town* Belgium 53 C11
Rogatica *Town* Bosnia & Herzegovina
   64 E8
Rogers *Town* Arkansas, US 10 D3
Roi Et *Town* Thailand 95 F9
Rokycany *Town* Czechia 63 B9
Roma *Town* Queensland, Australia 105 M5
Roma *see* Rome
Roman *Town* Romania 68 G5
Romania *Country* 68 E6
Rome *Capital* Italy 61 E9
Romny *Town* Ukraine 69 J2
Rondonópolis *Town* Brazil 29 I6
Ronne Ice Shelf *Ice feature* Antarctica 110 C5
Roosendaal *Town* Netherlands 53 D10
Røros *Town* Norway 48 C8
Rosario *Town* Argentina 30 F8
Rosario *Town* Paraguay 30 H5
Rosarito *Town* Mexico 18 C2
Roseau *Capital* Dominica 23 O6
Rosenheim *Town* Germany 57 F10
Roslavl' *Town* Russian Federation 73 B9
Ross *Town* New Zealand 107 D10
Ross Ice Shelf *Ice feature* Antarctica 110 D7

Rosso *Town* Mauritania 40 E4
Rossosh' *Town* Russian Federation 73 C10
Ross Sea *Antarctica* 110 D7
Rostock *Town* Germany 56 F4
Rostov-na-Donu *Town* Russian Federation
   73 C11
Roswell *Town* New Mexico, US 17 I5
Rothera *Research station* Antarctica 110 B5
Rotorua *Town* New Zealand 106 G6
Rotorua, Lake *New Zealand* 106 G6
Rotterdam *Town* Netherlands 53 E9
Roubaix *Town* France 54 F5
Rouen *Town* France 54 E6
Round Rock *Town* Texas, US 17 L6
Rovigo *Town* Italy 60 E6
Roxas City *Town* Philippines 97 J3
Rozdol'ne *Town* Ukraine 69 J6
Rožňava *Town* Slovakia 63 F10
Ruatoria *Town* New Zealand 106 I6
Rubizhne *Town* Ukraine 69 M4
Rudnyy *Town* Kazakhstan 78 E6
Rudzyensk *Town* Belarus 71 E10
Rufino *Town* Argentina 30 F8
Rukwa, Lake *Tanzania* 39 E13
Ruoqiang *Town* China 88 F5
Ruse *Town* Bulgaria 66 G5
Rushmore, Mount *Mountain*
   South Dakota, US 12 E4
Russellville *Town* Arkansas, US 10 E3
Russian Federation *Country* 78 G6
Rustavi *Town* Georgia 77 L3
Ruston *Town* Louisiana, US 10 E5
Rutland *Town* Vermont, US 9 I4
Rwanda *Country* 39 D12
Ryazan' *Town* Russian Federation 73 D9
Rybinsk *Town* Russian Federation 72 D8
Rybnik *Town* Poland 62 E8
Ryki *Town* Poland 62 G7
Ryukyu Islands *Island chain* Japan 93 A16
Rzeszów *Town* Poland 63 G9
Rzhev *Town* Russian Federation 72 C8

S

Saalfeld *Town* Germany 56 E8
Saarbrücken *Town* Germany 57 C9
Sab' Ābār *Town* Syria 80 F8
Šabac *Town* Serbia 64 F7
Sabadell *Town* Spain 59 M4
Sabah *Cultural region* Malaysia 96 H5
Sabaya *Town* Bolivia 27 D12
Sabhā *Town* Libya 37 K6
Sabinas *Town* Mexico 19 I4
Sabinas Hidalgo *Town* Mexico 19 J4
Sable Island *Québec, Canada* 7 M7
Sabzevār *Town* Iran 82 G5
Sacramento *Town* California, US 14 F6
Sacramento Mountains *New Mexico/
   Texas, US* 16 H5
Sacramento Valley *California, US* 14 F5
Şa'dah *Town* Yemen 83 C12
Şafāshahr *Town* Iran 82 F7
Safi *Town* Morocco 36 E4
Sagaing *Town* Myanmar 94 B6
Sāgar *Town* India 87 I4
Saginaw *Town* Michigan, US 13 L5
Sagua la Grande *Town* Cuba 22 E3
Sagunto *Town* Spain 59 K6
Sahara *Desert* North Africa 36–37, 40–41
Sahel *Desert* North Africa 41 K5
Saïda *Town* Lebanon 81 D9
Saiki *Town* Japan 93 C13
Saimaa *Lake* Finland 48 H8
St Albans *Town* England, UK 51 H10
Saint Albans *Town* West Virginia,
   US 11 I2
St Andrews *Town* Scotland, UK 50 F6
St. Anthony *Town* Newfoundland &
   Labrador, Canada 7 M4
Saint Augustine *Town* Florida, US 11 J6
St-Brieuc *Town* France 54 B6
St. Catharines *Town* Ontario, Canada 6 G8
St-Chamond *Town* France 55 F10
St-Claude *Town* France 55 G9
St Croix *Island* Virgin Islands 23 M5

St-Denis *Capital* Réunion 45 O6
St-Étienne *Town* France 55 F10
St-Gaudens *Town* France 55 D11
St-Georges *Town* French Guiana 26 I6
St. George's *Capital* Grenada 23 O8
St George's Channel *Europe* 51 D10
St Helena *Dependent Territory* UK,
   Atlantic Ocean 33 L6
St Helier *Capital* Jersey, Channel Islands
   51 G13
St-Jean, Lac *Lake* Canada 7 I6
Saint John *Town* New Brunswick,
   Canada 7 K7
St John's *Capital* Antigua & Barbuda 23 N5
St. John's *Town* Newfoundland & Labrador,
   Canada 7 N5
Saint Joseph *Town* Missouri, US 12 H7
Saint Kitts & Nevis *Country* 23 N6
St-Laurent-du-Maroni *Town*
   French Guiana 26 H6
St. Lawrence *River* Canada/US 7 J6
St. Lawrence, Gulf of *Canada* 7 L6
Saint Lawrence Island *Alaska, US* 4 D4
Saint Louis *Town* Senegal 40 E5
Saint Louis *Town* Illinois, US 13 J7
St. Lucia *Country* 23 O7
St Lucia Channel *Martinique* 23 O7
St-Malo *Town* France 54 C6
St. Moritz *Town* Switzerland 57 D12
St-Nazaire *Town* France 54 B8
St-Omer *Town* France 54 E5
Saint Paul *Town* Minnesota, US 13 I4
St Peter Port *Capital* Guernsey, Channel
   Islands 51 F13
Saint Petersburg *Town* Russian Federation
   72 C7
Saint Petersburg *Town* Florida, US 11 I8
St Pierre & Miquelon *Dependent Territory*
   France, Atlantic Ocean 7 M6
St-Quentin *Town* France 54 F6
Saint Vincent *Island* St Vincent and the
   Grenadines 23 O7
Saint Vincent & The Grenadines *Country*
   23 O7
Saint Vincent Passage *Strait* St. Lucia 23 O7
Sakai *Town* Japan 93 E12
Sakata *Town* Japan 92 F8
Sakhalin, Ostrov *Island* Russian Federation
   79 M6
Şäki *Town* Azerbaijan 77 M3
Salado, Río *River* Argentina 30 F6
Salamanca *Town* Chile 30 C7
Salamanca *Town* Spain 58 G5
Salamīyah *Town* Syria 80 E7
Saldus *Town* Latvia 70 D5
Salé *Town* Morocco 36 F4
Salem *Town* Nepal 87 I8
Salem *Town* Oregon, US 14 F3
Salerno *Town* Italy 61 F10
Salihorsk *Town* Belarus 71 E10
Salima *Town* Malawi 45 J3
Salina *Town* Kansas, US 12 G7
Salina Cruz *Town* Mexico 19 M9
Salinas *Town* California, US 14 F7
Salisbury *Town* Maryland, US 9 H9
Salonica *Town* Greece 66 E8
Salonta *Town* Romania 68 D5
Sal'sk *Town* Russian Federation 73 C11
Salta *Town* Argentina 30 E5
Saltillo *Town* Mexico 19 J5
Salt Lake City *Town* Utah, US 15 I5
Salto *Town* Uruguay 30 G7
Salvador *Town* Brazil 29 M5
Salween *River* Myanmar 94 C7
Salyān *Town* Nepal 87 J3
Salzburg *Town* Austria 57 F10
Salzgitter *Town* Germany 56 E6
Samalayuca *Town* Mexico 18 G3
Samar *Island* Philippines 97 K3
Samara *Town* Russian Federation 73 E10
Samarinda *Town* Indonesia 97 I6
Samarqand *Town* Uzbekistan 85 I4
Şamaxi *Town* Azerbaijan 77 N3
Sambalpur *Town* India 87 J5
Samoa *Country* 103 K6
Sampit *Town* Indonesia 96 G7

Samsun *Town* Turkey 76 H3
Samtredia *Town* Georgia 77 K3
Samui, Ko *Island* Thailand 95 D12
Samut Prakan *Town* Thailand 95 E10
San *Town* Mali 40 H6
Şan'ā' *see* Sana
Sana *Capital* Yemen 83 C12
Sanae *Research station* Antarctica 110 D3
Sanandaj *Town* Iran 82 D6
San Andrés Tuxtla *Town* Mexico 19 L8
San Angelo *Town* Texas, US 17 K6
San Antonio *Town* Chile 30 C8
San Antonio *Town* Texas, US 17 L7
San Antonio Oeste *Town* Argentina 31 E10
Sanāw *Town* Yemen 83 E11
San Bernardino *Town* California, US 14 G8
San Carlos de Bariloche *Town* Argentina 31 D10
San Cristóbal *Town* Venezuela 26 C5
San Cristóbal de Las Casas *Town* Mexico 19 N8
Sancti Spíritus *Town* Cuba 22 F3
Sandakan *Town* Malaysia 97 I4
Sand Hills *Mountain range* Nebraska, US 12 E5
San Diego *Town* California, US 14 G9
Sandpoint *Town* Idaho, US 14 H2
Sandvika *Town* Norway 49 B9
Sandy City *Town* Utah, US 15 I5
San Fernando *Town* Venezuela 26 E5
San Fernando *Town* Spain 58 G9
San Fernando *Town* Trinidad & Tobago 23 O9
San Fernando del Valle de Catamarca *Town* Argentina 30 E6
San Francisco *Town* California, US 14 F6
San Francisco del Oro *Town* Mexico 18 H5
San Francisco de Macorís *Town* Dominican Republic 23 J5
San Ignacio *Town* Guatemala 20 E2
San Ignacio *Town* Mexico 18 D5
San Joaquin Valley *Valley* California, US 14 F7
San Jorge, Golfo *Gulf* Argentina 31 E12
San José *Town* Bolivia 27 F12
San José *Capital* Costa Rica 21 J7
San José *Town* Guatemala 20 D5
San Jose *Town* California, US 14 F6
San Juan *Capital* Puerto Rico 23 L5
San Juan *Town* Argentina 30 D7
San Juan del Norte *Town* Nicaragua 21 J6
San Juan Mountains *New* Mexico/Colorado, US 16 H3
Sankt Gallen *Town* Switzerland 57 E11
Sankt-Peterburg *see* Saint Petersburg
Sankt Pölten *Town* Austria 57 H10
Sankuru *River* Democratic Republic of the Congo 43 G11
Şanlıurfa *Town* Turkey 77 I6
San Luis *Town* Guatemala 20 E3
San Luis *Town* Argentina 30 E8
San Luis Río Colorado *Town* Mexico 18 D2
San Luis Potosí *Town* Mexico 19 J6
San Marcos *Town* Guatemala 20 D4
San Marino *Country* 60 E7
San Marino *Capital* San Marino 60 E7
San Martín *Research station* Antarctica 110 B5
San Matías *Town* Bolivia 27 G12
San Matías, Golfo *Gulf* Argentina 31 F10
Sanmenxia *Town* China 91 J3
San Miguel *Town* El Salvador 20 F5
San Miguel *Town* Mexico 19 I4
San Miguel de Tucumán *Town* Argentina 30 E6
San Miguelito *Town* Panama 21 M8
Sanming *Town* China 91 K7
San Pedro *Town* Belize 20 F2
San Pedro de la Cueva *Town* Mexico 18 F4
San Pedro de Lloc *Town* Peru 27 A9
San Pedro Mártir, Sierra *Mountain range* Mexico 18 D3
San Pedro Sula *Town* Honduras 20 F3
San Rafael *Town* Argentina 30 D8
San Remo *Town* Italy 60 B6
San Salvador *Capital* El Salvador 20 F5
San Salvador de Jujuy *Town* Argentina 30 E5
Sansanné-Mango *Town* Togo 41 J6

San Sebastian *Town* Spain 59 J2
  see also Donostia
Sansepolcro *Town* Italy 60 E7
San Severo *Town* Italy 61 G9
Santa Ana *Town* California, US 14 G8
Santa Ana *Town* El Salvador 20 E4
Santa Barbara *Town* California, US 14 G8
Santa Clara *Town* Cuba 22 E3
Santa Cruz *Town* Bolivia 27 F12
Santa Fe *Town* New Mexico, US 16 H3
Santa Fe *Town* Argentina 30 F7
Santa Maria *Town* Brazil 29 J8
Santa Marta *Town* Colombia 26 C4
Santander *Town* Spain 59 I2
Santarém *Town* Brazil 29 I2
Santa Rosa *Town* Argentina 31 E9
Santa Rosa *Town* California, US 14 F6
Santa Rosa de Copán *Town* Honduras 20 F4
Santiago *Capital* Chile 30 D8
Santiago *Town* Dominican Republic 23 J5
Santiago de Compostela *Town* Spain 58 F3
Santiago de Cuba *Town* Cuba 22 G5
Santiago del Estero *Town* Argentina 30 E6
Santo Domingo *Capital* Dominican Republic 23 J5
Santo Domingo de los Colorados *Town* Ecuador 26 A7
Santorini *Town* Greece 67 G13
Santos *Town* Brazil 29 K7
Santo Tomé *Town* Argentina 30 H6
San Vicente *Town* El Salvador 20 F5
São Fransisco, Rio *River* Brazil 29 L4
Sao Hill *Town* Tanzania 39 F13
São José do Rio Preto *Town* Brazil 29 K6
São Luís *Town* Brazil 29 L2
São Paulo *Town* Brazil 29 K7
São Roque, Cabo de *Coastal feature* Brazil 29 N3
São Tomé *Capital* São Tomé & Príncipe 43 B10
São Tomé & Príncipe *Country* 43 B9
São Tomé *Town* Japan 92 H5
Sapele *Town* Nigeria 41 K8
Sapporo *Town* Japan 92 H3
Saqqez *Town* Iran 82 D6
Sarajevo *Capital* Bosnia & Herzegovina 64 E8
Sarakhs *Town* Iran 82 H5
Saraktash *Town* Russian Federation 73 G11
Saran' *Town* Kazakhstan 78 F7
Saransk *Town* Russian Federation 73 E9
Saratov *Town* Russian Federation 73 D10
Sarawak *Cultural region* Malaysia 96 G6
Sardegna *see* Sardinia
Sardinia *Island* Italy 61 A9
Sargasso Sea *Atlantic Ocean* 33 I3
Sargodha *Town* Pakistan 86 G2
Sarh *Town* Chad 42 E7
Sārī *Town* Iran 82 F5
Sariwŏn *Town* North Korea 91 L3
Sark *Island* Channel Islands, UK 51 G13
Sarmiento *Town* Argentina 31 D12
Sarnia *Town* Ontario, Canada 6 F8
Sarny *Town* Ukraine 68 G2
Sasebo *Town* Japan 93 B13
Saskatchewan *River* Saskatchewan, Canada 5 I8
Saskatchewan *Province* Canada 5 I8
Saskatoon *Town* Saskatchewan, Canada 5 I8
Sasovo *Town* Russian Federation 73 D9
Sassari *Town* Sardinia, Italy 61 B9
Sātpura Range *Mountain range* India 86 H5
Satsuma-Sendai *Town* Japan 93 B14
Sattanen *Town* Finland 48 G5
Satu Mare *Town* Romania 68 E4
Saudi Arabia *Country* 83 D10
Sault Ste. Marie *Town* Ontario, Canada 6 F7
Sava *River* Serbia 64 F8
Savá *Town* Honduras 20 H3
Savannah *Town* Georgia, US 11 J5
Savannah River *Georgia/South Carolina*, US 11 I5
Saverne *Town* France 54 H7
Savona *Town* Italy 60 C6
Savu Sea *Indonesia* 97 J8
Sawhāj *Town* Egypt 38 E5
Saxony *Region* Germany 56 G7
Saýat *Town* Turkmenistan 84 H4

Sayḩūt *Town* Yemen 83 F12
Saynshand *Town* Mongolia 89 J4
Say'ūn *Town* Yemen 83 E12
Scarborough *Town* England, UK 50 H8
Schaerbeek *Town* Belgium 53 D11
Schagen *Town* Netherlands 52 E7
Schefferville *Town* Newfoundland & Labrador, Canada 7 J4
Scheldt *River* Belgium 53 D10
Schenectady *Town* New York, US 8 I5
Schwandorf *Town* Germany 57 F9
Schwaz *Town* Austria 57 F11
Schweinfurt *Town* Germany 56 E8
Schwerin *Town* Germany 56 E5
Schwyz *Town* Switzerland 57 D11
Scilly, Isles of *Island group* England, UK 51 D13
Scotland *Political region* UK 50 E5
Scott Base *Research station* Antarctica 110 E7
Scottsbluff *Town* Nebraska, US 12 E5
Scottsdale *Town* Arizona, US 16 E5
Scranton *Town* Pennsylvania, US 8 H6
Seattle *Town* Washington, US 14 G2
Sébaco *Town* Nicaragua 20 H5
Sedan *Town* France 54 G6
Sedona *Town* Arizona, US 16 E4
Seesen *Town* Germany 56 E6
Segezha *Town* Russian Federation 72 D6
Ségou *Town* Mali 40 H6
Segovia *Town* Spain 58 H5
Séguédine *Town* Niger 41 M3
Seine *River* France 54 E6
Sejong City *Capital* South Korea 91 M4
Sekondi-Takoradi *Town* Ghana 41 I8
Selby *Town* South Dakota, US 12 F4
Selwyn Range *Mountain range* Queensland, Australia 105 K4
Semarang *Town* Indonesia 96 G8
Semey *Town* Kazakhstan 78 G7
Semnān *Town* Iran 82 F6
Sendai *Town* Japan 92 G8
Sendai-wan *Bay* Japan 92 G8
Senegal *Country* 40 E6
Senegal *River* Senegal 40 E4
Senj *Town* Croatia 64 B6
Senlis *Town* France 54 F6
Sennar *Town* Sudan 38 E8
Sens *Town* France 54 F7
Seoul *Capital* South Korea 91 M3
Sept-Îles *Town* Québec, Canada 7 J5
Seraing *Town* Belgium 53 F11
Serang *Town* Indonesia 96 F7
Serbia *Country* 64 G8
Serhetabat *Town* Turkmenistan 84 G6
Seremban *Town* Malaysia 96 E5
Serov *Town* Russian Federation 78 F5
Serpukhov *Town* Russian Federation 73 C9
Sérres *Town* Greece 66 E8
Sesto San Giovanni *Town* Italy 60 C5
Setana *Town* Japan 92 H3
Sète *Town* France 55 F11
Sétif *Town* Algeria 37 I3
Setté Cama *Town* Gabon 43 C10
Setúbal *Town* Portugal 58 E7
Sevan *Town* Armenia 77 L4
Sevastopol' *Town* Ukraine 69 J7
Severn *River* England, UK 51 F11
Severnaya Zemlya *Island group* Russian Federation 79 J3
Severnyy *Town* Russian Federation 72 H5
Severodvinsk *Town* Russian Federation 72 E6
Severomorsk *Town* Russian Federation 72 E4
Sevilla *see* Seville
Seville *Town* Spain 58 G8
Sevlievo *Town* Bulgaria 66 F6
Seychelles *Country* 99 I5
Sfântu Gheorghe *Town* Romania 68 F6
Sfax *Town* Tunisia 37 J4
's-Gravenhage *see* Hague, The
Shaanxi *Administrative region* China 90 H5
Shanxi *Administrative region* China 91 I4
Shackleton Ice Shelf *Ice feature* Antarctica 110 G6
Shāhrūd *Town* Iran 82 F5

Shandong *Administrative region* China 91 J4
Shanghai *Town* China 91 L5
Shangrao *Town* China 91 K6
Shannon *River* Ireland 51 C9
Shan Plateau *Myanmar* 94 C6
Shantou *Town* China 91 J8
Shaoguan *Town* China 91 J7
Shar *Town* Kazakhstan 78 G7
Shari *Town* Japan 92 H4
Sharjah *Town* United Arab Emirates 83 G9
Shchuchinsk *Town* Kazakhstan 78 F6
Sheboygan *Town* Wisconsin, US 13 J5
Shebshi Mountains *Mountain range* Nigeria 41 M7
Sheffield *Town* England, UK 51 G9
Shelby *Town* Montana, US 15 I2
Shenyang *Town* China 91 L2
Shepparton *Town* Victoria, Australia 105 K8
Sherbrooke *Town* Québec, Canada 7 I7
's-Hertogenbosch *Town* Netherlands 53 F9
Shetland Islands *Island group* Scotland, UK 50 F2
Shibirghān *Town* Afghanistan 85 I6
Shihezi *Town* China 88 F4
Shijiazhuang *Town* China 91 J3
Shikarpur *Town* Pakistan 86 F3
Shikoku *Island* Japan 93 E13
Shiliguri *Town* India 87 K3
Shimoga *Town* India 86 H7
Shimonoseki *Town* Japan 93 B13
Shindand *Town* Afghanistan 84 G7
Shingū *Town* Japan 93 E12
Shintoku *Town* Japan 92 G5
Shinyanga *Town* Tanzania 39 E12
Shiprock *Town* New Mexico, US 16 G3
Shirataki *Town* Japan 92 G4
Shīrāz *Town* Iran 82 F8
Shivpuri *Town* India 86 H4
Shizugawa *Town* Japan 92 G8
Shizuoka *Town* Japan 93 F11
Shkodër *Town* Albania 65 E11
Shouzhou *Town* China 91 I3
Shreveport *Town* Louisiana, US 10 D5
Shrewsbury *Town* England, UK 51 F9
Shu *Town* Kazakhstan 78 F8
Shumen *Town* Bulgaria 66 H5
Shuqrah *Town* Yemen 83 D13
Shwebo *Town* Myanmar 94 B6
Shymkent *Town* Kazakhstan 78 F8
Šiauliai *Town* Lithuania 70 D6
Šibenik *Town* Croatia 64 C8
Siberia *Region* Russian Federation 79 J5
Sibi *Town* Pakistan 86 F2
Sibir' *see* Siberia
Sibiu *Town* Romania 68 F6
Sibolga *Town* Indonesia 96 D5
Sibut *Town* Central African Republic 42 E8
Sibuyan Sea *Philippines* 97 J3
Sichuan *Administrative region* China 90 F5
Sichuan Pendi *Depression* China 90 G6
Sicilia *see* Sicily
Sicily *Island* Italy 61 E13
Sicily, Strait of *Mediterranean Sea* 61 E14
Sidas *Town* Indonesia 96 G6
Sīdī Barrīnī *Town* Egypt 38 C4
Sidi Bel Abbès *Town* Algeria 36 G4
Sidney *Town* Nebraska, US 12 E6
Sidney *Town* Montana, US 15 L2
Siedlce *Town* Poland 62 G7
Siegen *Town* Germany 56 C7
Siena *Town* Italy 60 D7
Sieradz *Town* Poland 62 E7
Sierra Leone *Country* 40 F7
Sierra Madre *Mountain range* Guatemala 20 D4
Sierra Madre Occidental *Mountain range* Mexico 18 G5
Sierra Madre Oriental *Mountain range* Mexico 19 J6
Sierra Nevada *Mountain range* Spain 59 I8
Sierra Nevada *Mountain range* California, US 14 G6
Sierra Vieja *Mountain range* Texas, US 17 I7

Sigli *Town* Indonesia 96 C4
Signy *Research station* Antarctica 110 B3
Siguiri *Town* Guinea 40 G6
Siirt *Town* Turkey 77 K6
Sikhote-Alin', Khrebet *Mountain range* Russian Federation 79 M6
Silchar *Town* India 87 L4
Silesia *Region* Poland 62 C7
Silifke *Town* Turkey 76 F7
Silistra *Town* Bulgaria 66 H5
Sillamäe *Town* Estonia 70 H4
Silvan *Town* Turkey 77 J5
Silverek *Town* Turkey 76 H6
Simferopol' *Town* Ukraine 69 K7
Simpson Desert Northern Territory/ Queensland/South Australia, Australia 105 J5
Sinai *Desert* Egypt 38 E4
Sincelejo *Town* Colombia 26 B5
Singapore *Country* 96 E6
Singida *Town* Tanzania 39 E12
Singkang *Town* Indonesia 97 I7
Singkawang *Town* Indonesia 96 F6
Siniscola *Town* Sardinia, Italy 61 C9
Sinnamary *Town* French Guiana 26 I6
Sinsheim *Town* Germany 57 D9
Sint Maarten *Island* Caribbean Sea 23 N5
Sint-Niklaas *Town* Belgium 53 D10
Sinŭiju *Town* North Korea 91 L3
Sioux City *Town* Iowa, US 12 G5
Sioux Falls *Town* South Dakota, US 12 G5
Siping *Town* China 89 M3
Siquirres *Town* Costa Rica 21 J7
Siracusa *Town* Sicily, Italy 61 F13
Sīrjan *Town* Iran 82 G8
Şirnak *Town* Turkey 77 K6
Sirte, Gulf of Libya 37 L4
Sittoung *River* Myanmar 94 C8
Sittwe *Town* Myanmar 94 A7
Siuna *Town* Nicaragua 21 I4
Sivas *Town* Turkey 76 H4
Sjælland *Island* Denmark 49 C12
Skagerrak *Sea* Norway 49 B11
Skaudvilė *Town* Lithuania 70 D6
Skegness *Town* England, UK 51 H9
Skellefteå *Town* Sweden 48 F7
Skopje *Capital* Macedonia 65 G11
Skovorodino *Town* Russian Federation 78 K6
Slagelse *Town* Denmark 49 C12
Slatina *Town* Romania 68 E7
Slavonski Brod *Town* Croatia 64 E7
Sligo *Town* Ireland 50 B8
Sliven *Town* Bulgaria 66 G6
Slonim *Town* Belarus 71 D9
Slovakia *Country* 63 E10
Slovenia *Country* 57 G12
Slov"yans'k *Town* Ukraine 69 M4
Słupsk *Town* Poland 62 D5
Slutsk *Town* Belarus 71 E10
Smallwood Reservoir Nova Scotia, Canada 7 K4
Smara *Town* Western Sahara 36 D6
Smederevo *Town* Serbia 64 G8
Smolensk *Town* Russian Federation 72 B8
Snake River Idaho/Oregon, US 14 H3
Snowdonia *Physical region* Wales, UK 51 F9
Sochi *Town* Russian Federation 73 B12
Société, Archipel de la *Island chain* French Polynesia 103 N7
Socotra *Island* Yemen 83 F13
Soc Trăng *Town* Vietnam 95 G12
Söderhamn *Town* Sweden 48 E9
Södertälje *Town* Sweden 49 E10
Sofia *Capital* Bulgaria 66 E6
Sofiya *see* Sofia
Sogamoso *Town* Colombia 26 C6
Sokal' *Town* Ukraine 68 F2
Sokhumi *Town* Georgia 77 J2
Sokodé *Town* Togo 41 J7
Sokone *Town* Senegal 40 E5
Sokoto *Town* Nigeria 41 K6
Solāpur *Town* India 86 H6
Sol, Costa del *Coastal region* Spain 58 H9
Soledad *Town* Colombia 26 B4
Solikamsk *Town* Russian Federation 72 G8

Solingen *Town* Germany 56 C7
Sollentuna *Town* Sweden 49 E10
Solok *Town* Indonesia 96 D6
Solomon Islands *Country* 102 H5
Solomon Islands *Island group* Papua New Guinea/Solomon Islands 102 F5
Solomon Sea Pacific Ocean 102 F5
Solwezi *Town* Zambia 44 H3
Sōma *Town* Japan 93 G9
Somalia *Country* 39 H10
Somaliland *Cultural region* Somalia 39 H9
Somerset *Town* Kentucky, US 10 H3
Somme *River* France 54 E5
Somotillo *Town* Nicaragua 20 G5
Somoto *Town* Nicaragua 20 H5
Songea *Town* Tanzania 39 F14
Songkhla *Town* Thailand 95 D13
Sonoran Desert Arizona, US 16 D5
Sonsonate *Town* El Salvador 20 E5
Sop Hao *Town* Laos 94 F7
Sopron *Town* Hungary 63 D11
Sorgun *Town* Turkey 76 G4
Soria *Town* Spain 59 J4
Sorong *Town* Indonesia 97 L6
Sortavala *Town* Russian Federation 72 C6
Sousse *Town* Tunisia 37 J3
South Africa *Country* 44 G7
Southampton *Town* England, UK 51 F12
Southampton Island Nunavut, Canada 5 K5
South Australia *State* Australia 105 J6
South Bend *Town* Indiana, US 13 K6
South Carolina *State* US 11 J4
South China Sea Pacific Ocean 91 L8
South Dakota *State* US 12 F4
Southeast Indian Ridge *Undersea feature* Indian Ocean 99 K7
Southend-on-Sea *Town* England, UK 51 H11
Southern Alps *Mountain range* New Zealand 107 C11
Southern Cook Islands *Island group* Cook Islands 103 L8
Southern Cross *Town* Western Australia, Australia 104 E6
Southern Ocean 110 G3
Southern Sudan *Country* 39 D9
Southern Uplands *Mountain range* Scotland, UK 50 E7
South Georgia & The Sandwich Islands *Dependent Territory* UK, Atlantic Ocean 33 J8
South Island New Zealand 107 D11
South Korea *Country* 91 M4
South Orkney Islands *Island group* Antarctica 110 B3
South Shetland Islands *Island group* Antarctica 110 B4
South Shields *Town* England, UK 50 G7
Southwest Indian Ridge *Undersea feature* Indian Ocean 99 I6
Southwest Pacific Basin *Undersea feature* Pacific Ocean 109 K7
Soweto *Town* South Africa 44 H7
Spain *Country* 58 H5
Spanish Town *Town* Jamaica 22 G5
Spartanburg *Town* South Carolina, US 11 I4
Spijkenisse *Town* Netherlands 53 D9
Spīn Būldak *Town* Afghanistan 85 I8
Spitsbergen *Island* Arctic Ocean 111 M7
Split *Town* Croatia 64 C8
Spokane *Town* Washington, US 14 H2
Springfield *Town* Massachusetts, US 8 J6
Springfield *Town* Illinois, US 13 J7
Springfield *Town* Ohio, US 13 L6
Springfield *Town* Missouri, US 12 H8
Spring Hill *Town* Florida, US 11 I7
Srbobran *Town* Serbia 64 F7
Srebrenica *Town* Bosnia & Herzegovina 64 F8
Sri Jayewardenapura Kotte *Capital* Sri Lanka 87 I9
Sri Lanka *Country* 87 J9
Stafford *Town* England, UK 51 F9
Stakhanov *Town* Ukraine 69 M4
Stalowa Wola *Town* Poland 62 G8

Stamford *Town* Connecticut, US 8 I6
Starachowice *Town* Poland 62 F8
Stara Zagora *Town* Bulgaria 66 G6
Stargard Szczeciński *Town* Poland 62 C5
Starobil's'k *Town* Ukraine 69 M4
Staryy Oskol *Town* Russian Federation 73 C10
State College *Town* Pennsylvania, US 8 F7
Statesboro *Town* Georgia, US 11 I5
Staunton *Town* Virginia, US 11 K2
Stavanger *Town* Norway 49 A10
Stavropol' *Town* Russian Federation 73 C11
Steamboat Springs *Town* Colorado, US 15 K5
Steinkjer *Town* Norway 48 C7
Sterling *Town* Illinois, US 13 J6
Sterlitamak *Town* Russian Federation 73 G10
Stevenage *Town* England, UK 51 H10
Stevens Point *Town* Wisconsin, US 13 J4
Stewart Island New Zealand 107 B14
Stillwater *Town* Oklahoma, US 17 L3
Stockholm *Capital* Sweden 49 E10
Stockton *Town* California, US 14 F6
Stockton Plateau Texas, US 17 J7
Stœng Trêng *Town* Cambodia 95 G10
Stoke-on-Trent *Town* England, UK 51 F9
Stonehenge *Ancient site* England, UK 51 G11
Stornoway *Town* Scotland,UK 50 D4
Storuman *Town* Sweden 48 E6
Stralsund *Town* Germany 56 F4
Strasbourg *Town* France 54 H7
Strelka *Town* Russian Federation 78 H6
Strumica *Town* Macedonia 65 H12
Stryy *Town* Ukraine 68 F3
Stuttgart *Town* Germany 57 D9
Subotica *Town* Serbia 64 F6
Suceava *Town* Romania 68 G5
Sucre *Capital* Bolivia 27 E12
Sudan *Country* 38 D7
Sudbury *Town* Ontario, Canada 6 G7
Sudd *Region* Southern Sudan 39 D9
Sudeten *Region* Poland 62 C8
Suez *Town* Egypt 38 E4
Suez, Gulf of Egypt 38 E4
Sühbaatar *Town* Mongolia 89 I2
Suhl *Town* Germany 56 E8
Sujāwal *Town* Pakistan 86 F4
Sukabumi *Town* Indonesia 96 F8
Sukagawa *Town* Japan 93 G9
Sukkur *Town* Pakistan 86 F3
Sukumo *Town* Japan 93 D13
Sulawesi *see* Celebes
Sullana *Town* Peru 27 A9
Sulu Archipelago *Island chain* Philippines 97 I5
Sulu Sea Pacific Ocean 97 J4
Sumatera *see* Sumatra
Sumatra *Island* Indonesia 96 E7
Sumbawanga *Town* Tanzania 39 E13
Sumbe *Town* Angola 44 D3
Sumqayit *Town* Azerbaijan 77 N3
Sumy *Town* Ukraine 69 K2
Sunderland *Town* England, UK 50 F7
Sundsvall *Town* Sweden 48 E8
Sungaipenuh *Town* Indonesia 96 D7
Sunnyvale *Town* California, US 14 F6
Suông *Town* Cambodia 95 G11
Superior *Town* Wisconsin, US 13 I3
Superior, Lake Canada/US, 13 I3
Suqutrā *see* Socotra
Şūr *Town* Oman 83 H10
Surabaya *Town* Indonesia 96 G8
Surakarta *Town* Indonesia 96 G8
Sūrat *Town* India 86 G5
Surat Thani *Town* Thailand 95 D12
Surdulica *Town* Serbia 65 H10
Surfers Paradise *Town* Queensland, Australia 105 N6
Surgut *Town* Russian Federation 78 G5
Suriname *Country* 26 G6
Surt *Town* Libya 37 L5
Surt, Khalīj *see* Sirte, Gulf of
Susa *Town* Italy 60 B5
Susteren *Town* Netherlands 53 F10
Susuman *Town* Russian Federation 78 L4
Suva *Capital* Fiji 103 J7
Suwałki *Town* Poland 62 G5

Suzhou *Town* China 91 K5
Svalbard *Dependent Territory* Norway, Arctic Ocean 111 F7
Svartisen *Glacier* Norway 48 D5
Svenstavik *Town* Sweden 48 D8
Svetlogorsk *Town* Belarus 71 F11 *see also* Svyatlahorsk
Svilengrad *Town* Bulgaria 66 G7
Svobodnyy *Town* Russian Federation 79 L6
Svyatlahorsk *Town* Belarus 71 F11 *see also* Svetlogorsk
Swansea *Town* Wales, UK 51 E11
Swaziland *Country* 45 I7
Sweden *Country* 48 D7
Świdnica *Town* Poland 62 D8
Świebodzin *Town* Poland 62 C7
Swindon *Town* England, UK 51 G11
Świnoujście *Town* Poland 62 B5
Switzerland *Country* 57 C11
Sydney *Town* New South Wales, Australia 105 M7
Syeverodonets'k *Town* Ukraine 69 M4
Syktyvkar *Town* Russian Federation 72 F7
Sylhet *Town* Bangladesh 87 L4
Syowa *Research station* Antarctica 110 F4
Syracuse *Town* New York, US 8 G5
Syria *Country* 80 F7
Syrian Desert Jordan 81 G10
Syzran' *Town* Russian Federation 73 E10
Szczecin *Town* Poland 62 C5
Szeged *Town* Hungary 63 F12
Székesfehérvár *Town* Hungary 63 E11
Szolnok *Town* Hungary 63 F11
Szombathely *Town* Hungary 63 D11

T

Tabora *Town* Tanzania 39 E12
Tabrīz *Town* Iran 82 D5
Tabūk *Town* Saudi Arabia 82 A8
Täby *Town* Sweden 49 E10
Tacloban *Town* Philippines 97 K3
Tacoma *Town* Washington, US 14 F2
Tacuarembó *Town* Uruguay 30 H7
Tademaït, Plateau du Algeria 36 H6
Tādpatri *Town* Bhutan 87 I7
Taganrog *Town* Russian Federation 73 B11
Taguatinga *Town* Brazil 29 K5
Tagus *River* Spain/Portugal 58 F6
Tahoua *Town* Niger 41 K5
Tainan *Town* Taiwan 91 K8
Taipei *Capital* Taiwan 91 L7
Taiping *Town* Malaysia 96 D5
Taiwan *Country* 91 L8
Taiwan Strait China/Taiwan 91 L8
Taiyuan *Town* China 91 I4
Taizhong *Town* Taiwan 91 L8
Ta'izz *Town* Yemen 83 C13
Tajikistan *Country* 85 K5
Takaoka *Town* Japan 93 E10
Takapuna *Town* New Zealand 106 F5
Takasaki *Town* Japan 93 F10
Takikawa *Town* Japan 92 F5
Takla Makan Desert China 88 E5
Talamanca, Cordillera de *Mountain range* Costa Rica 21 J8
Talas *Town* Kyrgyzstan 85 K3
Talavera de la Reina *Town* Spain 58 H5
Talca *Town* Chile 30 C8
Talcahuano *Town* Chile 31 C9
Taldykorgan *Town* Kazakhstan 78 G8
Tallahassee *Town* Florida, US 10 H6
Tallinn *Capital* Estonia 70 G3
Talnakh *Town* Russian Federation 78 H4
Talsi *Town* Latvia 70 E5
Talvik *Town* Norway 48 F3
Tamale *Town* Ghana 41 I7
Tamanrasset *Town* Algeria 37 I7
Tamazunchale *Town* Mexico 19 K7
Tambacounda *Town* Senegal 40 E5
Tambov *Town* Russian Federation 73 D10
Tampa *Town* Florida, US 11 I7
Tampa Bay Florida, US 11 I8
Tampere *Town* Finland 48 G8
Tampico *Town* Mexico 19 K6

Tamworth *Town* New South Wales, Australia 105 M6
Tana *Town* Norway 48 G3
Tanabe *Town* Japan 93 E12
Tanami Desert Northern Territory, Australia 104 H3
Tandil *Town* Argentina 31 G9
Tane Range *Mountain range* Thailand 94 D8
Tanezrouft *Desert* Algeria 36 H7
Tanga *Town* Tanzania 39 G12
Tanganyika, Lake Democratic Republic of the Congo 43 I12
Tanggula Shan *Mountain range* China 88 G7
Tangier *Town* Morocco 36 F3
Tangshan *Town* China 91 K3
Tan-Tan *Town* Morocco 36 D5
Tanzania *Country* 39 E12
Taoudenni *Town* Mali 40 H3
Tapa *Town* Estonia 70 G4
Tapachula *Town* Mexico 19 N9
Tapajós, Rio *River* Brazil 29 I3
Ţarābulus *see* Tripoli
Tarancón *Town* Spain 59 I6
Taranto *Town* Italy 61 H10
Taranto, Gulf Italy 61 H11
Tarapoto *Town* Peru 27 B9
Taraz *Town* Kazakhstan 78 F8
Tarbes *Town* France 55 D11
Târgovişte *Town* Romania 68 F7
Târgu Jiu *Town* Romania 68 E7
Târgu Mureş *Town* Romania 68 F5
Tarija *Town* Bolivia 27 E13
Tarim Basin China 88 F5
Tarnobrzeg *Town* Poland 62 G8
Tarnów *Town* Poland 63 F9
Tarragona *Town* Spain 59 L4
Tarsus *Town* Turkey 76 G6
Tartu *Town* Estonia 70 G5
Ţarţūs *Town* Syria 80 D7
Tarvisio *Town* Italy 60 F4
Tashkent *Capital* Uzbekistan 85 J0
Tash-Kumyr *Town* Kyrgyzstan 85 K3
Tasikmalaya *Town* Indonesia 96 F8
Tasmania *State* Australia 105 K9
Tasman Sea Pacific Ocean 105 M8
Tassili-n-Ajjer *Plateau* Algeria 37 I6
Tatabánya *Town* Hungary 63 E11
Tathlīth *Town* Saudi Arabia 83 C11
Tatra Mountains Slovakia 63 F9
Tatvan *Town* Turkey 77 K5
Taungdwingyi *Town* Myanmar 94 B7
Taunggyi *Town* Myanmar 94 C7
Taunton *Town* England, UK 51 F11
Taupo *Town* New Zealand 106 G7
Taupo, Lake New Zealand 106 G7
Tauranga *Town* New Zealand 106 G6
Taurus Mountains *Mountain range* Turkey 76 E6
Tawau *Town* Malaysia 97 I5
Taxco *Town* Mexico 19 K8
Taxiatosh *Town* Uzbekistan 84 F2
Taymā' *Town* Saudi Arabia 82 B8
Taymyr Peninsula Russian Federation 79 I3
Tbilisi *Capital* Georgia 77 L3
Tczew *Town* Poland 62 E5
Te Anau *Town* New Zealand 107 B13
Teapa *Town* Mexico 19 N8
Tebingtinggi *Town* Indonesia 96 D5
Tecomán *Town* Mexico 19 I8
Tecpan *Town* Mexico 19 J9
Tecuci *Town* Romania 68 G6
Tegal *Town* Indonesia 96 E8
Tegucigalpa *Capital* Honduras 20 G4
Tehrān *Capital* Iran 82 E6
Tehuacán *Town* Mexico 19 L8
Tehuantepec *Town* Mexico 19 M9
Tehuantepec, Gulf of Mexico 19 M9
Tehuantepec, Istmo de *Isthmus* Mexico 19 M8
Tejen *Town* Turkmenistan 84 F5
Te Kao *Town* New Zealand 106 E3
Tekeli *Town* Kazakhstan 78 G8
Tekirdağ *Town* Turkey 76 C3
Tel Aviv-Yafo *Town* Israel 81 C11
Temirtau *Town* Kazakhstan 78 F7
Temple *Town* Texas, US 17 M6

Temuco *Town* Chile 31 C10
Ténéré *Physical region* Niger 41 M4
Tennessee *State* US 10 G3
Tennessee River Alabama/Tennessee, US 10 G4
Tepic *Town* Mexico 18 H7
Teplice *Town* Czechia 62 B8
Tequila *Town* Mexico 19 I7
Teramo *Town* Italy 60 F8
Teresina *Town* Brazil 29 M3
Ternate *Town* Indonesia 97 K6
Terni *Town* Italy 60 E8
Ternopil' *Town* Ukraine 68 G3
Terrassa *Town* Spain 59 M4
Terre Haute *Town* Indiana, US 13 K7
Teruel *Town* Spain 59 K5
Teseney *Town* Eritrea 38 F8
Tessalit *Town* Mali 41 J3
Tete *Town* Mozambique 45 I4
Tetouan *Town* Morocco 36 F3
Tevere *River* Italy 60 E8
Texarkana *Town* Texas, US 17 N5
Texas *State* US 17 L6
Teziutlán *Town* Mexico 19 K7
Thai Binh *Town* Vietnam 94 G7
Thailand *Country* 95 D9
Thailand, Gulf of Pacific Ocean 95 E11
Thai Nguyên *Town* Vietnam 94 G6
Thakhèk *Town* Laos 94 F8
Thamarit *Town* Oman 83 G11
Thames *River* England, UK 51 G11
Thandwe *Town* Myanmar 94 B8
Thanh Hoa *Town* Vietnam 94 F7
Thar Desert Pakistan/India 86 F3
Thaton *Town* Myanmar 94 C8
Thayetmyo *Town* Myanmar 94 B7
The Fens *Physical region* England, UK 51 H9
Thessaloníki *see* Salonica
The Valley *Capital* Anguilla 23 N5
Thimphu *Capital* Bhutan 87 L3
Thiruvananthapuram *Town* India 86 H9 *see also* Trivandrum
Thracian Sea Greece 66 F3
Thun *Town* Switzerland 57 C11
Thunder Bay *Town* Ontario, Canada 6 E6
Thurso *Town* Scotland, UK 50 E3
Tianjin *Town* China 91 J3
Tianjin Shu *Administrative region* China 91 J3
Tianshui *Town* China 89 J6
Tiberias, Lake Israel 81 D10
Tibesti *Mountain range* Chad 42 E3
Tibet *Administrative region* China 88 F7
Tibet, Plateau of China 88 F6
Tichît *Town* Mauritania 40 G4
Ticul *Town* Mexico 19 O6
Tien Shan *Mountain range* Kyrgyzstan 85 L3
Tierra del Fuego *Region* Argentina/Chile 31 D14
Tifu *Town* Indonesia 97 K7
Tighina *Town* Moldova 68 H6
Tigris *River* Iraq 82 C6
Tiguentourine *Town* Algeria 37 J6
Tijuana *Town* Mexico 18 C2
Tikal *Ancient site* Guatemala 20 E2
Tikhoretsk *Town* Russian Federation 73 C12
Tikhvin *Town* Russian Federation 72 C7
Tiksi *Town* Russian Federation 78 J4
Tilburg *Town* Netherlands 53 E10
Timaru *Town* New Zealand 107 D12
Timbedgha *Town* Mauritania 40 G5
Timbuktu *Town* Mali 41 I4
Timişoara *Town* Romania 68 D6
Timor Sea Asia/Australasia 97 J9
Tindouf *Town* Algeria 36 E6
Tirana *Capital* Albania 65 F11
Tiranë *see* Tirana
Tiraspol *Town* Moldova 68 H6
Tirol *Region* Austria 57 F11
Tiruchchirāppalli *Town* India 87 I8
Tisa *River* Hungary 63 F11
Titicaca, Lake *Lake* Peru 27 D12
Tivoli *Town* Italy 61 E9

Tizi Ouzou *Town* Algeria 36 H3
Tiznit *Town* Morocco 36 E5
Tlaquepaque *Town* Mexico 19 I7
Tlaxcala *Town* Mexico 19 K8
Tlemcen *Town* Algeria 36 G4
Toamasina *Town* Madagascar 45 M5
Tobago *Island* Trinidad & Tobago 23 O8
Tobol'sk *Town* Russian Federation 78 G5
Tocantins, Rio *River* Brazil 29 K4
Tocopilla *Town* Chile 30 D4
Todi *Town* Italy 60 E8
Togo *Country* 41 J7
Tokar *Town* Sudan 38 F7
Tokat *Town* Turkey 76 H4
Tokelau *Dependent territory* New Zealand, Pacific Ocean 103 K6
Tokmak *Town* Kyrgyzstan 85 L3
Tokmak *Town* Ukraine 69 L5
Tokoroa *Town* New Zealand 106 G6
Tokushima *Town* Japan 93 D12
Tōkyō *Capital* Japan 93 G10
Toledo *Town* Spain 59 I6
Toledo *Town* Ohio, US 13 L6
Toliara *Town* Madagascar 45 L6
Tolitoli *Town* Indonesia 97 J6
Tolmin *Town* Slovenia 57 G12
Toluca *Town* Mexico 19 K8
Tol'yatti *Town* Russian Federation 73 E10
Tomakomai *Town* Japan 92 F5
Tomaszów Mazowiecki *Town* Poland 62 F7
Tombouctou *see* Timbuktu
Tomini, Gulf of Indonesia 97 J6
Tomsk *Town* Russian Federation 78 H6
Tonga *Country* 103 K7
Tongatapu Group *Island group* Tonga 103 J8
Tongchuan *Town* China 90 H4
Tonghe *Town* China 89 M2
Tongzi *Town* China 90 H6
Tongliao *Town* China 89 L3
Tongxin *Town* China 89 J6
Tongzi *Town* China 90 H6
Tonkin, Gulf of South China Sea 90 H9
Tônlé Sap *Lake* Cambodia 95 F10
Tonopah *Town* Nevada, US 14 H6
Tooele *Town* Utah, US 15 I5
Toowoomba *Town* Queensland, Australia 105 M6
Topeka *Town* Kansas, US 12 G7
Torez *Town* Ukraine 69 M5
Torgau *Town* Germany 56 F7
Torino *see* Turin
Torkestan Mountains *Mountain range* Afghanistan 84 H4
Toro *Town* Spain 58 H4
Toronto *Town* Ontario, Canada 6 G8
Toros Dağları *see* Taurus Mountains
Torquay *Town* England, UK 51 F12
Torre del Greco *Town* Italy 61 F10
Torrejón de Ardoz *Town* Spain 59 I5
Torrelavega *Town* Spain 59 I2
Torrente *Town* Spain 59 K6
Torreón *Town* Mexico 19 I5
Torres Strait Australia/Papua New Guinea 105 K1
Torres Vedras *Town* Portugal 58 E6
Torrington *Town* Wyoming, US 15 L5
Toruń *Town* Poland 62 E6
Torzhok *Town* Russian Federation 72 C8
Toscana *see* Tuscany
Toscano, Archipelago *Coastal feature* Italy 60 D8
Toshkent *see* Tashkent
Totness *Town* Suriname 26 H6
Tottori *Town* Japan 93 D11
Touggourt *Town* Algeria 37 I4
Toukoto *Town* Mali 40 G5
Toul *Town* France 54 G7
Toulon *Town* France 55 G12
Toulouse *Town* France 55 D11
Tourcoing *Town* France 54 F5
Tournai *Town* Belgium 53 C11
Tours *Town* France 54 D8
Tovarkovskiy *Town* Russian Federation 73 C9
Towada *Town* Japan 92 G7
Townsville *Town* Queensland, Australia 105 L3
Towson *Town* Maryland, US 8 G8

Toyama *Town* Japan 93 F10
Toyota *Town* Japan 93 F11
Tozeur *Town* Tunisia 37 I4
Trabzon *Town* Turkey 76 H3
Trang *Town* Thailand 95 D13
Transantarctic Mountains *Mountain range* Antarctica 110 D6
Transnistria *Cultural region* Moldova 68 H5
Transylvania *Cultural region* Romania 68 E5
Transylvanian Alps *Mountain range* Romania 68 E6
Trapani *Town* Sicily, Italy 61 D12
Trasimeno, Lago *Lake* Italy 60 E7
Tra Vinh *Town* Vietnam 95 G12
Tremelo *Town* Belgium 53 E11
Trenčín *Town* Slovakia 63 E10
Trenque Lauquen *Town* Argentina 31 F9
Trent *River* England, UK 51 G9
Trento *Town* Italy 60 E4
Trenton *Town* Pennsylvania, US 8 G7
Tres Arroyos *Town* Argentina 31 F9
Treviso *Town* Italy 60 E5
Trier *Town* Germany 56 B8
Trieste *Town* Italy 60 F5
Trincomalee *Town* Sri Lanka 87 I9
Trinidad *Island* Trinidad & Tobago 23 O9
Trinidad *Town* Uruguay 30 G8
Trinidad *Town* Bolivia 27 E11
Trinidad & Tobago *Country* 23 O9
Tripoli *Town* Lebanon 80 D8
Tripoli *Capital* Libya 37 K4
Tripolitania *Cultural region* Libya 37 K5
Tristan de Cunha *Dependent Territory* UK, Atlantic Ocean 33 L7
Trivandrum *Town* India 86 H9 *see also* Thiruvananthapuram
Trnava *Town* Slovakia 63 D10
Trois-Rivières *Town* Québec, Canada 7 I7
Trollhättan *Town* Sweden 49 C10
Tromsø *Town* Norway 48 E4
Trondheim *Town* Norway 48 C7
Troy *Town* New York, US 8 I5
Troyes *Town* France 54 F7
Trujillo *Town* Spain 58 G6
Trujillo *Town* Peru 27 A10
Trzcianka *Town* Poland 62 D6
Tshela *Town* Democratic Republic of the Congo 43 D11
Tshikapa *Town* Democratic Republic of the Congo 43 F12
Tsu *Town* Japan 93 E11
Tsugaru-kaikyō *Strait* Japan 92 F7
Tsuruga *Town* Japan 93 E11
Tsuruoka *Town* Japan 92 F8
Tuamotu Islands *Island group* French Polynesia 103 O7
Tuapse *Town* Russian Federation 73 B12
Tuba City *Town* Arizona, US 16 E3
Tubmanburg *Town* Liberia 40 F7
Ţubruq *Town* Libya 37 N4
Tucson *Town* Arizona, US 16 E5
Tucumcari *Town* New Mexico, US 17 I4
Tudmur *Town* Syria 80 F7
Tuguegarao *Town* Philippines 97 J1
Tukums *Town* Latvia 70 E5
Tula *Town* Russian Federation 73 C9
Tulancingo *Town* Mexico 19 K7
Tulcán *Town* Ecuador 26 B7
Tulcea *Town* Romania 68 H7
Tulsa *Town* Oklahoma, US 17 M3
Tuluá *Town* Colombia 26 B6
Tumbes *Town* Peru 26 A8
Tumuc-Humac Mountains *Mountain range* Brazil 29 I1
Tungaru *Island chain* Kiribati 103 I4
Tungsten *Town* Northwest Territories, Canada 4 G6
Tunis *Capital* Tunisia 37 J3
Tunisia *Country* 37 J4
Tunja *Town* Colombia 26 C6
Tương Đương *Town* Vietnam 94 G7
Tupelo *Town* Mississippi, US 10 G4
Turan Lowland *Plain* Central Asia 84 F2
Ţurayf *Town* Saudi Arabia 82 B7
Turbat *Town* Pakistan 86 E3
Turda *Town* Romania 68 F5
Turin *Town* Italy 60 B5

Turkana, Lake Kenya 39 F10
Turkistan *Town* Kazakhstan 78 F7
Turkey *Country* 76 F5
Türkmenabat *Town* Turkmenistan 84 H4
Turkmenbaşy *Town* Turkmenistan 84 D3
Turkmenistan *Country* 84 F4
Turks & Caicos Islands *Dependent Territory* UK, Atlantic Ocean 23 I3
Turku *Town* Finland 49 F9
Turnov *Town* Czechia 63 C9
Tuscaloosa *Town* Mississippi, US 10 G5
Tuscany *Region* Italy 60 D7
Tuticorin *Town* India 87 I9
Tutuala *Town* East Timor 97 K8
Tuvalu *Country* 103 I6
Tuxpán *Town* Mexico 19 K7
Tuxpan *Town* Mexico 19 I8
Tuxtepec *Town* Mexico 19 L8
Tuxtla *Town* Mexico 19 N8
Tuy Hoa *Town* Vietnam 95 H10
Tuz Gölü *see* Tuz, Lake
Tuzla *Town* Bosnia & Herzegovina 64 E7
Tuz, Lake Turkey 76 F5
Tver' *Town* Russian Federation 72 C8
Twin Falls *Town* Idaho, US 15 I4
Tychy *Town* Poland 63 E9
Tyler *Town* Texas, US 17 M5
Tynda *Town* Russian Federation 79 K6
Tyrrhenian Sea Mediterranean Sea 61 F11
Tyumen' *Town* Russian Federation 78 F5

U

Ubangi *River* Central Africa 42 F8
Ube *Town* Japan 93 C13
Uberaba *Town* Brazil 29 K6
Uberlândia *Town* Brazil 29 K6
Ubon Ratchathani *Town* Thailand 95 F9
Ubrique *Town* Spain 58 G8
Uchiura-wan *Bay* Japan 92 G6
Uchquduq *Town* Uzbekistan 84 H3
Udaipur *Town* India 86 G4
Udine *Town* Italy 60 F5
Udon Thani *Town* Thailand 94 E8
Udupi *Town* India 86 G7
Uele *River* Democratic Republic of the Congo 42 H8
Uelzen *Town* Germany 56 E5
Ufa *Town* Russian Federation 73 G10
Uganda *Country* 39 D11
Uitenhage *Town* South Africa 44 G9
Ukhta *Town* Russian Federation 72 G7
Ukmergė *Town* Lithuania 70 E7
Ukraine *Country* 68 G3
Ulaanbaatar *see* Ulan Bator
Ulaangom *Town* Mongolia 88 G3
Ulan Bator *Capital* Mongolia 89 J3
Ulan Qab *Town* China 91 J4
Ulan-Ude *Town* Russian Federation 79 J7
Ulft *Town* Netherlands 53 G9
Ullapool *Town* Scotland, UK 50 E4
Ulm *Town* Germany 57 D10
Ulsan *Town* South Korea 91 M4
Ulster *Cultural region* Northern Ireland, UK 50 C8
Uluru *Peak* Northern Territory, Australia 104 H5
Ulyanivka *Town* Ukraine 69 I4
Ul'yanovsk *Town* Russian Federation 73 E9
Uman' *Town* Ukraine 69 I4
Umeå *Town* Sweden 48 F7
Umm Ruwaba *Town* Sudan 38 E8
Uncía *Town* Bolivia 27 E12
Ungava Bay Québec, Canada 7 I2
Ungava Peninsula Québec, Canada 6 H2
Uniontown *Town* Pennsylvania, US 8 E8
United Arab Emirates *Country* 83 F10
United Kingdom *Country* 50 E8
United States of America *Country* 8 I7
Ünye *Town* Turkey 76 H3
Upington *Town* South Africa 44 F7
Uppsala *Town* Sweden 49 E10
Ural Mountains *Mountain range* Russian Federation 73 H9
Ural'sk *Town* Kazakhstan 78 E5

Ural'skiye Gory *see* Ural Mountains
Uraricoera *Town* Brazil 28 H1
Uren' *Town* Russian Federation 72 E8
Urganch *Town* Uzbekistan 84 G3
Uroševac *Town* Kosovo 65 G10 *see also* Ferizaj
Ŭroteppa *Town* Tajikistan 85 J4
Uruapan *Town* Mexico 19 J8
Uruguay *Country* 30 G8
Ürümqi *Town* China 88 F4
Uşak *Town* Turkey 76 D5
Ushuaia *Town* Argentina 31 D15
Usinsk *Town* Russian Federation 72 G6
Usol'ye-Sibirskoye *Town* Russian Federation 79 I7
Ussel *Town* France 55 E9
Ussuriysk *Town* Russian Federation 79 M7
Ust'-Ilimsk *Town* Russian Federation 79 I6
Ústí nad Labem *Town* Czechia 62 B8
Ustka *Town* Poland 62 D4
Ust'-Kamchatsk *Town* Russian Federation 79 M4
Ust'-Kamenogorsk *Town* Kazakhstan 78 G7
Ust'-Kut *Town* Russian Federation 79 J6
Ust'-Olenëk *Town* Russian Federation 79 J4
Ustyurt Plateau Uzbekistan 84 F1
Usulután *Town* El Salvador 20 F5
Utah *State* US 15 I6
Utica *Town* New York, US 8 H5
Utrecht *Town* Netherlands 52 E8
Utsunomiya *Town* Japan 93 G10
Uulu *Town* Estonia 70 F5
Uvalde *Town* Texas, US 17 K7
Uvaravichy *Town* Belarus 71 G11
Uwajima *Town* Japan 93 D13
Uxmal *Ancient site* Mexico 19 O6
Uyo *Town* Nigeria 41 L8
Uyuni *Town* Bolivia 27 E13
Uzbekistan *Country* 84 H3
Uzhhorod *Town* Ukraine 68 E4

V

Vaal *River* South Africa 44 H7
Vaasa *Town* Finland 48 F8
Vaassen *Town* Netherlands 52 F8
Vác *Town* Hungary 63 E11
Valdés, Peninsula Argentina 31 F11
Val-d'Or *Town* Québec, Canada 6 H6
Vadodara *Town* India 86 G5
Vaduz *Capital* Liechtenstein 57 D11
Valday *Town* Russian Federation 72 C7
Valdez *Town* Alaska, US 4 E5
Valdivia *Town* Chile 31 C10
Valdosta *Town* Georgia, US 11 I6
Valence *Town* France 55 F10
Valencia *Town* Spain 59 K6
Valencia *Town* Venezuela 26 D5
Valencia, Golfo de *Gulf* Spain 59 L6
Valera *Town* Venezuela 26 D5
Valga *Town* Estonia 70 G5
Valladolid *Town* Mexico 19 O6
Valladolid *Town* Spain 58 H4
Valledupar *Town* Colombia 26 C5
Vallenar *Town* Chile 30 C6
Valletta *Capital* Malta 61 E15
Valley, The *Capital* Anguilla 23 N5
Valls *Town* Spain 59 L4
Valmiera *Town* Latvia 70 F5
Valozhyn *Town* Belarus 71 E9
Valparaíso *Town* Chile 30 C8
Van *Town* Turkey 77 K5
Vanadzor *Town* Armenia 77 L3
Vancouver *Town* British Colombia, Canada 4 G5
Vancouver Island British Colombia, Canada 4 F9
Van Diemen Gulf Australia 104 H1
Vänern *Lakes* Sweden 49 D10
Van Gölü *see* Van, Lake
Van, Lake Turkey 77 K5
Vantaa *Town* Finland 49 G9
Vanua Levu *Island* Fiji 103 I7
Vanuatu *Country* 102 G7
Vārānasi *Town* India 87 J4
Varberg *Town* Sweden 49 C11

Vardar *River* Macedonia 65 H12
Varde *Town* Denmark 49 B12
Varese *Town* Italy 60 C4
Varna *Town* Bulgaria 66 H5
Vasa *see* Vaasa
Vaslui *Town* Romania 68 G6
Västerås *Town* Sweden 49 E10
Vatican City *Country* 61 E9
Vättern *Lake* Sweden 49 D10
Vaughn *Town* New Mexico, US 17 I4
Vawkavysk *Town* Belarus 71 C9
Växjö *Town* Sweden 49 D11
Velebit *Mountain range* Croatia 64 B7
Veles *Town* Macedonia 65 G11
Velikiye Luki *Town* Russian Federation 72 B8
Velikiy Novgorod *Town* Russian Federation 72 C7
Veliko Tŭrnovo *Town* Bulgaria 66 G6
Vellore *Town* India 87 I7
Velsen-Noord *Town* Netherlands 52 E8
Vel'sk *Town* Russian Federation 72 E7
Vendôme *Town* France 54 D7
Venezia *see* Venice
Venezuela *Country* 26 E5
Venice *Town* Louisiana, US 10 F7
Venice *Town* Italy 60 F6
Venice, Gulf of Italy 60 F6
Venlo *Town* Netherlands 53 G10
Ventimiglia *Town* Italy 60 B6
Ventspils *Town* Latvia 70 D4
Veracruz *Town* Mexico 19 L7
Vercelli *Town* Italy 60 C5
Verkhoyanskiy Khrebet *Mountain range* Russian Federation 79 K4
Vermont *State* US 9 I4
Verona *Town* Italy 60 D5
Versailles *Town* France 54 E7
Verviers *Town* Belgium 53 F11
Vesterålen *Island group* Norway 48 D4
Vesuvius *Volcano* Italy 61 F10
Veszprém *Town* Hungary 63 E11
Veurne *Town* Belgium 53 B10
Viangchan *see* Vientiane
Viareggio *Town* Italy 60 D6
Vicenza *Town* Italy 60 E5
Vichy *Town* France 55 F9
Victoria *Capital* Seychelles 99 I5
Victoria *Town* British Colombia, Canada 4 G9
Victoria *Town* Texas, US 17 M7
Victoria *State* Australia 105 K8
Victoria Falls *Waterfall* Zambia 44 G4
Victoria Island Northern Canada 5 I5
Victoria, Lake East Africa 39 E11
Victoria Land *Region* Antarctica 110 E7
Vidin *Town* Bulgaria 66 D5
Vienna *Capital* Austria 57 H10
Vientiane *Capital* Laos 94 E8
Vierzon *Town* France 54 E8
Vietnam *Country* 94 G8
Vieux Fort *Town* St. Lucia 23 O7
Vigo *Town* Spain 58 E3
Vijayawāda *Town* India 87 I6
Vila Nova de Gaia *Town* Portugal 58 E4
Vila Real *Town* Portugal 58 F4
Villa Acuña *Town* Mexico 19 I3
Villach *Town* Austria 57 G11
Villahermosa *Town* Mexico 19 N8
Villa María *Town* Argentina 30 F7
Villa Martín *Town* Bolivia 27 D13
Villa Mercedes *Town* Argentina 30 E8
Villarrica *Town* Paraguay 30 H5
Villavicencio *Town* Colombia 26 C6
Villeurbanne *Town* France 55 G9
Villingen-Schwenningen *Town* Germany 57 D9
Vilnius *Capital* Lithuania 70 E8
Viña del Mar *Town* Chile 30 C8
Vinaròs *Town* Spain 59 L5
Vindhya Range *Mountain range* India 86 H4
Vineland *Town* New Jersey, US 8 H8
Vinh *Town* Vietnam 94 G8
Vinnytsya *Town* Ukraine 68 H4
Vinson Massif *Mountain* Antarctica 110 C5
Viranşehir *Town* Turkey 76 H6

Virginia *State* US 11 K2
Virginia Beach *Town* Virginia, US 11 L3
Virgin Islands *Dependent territory* US, Atlantic Ocean 23 M5
Virôchey *Town* Cambodia 95 G10
Virovitica *Town* Croatia 64 D6
Virton *Town* Belgium 53 F14
Virtsu *Town* Estonia 70 F4
Visaginas *Town* Lithuania 70 F7
Visākhapatnam *Town* India 87 J6
Viscount Melville Sound *Bay* Canada 5 I4
Viseu *Town* Portugal 58 F5
Vitebsk *Town* Belarus 71 H9 *see also* Vitsyebsk
Viterbo *Town* Italy 60 E8
Viti Levu *Island* Fiji 103 I7
Vitória *Town* Brazil 29 M6
Vitória da Conquista *Town* Brazil 29 L5
Vitoria-Gasteiz *Town* Spain 59 I3
Vitsyebsk *Town* Belarus 71 H9 *see also* Vitebsk
Vittoria *Town* Sicily, Italy 61 F13
Vizianagaram *Town* India 87 J6
Vlaardingen *Town* Netherlands 53 D9
Vladikavkaz *Town* Russian Federation 73 C13
Vladimir *Town* Russian Federation 72 D8
Vladivostok *Town* Russian Federation 79 M7
Vlagtwedde *Town* Netherlands 52 G6
Vlijmen *Town* Netherlands 53 E9
Vlissingen *Town* Netherlands 53 C10
Vlorë *Town* Albania 65 E12
Vojvodina *Region* Serbia 64 F6
Volga *River* Russian Federation 73 D11
Volgodonsk *Town* Russian Federation 73 C11
Volgograd *Town* Russian Federation 73 D11
Volkhov *Town* Russian Federation 72 C7
Volnovakha *Town* Ukraine 69 L5
Vologda *Town* Russian Federation 72 D7
Vólos *Town* Greece 67 E10
Vol'sk *Town* Russian Federation 73 E10
Volta *River* Ghana 41 J8
Volta, Lake Ghana 41 I7
Volturno *River* Italy 61 F9
Volzhskiy *Town* Russian Federation 73 D11
Vóreioi Sporádes *see* Northern Sporades
Vorkuta *Town* Russian Federation 72 H5
Voronezh *Town* Russian Federation 73 C10
Vostok *Research station* Antarctica 110 F6
Voznesens'k *Town* Ukraine 69 I5
Vratsa *Town* Bulgaria 66 E6
Vrbas *Town* Serbia 64 F6
Vršac *Town* Serbia 64 G7
Vung Tau *Town* Vietnam 95 G11
Vyborg *Town* Russian Federation 72 C6

W

Waal *River* Netherlands 53 F9
Waco *Town* Texas, US 17 M6
Wadayama *Town* Japan 93 D11
Waddān *Town* Libya 37 L5
Waddeneilanden *see* West Frisian Islands
Waddenzee *Sea* Netherlands 52 E6
Waddington, Mount *Mountain* British Colombia, Canada 4 G8
Wadi Halfa *Town* Sudan 38 E6
Wad Medani *Town* Sudan 38 E8
Wagga Wagga *Town* New South Wales, Australia 105 L8
Wāh *Town* Pakistan 86 G1
Wahai *Town* Indonesia 97 L7
Waiouru *Town* New Zealand 106 G7
Wairoa *Town* New Zealand 106 H7
Wakayama *Town* Japan 93 E12
Wake Island *Dependent Territory* US, Pacific Ocean 109 I4
Wakkanai *Town* Japan 92 F4
Wałbrzych *Town* Poland 62 D8
Wales *Political Region* UK 51 F10
Wallachia *Cultural region* Romania 68 E7
Wallis & Futuna *Dependent Territory* France, Pacific Ocean 103 J6
Walvis Bay *Town* Namibia 44 E6

Index

Acknowledgments

For the 2017 edition, Dorling Kindersley would like to thank:

Bharti Bedi, Priyanka Kharbanda, and Antara Raghavan for editorial assistance; Heena Sharma for design assistance; Shanker Prasad for CTS assistance; Deepak Negi for picture research assistance; and Simon Mumford for the Earth globe images.

Internet usage data has been sourced from Internet World Stats, www.internetworldstats.com

The publisher would like to thank the following for their kind permission to reproduce their photographs: (Key: a-above; b-below/bottom; c-center; f-far; l-left; r-right; t-top)

i Corbis: B.S.P.I. (bl); Steve Rayner (fbr). Photoshot: World Pictures (fbl, br). ii Corbis: Stephanie Maze (tl). Getty Images: Jim Cummins / Stone (cra). Science Photo Library: 1995 Worldsat International, and J. Knighton (l). iii Corbis: Sergio Pitamitz (br). Robert Harding Picture Library: Robert Frerck (cl); Frans Lemmens (cra). v Corbis: Frans Lanting (clb); Ludovic Maisant (bl); Werner H. Mueller (cla/dunes). vi Corbis: Howard Davies (br). viii Corbis: Jacky Naegelen / Reuters (cra). 2 Corbis: Alan Schein Photography (bl). Robert Harding Picture Library: John Miller (cra). 3 Corbis: Peter M. Wilson (clb). Science Photo Library: 1995 Worldsat International, and J. Knighton (globe). 4 Alaska Stock: (clb). Corbis: Gunter Marx Photography (br); Charles O'Rear (br). Photoshot: World Pictures (bc). 5 Corbis: Staffan Widstrand (tc); Peter M. Wilson (br/mountain background). NHPA / Photoshot: T. Kitchin and V. Hurst (tr); Andy Rouse (fbr/bear). 6 Cephas Picture Library: Fred R. Palmer (tr). Corbis: Benjamin Rondel (bl/Toronto.). Press Association Images: Tony Marshall / EMPICS Sport; (bc). 7 Corbis: William A. Bake (tr); Richard J. Nowitz (cra). Photoshot: Egmont Strigl / imagebroker; (tr); World Pictures (tl). 8 Pictures Colour Library: (ca). Robert Harding Picture Library: Stuart Pearce / Age Fotostock (bl). 9 Corbis: Alan Schein Photography (br); Paul Barton (crb); Ralf-Finn Hestoft (tl); Farrell Grehan (c). Robert Harding Picture Library: Andy Caulfield / Panoramic Images (tr). 10 Corbis: Owen Franken (crb). Getty Images: Andy Sacks (cla). Redferns: (bc). Robert Harding Picture Library: Peter Lilja / Age Fotostock (br). 11 Corbis: Tony Arruza (br); Flip Schulke (cra). Getty Images: Matthew Stockman (tr). 12 Corbis: Blaine Harrington III (cl/buffalo). Dorling Kindersley: American Museum of Natural History, London (fcl). Rex Features: Sipa Press (bl). Robert Harding Picture Library: Sergio Pitamitz (bl). 13 Corbis: Philip Gould (br); Julie Habel (tl). Getty Images: Jim Cummins / Stone (crb). 14 Robert Harding Picture Library: Liane Cary / age fotostock (tc); Melissa Farlow / National Geographic (tc). 15 Corbis: Dean Conger (ca); Jong Beom Kim / TongRo (clb); Lester Lefkowitz (br). Rex Features: Sipa Press (br). Robert Harding Picture Library: Louise Murray (tr). Science Photo Library: George Bernard (bl). 16 Corbis: B.S.P.I. (br); Richard Ransier (fbr). Dorling Kindersley: Hopi Learning Centre (br/doll). Getty Images: Eric Schnakenberg / Photographer's Choice (tr). Robert Harding Picture Library: Tony Gervis (bl). 17 NASA: (tr). Robert Harding Picture Library: Walter Rawlings (tr). 18 Corbis: Keith Dannemiller (tr); Danny Lehman (br). Robert Harding Picture Library: Robert Frerck / Odyssey / Chicago (cl). Still Pictures: Julio Etchart (br). 19 Corbis: Macduff Everton (br); Tim Thompson (tc). Getty Images: Bruce Stoddard / Stone (ftl). 20 Corbis: Stephen Frink (cl); Sergio Pitamitz (crb). Eye Ubiquitous / Hutchison: Robert Francis (b). Photoshot: World Pictures (bl). 21 Corbis: Poisson d'avril / Photocuisine (ca); Arvind Garg (tl). Eye Ubiquitous / Hutchison: Robert Francis (clb). Photoshot: World Pictures / Intervision: Jose Enrique Molina / age fotostock (crb). 22 Corbis: Bill Gentile (cl). Photoshot: Martin Engelmann (bl). 23 Corbis: Wolfgang Kaehler (cb); Peter Turnley (clb). Eye Ubiquitous / Hutchison: John Fuller (tl). Photoshot: World Pictures (ca). Robert Harding Picture Library: John Miller (tr). 24 Robert Harding Picture Library: P. Narayan / Age Fotostock (cra). South American Pictures: Jason Howe (b). 25 Photoshot: World Pictures (clb). Science Photo Library: 1995, Worldsat International and J. Knighton (globe). 26 Corbis: Pablo Corral V (cr). Photoshot: World Pictures (cr). South American Pictures: (tl). 27 Dorling Kindersley: British Museum (b). Eye Ubiquitous / Hutchison: H. Jelliffee (tr); Paul Seheult (tl); Eric Lawrie (cra). Photoshot: World Pictures (bl). Robert Harding Picture Library: Gavin Hellier (cr). 28 Corbis: Yann Arthus-Bertrand (cr). Eye Ubiquitous / Hutchison: Dr Nigel Smith (tr). Robert Harding Picture Library: (clb). South American Pictures: Jason Howe (bl). 29 Corbis: Stephanie Maze (cra). Photoshot: Tomek Sierek (tr). 30 Corbis: Tony Arruza (tr). Photoshot: World Pictures (bc). Robert Harding Picture Library: Bildagentur Schuster / Gluske (cla); Ken Welsh / Age Fotostock (tr). 31 Corbis: Fulvio Roiter (tr). Photoshot: World Pictures (cla). Robert Harding Picture Library: Victor Englebert (bl); P. Narayan / Age Fotostock (tl). South American Pictures: (br). 32 Corbis: Carlos Dominguez (crb); Wolfgang Kaehler (bl). NHPA / Photoshot: B. & C. Alexander (bl). Robert Harding Picture Library: (tr); Roy Rainford (cra); Adam Woolfitt (cl). 33 Corbis: George D. Lepp (br); Hans Strand (tl). 35 Science Photo Library: Tom Van Sant, Geosphere Project / Planetary Visions (t). 36 Eye Ubiquitous / Hutchison: Mary Jelliffee (br). Photoshot: World Pictures (tr, cl). 37 Corbis: Benjamin Lowy (b). Dorling Kindersley: British Museum (tc). Getty Images: Frans Lemmens / The Image Bank (crb). Photoshot: World Pictures (tr). Robert Harding Picture Library: T.D. Winter (tl). 38 Corbis: Michael Hanson / National Geographic Society (tr). Photoshot: World Pictures (br). Robert Harding Picture Library: Nakamura (ca). 39 Corbis: Karl Ammann (br). Eye Ubiquitous / Hutchison: (tr); Jeremy Horner (bl); Sarah Errington (bc). 40 Dorling Kindersley: Barnabas Kindersley (bl). Panos Pictures: Teun Voeten (br/diamond). Robert Harding Picture Library: J. Lightfoot (cla). 41 Corbis: Charles & Josette Lenars (bl). Eye Ubiquitous / Hutchison: Crispin Hughes (cr, br). Panos Pictures: Clive Shirley (tl). 42 Corbis: Skip Brown / National Geographic Society (tl). Dorling Kindersley: Powell Cotton Museum (bc). Eye Ubiquitous / Hutchison: Sarah Errington (br). Photoshot: World Pictures (tc). 43 Dorling Kindersley: Natural History Museum, London (cra/copper). Eye Ubiquitous / Hutchison: (c); Trevor Page (br). Getty Images: Nicolas Cotto / AFP (tr); Per-Anders Pettersson / The Image Bank (bl). 44 Corbis: Anthony Bannister (cra). Photoshot: (bl). Robert Harding Picture Library: Alain Evrard (bc). 45 Alamy Images: AfriPics.com (br/buffalo background). Corbis: Peter Turnley (bl). Dreamstime.com: Eric Isselée (fbr/lion). Eye Ubiquitous / Hutchison: Sarah Errington (tl); Liba Taylor (tr); Crispin Hughes (tc). Robert Harding Picture Library: Chris Mattison / age fotostock (crb/lemur). 47 Photoshot: World Pictures (cr). Science Photo Library: Tom Van Sant, Geosphere Project / Planetary Visions (t). 48 Corbis: Charles & Josette Lenars (tl). Photoshot: Paul Thompson / World Pictures (br). Robert Harding Picture Library: Kim Hart (ftl). 49 Corbis: Jean-Pierre Amet / Sygma (tl); Dave Bartruff (tr); Stephanie Maze (br). TopFoto.co.uk: Francis Dean / Imageworks (crb). 50 Corbis: David Paterson / WildCountry (tr); Michael St. Maur Sheil (br). Pictures Colour Library: (bc). Robert Harding Picture Library: Eye Ubiquitous (tc). 51 Corbis: Tommy Hindley / NewSport (bc). Eye Ubiquitous / Hutchison: Philp Wolmouth (br). Pictures Colour Library: Charles Bowman (cr). Robert Harding Picture Library: Mark Mawson / Robert Harding World Imagery (tr). 52 Corbis: Owen Franken (br). Photoshot: World Pictures (bc). Robert Harding Picture Library: Adam Woolfitt (tl). 53 Corbis: Dave Bartruff (bl); Ray Juno (br); Owen Franken (tr, tl). 54 Corbis: G. Bowater (cb); Roger Ressmeyer (ftl). Photoshot: (tl). 55 Corbis: Pierre Perrin / Sygma (bl); Kim Sayer (tr); Mike Powell (cra). Photoshot: Carol Pucci / Seattle Times / MCT (cr). 56 Corbis: Arnd Wiegmann / akw / Reuters (tl). Getty Images: Michael Rosenfeld (bc). Masterfile: Didier Dorval (tr). Rex Features: Sipa Press (br). 57 Corbis: Dominic Ebenbichler / Reuters (cr). Getty Images: Sylvain Grandadam (tr); Jess Stock (br). 58 Corbis: Morton Beebe (bl). Dreamstime.com: Photooiasson (Álvaro Germán Vilela) (tl). Robert Harding Picture Library: Jesus Nicolas Sanchez / age fotostock (cla). 59 Corbis: Patrick Ward (br). Getty Images: AFP (tr). Panos Pictures: David Constantine (tr). Pictures Colour Library: © FMGB Guggenheim Bilbao Museoa. Photo by Charles Bowman. All rights reserved. Total or partial reproduction is prohibited. (tl). Robert Harding Picture Library: Robert Frerck (bl). 60 Corbis: Jörg Carstensen / DPA (cl). Rex Features: Enrica Scalfari (tr). Robert Harding Picture Library: R. Richardson (br). 61 Art Directors & TRIP: (cra). Eye Ubiquitous / Hutchison: Trevor Page (bc). Photoshot: World Pictures (r). Pictures Colour Library: (clb). 62 Dreamstime.com: Taratorki (Ewa Rejmer) (tr). Panos Pictures: David Constantine (cla). Robert Harding Picture Library: (tl). 63 Eye Ubiquitous / Hutchison: Liba Taylor (cb). Photoshot: Rick Strange / World Pictures (tl); World Pictures (tr, br). 64 Eye Ubiquitous / Hutchison: (ca). Press Association Images: Tony Marshall (bc). Photoshot: World Pictures (tl). 65 Corbis: John Heseltine (cb). Eye Ubiquitous / Hutchison: David Watson (b). Robert Harding Picture Library: G. R. Richardson (tr); Phil Robinson (bl). 66 Corbis: Marco Cristofori / Robert Harding World Imagery (tl). Eye Ubiquitous / Hutchison: Melanie Friend (crb, br). Robert Harding Picture Library: (tr). 67 Corbis: Dallas & John Heaton / Free Agents Limited (cb); Clay Perry (tl). Photoshot: Lorraine Nicol / World Pictures (bl); World Pictures / Mauritius Images (br). 68 Art Directors & TRIP: P. Mercea (br). Eye Ubiquitous / Hutchison: Nick Haslam (clb). Photoshot: World Pictures (bl). Pictures Colour Library: (cla). 69 Art Directors & TRIP: D. Mossienko (tr); N.& J. Wiseman (cr). Corbis: Barry Lewis (bl). Eye Ubiquitous / Hutchison: Liba Taylor (br). 70 Art Directors & TRIP: T. Noorits (tl). Robert Harding Picture Library: Angelo Cavalli (bc). 71 Corbis: Serge Attal / Sygma (bl); Dimitri Iundt / TempSport (tr); Niall Benvie (fcra); Nik Wheeler (tl); Staffan Widstrand (br). Photoshot: Paul Thompson / World Pictures (br). 72 Corbis: Robbie Jack (bc); Steve Rayner (tr). Photoshot: World Pictures (cla). 73 Art Directors & TRIP: D. Iusupov (ca). Corbis: Gavin Hellier / Robert Harding World Imagery (br). Dorling Kindersley: Pitt Rivers Museum (b). Eye Ubiquitous / Hutchison: Victoria Ivleva-Yorke (tr); Liba Taylor (bl, tl). 75 Science Photo Library: Tom Van Sant / Geosphere Project / Planetary Visions (t). 76 Corbis: Dave G. Houser (b); Lawrence Manning (cl); Adam Woolfitt (cra). Robert Harding Picture Library: Adina Amsel / World Pictures (bl). 77 Corbis: Arne Hodalic (bl); David Turnley (tr); Nik Wheeler (cr). 78 Corbis: Peter Turnley (bc). Eye Ubiquitous / Hutchison: Sarah Errington (bl). 79 Alamy Images: Arcticphoto (tr). Corbis: Wolfgang Kaehler (bl); Gregor Schmid (crb). Pictures Colour Library: (cr). Robert Harding Picture Library: Morales (br). 80 Corbis: David Turnley (cla). Photoshot: José Nicolas / Hemis.fr / World Pictures (cb); Rick Strange / World Pictures (br); World Pictures (fcla). 81 Corbis: Christine Osborne (fcrb/police officer). Eye Ubiquitous / Hutchison: Bernard Gerard (bl); James Henderson (tr). Photoshot: Jonathan Carlile / Imagebrokers (tr). Robert Harding Picture Library: Michael Short (br/landscape). 82 Dorling Kindersley: British Library (c). Eye Ubiquitous / Hutchison: Bernard Gerard (b). Getty Images: Bruno Morandi (tc). Rex Features: Stuart Clarke (tl). 83 Dorling Kindersley: Barnabas Kindersley (br). Eye Ubiquitous / Hutchison: John Nowell (crb). Robert Harding Picture Library: Mohamed Amin (bl); Walter Bibikow (tl). 84 Corbis: S. Sabawoon (b). Getty Images: Shah Marai / AFP (cb). 85 Corbis: David Turnley (cr); Nevada Wier (cb, tr/mountains, tr). Robert Harding Picture Library: Ivan Vdovin (br). 86 Corbis: Keren Su (br). Eye Ubiquitous / Hutchison: Sarah Errington (clb). Getty Images: Martin Puddy (cl). 87 Alamy Images: Tibor Bognar (br). Eye Ubiquitous / Hutchison: Horner (bl). Getty Images: Indranil Mukherjee / AFP (crb). Robert Harding Picture Library: David Beatty (tl); Frans Lemmens (bl). 88 Eye Ubiquitous / Hutchison: Sarah Murray (b); Stephen Pem (cb). 88-89 Robert Harding Picture Library: Philippe Michel (tc). 89 Eye Ubiquitous / Hutchison: Melanie Friend (bl); Stephen Pern (tr). Photoshot: Rudi Pigneter (clb). Robert Harding Picture Library: G. Hellier (tr); Doug Traverso (cr). 90 Corbis: Douglas Peebles (tr). Eye Ubiquitous / Hutchison: Melanie Friend (cb); Jeremy Horner (bl). Photoshot: World Pictures (cla). 91 Corbis: Michael S.Yamashita (bc). Eye Ubiquitous / Hutchison: Trevor Page (tl); Christine Pemberton (br). Getty Images: Kim Jae-Hwan / AFP (cra). Photoshot: World Pictures (crb). 92 Corbis: Robert Holmes (tl). Getty Images: Paul Chesley / Stone (cl). Photoshot: World Pictures (br). Pictures Colour Library: (br). 93 Corbis: Michael S.Yamashita (br). Eye Ubiquitous / Hutchison: Jon Burbank (tl); N. Haslam (clb). Getty Images: Panoramic Images (tr). Robert Harding Picture Library: Gavin Hellier (cr). 94 Corbis: (cla). Eye Ubiquitous / Hutchison: Rene Giudicelli (tl). Photoshot: (tc); World Pictures (tr). 95 Eye Ubiquitous / Hutchison: Norman Froggatt (cr). Photoshot: Stuart Pearce / World Pictures (clb); Alain Evrard (tr). 96 Corbis: (cl); Tom Brakefield (tr). Eye Ubiquitous / Hutchison: John Halt (br); Juliet Highet (bl). Rex Features: Tim Rooke (cra). 97 Corbis: Dean Conger (br). Eye Ubiquitous / Hutchison: Michael Macintyre (cla); Dr Nigel Smith (cr). Rex Features: Sipa Press (tr). 98 Eye Ubiquitous / Hutchison: Isabella Tree (tr). Photoshot: Josef Beck (cla); Hartmut Röder (cr); World Pictures (br). Still Pictures: Roland Seitre (cb). 99 Corbis: Theo Allofs (cra). Photoshot: Eye Ubiquitous / Hutchison (tr). Rex Features: Wilhemsen (br). 100 Corbis: Sergio Pitamitz (bl); Keren Su (cra). Photoshot: Wolfgang Kaehler (br). Getty Images: Travel Pix (cr). Science Photo Library: 1995, Worldsat International and J. Knighton (globe). 102 Corbis: B.S.P.I. (tr). Dorling Kindersley: Mark O'Shea (bl). Eye Ubiquitous / Hutchison: Michael Macintyre (tr). 103 Corbis: Wolfgang Kaehler (bl). Eye Ubiquitous / Hutchison: Nick Haslam (cra); Michael MacIntyre (tr). Robert Harding Picture Library: Upperhall Ltd (tl). 104 Corbis: Penny Tweedie (tl). Eye Ubiquitous / Hutchison: N. Durrell McKenna (clb). Getty Images: Panoramic Images (cla/landscape background). Press Association Images: Phil Walter / EMPICS Sport (bc). Robert Harding Picture Library: Ken Gillham (tr). 105 Corbis: Sergio Pitamitz (br). Eye Ubiquitous / Hutchison: Robert Francis (br). Getty Images: Jeff Hunter / Photographer's Choice (cra). Robert Harding Picture Library: Neale Clark (crb). 106 Photoshot: Rick Strange / World Pictures (crb); Paul Thompson / World Pictures (tl); World Pictures (br). 107 Corbis: Jeny McMillan (tr). Rex Features: Simon Runting (bl). Robert Harding Picture Library: Jeremy Bright (tl); Julia Thorne (tl). 108 Getty Images: Andy Hall / Australian Defense Force (clb); Jeremy Woodhouse / Photodisc (cra). Photolibrary: Seiden Allan / Pacific Stock; ; (tr). Robert Harding Picture Library: Andoni Canela (bl). Verena Tunnicliffe: (crb). 109 Corbis: Wolfgang Kaehler (br); Stephanie Maze (br). Robert Harding Picture Library: Warren Finlay / International Stock (cra). 110 Eye Ubiquitous / Hutchison: Isabella Tree (bl). NASA: (cla). Robert Harding Picture Library: Thorsten Milse (br); Geoff Renner (tr). Still Pictures: Marc Steinmetz / VISUM; (clb). 111 Corbis: Composite Image / Alaska Stock LLC (tr); Tim Davis (cla); Vince Streano (cla); Torleif Svensson (crb).

All other images © Dorling Kindersley

For further information see: www.dkimages.com